Researching with Communities

Grounded perspectives on engaging communities in research

Edited by Andy Williamson and Ruth DeSouza

Researching with communities presents a range of personal and grounded perspectives from academics, researchers and practitioners on undertaking research in ways that promote and privilege the voice of the community, is respectful of local or indigenous practices and is culturally safe.

muddycreek**press**

auckland | london

Researching With Communities: Grounded perspectives on engaging communities in research

Edited by: Andy Williamson and Ruth DeSouza

Published by:

muddycreekpress
auckland | london

Muddy Creek Press
PO Box 60-517
Titirangi
Waitakere City
Aotearoa/New Zealand

www.muddycreekpress.com

ISBN 978-0-9556941-0-3

Copyright © 2007 Andy Williamson and Ruth DeSouza. Individual authors retain copyright to their chapters. This work is copyright and must not be reproduced by any process without the written permission of the copyright holder and full acknowledgement of the original publication.

Contents

Acknowledgements iii

Introduction 1
Andy Williamson

Creative tensions in the new community based research................................... 7
Randy Stoecker

Engaging communities

Health and home place: Close contact participatory research with Gypsies and Travellers... 25
Marion Horton

Is community research possible within the Western academic tradition? 39
Shannon Faulkhead, Lynette Russell, Diane Singh and Sue McKemmish

Overcoming obstacles to accessing participants in community health research 57
Alfred Joseph Banya

Community network analysis: Communications, neighbourhood and action (CNA^2)........ 67
Peter Day and Clair Farenden

Children in communities affected by conflict and natural disaster in north and east Sri Lanka 87
Jaya Earnest and Robert P. Finger

Hearing the voices of service users: Reflections on researching the views of people from South Asian backgrounds.. 103
Cathy Lloyd, Mark Johnson, Jackie Sturt, Gary Collins and Anthony Barnett

The doors to Aleut orthodoxy 113
Don Wren

Research as a living partnership

Soulful research: Using an arts-based methodology to authentically engage with local communities 123
Victoria Foster

Issues in researching the health of Irish people in the UK............................... 137
Paula McGee

Participation in health research: The need for a second mirror 151
Gaby Jacobs

Involving refugees in focus group research 167
Maria Higgins and Catherine O'Donnell

The Gudaga Project: Researching with our local Aboriginal community......... 181
Jennifer Knight, Elizabeth Comino, Elizabeth Harris, Lisa Jackson Pulver, Cheryl Anderson and Pippa Craig

NGO-University partnerships: Practicing what we preach 197
Claudette Legault and Madine VanderPlaat

The stranger within: Rethinking distance and proximity of the researcher as community member 209
Uzma Jamil

Recording oral memory: Views of Indigenous Victorians 219
Graeme Johanson, Kirsty Williamson and Don Schauder

Soalapule – The sharing of power: Reflections on community initiated research 243
Alison Greenaway, Jennifer Margaret and Robyn Allpress

Methodology and process

17 ways that 'community talk' misguides research 263
Bernard Guerin and Pauline Guerin

Direct qualitative analysis of data from digital audio sources 275
Andy Williamson and Ruth DeSouza

Researching inequalities: Lessons from an ethnographic study 285
Ghazala Mir

Lessons in research collaboration: Strengths Model research in New Zealand 301
Monika Divis

Researching communities with community participation in a metropolitan municipality in South Africa 309
Udo Richard Averweg

Blending commitment, passion and structure: Engaging cultural linguistic communities in collaborative research 323
Joanna Ochocka and Rich Janzen

Moving towards increased cultural competency in public health research 339
Lisa Gibbs, Elizabeth Waters, Andre Renzaho and Maree Kulkens

Innovative assessment of human development: The case of Bougainville 357
Jim Chalmers, Udoy Sankar Saikia and Gouranga Dasvarma

Using interviews effectively in Community Informatics 371
Larry Stillman

Engaging Asian communities in Aotearoa New Zealand: An exploration of what works in community research 385
Terry McGrath, Andrew Butcher, Yvette Koo, John Pickering and Hilary Smith

Contributors 399

Acknowledgements

This book has been a collaborative effort. Most obviously it has emerged from the work of the editors and authors, but in reality it is also the product of the communities in which the projects occurred.

The original motivation for this book comes from the editors' experiences of working with marginalised groups who were wary of yet more academics intruding and making off with the stories of their lives. This antipathy to and fear of the colonisation of community knowledge was re-enforced time and again on many different projects and in many different settings. What we learnt from these experiences was that there are alternative ways to work with a community so that useful research is produced which not only satisfies our funders, governments and universities but which actually – and perhaps most importantly – also contributes something back to the community being researched.

The editors are extremely grateful to the authors for agreeing to write for this book and for being so willing to share their experiences so that we can all gain new and valuable insights into what community-based research is about.

Since each chapter has gone through a rigorous double-blind peer review process we are also extremely grateful to the numerous reviewers for their generous contribution to this project.

Introduction

Andy Williamson

The 7th century-BC Chinese philosopher, Lao Tzu, said

> Go to the people. Live with them. Learn from them. Love them. Start with what they know. Build with what they have.

The ideal motto, perhaps, for a growing group in the research and evaluation community who are undertaking research with, rather than on, communities? It certainly suggests that community based research can be done better. And this becomes more important when you listen to the voices of community members when asked about research. I am reminded of an elderly Pacific Island lady sitting quietly in a focus group. After a while she rose to her feet and said, in a measured and calm way, that the trouble with research was that

> white men in suits come along and steal our ideas, they take them off on a plane to their conferences and what are we left with? Nothing!

This comment touched me deeply. It resonated not only because it was, in my experience, true, but also because I knew that there was another way. Reflexively, I was forced to challenge my own place in society (undeniably white, middle-class and liberal), my role as a researcher (to discover) and, consequently, the power that lay in my hands to choose what I might do with her ideas. Her stories. Her life.

And so the original seed behind this book was sown through the editors' research practice in Aotearoa New Zealand. Yet the idea has reverberated and was nourished through the similar experiences of colleagues in South Africa, Canada, Australia and the UK. The concepts in this book are global yet the impact of research is often profoundly local. The earlier example is just one of many clashes between traditional 'academic' research or programme evaluation and our communities.

Whilst a shift to more inclusive and grounded research is certainly desirable, it is not without its challenges – for both the researcher and the researched. There has been an historical tendency within the western academic tradition towards excluding the views of ordinary people. How often do we ask our research subjects how to go about carrying out our research or what we should do with the results? There are, of course, times when this would be inappropriate even impossible. However, sometimes it is not only appropriate that we hold stakeholders at the heart of our research, as this book demonstrates, there are times when it is vital to the success of the project and to the future wellbeing of the community. Research does not have to be about consuming ideas, as Freire (1985) suggested, it can be about creating and recreating them. Surely a community that is actively engaged in research about itself has more opportunity to learn and transform as a result of that research?

'Researching with communities' presents a diverse range of personal and grounded perspectives from academics, researchers and practitioners on undertaking research in ways that promote and privilege the voice of the community, are respectful of local or indigenous practices and are culturally safe. This book does not attempt to provide solutions to all of these difficulties one might encounter and it most definitely is not intended to be 'tick list' for approaching community-inclusive research. This book makes no claim to have all the answers! What I hope it does do is provide some examples, guides and discussion about the experiences of doing research respectfully and inclusively. It does this by drawing on the perspectives of researchers and community practitioners and by providing a range of reflective chapters that explore what community-based research means in a range of settings and for a range of people. Like the communities in which they are grounded, undertaking research in this way is always a unique experience.

It is hoped that this book is of value to a wide audience. It was never written as a purely academic text or reference, though hopefully it will be valuable as such. It was intended to support the community being researched – or wanting to research itself – as much as students and researchers, whether experienced or emerging. It is hoped that this book can contribute, however modestly, to a wider debate on the value of grounded, community based research and towards developing and supporting policies and programmes that directly affect communities.

What do we mean when we talk about a 'community'? They are not rigid monoliths that we can neatly label. Communities come and go. They evolve, grow and die. Definitions of 'community' are inevitably problematic and the term remains rightly contestable and malleable. The communities represented and described in this book include local, ethnic and religious but what makes a community can equally be a single point of connection, an up-to-date issue or a shared history. The only common thread in defining a 'community' is that it requires people to come together and this occurs in three, potentially overlapping, forms (Crow & Allan, 1994; Gaved & Anderson, 2006; Willmott, 1986, 1989):

Locality	Geographical or place-based community.
Interest	Topical community of those who share common interests.
Attachment	The weakest form of community, suggesting a common sense of identity and a level of interaction with others.

For me, the term 'community' engenders a feeling of belonging and a desire to retain that connection over a period time (see Bauman, 2000). It is also not easy to measure the strength or value of a community. It is often intangible, varies depending on an individual's commitment or sense of belonging and is not always obvious to outsiders.

Real life is not a theoretical exercise, yet so often research can be dehumanising. You cannot separate individuals from their lives and the communities to which they belong (Reason, 1994). The everyday folksonomies of community and kin are as valuable and important as our more formally instantiated taxonomies of knowledge, so prized by academia and government.

As we become more familiar with a community we see that it has itself got layers and differences. An example of this is provided by Maria Higgins and Catherine O'Donnell, who warn us to beware of assumed homogeneity when working with even relatively small, minority communities. Their experience of working with asylum seekers and refugees in Scotland shows that division and difference is as likely to be the norm, rather than the exception. Bernard and Pauline Guerin warn in their chapter, assumed homogeneity is dangerous for researchers who fail to understand that an individual or group almost certainly do not speak for all the community. On a more positive note, difference does not have to be a problem if it is understood and acknowledged. The diverse and contested nature of community, Peter Day observes, can be seen as a strength, rather than a weakness, because it facilitates an environment in which social creativity and innovation can be nurtured in ways that stimulate and promote community learning.

The value of civil society is not drawn from the good intent of the individual but in the way those individuals are connected and embedded within what Putnam refers to as "dense network of reciprocal relations" (2000, p.19). Such semi-institutionalised relationships of mutual acquaintance and recognition provide members with a degree of backing from the collective, providing both support and credibility. Relationships are socially instituted and community based research is to a large degree about relationships.

Social capital is one measure applied to communities and groups. A theoretical concept, it emphasises the importance of social ties and shared norms, measuring the connectedness of individuals to each other and the "social networks and norms of reciprocity and trustworthiness that arise from them" (Putnam, 2000, p.19). As Coleman (1988, p.1) suggests, "unlike other forms of capital, social capital adheres to the structure of relations between and among actors." Whilst strong social capital can be difficult to measure and risky to compare across different communities, strong communities are important.

The above is an important point for those of us wishing to undertake community based research because, in some small way, when we do, we become a part of that community and exchanges inevitably occur (for good or for bad). This leads on to a reflexive discussion about how we might accurately represent communities, as both an etic (outsider) or an emic (insider) researcher, considering of course that researchers are never wholly on the inside given the issues of trust, power and social desirability bias that affect what we do. Reflexivity and negotiation are paramount if we are to avoid making assumptions about the nature of community and, as Gaby Jacobs suggests, about the very nature of participatory research. Jacobs poses four questions which researchers might ask themselves:

1. What do we mean by participation?
2. Why do we think participation is important?
3. Who benefits from the research and in what way?
4. How do we judge the success of participation and how is participation involved in this?

Paula McGee identifies a conflict between taking a collaborative approach and meeting the demands of research governance. As Reason (1994) argues, research can only be conducted *with* people if the researcher engages with them as people because, while "understanding and action are logically separate, they cannot be separated in life: so a science of persons must be an action science" (p.10). This requires us as researchers to accept our place in the world, not as disconnected, soul-less bodies but as real people with beliefs, biases and different points of view. Subjectivity is not a problem, it is central to what we do and does not stop us being rigorous in our research, it just acknowledges that researchers too are human.

We must negotiate community boundaries carefully. Even as an insider our status changes when we undertake research. This is especially the case when, as Randy Stoecker suggests, the research is managed by an external body, such as a university, with its own often inward-looking processes. As outsiders we are often on the look-out for the 'mavens' and 'gatekeepers' who provide access to a community and, with it, the credibility for us to start our research. Whilst we look for these links in the community being researched, we also need them in the institutions that allow us to do research. Entry to a community is not enough, as Stoecker (2005) argues when describing the difficulties that researchers experience when establishing their own legitimacy.

Establishing trust is a pre-cursor to effective community engagement. Even more so when entering a community without invitation or existing social capital. Yet, despite these challenges, when community based research succeeds and trust is built we as researchers will often become the conduit between institutions, agencies or government and a community that is distrusting, feels let down or badly treated and which is sceptical of outsiders. This is a tenuous place to be and so, as Claudette Legault and Madine VanderPlaat remind us, the challenge for any collaborative relationship is to ensure that the collaboration is actually genuine!

Engaging in community based research is difficult when we are committed to representing the true voices that we hear. Grounded research is subjective and it is the same in this book; just as the contributors have attempted to retain the voices and values of the communities in which they work, we as editors have also attempted to allow the author's own voice and individual styles to come through. As I mentioned earlier, do not expect homogeneity, even in a small community!

Privileging the voices of participants is about respect. Language is a matter of power and control, of colonisation and submission. For example, notice how, in this book, indigenous peoples are often assigned names by the coloniser. Sometimes this is accepted (or at least tolerated and used) but often that community chooses a different name to refer to itself. What we call ourselves can be the tip of the epistemological iceberg; many indigenous groups do not subscribe to a western-oriented worldview and this presents further challenges for researcher and researched alike. As Shannon Faulkhead, Lynette Russell, Diane Singh and Sue McKemmish conclude "attempting to match these two systems of knowing often results in one system being subsumed by the other, or one being presented as an alternative to the other; not in them being equal but different worldviews." This book is itself set in a Western academic tradition but it does at least attempt to break free from the positivist paradigm and give voice to individual stories and worldviews.

This book is not limited to a single discipline, rather it tries to draw out different experiences from a range of disciplines – the book's commonality lies in what the authors have set out to achieve, not the fields in which they undertake research. A number of the authors have commented on how, in writing their chapters, they have themselves been given the opportunity to be reflexive about their own research – a luxury in an output-oriented academic sector and a challenge for practitioners who are often overworked and under-resourced. All too often our outputs report the findings but fail to reflect on or describe the research experience.

The book is divided into four parts. The first two chapters (this introduction included) attempt to set the scene for community based research. In section two, 'engaging communities', the focus is on strategies to engage with community partners and the third section focuses on a discussion around how the research itself can be participatory and grounded. These two sections obviously overlap and, in many ways, most chapters would sit comfortably in the other section.

The fourth section of the book is about method and methodology; the process of undertaking the research. Each chapter is grounded in a piece of research but this book is not about reporting that research per se, it is about reflecting on the process, the method and the experience.

The authors are drawn from a wide variety of disciplines and backgrounds and from a diverse range of locations. This was always our intention as we wanted to create a global account of community based research (albeit, we accept, from a predominantly Anglo-European standpoint). There is a, of course, a common thread throughout this book, which is that community based research is about mutuality, reciprocity and respect. Above all else, it is about people:

> E patai atu ahau ki a koe,
> He aha te mea nui o te Ao?
> He tangata, he tangata, he tangata[1].

References

Bauman, Z. (2000). Community: Seeking safety in an insecure world. London: Polity.

Crow, G., & Allan, G. (1994). Community Life: An introduction to local social relations. Hemel Hempstead, UK: Harvester Wheatsheaf.

Freire, P. (1985). The Politics of Education: Culture, Power and Liberation. London: Macmillan.

Gaved, M., & Anderson, B. (2006). The impact of local ICT initiatives on social capital and quality of life. Ipswich, UK: Chimera, University of Essex.

Stoecker, R. (2005). Research methods for community change: A project-based approach. Thousand Oaks: Sage Publications.

Reason, P. (1994). Inquiry and alienation in Participation in Human Inquiry, ed. P.Reason, pp.9-15. London, Sage Publications.

Willmott, P. (1986). Social networks, informal care and public policy. London, UK: Policy Studies Institute (PSI Research Report 655).

Willmott, P. (1989). Community Initiatives. Patterns and prospects. London, UK: Policy Studies Institute.

---

[1] Let me ask you / What is the most important thing in this world? / It is people, it is people, it is people (Māori proverb).

Creative tensions in the new community based research

Randy Stoecker

The Goose Approach to Research

There has been a story circulating for some years now about how geese behave:

> Next fall, when you see Geese heading south for the winter, flying along in V formation, you might consider what science has discovered as to why they fly that way: as each bird flaps its wings, it creates an uplift for the bird immediately following. By flying in V formation the whole flock adds at least 71% greater flying range than if each bird flew on its own.
>
> When a goose falls out of formation, it suddenly feels the drag and resistance of trying to go it alone and quickly gets back into formation to take advantage of the lifting power of the bird in front.
>
> When the Head Goose gets tired, it rotates back in the wing and another goose flies point.
>
> Geese honk from behind to encourage those up front to keep up their speed.
>
> Finally, and this is important, when a goose gets sick, or is wounded by gunshots and falls out of formation, two other geese fall out with that goose and follow it down to lend help and protection. They stay with the fallen goose until it is able to fly, or until it dies. Only then do they launch out on their own, or with another formation to catch up with their group.

If only we could have as much sense as a goose[2].

---

[2] Attributed to Dr. Harry Clarke Noyes ARCS NEWS, Vol. 7, No. 1, January 1992 at www.hotelnewsresource.com/studies/study0195.htm, but also attributed to anonymous.

Well, we're getting there. And we're doing it through a practice that many are calling community-based research or CBR. It goes by many other names – participatory research, action research, participatory action research, collaborative research, community-based participatory research, community-directed research, and popular education. It also goes by no name in those many places where people are doing the work without having read the literature or taken a course in it because they have already achieved the sense of a goose. In short, all of these models have in common a partnership between professional researchers and community groups integrating research and action for social justice.

So how is CBR like a flock of geese?

First, and perhaps most importantly, just like geese migrating, CBR is about getting somewhere. It is not about producing 'shelf research' whose only impact is to fill a space in a dusty row of books. Research is but a small part of the overall process. In the best CBR projects, people are also planning strategy, recruiting participants, changing organizations, and producing policy.

When I do CBR training workshops I often use two sets of circles. The first set shows a big 'research' circle with a little 'action' circle inside of it, which is how many professional researchers approach CBR.

The next set of circles shows a big 'action' circle with a little 'research' circle inside of it, which is how community workers and members more often see the work.

There are times in this research and action combination when different people fly point. In one recent CBR project, my job was to guide the group through planning and outlining a program evaluation and then implement the research. Once we wrote up the report, however, leadership shifted back to the program director, who then took the group through a planning process to make changes based on the research. Leadership also shifts during a project as a result of the varied expertise that community members and academics bring. Sometimes, such as when diagnosing a community problem, community members' in-depth expertise of their own situation will be indispensable. Other times, such as when a group is trying to develop solutions to a problem, the academic's broad expertise on the array of possible solutions and their theoretical fit will be important (for a discussion of these different forms of expertise, see Nyden, Figert, Shibley, & Burrows, 1997).

There is also a lot of honking in a good CBR effort, because of its social justice focus. This, too, can be challenging for traditionally trained researchers who were taught to be dispassionate, distanced, and objective. All that honking can feel like pressure to skew the interpretation. And becoming one of the honkers can lose one's credibility among those who hold to the old standards of dispassion, distance, and objectivity. It is important to remember, however, that objectivity was only ever a method, never a goal in itself. The goal is accuracy, not objectivity. The important thing is to get the group to its destination, and bad data can't do that anymore than bad parenting for a goose can get it to its winter feeding ground. There is no more of a problem facing an activist researcher doing research for a social justice cause than there is for a medical researcher doing research on a new treatment for a dreaded disease.

Most importantly, CBR is about partnering with those who have been wounded – who lack decent housing, decent jobs, decent rights and freedoms – to move the entire flock. One of my favourite quotes comes from Lilla Watson, an Australian Aboriginal activist, who says "If you have come here to help me, you are wasting your time... But if you have come because your liberation is bound up with mine, then let us work together." The community partners in this work are only wounded, not incapacitated. And their participation in our joint work informs the work of academics as much as academic research can inform community work.

The most powerful illustration of the importance of community leadership in research, told by Canada's David Suzuki and others, comes from a deadly disease that struck the Navajo community in 1993. When the Centers for Disease Control tried to investigate what was killing members of the Navajo Nation in New Mexico, they went in without understanding cultural norms of mourning the dead and community privacy standards. As a consequence, the people they interviewed told them anything just to get them out of the way. The CDC ended up, unknowingly, with useless data. In the interim, more people died. Eventually, a Navajo public health researcher, consulting with a local Navajo Medicine Man, helped manage the cultural differences and they discovered the killer was the mouse-borne Hantavirus. It appears that this virus had already been diagnosed through Navajo 'myth' which told of the relationship between excess rainfall and growth in the mouse population, and the bad luck that would befall you if a mouse ran across your clothing (Alvord & Van Pelt, 1999; Suzuki, 2000). The Centers for Disease Control now cites the knowledge of traditional Navajo healers in its information on Hantavirus[3] and has established community advisory committees around the United States to link community-based knowledge with scientifically-derived knowledge[4]. Lives were lost by ignoring community knowledge, and others were saved by treating that knowledge as legitimate. And the Centers for Disease Control is becoming liberated from old damaging and dangerous knowledge models.

The Theory and History of CBR

For many of us, there are two kinds of research models for working with communities, based in two different theories of society – functionalist theory and conflict theory. The

---

[3] Centers for Disease Control, 2000, Navajo Medical Traditions and HPS, www.cdc.gov/ncidod/diseases/hanta/hps/noframes/navajo.htm

[4] Chronic Disease Reports and Notes, Centers for disease control and prevention15(1). www.cdc.gov/nccdphp/cdnr/cdnr_winter0207.htm

split between these two theoretical approaches have expressed themselves across the social sciences, and especially in sociology, which I will focus on here.

Functionalist theory argues that society tends toward natural equilibrium and its division of labour develops through an almost natural matching of individual talents and societal needs. For functionalists, healthy societies maintain some basic degree of equilibrium and place all of their members into the roles for which they are fit. This theory also assumes that people have common interests even when they have different positions in society. Healthy, persistent societies are in a constant state of gradual equilibrium-seeking improvement. Thus, a group organizing to force change is actually unhealthy, as it can throw off equilibrium, and cooperation to produce gradual change is a better alternative (Eitzen & Zinn, 2000; Morrow, 1978). In this model, poor people only need opportunity, not power, and cooperation between the haves and the have-nots is the best means to provide opportunity.

Conflict theory sees no natural tendency toward anything but conflict over scarce resources. In this model society develops through struggle between groups. Stability in society is only fleeting, and to the extent that it is achieved even temporarily, it's not because society finds equilibrium but because one group dominates the other groups. Conflict theory sees society as divided, particularly between corporations and workers, men and women, and whites and people of colour. The instability inherent in such divided societies prevents elites from achieving absolute domination and provides opportunities for those on the bottom to create change through organizing for collective action and conflict (Eitzen & Zinn, 2000; Morrow, 1978).

Functionalist theory fits with social service practices that peacefully integrate people into existing institutional structures (See for example Munson, 1978). Conflict theory fits with social movement practices that confront and attempt to change existing institutional structures. Likewise, in community-based research, those working from different theoretical worldviews tend to use different research models, which I will call action research and participatory research, using their original labels.

The origin of action research is most associated with Kurt Lewin (1948). He and his colleagues focused on attempting to resolve inter-racial conflicts, along with conducting applied research to increase worker productivity and satisfaction. Action research emphasizes the integration of theory and practice, and does not challenge the existing power relationships in either knowledge production or material production. It has been used in education settings, and in union-management collaboration in research to save jobs and improve worker satisfaction (Whyte, 1991). Action research values useful knowledge, developmental change, the centrality of individuals, and consensus social theories, and professional researchers are central to the process. The action research model emphasizes collaboration between groups, and does not address the structural antagonism between those groups, reflecting the basic worldview of functionalist theory.

Participatory research and popular education were influenced by the third world development movement of the 1960s. Academics, activists, and indigenous community members collaborated to conduct research, develop education programs, and create plans to counter global corporations attempting to take over world agriculture. Their research, education, and planning processes led to sustainable, community-controlled agricultural and development projects. The 'participatory research' and 'popular education' models resulting from this movement across India, Africa, and South America, have been the leading models around much of the world (Brown & Tandon, 1983; Freire, 1970; Hall, 1993). These models also emphasize people producing knowledge to develop their own consciousness as a means for changing oppressive social structures (Gaventa, 1991), consistent with conflict theory. Consequently, the highest form of participatory research is that which is completely controlled and conducted by the community. It is interesting in this regard that the most well-known practitioners of this model, such as the Highlander Research and Education Center, the Applied Research Center, and Project South, are all organizations outside of academia.

Today, however, you can't depend on knowing someone's practice based on the labels they use. Today's action researcher is as likely to be doing participatory research as today's participatory researcher is to be doing action research.

A further complicating factor that affects the CBR model one uses is their organizational or institutional standpoint. United States practitioners tend to divide the community work industry into the advocacy, service delivery, community development, and community organizing. Advocacy – trying to create social change on behalf of others (such as children or illegal immigrants who are unable to advocate for themselves) – and service delivery – what we normally think of as social services – both tend to occur through mid-range mid-level organizations. Community development – defined in the U.S. as providing housing, business, and workforce development – and community organizing – building powerful self-advocacy organizations--are more likely to occur through grass-roots community organizations. Advocacy and community organizing are based more on conflict theory, while service delivery and community development are based more on functionalist theory. As you can see, service provision fits consistently with Action Research and community organizing fits consistently with Participatory Research/Popular Education. Advocacy and community development are 'mixed' models, and we don't yet know for sure how well they might combine with action research versus participatory research models.

So why do we call it the new CBR?

For the first time in its history, the process of doing action- and participation-oriented research with communities is being institutionalized. You can see it everywhere – in federal funding priorities in the U.S. and Canada – and in the development of official college and university programs to engage in a wide variety of 'civic engagement' activities. Now, I'm not sure that is necessarily a good thing, even though I and many others have been fighting for it. But despite ourselves we are beginning to institutionalize CBR.

There are two dimensions to the model – one focusing on who is involved in a CBR process and the other on what those people do in a CBR process. The 'who' dimension can include community residents, community workers, researchers, students and, sometimes, funders.

The goal is for community residents, whether they are the members of a place-based community such as a neighbourhood or a race-, ethnicity-, sexuality-, or other-based identity community, to be integrally involved in the process. Most of us believe that the research question should be generated primarily from community residents, and that they should play a decisive role throughout such a process.

What we often find in CBR projects, however (and this includes mine) is that community workers are often more involved than community residents in the actual project decision-making. Social workers, community development workers, community organizers, and ministers, often have the capacity and time to attend the many meetings required of a good CBR project. This process of 'working from the middle' rather than from the grass roots is especially important in disorganized communities. In the best cases, however, those community workers will find ways of building increasing resident involvement into the project.

The researcher can also take a variety of different roles in the new CBR, which can roughly be divided up into the initiator, the consultant, and the collaborator (Stoecker, 1999). In many cases, for good or bad, researchers find themselves in the position of being an Initiator, approaching the community with a project. As we will see, there are many potential challenges with this. In other cases, the community approaches the researcher, looking for consulting on specific research services. Rare, but in some ways the most enriching, are those situations where community members and researchers combine their talents in a truly collaborative fashion.

Because CBR has become so higher education centred lately, and so connected to service learning, students have also become important to the process. Their involvement ranges from providing basic labour, to sometimes even taking leadership on projects.

Finally, we must not forget funders, who may seem an unlikely group of people to include in a CBR project. And yet, I have worked with two CBR projects where funders were integrally involved, and the project was better for it as the funders became better informed of the challenges facing the project and project organizers were able to more directly negotiate the funders' expectations.

The CBR Research Process

When we think of all the possible ways that these five categories of people – the community resident, community worker, researcher, student, and funder – can be involved in a CBR project, it quickly becomes clear that there is no single best combination of roles and actors. I regularly do training workshops where I ask people to try and determine which of the five categories of actors should be involved at each stage of the research process: Choosing the question, designing the method, gathering the data, analyzing the data, and reporting or acting on the research. Every time I do such a workshop people find new combinations and new justifications. So I will discuss just a few of the possible combinations here.

Choosing the question

Choosing the question involves building a relationship with a community or community group, understanding how the research will fit in with their social change goals, and combining the academic's research expertise with the community group's situational expertise. The Appalachian Center for Community Service at Emory and Henry College held focus groups that involved over 100 people from area community organizations to identify research and service opportunities and support relationship-building between the organizations themselves in the hopes of doing mutually beneficial projects. A number of higher education CBR centres also send a request for proposals to area community organizations to identify possible research questions, and to make an initial contact that can lead to lasting relationships.

Designing the method

Designing a research method is not a purely technical task. It may also include considerations of how involved the community group wants to be in the actual research, perhaps to build members' skills, to facilitate community education, or even to build community relationships. Surveys might get good information, but face to face interviews might also build relationships. When Professor Thomas Plaut started working with a local physician to improve health care in the communities around Mars Hill College, they started by doing surveys of people's health care needs. But community people who had been surveyed before, and stereotyped by them as poor and dumb, were very reluctant to participate. Instead, the researchers began an 18 month focus group process that ultimately led to a regional emergency 911 phone system. Research methods can also involve intensive water, soil, air, and other testing procedures when health and environmental factors are involved. Helping communities effectively deploy these highly technical research methods becomes paramount in such cases[5].

---

[5] See, for example the story of Yellow Creek in Williams (1997).

Collecting the Data

Collecting data goes beyond simply getting good information to also involving community members, as they may be able to build and skills and relationships by collecting data together and from each other. Students also enter into this equation as a cheap and eager labour force who can learn a great deal from the hands-on experience. Academic researchers may need to be closely involved when the stakes are high and measurement accuracy is paramount. At the University of Denver, Professor Nick Cutforth and a group of graduate students conducted an evaluation of area after-school programs in partnership with the Piton Foundation and the school administrations. The graduate students designed an evaluation instrument, and trained high school students to interview middle-school students participating in the after school program.

Analyzing the Data

Academics used to data analysis being a quiet solitary process may find data analysis to in fact be quite boisterous. The academic researcher might only do a rough categorization of information for community meetings where the meaty interpretation is done. Students and community members might sit around a table going over rough drafts to collaboratively shape a report. In Washington DC, the Georgetown University-sponsored Youth Action Research Group gave a workshop on tenant issues in the Mt Pleasant/Columbia Heights neighbourhood, using their research data and the workshop analysis led residents to form a tenant's association and start focusing on the problem of absentee landlords.

Reporting the Results

Finally, the research report could be an oral report at a community meeting, it could be testimony at city council, it could be a glossy brochure, it could be a web site, it could even be (gasp!) a protest. One result of the Old Ashboro mapping project, done with Guilford College students in Greensboro North Carolina, was a mailing to all the absentee landlords owning property in the neighbourhood reminding them of the importance of maintaining their properties. In Toledo, Ohio, a neighbourhood conducted intensive research on the city budget, and presented their recommendations for dealing with a severe city budget shortage on the steps of city hall to the tune of 'We Wish You a Merry Christmas' retitled 'We Wish you Would Fix the Budget'.

Creative Tensions in the New CBR

As CBR has been brought into institutions of higher learning, combined with compromised forms of service learning, controlled by university grants budgeting formulas, and subjected to traditional academic standards, we are seeing a number of tensions in its practice.

The tensions are not fatal, however. They may even be something to look forward to. What are creative tensions? Kenneth Benson's 'dialectical methodology' (Benson, 1977, 1983) uncovers the contradictions between the goals of an organization and the practice of those goals which may create internal tensions. For any project trying to do something creative, such contradictions, or tensions, will exist. In fact, tensions give rise to many creative projects, as people struggle to define their dissatisfaction with the status quo.

Dealt with openly and constructively, creative tensions are healthy conflicts. They are not weaknesses in a program, but simply realities – usually rooted in social structural conditions. Understood this way, participants can see personality conflicts as rooted in external conditions of inequality and make the outside world, rather than each other, the target (Andrews, 1996; Grills, Bass, Brown, Akers, 1996; Wadsworth, 1991). People's collective identification of creative tensions, and their collective attempts to manage them, lead to even more program innovations (Uphoff, 1991).

What are the creative tensions in CBR?

Community versus Academy

This may be the most important creative tension in CBR. It begins with the different structural realities of communities and higher education institutions. First, there is the problem of schedules. Community issues arise and must be dealt with sometimes on a daily basis. A community organization that suddenly finds out about a government proposal to reduce bus service, with a hearing one month away, needs to marshal its troops and its data in short order. But universities and colleges set their course schedules, and academics make their research commitments, far ahead of time, with little flexibility left for last minute projects. Never mind that community projects rarely start and end on an academic term schedule, requiring academic researchers and students to commit to the project outside of the regular academic term schedule.

This creative tension also manifests itself in the different standards for knowledge that exist between universities and communities. Remember, it took the urgency of death to get the Centers for Disease Control to think differently about how it treated the oral traditions of indigenous communities. Those researchers who are sympathetic to less formal forms of knowledge used by communities may find their status and even employment in the university threatened by showing too much sympathy.

Of course, there is also the challenge of who leads in a partnership where the partners may have such different knowledge cultures and power positions. Some researchers attempt to impose their own agendas on communities rather than finding out the community's agendas. The Australian community-based researcher Ernie Stringer cautions that, "When we try to 'get' people to do anything, insist that they 'must' or 'should' do something, or try to 'stop' them from engaging in some activity, we are working from an authoritative position that is likely to generate resistance." (Stringer, 1996, p.43).

There are, of course, many other more specific forms of this tension, over who controls the data being produced by the research, what responsibilities each side has for the overall project, who gets what proportions of any grant funds supporting the project, and other issues that are endemic to any partnership.

Research versus Action

In some ways this could be seen as an extension of the academy vs. community tension, but it occurs even when the project is managed completely within a community. I do a lot of participatory evaluation research with community organizations and community-university partnership efforts. One of the challenges we confront time and time again is that community staff and leaders are running full out just trying to make the program happen. They have little time to devote to planning and contributing information to an evaluation effort – even when it may help them in the end. This can be a serious issue. If the evaluation is dependent on getting access to individuals for interviews, for example, someone has to supply the names and contact information. Making the situation worse, many funders still require recipients to conduct formal evaluations, but provide no extra funds to support those evaluations.

Beyond the resource-derived source of this tension, there is also a cultural source. I am currently engaged in a project trying to understand the research and data needs of Toledo's non-profit organizations – basically asking what research and data they need to write better grant applications, conduct more useful evaluations, and plan better programs. After one week, with a survey sent out to over 200 organizations, we have a grand total of 10 replies. Research is still seen as something that gets in the way of action, slows it down, and even misdirects it. We could even call it anti-intellectualism if there weren't so many examples to support the groups' charges about the negative impacts of research. Those of us doing CBR, of course, have seen how a very different form of research – one that is controlled by community participants and is focused on meeting community-set goals – can benefit organizations. But we have not been able to fully impact the anti-research culture of community people who have filled out too many forms, submitted to too many externally-controlled evaluations, and been subjected to too many demands for their information without ever seeing a practical result.

Training Students versus Solving Problems

In those cases of CBR projects that engage students, we confront another manifestation of the academy vs. community tension, this time focusing on the role of students in CBR, and based in institutional definitions of service learning that have been imported into CBR. Too often, the purpose of service learning is to provide students with a better education rather than to provide communities with better service. Service learning trainers even go so far as to say that the community should be used as a laboratory for students, an approach which leads a community activist friend of mine to ask 'what does that make us, dead frogs?' (Beckwith, 1996). There is also an overwhelming bias within the service learning field toward charity service learning – providing back-end services to those excluded from the system – rather than social change service learning – creating structural change that reduces the need for charity (Mooney & Edwards. 2001). Among other negative impacts of such a bias is a danger that it reinforces students' stereotypes of the excluded as helpless and incompetent (Eby, 1998).

The tension in such cases is that communities are looking for qualified and committed assistance in social change projects, but receive students who are neither fully trained nor fully committed to taking guidance from the community and discover that the supervision and training burden they have to endure actually reduces their organizational effectiveness and efficiency. In addition, students are typically unable to commit to a CBR project beyond the end of the term, leaving either the community or the supervising professor to try and pull the project together and actually meet the community's needs.

Service versus Social Change

Service versus social change is the biggie. This tension goes back to our early discussion of functionalist versus conflict theory, and whether one believes cooperation or confrontation is the most fundamental social change strategy. This tension is as basic as the debate between whether we need to train individuals to make them ready for the responsibilities of homeownership, or whether we need to change the regulation of the mortgage and housing markets to make homeownership more realizable.

This is a particularly important tension for those of us working in, or partnering with, social service organizations. For most service organizations are not organized to promote the participation of their clientele in organizational goal setting. Imagine, for example, a homeless service organization run by a board of homeless individuals. I am told of one homeless agency that commissioned a study of the most important issues facing the homeless. Well, as you might guess, the results came back with the usual stuff like education, employment, mental health services, etc. But then a community organizing group came along, and involved homeless folks in determining what their greatest needs were. Their greatest expressed need focused on the indignity of having to stand in line every day to receive three sheets of toilet paper. That was the issue they cared about the most, and was the starting place for building a sense of dignity from which they could move on to other issues[6]. It's not that social service agencies oppose social change. Indeed, the staffs of such organizations are often on the front lines of advocacy efforts. But their organizations are not structured for such efforts any more than educational institutions are. In many cases, then, using CBR for actual social change often rests on the shoulders of mavericks both on the higher education side and on the non-profit side.

---

[6] Willie's tp story.

Creative Tension Innovations

So what innovations can come from such tensions?

Academy versus Community

One of the most interesting innovations being produced by this tension is what one day may be called the 'flash seminar'. In the two cases of this that I know of, an organization received a grant that included funds for community-based research. Those funds released a professor from a regular course, in its place creating a special seminar for students interested in working on the community project. I was one of those professors. It wasn't easy – kind of like setting up dominoes. You have to find someone to teach the course you were originally signed up for, and you have to find students willing to sign up for your seminar. In these two cases only a handful of students signed up. Thankfully, in my case, three of those students were willing to continue through independent study to finish the project in the summer.

Another important innovation that has come from the tension between community and academy is the memorandum of understanding, also called a memorandum of agreement. This is a semi-formal document detailing what responsibilities each partner has in the project, what resources they will contribute, the project timeline, and ownership and use of the data. It is not quite at the level of a legal agreement, since that would require the university lawyers getting involved and who would want that! But it forces each party to make a commitment to the project and be held accountable for its part (Strand, Marullo, Cutforth, Stoecker, & Donohue, 2003).

A third innovation to come from this creative tension is the publication of CBR work, in some cases by community-university author teams. There are now many journals that will consider CBR-related papers. Journals such as the Michigan Journal of Community Service Learning, which also publishes CBR work, have seen exponential growth in subscribership. And we are getting books published as well, including the joint-authored book on CBR that I was part of and a second book I am currently finishing. It's still not getting into the top disciplinary journals except in rare cases, which makes it difficult for junior faculty at the most haughty PhD-granting institutions to do CBR, but for the rest of us there is now a margin of safety.

Research versus Action

Integrating research and action continues to be challenging under our current resource-poor circumstances. But even here there are some interesting innovations. The Centers for Disease Control in the United States poured large sums of money into community-based participatory research centres devoted to public health concerns. Canada's own Community-University Research Alliances program is actually a step ahead of the United States program in supporting not just university-based CBR projects, but actual community-based CBR projects. I also sit on the board of the Sociological Initiatives Foundation, which funds projects integrating research and action.

The struggle to change cultural attitudes toward research both within and without the academy has also produced innovations. The Loka Institute sponsored regular gatherings of community organizations who are doing their own community-based research. A recently completed project, sponsored through the Corella and Bertram Bonner Foundation, helped build CBR networks in five metropolitan areas and Appalachia. This symposium is one of many local gatherings occurring to help academics and community workers and leaders think further about the integration of research and action, and I tip my hat to the organizers who scraped this thing together even without the grant they had worked so hard for.

Training Students versus Solving Problems

As intractable as this tension seems, here too we are seeing important innovations. One, pioneered by Pat Donohue at Middlesex County College in New Jersey, uses community service, service learning, and community-based research as graduated steps. Community service activities are disconnected from any classroom learning objectives. Service learning takes the model to the next step, linking that volunteer service work with in-class learning objectives. CBR is yet another advance, as students trained in various research methods put their skills into practice on a real community-based project. At Middlesex County College, the Community Service Corps is the recruiting ground for faculty looking for students to participate in service learning and advanced CBR projects. In some cases, students expand their work with the same agency, as when the community service students who were dishing out food at a shelter received training to conduct an evaluation for that shelter that involved getting participation from the people using shelter services. The Center for Assessment and Research Alliances (called CARA) at Mars Hill College recruits students from research methods classes as 'apprentices' to CARA for basic data gathering, entry and cleaning work. Those who excel can be trained as CARA staff 'sojourners', who help design projects and carry them through to completion. Each year two or three students are named CARA Fellows, who are responsible for running the centre, helping organize projects and training and supervising apprentices and sojourners.

There are also those who are pushing the envelope to bring students into social change work. Tony Robinson's work at the University of Colorado at Denver engages students in research with housing advocates, environmental activists, and other groups (Robinson, 2000a, 2000b). And he is not alone. It is harrowing, messy work in some cases (Staudt & Thurlow Brenner, 2002), but these and other scholars are building models of how to use CBR to shift students from charity to social change work.

Service versus Social Change

Service versus social change is the most difficult tension to develop creativity from. We live in very difficult times in the United States, where questioning and confronting power is seen as more treasonous than at perhaps any time since the 1950s. At the same time, United States academic and community cultures have become conflict avoiding at almost any cost. The rejections of confrontational models of community organizing in favour of unrealistic 'win-win' mythologies, where corporate lions and community lambs supposedly can lay side by side for mutual benefit, are at an all-time high. In Canada, where confrontation has not been as necessary to receive minimal levels of social safety net services, a call for more conflict may seem grotesquely characteristic of your naughty neighbour south of the border. But those of us living there are convinced of its necessity as we watch the gap between rich and poor, healthy and sick, powerful and powerless, grow while we all mind our manners. Perhaps the most important innovation in relation to this tension is not connected to what is happening inside the academy, but what is happening outside of it, as more confrontational groups such as ACORN – the Association of Community Organizations for Reform Now – engage their members more and more in activist research around issues such as predatory lending.

Conclusion

So the next time you look up in the sky, to see a flock of geese flying in V formation, think of how well evolution has served them, and how far we have yet to go. And, in classic CBR fashion that seeks and respects knowledge from all things great and small, think of what we can learn from them, what we can learn from each other, and how we can together change the world.

Acknowledgement

This chapter has developed from a keynote address originally presented at the Community-based Research Network Symposium, Carleton University, Ottawa, Canada in May 2004.

References

Alvord, L.A. & Van Pelt, E.C. (1999), The Scalpel and the Silver Bear, New York: Bantam.
Andrews, A.B. (1996). Realizing Participant Empowerment in the Evaluation of Nonprofit Women's Services Organizations: Notes from the Front Line. in D.M. Fetterman, S.J. Kaftarian, and A. Wandersman (eds.) Empowerment Evaluation: Knowledge and Tools for Self-Assessment and Accountability. pp.141-158. Thousand Oaks: Sage.
Beckwith, D. (1996). Ten Ways to Work Together: An Organizer's View. Sociological Imagination 33:164-172. Retrieved from uac.rdp.utoledo.edu/docs/si/sihome.htm
Benson, K. (1983). A Dialectical Method for the Study of Organizations in G. Morgan (ed.) Beyond Method: Strategies for Social Research. Pp.331-346. Beverly Hills: Sage.
Benson, K. (1977). Organizations, a Dialectical View. Administrative Science Quarterly 22: 1-21.
Brown, L.D, & Tandon, R. (1983). Ideology and Political Economy in Inquiry: Action Research and Participatory Research. Journal of Applied Behavioral Science, 19, 277-294.
Eby, J.W. (1998). Why Service-learning is Bad. Retrieved from www.messiah.edu/agape/pdf

files/wrongsvc.pdf.

Eitzen, S. & Baca Zinn, M.B. (2000). In Conflict and Order: Understanding Society, 9e. Boston: Allyn and Bacon

Freire, P. (1970). Pedagogy of the oppressed. New York: Continuum.

Gaventa, J. (1991). Toward a Knowledge Democracy: Viewpoints on Participatory Research in North America in O. Fals-Borda and M.A. Rahman (eds) Action and Knowledge: Breaking the Monopology with Participatory Action-Research. Pp. 121-133. New York: Apex Press.

Grills, C.N., Bass, K., Brown, D.L. & Akers, A. (1996). Empowerment Evaluation: Building upon a Tradition of Activism In the African American Community in D.M. Fetterman, S.J. Kaftarian, and A. Wandersman (eds.) Empowerment Evaluation: Knowledge and Tools for Self-Assessment and Accountability. pp.123-140. Thousand Oaks: Sage.

Hall, B. (1993). Introduction. In P. Park, M. Brydon-Miller, B. Hall & T. Jackson (eds.) Voices of Change: Participatory Research in the United States and Canada. Westport, Connecticut: Bergin and Garvey.

Lewin, K. (1948) Resolving social conflicts; selected papers on group dynamics. G.W. Lewin (ed.). New York: Harper & Row.

Mooney, L.A. & Edwards, B. (2001). Experiential Learning in Sociology: Service-learning and other community-based initiatives. Teaching Sociology, 29, 181-194.

Morrow, P.C. (1978). Functionalism, Conflict Theory and the Synthesis Syndrome in Sociology. International Review of Modern Sociology. 8, 209-225.

Munson, C.E. (1978). Applied Sociology and Social Work: A Micro Analysis. California Sociologist, 1, 89-104.

Nyden, P., Figert, A., Shibley, M., & Burrows, D. (1997). Building community: Social science in action. Thousand Oaks: Pine Forge Press.

Robinson, T. (2000a). Service-learning as justice advocacy: Can Political Scientists do politics? Political Science and Politics, 33, 605-12.

Robinson, T. (2000b). Dare the School Build a New Social Order? Michigan Journal of Community Service-learning, 7, 142-157.

Staudt, K. & Thurlow Brenner, C. (2002). Higher Education Engages with Community: New Policies and Inevitable Political Complexities. Paper presented on COMM-ORG: The OnLine Conference on Community Organizing and Development. Retrieved from comm-org.wisc.edu/papers2002/staudt.htm.

Strand, K., Marullo, S., Cutforth, N., Stoecker, R., & Donohue, P. (2003). Community-Based Research and Higher Education: Principles and Practices. San Francisco: Jossey-Bass.

Stoecker, R. (1999). Are Academics Irrelevant? Roles for Scholars in Participatory Research. American Behavioral Scientist 42:840-854.

Stringer, E.T. (1996). Action Research: A Handbook for Practitioners. Thousand Oaks, CA: Sage.

Suzuki, D. (2000). Hidden Killer: Portrait of an Epidemic. The Nature of Things, CBC Television, Sunday, June 18 at 5pm.

Uphoff, N. (1991). A Field Methodology for Participatory Self-Evaluation. Community Development Journal 26:271-286.

Wadsworth, Y. (1991). Everyday Evaluation on the Run. Melbourne: Action Research Issues Association.

Whyte, W.F. (Ed.) (1991). Participatory Action Research. Newbury Park, CA: Sage.

Williams, L. (1997). Grassroots Participatory Research: A Working Report from a Gathering of Practitioners, University of Tennessee, Knoxville Community Partnership Center.

Randy Stoecker

Engaging communities

Health and home place: Close contact participatory research with Gypsies and Travellers

Marion Horton

> This chapter describes and analyses the methods, values, and processes essential for rigorous, academic yet participative community research with and for an excluded and marginalised group – the Gypsies and Travellers of the UK. A case study of research was used which described the work of an independent researcher commissioned by a number of statutory and voluntary sector (NGO) organisations to conduct an assessment of the health and (caravan) site needs of transient (travelling) Gypsies and Travellers around the city of Leeds. The research was conducted within a national and local political context whereby the acute health and site needs of Gypsies and Travellers were being raised by politicians and Gypsy and Traveller organisations.
>
> The method of close contact qualitative research interviewing was chosen for the research. Participative methods deployed emphasised the development of equal, respectful, culturally sensitive and trusting research relationships with Gypsies and Travellers. The process of the research is described in terms of flexibility, opportunism and constant reflections on data and methods. Practical examples of research encounters and 'special moments' are used to illustrate theories and methods.
>
> Established methods of participative community research are extended to develop processes which capture 'really useful knowledge'. The role of an engaged researcher in a highly politicised research environment is explored in terms of collecting and reporting on robust data in the context of solidarity, rejection of deficit theories to explain Gypsy and Traveller lives, and using research results and reports for political lobbying by Gypsy and Traveller organisations and their allies.

In this chapter I will outline the difficulties and joys of researching 'with' what are perceived to be a 'hard to reach' and at times a 'hostile' group outside the norms of society using methods of close contact qualitative and participative research. British Gypsy and Traveller culture is almost unknown in society as a whole. Prejudice, racism and indeed institutional racism against them are almost accepted by society as 'common sense' (see Acton 1997; Clark & Greenfields, 2006).

I will detail why I think the political and historical context I work in is important, as I feel, that context is a vital and much overlooked concept, which is an important asset, not only to understanding but also to changing perceptions and in the implementation of any research results. I will review the research process, partnerships and the implications of power relationships within the research. When evaluating the research process, I will also look at the emotional investment of both the researcher and the 'researched' and the necessity of commitment and engagement in this close contact qualitative and participative research. I will give a short review of the Gypsies and Travellers who took place in the research in order to encourage an understanding of the culture and difficulties for this ethnic minority and conclude with the political use made of my final report.

The research

This research (see Horton 2004) was commissioned, originally, as two separate pieces of qualitative research to provide a snapshot of the health and site needs of transient Gypsies and Travellers whose home place is their caravan and who were travelling in Leeds between May and November 2004. The combined research budgets were tiny and there was pressure for 'results' over process. In the course of the research it was found that the health and site needs of Gypsies and Travellers are interconnected and therefore the research methodology was adjusted slightly by allowing the semi structured interviews to cover both subjects and the final reports were combined and published as one report. In addition to the lack of resources, which for a freelance consultant is not easy, a small budget can create the impression in the minds of some of the members of a research steering group that the research is merely a 'small, local, qualitative piece of work' rather than a serious academic work, which provides immense value for money. This perception is something that the steering group need to deal with positively by encouraging context setting.

Forty-nine semi structured in-depth interviews were held with Gypsies and Travellers. A small number of interviews, some by telephone were carried out with stakeholders from the statutory sector and voluntary sector (Non-governmental organisations – NGO's).

The steering group for the research

The steering group was organised as a partnership of two voluntary organisations (NGO's), one who promoted 'health for all' in south Leeds and the other who existed to promote the exchange of information for Gypsies and Travellers. A Primary Care Trust (PCT) (which is a management body within the National Health Service) and Travellers Education Service (a statutory service within the local school system, which encourages participation of Gypsy and Traveller children of school age) and there were two representatives from the Local Authority Gypsy and Traveller liaison team.

'Partnership working' of this kind has its problems for research. There are inevitable tensions and power inequalities between different institutional cultures and members and professional interests (See Byrne, 2001).

The Steering group was interested in the status of the research and chose me because they felt I would access and involve the Gypsies and Travellers and build trust but perhaps, a university would have been their first choice. Often steering groups need persuading of the value of qualitative as against quantitative research. The 'evidence based' culture particularly in the public sector crudely prioritises statistical reports. Crude 'value for money' notions again forefront actual numbers of people interviewed rather than attempting to understand sampling techniques or the quality of close contact in depth research. I produced in the end a research report which I felt followed the principles and values of an engaged researcher who built trust with Gypsy and Traveller people I worked with as well as carrying out the largest health and site survey of transient Gypsy and Traveller people in the UK

Working with a steering group for this type of research I feel inevitably produces tensions placed within a research and political culture not of our making. The Leeds experience suggested

1. That where a Steering Group is sceptical of using participative and democratic research methods then the debate between researcher and Steering Group can be a useful learning experience for the Steering group.
2. A researcher can find ways of mobilising the skills and contacts of the Steering Group to resource and support the research. The Leeds steering group produced a really effective summary of the report for circulation to agencies and Gypsies and Travellers, using their contacts with designers and printers with the relevant experience.
3. A participative community researcher can gain the support of a Steering Group by demonstrating the support and trust generated by the process of the research with the group s/he is working with. Certainly the feedback Steering group members were getting from Gypsies and Travellers and those working with them about the research helped relationships.

In controversial areas of community based research, 'partnership' steering groups who commission research, are often formed to smooth out conflict and try and make sure uncomfortable truths do not emerge. Effective research with and for oppressed minorities like Gypsies and Travellers, who are developing their own organisations and movements, is inevitably and justifiably conflictual, rather than aimed at a false consensus. British Gypsies and Traveller people and their organisations are currently 'changing their worlds' and they are part of what Sidney Tarrow has called 'contentious' social movements (Tarrow, 1998, p.6). Engaged researchers, like me, whilst insisting on rigorous research standards and methods are part of this 'political' process. Having a background in radical community work practice allows a useful role to be developed which is valuable to the group one is working with and for. As Popple has argued:

> We can therefore, simultaneously hold different and apparently contradictory and inconsistent interpretations of the world – one determined and shaped by the dominant ideology, and the other determined by our everyday experiences in communities which gives us 'common sense' knowledge. In this paradigm community workers are situated in a pivotal position within the civil society, for although they are often employees of the state and are required to play a part in maintaining the social system, they are not necessarily in agreement with its ideology. Accordingly community workers have opportunities to work alongside members of communities as they articulate their contradictory understanding of the world and their situation within it. This theory also proposes that community work is concerned with moving from the terrain of ideas and discussion and into transforming action to change people's material situation (Popple, 1995, p.46).

Ownership and participation

A young woman member of the largest local transient extended Gypsy family was also an official member of the steering group. Her membership gave the final report some credibility that some Gypsy and Traveller participation had been included in the design of the research. Unfortunately her transient lifestyle and family commitments prevented her from fully participating and she rarely attended research meetings. She was however a direct link into her extended family and travelling group which proved to be extremely useful in the initial stages of the research. Her difficulties in playing an active part in the Steering Group does highlight the tensions between informal effective ownership of community research by disadvantaged and oppressed groups, and more formal membership of steering groups. Other research I have been involved in with Gypsies and Travellers has built in advisory workshops where people can comment on the process of research and raise issues but also contribute materially to research by suggesting avenues of research or people to contact.

The Leeds research lacked consistent formal involvement in the Steering Group from the transient Gypsy and Traveller population – but after all that is why they are transient, constantly travelling, refusing to relate to gadjo formalities which they feel can entrap them.

The crucial issue of trust perhaps can augment formal involvement. The small world of Gypsies and Travellers would have closed their caravans and encampments to me if they had not felt that the research and the researcher were in solidarity with their interests and way of life.

Perhaps also the issue of ownership does raise the question of whether Gypsy and Traveller research should be carried out by Gypsy and Traveller people to be authentic. I believe that 'close contact' can be achieved in research terms through solidarity and political understanding. The debate will no doubt continue, but pragmatically in the UK the most effective political campaigns have combined the skills and research resources of gadjo academics and research workers with Gypsy and Traveller organisation. The only Professor of Romani Studies in the UK Thomas Acton is a gadjo (Romani word for a non-Gypsy), not a Romani Gypsy, and revered by the Gypsy and Traveller people and their organisations.

Gypsies and Travellers in Leeds

I was commissioned to undertake the research because I am a freelance community development consultant therefore I am not attached to any institution and have an independent status and ethos. More importantly I have a track record and good reputation for my work with Gypsies and Travellers in Leeds and elsewhere in the region. I am open and honest about my values and principles and the value framework of my work.

The research was commissioned for several interconnected reasons, which had primarily come to the forefront of professional agendas because of recent changes in United Kingdom legislations. There were increasing concerns about the needs of travelling Gypsies and Travellers who, not only had unmet needs, but it was clear, that both locally and nationally, service providers knew little about meeting their needs in a culturally acceptable and sensitive way. There was also recognition that the lack of official site provision meant that the enforcement of the law in evicting people who encamped on public land was costing the City Council and therefore the local taxpayers a vast amount of money (see Morris & Clements, 2002; Robinson, 2006).

A range of research over the last few years has demonstrated that the health of Gypsies and Travellers, who are recognised as an ethnic minority in UK law, is much worse than the general population in the UK and Ireland. This is shown in reduced life expectancy, higher infant mortality, and a range of chronic health conditions and high rates of disabilities (see Horton, 2004; Parry et al., 2004). Research in Bristol suggested in 2003 Gypsy men have a life expectancy of more than a decade less than the general male population (see Chamberlain, 2004). Earlier research in Ireland had suggested three to twelve years less (see Barry, 1989), and a massive 27 years less in a study of the UK in 1988 (see Pahl & Vail, 1988). Gypsies and Travellers have worse health than working class people in general, and worse than other ethnic minorities in England (see Chamberlain, 2004). Studies have also demonstrated the poor site and living conditions are the main explanations for poor health along with a lack of culturally sensitive health service provision (see Goward, 2006; Horton, 2004).

The research group were transient Gypsies and Travellers who were without 'legal' stopping places or conventional sites in which to stay, even on a temporary basis, and who were travelling around the City of Leeds in West Yorkshire, which is a major urban city with a small semi-rural hinterland. They park their caravans and live on what is generally termed 'illegal', and what I would prefer to refer to as 'unauthorised' places, like the grass edges of roads, under motorways, industrial waste sites or even large car parks. The number of caravans in these entourages of extended families varied between 5 and 20 caravans travelling together. They stay for a variety of reasons, some to visit relatives as the large extended family is important in the culture, some searching for work and some just travel for the joy of travelling in the same way as people travel for holidays. They stay for varied periods of time from overnight to a week. In some cases they can find a site which is 'tolerated' and the local authority or landowner may 'turn a blind eye' and allow them to stay for a few weeks and perhaps as long as one month. For many the real reason that they continue travelling around is that they have no choice and they are in search of a permanent, safe homeplace without resorting to their fear of living in a bricks and mortar house.

One large extended family whose members I interviewed in depth had been travelling around Leeds for thirty years without finding a permanent homeplace. They travel as independent units, providing for their own daily needs but rarely have access even to a basic necessity like running water. National and local authorities and indeed the general public perceive Gypsies and Travellers, in particular those who travel around, as an unhealthy, problematic group of people, who create environmental vandalism and who are, at the very least, to be avoided and even feared for their stance of remaining outside society. In fact as Richardson has pointed out the only things talked about as far as Gypsies and Travellers, particularly in the British media are concerned, are dirt and mess and their 'illegal' status (see Richardson, 2006). The Gypsies and Travellers experience racism every day of their lives and are stereotyped in ways, which make members of the general, unthinking society treat them as 'outcasts'. Anti-gypsyism is commonplace throughout Europe, Turkey and the United States and Canada (see Hancock, 2002).

Gypsy and Traveller people are still fighting for the right to be different. Clark and Dearling argue for valuing cultural diversity not conformity and assimilation.

> Gypsies and Travellers are an obvious example of people who are discriminated against both on grounds of 'race' and 'lifestyle' (Clark & Dearling, 2003, p.44).

This local and national historical and political context in which research is carried out is vital to understanding what sort of methodology process is needed, how the results of the research should be presented, how it can be taken forward and any recommendations implemented.

Any research must obviously be handled with sensitivity to the political and historical environment and may be difficult where there is a long legacy of distrust (McKee, 1997, p.1172).

It is also important that the result of qualitative research is grounded in a theoretically sound academic framework in order that it 'fits' into the important wider political debates. It is therefore not only essential to have a good practitioner knowledge and understanding but to conduct rigorous 'academic' desk research. This turns the small local research project into one, which does not 're-invent the wheel', e.g. simply repeating work done on other local research projects. It also allows the research to connect to knowledge networks nationally and even, increasingly importantly, globally. The sustainability of the research results is more likely to be secured if all concerned understand this process of context setting and see their roles and lives connected to national NGO's and campaign groups and European Union and International human rights debates.

The realisation that every day existence is due, or at least can be traced to, legislation, political or historical factors, is liberating. The personal is political and a participative research process can start making the links between personal and group identities and histories, and give people the confidence to critique and challenge images of themselves they encounter in the local health, education or police services.

Foucault argues that society's reality is perceived through the institutions of the state (Foucault, 1980). If we are to make an impact with any research and ensure social, cultural and political change it has to be placed within an all-embracing perspective, which challenges limited thinking determined by state institutions. As Thomas Acton, the only Professor of Romani Studies in the UK and a gadjo himself argues:

> If political practice, community activism, and policy planning are to change rather than reinforce the deeply embedded structures of Romani – gadjo misunderstanding they have to be grounded in a profound understanding of how Romani – gadjo relations have developed (Acton, 2005, p.30).

Choosing the methodology

The difficulties of this kind of qualitative research cannot be under estimated. However, other forms of research would not have been successful.

- Questionnaires would have been unacceptable and indeed could have been divisive between people who can read and the many who cannot read. If questionnaires had been circulated the Gypsies and Travellers would, I think, have wanted to complete them because they want to improve their health and site opportunities. However, they would have had to confide in those who read and write and I was told that they might not have been as open with other Gypsies and Travellers, as with an independent but sympathetic researcher who they felt they could trust. The quality of information would therefore have been open to question and would have been variable.

- Peer group research, after appropriate training, was considered but rejected on the same grounds, but also it was felt that the issues were too politically and personally sensitive. The politicians who were to receive the report may also have cast doubts about the authenticity of the research if not carried out by a 'researcher'.
- The idea of focus groups was also rejected because it was felt that there would be difficulty in getting people to attend and if they did attend getting to the more sensitive information surrounding health and site needs. It would have been difficult in such a small budget to pay expenses to those who travelled to attend focus groups.
- Building trust and endeavouring to design a fully participative action research project with a group of people who had experienced a lifetime of prejudice and were constantly moved on inhibited some aspects of the research. Some people I could only visit once but others I was able to establish a relationship and was invited to meet them several times, giving me a valuable insight into their culture and biological life history research. I was given trust enough to be told about such emotional subjects and intimacies as sex, pregnancies, birth and bereavement. These are all important rites of passage within Gypsy and Traveller culture.
- Qualitative research is more time consuming but more effective in gathering data. The use of face-to-face semi structured interviews in situations, which were part of the everyday lives of interviewees. I was going into their world and not asking them to come into anything unfamiliar. I was therefore ensuring that power was more equal between us.
- The qualitative research assumes gender was important. The methods I use are greatly influenced by feminist research methods, which emphasise the importance of informal conversation, 'chatting' and even what can be described as friendly gossip as important sources for data and information (See Roberts, 1981).

Close contact participative qualitative research fuses a range of methods which allow the 'close contact' with a culture, and people. It borrows from sociology and anthropology, feminism, and development techniques. Close contact means in practice

- A personal, political and emotional engagement with the people involved in the research. A belief that such engagement handled intelligently produces robust, effective research results able to be defended in the academic research community;
- The development of trust in the research process so that one is literally 'invited into' the culture, the homeplace;

- A rigorous research approach to value the 'really useful knowledge' of interviewees as rich data; and
- An awareness that close contact involves responsibilities – to make the research available and effective for use in political and community struggles for changing the world.

Theory and practice – the praxis of qualitative community research

The skill of the close contact qualitative researcher is in building trust. Sometimes this has to be done very quickly, rarely with the luxury of time and sometimes in the most awkward of situations. Trust is built through giving respect and building mutual respect. Gaining respect is only done through completely open and honest encounters. My first introduction to the mother of the Gypsy steering group member was not the expected friendly reception but a rather hostile 'Why should I help you?' and 'what are you going to give me?' questioning. Questions I could not answer in any other way than to tell the truth – and I simply stated 'nothing'. I explained I had nothing to offer, I could not guarantee anything helpful, I had no power to change anything and I had no resources or finance to improve her life. I could however, offer my commitment to listen to her, to offer complete confidentiality and that I would write a good report which would make recommendations, that if implemented would change the world a little. She smiled, looked directly into my eyes and said with some surprise "Well! At least you're honest; come in".

This brave and intelligent woman could see that I was offering a process, which changed our power relationship to be more equal. I offered a process, which could continue after my disappearance as she and her family could use the report as evidence in any future encounters with those who have power. Most importantly I offered her an opportunity to have her voice heard within the research.

As other researchers who have used this approach have pointed out

> it is particularly important for groups who tend to have least power in research relationship and in other relationships too and whose contributions are often dismissed…. Participatory research can also enhance people's awareness of their rights and strengthen their claims on society more generally (Bennett & Roberts, 2004. p.7).

Thus the practice of the research is based on theoretical principles of developing trust and giving a space for 'voice'. Methodology needs to be grounded in academic theory and the values and principles of the research must be clearly understood by all. The 'Principles of Participatory Action Research' (Chambers 1994), developed to relate to the extreme poverty of the South, gives a good foundation for ethical qualitative research, which values the 'researched' person. Chambers and others have demonstrated how it is the collective knowledge of the group we are researching that hold the key to, not only solutions to problems, but when really listened to, they show us how to proceed throughout the process of the research. The process changes and develops through self-reflection of the researcher, reflection of the process and of the results as we gather information.

Starting out: What's in it for me?

Sensitive, close contact qualitative research has to evolve but the starting point has to be consideration of why people should get involved in the research in the first place. Ask from the outset 'what will they gain?' and devise a programme that does not treat the researched as a passive person but one who deserves to gain through the process. We have seen how this can be through finding a voice through the research but it can be also be through research methods which bring with them information giving, networking, signposting or just fun.

One technique I have used in my qualitative research is to organise with groups 'Action Days' with a carnival atmosphere. These can be useful celebration days for information gathering and giving. These research action days are excellent for gaining a lot of in-depth information, and are set up to be informal, fun and helpful. In the past I have organised days with a whole range of professions from architects to health professionals, who have welcomed the opportunity to talk informally whilst talking about their specialist subjects. I have had health professionals offering information, checking blood pressure or giving information about childhood diseases or pregnancy, and health promotion issues. Information about domestic violence, rape or sexual abuse can be discreetly obtained in amongst information about healthy eating or more 'ordinary' life events.

In the Leeds research budget restraints and the difficulties of encouraging people who are unused to mixing in public gatherings made any 'action days' undesirable. However, I coordinated my visits with the visits of the 'Health Bus', which is a very small mobile health room staffed by nurses and health professionals, sometimes a doctor and occasionally a dentist. The bus is usually accompanied by Travellers Education Services who provide mobile crèche facilities so the women can attend alone or in groups for a consultation. The bus and staff are welcomed onto site and this provides a focus for an almost celebratory communal gathering in a helpful, non-invasive way.

Really useful knowledge

The commitment of the engaged researcher to change the world with and for, in this case Gypsies and Travellers, means we challenge surface notions of conventional wisdom or common sense. We are trying to release in the qualitative research process what is generally referred to as tacit knowledge. However, the real goal must be to a step further, to build trust and relationships, which encourages the researched person to impart their 'really useful knowledge' which can be the key to them themselves finding connections and methods to change their worlds. Researchers can learn from adult educators who have used the idea of 'really useful knowledge', since the 19th century as a central theme in radical theories of adult education. Their focus is on notions of developing and applying this 'really useful knowledge' a term which still holds the resonance of the classic social movements of early industrial England. One radical workingman described it then (in 1834) as the knowledge, which will give him the methods on "how to get out of our present troubles" (Clarke, 1979, p.84).

Concentrating on the value of 'really useful knowledge' also means an open rejection of theoretical perspectives, which see poor people as a problem and in terms of what they lack, depending on a presentation of negative images. We have to start from a positive perspective and this means a rejection of deficit theory. Our starting point must be that people are interesting, skilled and are able to, not only solve, but also to define what their real problems are. If society wants to change to give opportunities to poor people then we must learn what their problems really are, not what we perceive them to be.

Starting from a rejection of deficit theory I have developed a simple research technique which can succeed in building trust and interest. When asked to self define, I found that many Gypsies and Travellers would not admit to official bodies or outsiders their ethnic origins. When I asked them they would hesitate and then tell me they were a Gypsy or a Traveller. My reply to this is always a simple but positive 'good!' I go on to encourage expressions of their cultural pride, which they have become accustomed to hiding. I use positive images and role models in my reports. Finding examples are usually easy after meeting such interesting and colourful characters.

Solidarity, building on trust

During the process of this research I observed an interesting shift of perception of me, no longer just the researcher but as an 'outsider' who had solidarity with the Gypsies and Travellers. This privileged position gained me a place to continue and gather really sensitive information.

An extended family of about twenty caravans had encamped on a piece of local authority land and had gained through the judicial process permission to stay for approximately three months. They were given portable toilets and refuse collection, albeit inadequate refuse collection as they were blamed for local tipping of rubble and rubbish. I had visited this encampment several times and one day one of the men who had avoided being interviewed asked who I was and what I was doing. The police had raided the site in the dawn hours and had, he explained, frightened the children and acted in what he felt was an aggressive and provocative way, making people get out of bed and stand in the field whilst they searched the caravans. They found nothing and made no arrests. He asked what I could do and I felt powerless to offer any real help. I did however visit the site from dawn on a number of mornings. I sat in my car and didn't speak to anyone. I did not witness any raids but the fact that I had turned out to observe was noted. I thought about it carefully and decided on a subsequent visit to take breakfast for the families. Not in a patronising or philanthropic way, but in the same way as I would take a bottle of wine to a party, I took bacon, eggs, bread, cereal and milk and we all had breakfast in what became a celebration of eating outside and sharing stories of past encampments. This was one of the many special moments which Judith Okley describes as "heaven sent moments" of research (Okley, 1983, p.v) and an opportunity to be welcomed into the homeplace, which is often "a site of resistance" (Kendall, 1997, p.75) to gadjo society, and not often afforded the stranger researcher.

I wanted to build on this experience and I invited one woman Gypsy, who was about the same age as me and I had developed a good relationship with, to accompany me to a very pleasant destination where we could talk confidentially and I would ensure she was well looked after. My desire was to somehow thank her for participation by 'treating her', perhaps like I would have 'treated' a sister or my Mother. The invitation was understandably rejected because in an attempt to understand her world I was taking her out of her comfort zone and into my world. This was an honest mistake but one well learned in my research which demonstrated some of the limits of the approach.

During this research I learnt to be opportunistic, to conduct interviews in the most awkward situations. I have learnt to take both written and mental notes whilst standing outside a caravan or in the rain, anywhere, when the opportunity presented itself. I once asked for an interview but was told there was not enough time as my interviewee was going shopping; I proceeded to be kept in conversation for more than an hour, whilst she crouched down and I leaned across the empty passenger seat out of my car window. I think the real reason was that entering the caravan, which I had visited many times before when it was full of people, was not acceptable when there was no one else around and the space to be confidential was too threatening.

Reports and their uses

The 60-page report of the research was written using case studies, which illustrated the lives of the Gypsies and Travellers I met. Positive images and recommendations were developed for a range of organisations and state institutions to take forward (Horton, 2004). It was made available on the internet through the Travellers Education Service[7]. The report was also adapted by the steering group who produced a small booklet with a colourful range of positive image photographs, quotes from the Gypsies and Travellers and

---

[7] See: www.travellersinleeds.co.uk/academic

the recommendations. This was a step towards providing an accessible form of the report for people who cannot read.

The tiny research budget and the nature of the travelling patterns of the researched group of Gypsies and Travellers restricted a formal presentation of the research findings to a research seminar. However, informally I visited as many of the research participants and told them about the report and how it could be accessed. The report was widely used within Leeds and presented to politicians. The report contributed to Gypsy and Traveller campaigns on health and became a main part of a conference, which was organised by Gypsies and Travellers in the region. It has been quoted in other research (see Thomason, 2006) and was one of the influencing factors used by Senior Civil Servants at the Department of Health to invest more funding in the health needs nationally of Gypsies and Travellers.

Conclusion

This chapter has provided a case study demonstrating an approach to community participative research using a process of innovative qualitative methodology. It also demonstrates that research with a marginalized and oppressed ethnic minority like Gypsies and Travellers demands culturally sensitive approaches, and a commitment to values and solidarity. I feel that it is possible for an engaged researcher working closely with and for Gypsies and Travellers to produce a robust and academically recognised piece of local research. The research may start out to be local but one of the aims of research is to change the world, albeit step by step... and hopefully as Thomas Acton has pointed out "... will also be a re-humanising of inter-cultural relations in general" (see Acton, 2006).

References

Acton, T. (2006). Romani politics, scholarship, and the discourse of nation building: Romani Studies in 2003. In Marsh A and Strand E. Gypsies and the problems of Identities. (pp 27-37). Istanbul: Swedish Research Institute in Istanbul.
Barry, J. et al. (1989). The Travellers Health Status study 1987. Dublin: The Health Research Board.
Bennett, F. and Roberts, M. (2004). Participatory approaches to research on poverty. Poverty 118 p.5-8
Byrne, D. (2001). Partnership – Participation – Power: the meaning of empowerment in post-industrial society. In Balloch S. and Taylor M. eds. Partnership Working: Policy and practice. Bristol: Policy Press (pp 243 – 260).
Chamberlain, P.(2004). Unhealthy issues. Big Issue, August.
Chambers, R. (1994). Participatory Rural Appraisal (PRA): Analysis of Experience. World Development. 22(9).
Clark, C. and Dearling, A. (2001). Ethnicity, Nomadism and 'Traveller' identity: in Pursuit of Common Ground. Social Work in Europe. 7(1), 42-50.
Clark, C. and Greenfields, M. (2006). Here to Stay: the Gypsies and Travellers of Britain. Hatfield:

HUP

Hancock I. (2002). We are the Romani people. Hatfield: UHP

Clarke J. et al eds. (1979). Working Class Culture – Studies in History and Theory. London: Hutchinson

Foucault, M. (1980). Power/Knowledge. Brighton: Harvester Press

Goward, P et al. (2006). Crossing boundaries. Identifying and meeting the mental health needs of Gypsies and Travellers. Journal of Mental Health June 15 (3): 315 - 327

Horton, M. (2004). Health and Homes: the health and site needs of transient Gypsies and Travellers in Leeds. Leeds: Leeds Voice

Kendall, S. (1997). Sites of Resistance: places on the margin- the Traveller 'homeplace'. In Acton T. ed. Gypsy politics and Traveller Identity. (pp70-89) Hatfield: University of Hertfordshire Press (UHP)

McKee, K. (1997) The Health of Gypsies (Editorial) British Medical Journal November 8. 315(7117), .1172-3

Morris, R. and Clements, L. (2002). At what cost: the economics of Gypsy and Traveller encampments. Bristol: Policy Press

Okely, J. (1983). Changing Cultures – The traveller-Gypsies. Cambridge: Cambridge University Press

Pahl, J. and Vaile, M. (1988). Health and health care among Travellers. Journal of Social Policy 17, 195-213

Parry, D. et al. (2004). The health status of Gypsies and Travellers in England. Sheffield: University of Sheffield.

Popple, K. (1995). Analysing Community Work – its Theory and Practice. Buckingham: Open University

Richardson, J. (2006). Talking about Gypsies: the Notion of Discourse as Control. Housing Studies, 21(1), 77-96

Roberts, H. (1981). Doing Feminist Research London: Routledge

Robinson, A. (2006). Tax-payers fork out £750,000 for illegal travellers' camps. Yorkshire Post March 8th

Thomason, C. (2006). Here To Stay. Chester: Cheshire, Halton and Warrington Racial Equality Council

Tarrow, S. (1998). Power in Movement: Social Movements and Contentious Politics. Cambridge: Cambridge University Press

Is community research possible within the Western academic tradition?

Shannon Faulkhead, Lynette Russell, Diane Singh and Sue McKemmish

> The research project 'Trust and Technology: building archival systems for Indigenous oral memory' has taught the research team as much as the project itself has learned. During self-reflective analyses of these lessons, it became obvious that many of the challenges faced by the team link back to the contradictory needs of community groups and Western systems of learning and research, leading to the question: is community research possible within the western academic tradition? This chapter represents an attempt to think through some of the difficulties and challenges presented by the 'Trust and Technology project' (T&T); the most significant being the challenge of what we now refer to as 'irreconcilable ontologies' (Russell, 2005). By recognising the irreconcilable nature of these ontologies – western and Indigenous – and addressing its implications, we believe we have added tremendously to the overall understandings that have come out of the project, and overcome, at least in part, some of the shortcomings inherent in its conception within a western academic tradition. This chapter reflects on T&T in relation to making linkages between Indigenous and western knowledge systems; the challenges of undertaking Koorie community protocols within academia; and some of the lessons that the authors feel are important for a wider audience. In this chapter we explore these issues as part of the self-reflective, critically engaged methods employed in this multi-disciplinary, multi-phased project.

This chapter begins by asking a simple yet profound question: 'is community research possible within the western academic tradition?' We ask this in part in an attempt to differentiate between two different knowledge systems, i.e. western and Indigenous. Substantively there is a desire to draw attention to these differences, not only as they might be observed in divergent methodologies but rather in the end product, the research outcome. We also ask this question to interject and elaborate the complexity of community research, and the extensive and crucial protocols it requires.

Our illustrative case study is the 'Trust and Technology: building an archival system for Indigenous oral memory' project (T&T). T&T is an Australian Research Council Linkage project, with a partnership between Monash University, the Public Record Office Victoria, the Koorie Heritage Trust Inc., the Victorian Koorie Records Taskforce, and the

Australian Society of Archivists, Indigenous Issues Special Interest Group. The focus of the T&T project is on oral memory as captured within narratives that constitute Koorie knowledge and the mainstream narratives in government and institutional archives.

The terms oral memory and Indigenous or Koorie knowledge are used to denote a living, dynamic knowledge system encompassing all forms and types of knowledge. Oral memory is defined as Australian Indigenous knowledge that originates and/or is knowledge reinterpreted as orally transmitted narratives or stories. In a discussion of the concept of oral memory, Faulkhead and Russell (2006) link it to a broad concept of Australian Indigenous oral history, encompassing both the transmission of knowledge orally and the recording of Indigenous knowledge. Oral transmission of knowledge continues to be fundamental to Indigenous personal and group identity, and may take many forms, including the spoken word, song, music, dance and ritual.

The three stages of T&T are:

Stage One A user needs analysis, involving 72 interviews, collected Koorie views on storytelling and recording; trust and authenticity in oral and written records; and issues relating to control, ownership, custodianship, accessibility and privacy. The interviewees from throughout Victoria form a 'purposive sample', with the key characteristics represented being, gender, age, place of abode and community roles. From this analysis a set of 'scenarios' were developed to illustrate various user needs;

Stage Two A case study using the scenarios from Stage One to explore the services currently provided by the Koorie Heritage Trust Inc. and the Public Record Office Victoria. It involved interviewing 22 Koorie clients of archival services, mediators and service providers, and the development of models of trust and distrust of archival systems and services; and,

Stage Three A response to a key need identified in Stages One and Two, involves developing a framework and set of functional requirements for a trusted Koorie Annotation System that will allow Koorie communities to add their stories and perspectives, comment on or challenge the version of events in the archival records, and provide information about their context.

T&T has also employed critically engaged methods of self-reflectivity. This process has encouraged the authors, three of whom are members of both the T&T project team and the Koorie community, to present this reflective view of the project.

Koorie is a term of self-identification used by some Australian Indigenous people from Victoria and southern parts of New South Wales, meaning 'our people', 'man' or 'person'. We recognise and respect that this is not a blanket term adopted by all Indigenous people from this region. Many prefer their own clan, nation, or state title, or the generic terms 'Indigenous Australian' or 'Australian Aboriginal and Torres Strait Islander'. There are also those within the Koorie community who, whilst proud of their ancestry, feel that their identity lies in being 'who they are'; 'themselves'; 'Australian'; of 'mixed race'; or a 'hybrid', with hybridity defined as recognising and embracing the concept of being of more than one culture, whilst not attaching exclusively to any. The self-identification of a person, however, does not prevent the Koorie community from identifying and claiming these people as their own, placing responsibilities upon them as community members, or the individuals from accepting their responsibilities as a community member. When referring to Australia as a whole in this chapter, the term Indigenous Australian is used.

The connection between the project's self-reflective methodology and issues of individual and group identity is not coincidental. Team members have used various techniques for reflecting on such issues and considering their own relationship to the project, including personal journals tracking shifts in sensitivities, and regular talk fests. This self-reflection has fed reflexively back into decisions about working with communities and the direction of the project. An example of this is the re-development of Stage Three to specify a Koorie Annotation System rather than build a prototype archival system for oral memory as originally proposed. Another example was the undertaking midway through the project of a major review of the community and project relationships, the project data management, and the role of project participants, taking into account feedback from all areas of the research project community, and leading to recommendations that have since been implemented through the rest of the project. The Final Project Report, currently under development, will include a set of recommendations that address the lessons we have learnt about researching together with communities through proposed changes to academic research frameworks.

Much of this chapter is framed by issues relating to the (ir)reconcilability of Indigenous and western knowledge systems, and the problems encountered when research of one system is undertaken within another. The argument is structured into three parts. First, we look at the relationship between Indigenous and western knowledge systems; second, we reflect on Koorie community protocols and the challenges to T&T to achieve these; and finally we present the lessons we have learnt.

Indigenous and Western Knowledge Systems

Whilst working on a project that was attempting to match western and Indigenous Australian weather cycles, Russell adopted the term 'irreconcilable ontologies' (2005) to explain the impossibility of reducing western and Indigenous Australian knowledge systems so that they are equivalent (see also Attwood, 2001). These two knowledge systems work within different frameworks and are based on different ways of viewing the world. Clearly it is difficult, if not impossible, for academics schooled in western-positivist science to meaningfully engage with differing worldviews. Attempting to match these two systems of knowing often results in one system being subsumed by the other, or one being presented as an alternative to the other; not in them being equal but different worldviews.

The concept of irreconcilable ontologies suggests that mutual understanding will only come via an acknowledgment of and respect for the differing worldviews in all their complexity, but there is an inherent problem in this. Any researcher is always trying to understand the worldview of the other from within his/her own worldview. For example in one worldview narratives, histories or stories from another might be labelled mythic and characterised as fictitious or imaginary. We are optimistic about the potential to transcend this and reach a reconciled understanding. Within a framework that acknowledges differing ontologies, it is possible to place narratives from one ontology alongside narratives from the other. Thus, a creation story would sit beside, and be seen as equally valid to, a geological reading of landscape history. Accepting the differing views of the academic community and the Indigenous community can involve a close reading of the subtexts of meanings and the subtleties of expression.

It can be too readily assumed that the challenges of dealing with differing worldviews can be easily overcome within a project like T&T, with its interpretivist-qualitative approach, its multidisciplinary and multicultural research team, and its concern with the different ways people make sense of their world and construct their own realities. Our experience suggests it is possible by working and learning together to achieve a different perspective that both transcends and transforms our own worldview, as well as that of the community with whom we are working. This, however, is not always easy within a perceived mainstay of the western knowledge system, academia. One way of achieving this is by developing a coalition of community and academia in which one does not overshadow the other. Key to the success of our approach has been the feedback and self-reflection we have generated within the group of researchers. In our case this was not built into the original project plan, but it is one of the most significant lessons we have learned along the way.

Two Monash University schools are involved in T&T, the Centre for Australian Indigenous Studies (CAIS), and the Caulfield School of Information Technology. For a number of years research staff at CAIS have worked towards including Australian Indigenous communities in academic research projects as a matter of necessity. This is done in conjunction with a commitment to taking academic research out into the public arena, and has been achieved in a number of ways, including the production of 'plain English' research reports which are distributed to communities along with the more traditional academic papers and books. One of the most successful means of getting academic research outcomes accepted and acknowledged by the Indigenous community has been through the production of large format research posters.

The School of Information Technology has been similarly working towards community involvement within academia by connecting communities (not specifically Indigenous) and the disciplines of information technology, and community informatics. The establishment of the Centre for Organisational and Social Informatics and the Centre for Community Networking Research are leading examples of linking communities and informatics.

The Centre for Organisational and Social Informatics (COSI) contributes to the development of individuals, organisations, and society through research relating to human-centred design and deployment of information and communication technologies (ICT). COSI focuses on understanding the people and organisational dimensions, the complexities and needs of the social networks that ICT serves, in order to optimise its social, cultural and economic benefits (COSI, 2007).

Similarly the Centre for Community Networking Research:

> ... aims to understand how communities and community organisations are using new technologies. We are interested in the practicalities of information and technology usage and broader issues of community and institutional culture and memory as they are shaped through different understandings and uses of technologies (CCNR, 2007).

With this combination of schools and a project team with members from a range of disciplinary perspectives, T&T is viewed as both a community informatics and a Koorie community project.

Essentially community informatics, which came into prominence as an academic discipline in the 1990s (Wikipedia, 2006b), is engaged in developing principles and practices to help communities achieve their goals through matching community needs and technology. From the perspective of this emerging discipline, T&T is a community informatics project as it is aiming to use information technology to 'empower' Victorian Koorie communities through sharing, collecting and providing access to Koorie oral memory. This also defines T&T as a Koorie community project.

Whilst T&T straddles two areas of community research, most of the team have been integrally involved in either community informatics or Koorie community research, with the other area being relatively unknown to them. There is a concern though that viewing T&T, even in part, as a community informatics project may risk subsuming it to the dominant western research paradigm.

Whilst the principles of community informatics potentially challenge existing research paradigms, it is still an embryonic discipline. It is developing models of participatory community research based on action research, which engages the community in ways that are pioneering in the IT discipline by:

1. Researchers including the community as equal partners with no hierarchy of research roles, though it is acknowledged that there are skilled expert researchers to guide and facilitate.

2. Research emanating from a community-identified problem, expressed in the community's terms.

3. The community staying involved with the research, including participation in the choice of content, form and channel for the outputs of results.

4. The research being 'owned' by all participants.

5. Research processes being iterative, based in the community, incorporating investigation, reflection, and action.

6. The research seeking validation in the approval of the community that it serves as well as in external validation mechanisms. (Stoecker, 2005 & Wikipedia, 2006a).

Such models present fundamental challenges to the frameworks in which research is currently conducted in universities in Australia. For the moment though, community informatics is largely operating within these frameworks, and indeed is challenged to prove itself therein.

These principles of community informatics echo other community research protocols, including Indigenous ones. However, the Australian Indigenous community has been challenging the western paradigm since colonial-invasion. They have been developing methods, principles and protocols for research within their communities that have been visibly noticeable within academia since the late 1960s, early 1970s, and have influenced the ways that academics in some parts of academia have been engaging with Indigenous communities.

From our experiences, we consider the strength of community informatics still lies more in information networks and systems, with the community aspect still emergent. We find the developing nature of community informatics exciting, especially as it resonates with the background of other team members, who have been involved in previous attempts to get IT projects to position the needs of Indigenous communities at the heart of the systems they are developing.

Koorie Community

In the research context, reciprocity implies inclusion and means recognising partners' contributions, and ensuring that research outcomes include equitable benefits of value to Aboriginal and Torres Strait Islander communities or individuals. ... Reciprocity requires the researcher to demonstrate a return (or benefit) to the community that is valued by the community and which contributes to cohesion and survival. It is important to remember that Aboriginal and Torres Strait Islander Peoples may place greater or lesser value on the various returns than researchers. Reciprocity involves exchange although in the context of research this often involves unequal power relationships. In negotiating the conduct of research, Aboriginal and Torres Strait Islander communities have the right to define the benefits according to their own values and priorities (National Health & Medical Research Council (Aust.), 2003, p.10).

Indigenous groups worldwide have developed research protocols to ensure that any research engages the simple fundamentals of reciprocity and ethically sound practice. These protocols have been established to address the continuing practices of colonial or dominant cultural research paradigms. Indigenous groups historically have been treated as research subjects under these dominant research paradigms, with research concentrating on the differences between peoples and cultures, often in stark contrast to research that benefits the community.

> Community Consultation builds relationships between Indigenous communities and researchers, and gives control of what information is shared with researchers to the community (Vickery, Faulkhead et al., 2004, p.37).

As explored further by Vickery, Faulkhead et al. (2004, p.37), Community Consultation consists of recommended protocols aimed at producing a project that benefits all parties without disadvantaging or disrespecting the community involved. For many communities the primary protocol is that the project be developed though discussions with representatives of the community, allowing for it to address a particular problem or knowledge gap that the community identifies as important. This protocol is essential for community and researchers to develop a truly joint partnership.

Although vital, undertaking this protocol can be viewed as time consuming, especially by researchers not belonging to, or who do not have an existing relationship with, the partner community. This is particularly true when communities and individuals have negative experiences with previous researchers.

Community protocols and T&T

Initially T&T seemed to be aiming at outcomes that both benefited the Koorie community and develop academically rigorous research, with the original aims of the project being to:

- explore what the emphasis of Indigenous people on oral memory implies for the provision of archival services.

- examine how trust is engendered within Indigenous groups relating to authenticity, intellectual property and access to archives
- investigate how well government and other archival services meet the needs of Indigenous people for access to oral memory
- examine how archival techniques and IT can be used to build trusted archival systems to meet the needs of Indigenous people.
- build a prototype preservation and access system.

T&T had followed through on comments from the Koorie community that suggested that there existed a lack of cultural understanding around the issue of oral knowledge, and a concomitant lack of cultural respect by existing archival repositories for Indigenous communities. Indeed it seemed to many that the normative position was that archives were for Anglo Australians, and that both Indigenous and migrant communities were being overlooked. T&T was developed in an attempt to address this, mindful of the need to be culturally respectful. However the very foundations of the project were yet to engage fully with these normative and culturally biased assumptions.

Koorie communities want cultural respect from archival institutions, and recognition that oral knowledge is a respected knowledge source. Although uncertain as to whether or not Koorie communities wanted archival services in regards to their oral memory, T&T aimed 'to discover how to capture it and make it accessible to the relevant communities' over time (SIMS, FIT, 2005). The aims of T&T were based on an untested assumption that Koorie communities wanted to engage with archival institutions in this way – untested in the sense that the aims were developed without consultation with the Koorie community. Not posited in developing the research scope and design was that Koorie communities might simply be after cultural respect from archives, while wanting to make their oral memory accessible through their own knowledge systems. It is important to reflect on how T&T came to its initial premise and aims; especially given two of us were involved in the project from the outset. It is possible that T&T could be viewed as an attempt to control a system of knowledge that is not currently contained within the rigours of Western academia; however this was never the intention. T&T was undertaken as an attempt to produce more culturally inclusive archival institutions – but the question of whether that was an aspiration shared by the Koorie community was not explicitly posed at the outset.

The Public Record Office Victoria, along with Monash University, initiated T&T. The Public Record Office had identified a gap within their responsibilities relating to expanding community access to their collections, and addressing issues relating to oral memory and the archives. Identifying this gap occurred through the long-standing relationship between the Public Record Office Victoria, the Koorie Heritage Trust Inc., and the Victorian Koorie Records Taskforce.

> And most people, when they hear the name of Koorie Heritage Trust, they sort of feel that, well they can trust, because they know people who work

> there and there's a lot of faith in that place, and that's where they like their information sort of stored eventually, and I know the Koorie Heritage Trust are working alongside the Public Records Office, so, I think that feels safe (Singh, 2006, p.6).

Community consultation and the development of relationships require time that, disappointingly, is not factored into the grant application process or adequately funded by the granting agencies. Community projects should ideally involve a pre-project development stage when the project aims, research design and methodologies are worked out in parternership with community members. Project seeding funding is needed for such a stage – to support all participants, including the community members. In the absence of such support, to get project funding approved, many projects source a community organisation to mediate or represent the partner community. This in itself produces problems, as many community organisations do not have the funds or staff to dedicate to this responsibility. The T&T project followed this pattern and experienced related difficulties. Whilst the Koorie Heritage Trust Inc. committed itself to T&T, the project commenced later than expected. Due to other commitments at the time of commencement, there were no in-kind resources available from the Koorie Heritage Trust Inc. to engage with community until after the research design and data collection for Stage One had begun.

Despite the lack of detailed knowledge that would have eventuated from substantial consultation regarding the Koorie community's hopes and aspirations for T&T, the Stage One user needs analysis has indicated that archiving Koorie oral memory is desirable. However, it is acceptable only in certain circumstances and conditions such as Koorie communities, families and individuals retaining control of the archive and their oral memories. One of the main reasons for this is distrust of how these records will be used. Ross, McKemmish, & Faulkhead have discussed the findings of Stage One in detail (2006).

Community Involvement

> There is a need for a Koorie person to be on [research projects], but the thing is we don't want to be just tokens, we want to be utilised (Singh, 2006, p.34).

Another aspect of the initial research design that required substantial re-working was the role of the project's Community Liaison Officer. There was funding in Stage One for the employment of a Community Liaison Officer. It quickly became evident that for the project to have any validity or meaning for the Koorie community, then the Community Liaison Officer should play a role throughout the entire project. Therefore funds were reallocated within T&T, whilst other funds were sourced from outside to ensure the ongoing employment of the Community Liaison Officer.

Employing a community member as a Community Liaison Officer is also a recommended Koorie community protocol; however, it comes with conditions. Koorie people employed in these roles are to play a vital role in the project and not a token one, and they should receive training in their role. On reflection we could have done this much better. A key problem was that the Community Liaison Officer was only brought onto the team after the project had been approved and funded by the Australian Research Council; by this stage, the research design and methods were developed, and the role of the Community Liaison Officer defined,

> ...to be quite honest, I wasn't really aware what I was getting myself into at the time. I didn't actually see what I was doing until I actually signed the contract and came in (Singh, 2006, p.34).

Whilst no-one questions the amazing job the Community Liaison Officer undertook in arranging and supporting the interviewees for Stage One, team members seemed confused about the role. Some viewed it as an essential administrative role in contacting community, but not as a researcher; whilst others viewed the position as a vital community conduit that included research. This led to an unfortunate impression for some that the Indigenous postgraduate student and the Director of the Centre for Australian Indigenous Studies held more vital roles. Their academic standing was being given preference over the community standing of the Community Liaison Officer. Clearly this is not a situation that any community research project wants or can tolerate, especially if this impression flows out into the community. This misunderstanding was rectified when realised. In hindsight, once the team had come together and before launching into the project as designed, time should have been spent revisiting the research design, and negotiating the roles of the various team members.

> ... you can sort of sense there is a little bit of sort of agitation on 'when is this interview going to finish', how come there are so many questions, and although I haven't really felt that the questions were, when you sort of look at the list of questions, you don't sort of feel that they're sort of intimidating, but I guess that depends on the person who's answering them, so I can't speak for them. But I guess if I was in their place and they touched on a few raw nerves I guess I'd become a little bit agitated too, because the questioning also opens up, triggers off other memories... (Singh, 2006, p.2).

Whilst it is difficult to know to what extent, if any, this misunderstanding may have impacted on the data collected in Stage One, it has been anecdotally shown that research developed and conducted in conjunction with a Koorie community member tends to produce different, and possibly more extensive, information. The project process was not unethical according to current academic frameworks, but it did not fully meet the requirements of Koorie research protocols. Our processes of self-reflection led to the Community Liaison Officer having a more hands-on role in the data collection interviews in Stage Two, much to the delight of the Community Liaison Officer and the project team as a whole.

> I find that a lot of community members, if they know you or they know of somebody who you can speak to, it's really good to get the names of people that they know and then they're a little bit more trusting also (Singh, 2006, p.2).

The Community Liaison Officer arranged for seventy-two people from Victorian Koorie communities to be interviewed for Stage One. This was achieved through Koorie community protocols that differ from the protocols normally recommended by university ethics regimes. Koorie protocols require being part of, or well known, by the Koorie community, an added bonuses of employing a Koorie person in this role. Through her methods, the Community Liaison Officer was able to provide not only a cross-section that represented age, gender, and urban and country, she also addressed the community requirements of representation of Elders, and the various Koorie communities of Victoria. Convincing people to be interviewed is not an easy:

> I've always sort of put myself in the place of the interviewees, ... [In the past] I've been asked to take part in research, but it's never been recorded research, and I think that's a little bit harder, because people, well people always sort of think, 'well what's going to happen to this? Where's it going to go?' And, 'are we as Indigenous people going to be exploited again?' I'm sure there's a lot of things' going through people's minds, and because of past injustices to our mob, I think that people do think that way. They sort of say 'well in the past when our people have sort of cooperated with non-Indigenous people, that knowledge that we've recorded, has been taken away and we've never ever seen it again', or ... 'we don't know what the outcome of it is, we just see it when someone's got a big PhD at the back of them, at the back of their names (Singh, 2006, p.4).

The Community Liaison Officer faced other frustrations – many of which were linked to her employment beginning after the project commenced. The first was that she was not involved in the university ethics application processes. As a result the ethics application followed general practice and did not fully take into account community needs. Ethics approval was based upon the recommended approach, which specified that the interviewees be anonymous. It also did not make allowances for further follow up contact. The Community Liaison Officer's suggestions that some of the interviewees would like to have copies of the sound recordings of their interviews, be involved in consulting on the findings of the research, and have their names attached to their knowledge when quoted in publications, led to a rethinking of how ethics applications could be more participant friendly, or community orientated:

> ...we've lost another Elder – well I know he has been recorded quite a bit, but it's just nice that maybe his family would like that tape, that it just was sort of candid interview more or less (Singh, 2006, p.5).

Providing a copy of both the transcript and of the sound recording is a common courtesy usually requested by Indigenous community protocol, but was overlooked in the rush to commence this project, with only transcripts being provided.

Perhaps the above issues should have been identified within the ethics process, however many academic ethics processes are steeped in Western traditions relating to privacy, informed consent, and the ownership and control of data by the academics involved in a project. As a result they are more geared to protecting the interests of the university than the community or individual. Although it is possible to vary the standard approaches to managing relationships with community partners and handling research data, the standard approaches reveal a lack of sensitivity to community protocols, with it being possible for community projects to gain ethics approval without adequate community consultation, or full compliance with community protocols. This stems in part from the place assigned to community members in the western research paradigm – as subjects of research, rather than partners and participants in research as envisaged by community protocols and models of participatory research.

Other obstacles encountered by the Community Liaison Officer included ensuring that all relevant documentation was converted to plain English, and the renaming of the position to something more down to earth – the original position was Cultural Attaché/Protocol Officer.

Another critical issue faced, which impacted on the whole project, related to the Advisory Committee. Koorie community protocols suggest that a group of relevant representatives from the Koorie community be formed, who are to be called upon for regular input and advice, especially at the beginning and end of the project, with regular meetings throughout the project. This provides the Koorie community with the capacity to be an involved and proactive partner. The Advisory Committee formed for T&T differed from this model in several key respects.

Members of the T&T Advisory Committee were selected due to their vested interest in the project's outcomes, such as: members of the Koorie community, representatives of archival repositories, and online archival experts. Only four of the twelve members of the Advisory Committee were Koorie. The committee was established to provide feedback, advice and discussion throughout T&T whilst meeting as a group twice a year. It soon became apparent that the Advisory Committee was not working effectively as indicated by lack of interest by some members, complaints regarding the lack of discussion, and withdrawal from the project by a Koorie Elder. The breakdown of the Advisory Committee could be linked to a number of things including confusion of purpose, infrequency of meetings, and lack of communication. It was felt that the meetings had become project team information sessions, instead of occasions for the Advisory Committee to provide advice.

Unsuccessful attempts to review the Advisory Committee occurred. Whilst individual members of the Advisory Committee were being called upon for advice, the committee as a group appeared to be defunct. Following consultation with the Koorie Elders on the Advisory Committee, we came to the view that the community representation we needed to be consulting with in relation to our research was made up of all the Koorie interviewees who are engaged with the project, and that in terms of seeking advice, recommendations, feedback and validation of the research, we needed to consult with this group as a whole. T&T is currently undertaking processes to achieve this change from an Advisory Committee of interested parties to a Reference Group of Koorie community members.

The problems associated with the Advisory Committee were in no way a reflection of the members. They have all been extremely interested in and dedicated to the project. It is, however, a reflection of a lack of clarity regarding the purpose of the group, and possible differences between a community project and an academic project. As T&T considers the opinions of the Advisory Committee's members as of vital interest to the project, they will also be involved in the consultation process of the project's outcomes.

Whilst this process has been a positive learning experience for the project team, it has also been frustrating, especially for the community members involved in the project, as many of them have had positive experiences with project reference groups in the past. Through this frustration, though, other methods of providing feedback to the Koorie community were developed, such as the Community Liaison Officer keeping in touch with interviewees by telephone and a project newsletter sent to community groups and individuals, providing project up-dates. These methods are keeping community involved and allowing for interaction between the project team and the Koorie communities of Victoria:

> And I think as project's go, I think we've kept the community fairly well up-to-date, because I've been, I've taken part in surveys and things in the past and once you cross those lines and put true or false and give it back, you never see nor hear from it anymore. So I think, really and truly the committee's been trying to do everything in its power, and more I think (Singh, 2006, p.8).

Issues relating to the inclusion of community protocols in western academic research processes have not been the only obstacle to full community involvement. There have also been frustrations within the university administration. Most recently we endured an experience in which it became obvious that the western academic system and the premise of community research are at odds. The university, as it prepares itself for the Research Quality Framework, has reviewed all 'research only' academic positions, and decided that all staff designated 'research' staff must have a research profile and produce independent research outcomes. This led to the Community Liaison Officer position, crucial facilitating T&T and all its research outcomes, being reclassified as a research facilitator; an administrative position. There is no mechanism within the system to recognise that the work involved in keeping community involved and informed is equivalent to a number of research outcomes in itself.

Another example of an administrative obstacle relates to supporting community representation of the project at domestic and International forums. As partners in, and beneficiaries of the project, it is ideal to provide financial support for community representatives to present on the project. Whilst it is possible to book accommodation and flights for community representatives, there are no facilities available to provide a cash advance for travel costs to a non-university staff member. It is rare that a community representative would be able to fund these travel costs up front. This situation could lead to financial hardship for the representative's family, and/or stop community representatives from travelling to represent the project.

Community relations on T&T have been evolutionary, with the project team adapting and developing methods of community engagement, but our experience tells us that true community involvement still faces many obstacles within the western academic paradigm.

Lessons Learnt

The project team came to realise that:

- Communities need to be informed partners, full participants in all stages of a project.
- Community consultations need to occur prior to project funding applications to make sure that the project benefits the community.
- The community organisation and/or representatives, the Community Liaison Officer and the community Reference Group need to be fully engaged prior to commencement of the project.
- The roles of all participants need to be negotiated and agreed.
- We cannot go into a project assuming that the whole team has the same worldview or understands that there are inevitably differing and potentially irreconcilable worldviews when undertaking a community project. Reflexive methods have to be built in to the project to address this.
- Research methodologies, ethics agreements, project management, and research data management systems need to be designed to engage communities as equal partners and participants, with a role in research design and governance, negotiated rights in research data and outcomes, and a role in validating research findings.

To follow through on the lessons learned, we believe we need to work together with communities on two levels – at individual project and systemic levels. For example, a longer period of community engagement before the project started would have significantly re-shaped the initial direction of the research as later stages have been re-shaped by closer community engagement and better understandings. However, it takes time to build trusted research relationships and funding to engage with communities before a project commences. Current research funding models do not support the development of such sustained long-term relationships. Indeed the system encourages so-called 'hit-and-run scholarship'. Similarly, if we are to position community and academic participants as equal partners, we need to work to transform our own research designs and practice, as well as our research governance frameworks, ethics regimes, and models for ownership of and rights in research data.

Conclusion

This chapter has been an extended reflection on the question posed at the outset: 'is community research possible within the western academic tradition?' Our response right now is a somewhat under whelming, yes, well no, maybe? It is not completely impossible to envisage a transformation of academia that would make community research of the kind envisaged here possible, but to achieve this we have to address the challenge of irreconcilable ontologies in our own practice and in our systems. Protocols for researching Indigenous communities have been evolving for a very long time, but it is only recently that the academy has begun to incorporate them into its processes. At this stage, it seems this is essentially being attempted by subsuming community protocols and the constructs of ethical research that underpin them to the western academic tradition.

Throughout our experiences of working together and learning together, we have struggled to find a way that makes community research a reality, which has involved extensive self-reflection, reiteration and reviewing of our methods, motivations and outcomes, and a challenging of the tradition in which we work. We have asked questions of our frameworks, our methods, our colleagues, our communities and ourselves. Reflecting on the question we posed at the start of this sojourn, we would like to revisit it and suggest that the question is not 'is community research possible within the western academic tradition', but 'does the academy want to achieve community based research'? Involving community in academic research can be problematic and time consuming, however the benefits of producing something that will profit or even transform the community, instead of being merely a report on a shelf or another entry in the academic's list of publications, should be enough to encourage changes to occur within academia. Furthermore as universities and other government-funded institutions are increasingly asked to demonstrate their relevance, what better way to do this than to engage in research with all range and manner of communities?

We believe that community and academia can work together, but it needs to be in partnership, not as one within the other. This may involve partnership projects where research methods, results and outcomes are collectively owned. Clearly provisions for the approval of publications and other research outcomes would need to be thought through carefully and continually revisited. In the experience of at least one of the authors this is not nearly as onerous a task as it might appear. In countless community projects, collaborative arrangements have worked successfully. Importantly in these projects, there has never been an occasion where academic results were censored or a community chose not to allow publication, although one occasion it did warrant further negotiation.

Finally community informatics is an area that is illustrating how academia can produce outcomes that are beneficial in the world beyond research. Whilst community informatics is a developing area, it does have a future, especially if takes into account community worldviews and protocols when working within the Indigenous community arena, and is prepared to address the challenge of irreconcilable ontologies as explored in this chapter. Our journey towards reconciled understandings encourages us to be optimistic that the future for communities, academia and the nexus between the two has never been brighter.

Acknowledgement

Whilst this chapter is based on the thoughts and experiences of specific members of the research team, the research team has been extremely supportive with encouragement, advice and discussions. We therefore gratefully acknowledge the ARC Linkage Project, 'Trust and Technology: Building an archival system for Indigenous oral memory' (T&T) team. This team includes the Chief Investigators Professor Lynette Russell, Centre for Australian Indigenous Studies, Monash University, Professor Sue McKemmish, Faculty of Information Technology, Monash University, Professor Don Schauder (2003-6), Associate Professor Graeme Johanson (from 2005), and Dr Kirsty Williamson (2003-4), with Partner Investigator Justine Heazlewood, Director and Keeper, Public Record Office Victoria. The industry partners are Public Record Office Victoria, the Koorie Heritage Trust Inc., the Australian Society of Archivists Indigenous Issues Special Interest Group, and the Victorian Koorie Records Taskforce. Past and current members of the Research Team include: from the Public Record Office Victoria Andrew Waugh, Rachel U'Ren (also of Faculty of Information Technology), Emma Toon, and Merryn Edwards; from the Faculty of Information Technology, Dr Stefanie Kethers, Fiona Ross, Carol Jackway, Jen Sullivan, and Sharon Huebner (also from Koorie Heritage Trust); from the Centre for Australian Indigenous Studies Diane Singh, and the Australian Postgraduate Award (Industry) PhD researcher is Shannon Faulkhead. We would like to also thank our Advisory Committee. Finally we would like to acknowledge and thank the eighty-four participants who agreed to be interviewed as part of the project; who shared their views and experiences with us.

References

Attwood, B. (2001). Learning about the truth: the stolen generations narrative. In B. Attwood, & F. Magowan (Eds.), Telling stories: Indigenous history and memory in Australia and New Zealand (pp.183-212). Crows Nest, NSW: Allen & Unwin.

Centre for Community Networking Research (CCNR), Faculty of Information Technology, Monash University. Accessed on 1 February 2007 at: www.ccnr.net.

Centre for Organisational and Social Informatics (COSI), Faculty of Information Technology, Monash University. Accessed 1 February 2007 at: www.infotech.monash.edu.au/research/centres/cosi/index.html

Faulkhead, S., & Russell, L. (2006). What is Australian Indigenous oral history? International Oral History Association Conference, Sydney. Unpublished.

National Health & Medical Research Council (Aust.). (2003). Values and ethics: guidelines on ethical conduct in Aboriginal and Torres Strait Islander health research. Canberra: The Council.

Ross, F., McKemmish, S., & Faulkhead, S. (2006). Indigenous knowledge and the archives: designing trusted archival systems for Koorie communities [Article is based in part on a paper delivered at the joint ARANZ ASA Conference, Archives and Communities (2005): Wellington.] Archives & Manuscripts, 34:2, 112-151.

Russell, L. (2005). Indigenous knowledge and archives: accessing hidden history and understandings. In M. Nakata & M. Langton (Eds.), Kingston (ACT), Australian Indigenous Knowledge and Libraries.

SIMS, FIT (School of Information Management & Systems, Faculty of Information Technology, Monash University). (2005). Trust and Technology Project: Building archival systems for Indigenous oral memory. Accessed 4 June 2006 at: www.sims.monash.edu.au/research/eirg/trust/index.html

Singh, D. (2006). Researching Together Interview 23 March. CAIS: Monash University, Unpublished.

Stoecker, R. (2005) Research Methods for Community Change; a Project-based Approach, (California: Sage)

Vickery, J., Faulkhead, S., Adams, K., & Clarke, A. (2004). Indigenous Insights into Oral History, Social Determinants, and Decolonisation. Cooperative Research Centre for Aboriginal Health Workshop, Adelaide.

Wikipedia The Free Encyclopedia. (2006a). Community-based participatory research. Accessed 6 August 2006 at: en.wikipedia.org/wiki/Community-based_participatory_research

Wikipedia. (2006b). Community Informatics. Accessed 23 October 2006 at: en.wikipedia.org/wiki/Community_informatics

Shannon Faulkhead, Lynette Russell, Diane Singh and Sue McKemmish

Overcoming obstacles to accessing participants in community health research

Alfred Joseph Banya

> In this chapter I describe how, in studying community involvement in a public health programme, I applied a participatory methodology to overcome obstacles to accessing the research participants. The chapter is based on a study I conducted on the development of a government public health programme called Health Action Zone (HAZ) in England between 1999 and 2002. I give the context of my study, which included ongoing debates in public health about the individual and society's responsibility for health, as well as the national and local HAZ policy on the involvement of communities in health programmes. In the study, I investigated how, in one of the HAZ projects in the North of England, lay people were recruited as 'Health Activists' to promote health. I describe how the organisation of the HAZ and the different priorities between the Health Activists and the professionals had caused tension that became an obstacle to my efforts to recruit research participants. I explain how my identity as a Black African male researching a white and predominantly female group in one of the most deprived areas of the UK compounded this obstacle. I describe how I overcame this by applying a methodology based on participatory research and the work of Paolo Freire, as well as my own professional experience and life as an African.

Over the years there has been an ongoing debate in public health about the potential benefits of community participation in promoting health and wellness, and preventing illness, disease and injury. The debate has been conducted against the background of arguments that Western society in particular is obsessed with the assessment of risk. Evidence of this is the growth of health promotion and disease prevention activities, as well as the environmental movement. Social theorists have also entered the debate about risk. Beck (1992) and Giddens (1991) have, for example, argued that the current period we live in is one in which life tends to be characterised by how both lay people and professionals organise their social worlds around risk. There is also a perception that the state is increasingly assigning responsibility to individuals and communities to look after their own health.

During the early period after the Labour government came to power in 1997 in the UK, it introduced a number of health policies aimed at enabling partnerships between communities and professionals in tackling factors that put people's health at risk. One such policy introduced the Health Action Zone (HAZ) as a public health programme targeted at the most deprived areas of England. I concentrate in this chapter on one HAZ in the North of England that I focused on in my research. I use this to illustrate some of the tensions that can arise between professionals and lay people in translating such policy initiatives into practice. I particularly describe how such tension can arise when programmes such as the HAZ are organised in ways that marginalise lay or community participation in the governing structures. I also describe the challenges I faced as a Black African male researching a group that was all white and mainly female. I explain how the differences between the professionals and lay people, compounded by my ethnicity and gender, made me an 'outsider' to those I intended to recruit as my research participants. I describe how I overcame these obstacles by applying a methodology based on participatory research, and on sharing some of my life experience, to facilitate access to the research participants.

The HAZ public health programme: A community and professional partnership for health?

When the Labour government came to power in 1997 in the UK, one of its 'Big Ideas' for improving health was the introduction of health policy reforms, one of which was the establishment of the HAZ. The public health White Paper Saving Lives: Our Healthier Nation (Department of Health, 1999) introduced the idea of the HAZ as a public health programme. This was based on the recognition by the government that improving health and reducing health inequalities between population groups was a complex policy problem that required various agencies and departments to work together across their conventional organisational and professional boundaries. Central to this was the involvement of communities. Between 1998 and 1999, the government established a total of 26 HAZs across the country. The HAZs were established in the most deprived parts of England. These areas also had populations with worse health than those in other parts of the country. The government funded the HAZs on condition that the responsible health authorities worked in partnership with communities, the local authority and voluntary organisations to develop and implement a plan for improving health and reducing health inequality.

The introduction of the HAZ provided a unique opportunity for the study of how partnerships in such a public health programme would translate in practice. Of particular interest was the extent to which lay people and communities would be involved in prioritising health problems and delivering health interventions. This is because the knowledge and expertise that lay people develop from their personal experience and use to tackle risk, is often marginalised and rarely considered valid knowledge. Writers, such as Williams and Popay (1997), have argued for the need to value lay experience in helping to bridge the gap between epidemiology that informs much of professional public health practice, and the theories postulated by sociologists. Other writers, such as Petersen and

Lupton (1996), Crawshaw, Bunton and Gillen (2003), have also argued that the 'new' approaches to public health that claim to work in partnership with the public has developed within a framework of dominant professional knowledge, informed by 'scientific' epidemiology. According to these writers, this is just another way of using power and knowledge to control individuals and society. In their view, the so-called new approaches offer very little opportunity for challenging the power relations or for individuals to take autonomous action on health. These views are reflected in findings about the type of research methodologies that dominate public health research. Millward, Kelly and Nutbeam (2003) have reported that, despite policy commitment in the UK to expand the public health practice evidence base, only 0.4% of research on public health issues are about prevention compared to cure. Moreover, very little of the published research from which the evidence is drawn is based on qualitative methodologies that could explore in more depth the complexities of getting individuals to participate in looking after their health and that of the public. From a community research perspective, Stoecker (2005) has also noted that research carried out by community workers and community members on the ground does not often get recognised as producing legitimate knowledge and is rarely published.

The introduction of programmes such as the HAZ offer opportunities for changing public health practice. However, the tension between the practices in health that create boundaries between key players, and those that try to dismantle such boundaries presents a tremendous challenge to such change. Rothman (2001) has conceptualised three 'modes' of community intervention. He has also described the tensions that can occur between practices based on the different modes. The first of Rothman's community intervention mode is the locality development approach and is underpinned by community consensus in setting priorities for action. The second mode is social planning and is based on priorities of policy makers who are often external to the potential beneficiaries. The third community intervention mode is social action and is characterised by the community taking control and acting to change power relations in order to solve problems affecting the community. A balance in the appropriate use of different elements of these modes of community intervention is a major challenge for partnership working.

A key aspect of my study of the HAZ was to explore whether government interest in community participation in public health was a mere extension of power and control, or a genuine commitment to creating an opportunity for both lay people and professionals to work together to improve health. The HAZ in the North of England was ideal for my study. This was because it had a specific work programme on community involvement. This was the Local Governance and Community Health work programme whose main aim was to create opportunities for communities to define their priorities and to take action to improve their health. The Health Activists' scheme was crucial to the achievement of this aim.

The problem of community exclusion from the HAZ organisational structure and governance

When the government introduced the HAZ programme, each HAZ was required to establish a partnership board as the governing body to plan and oversee the implementation of local health improvement programmes. This partnership was to include the community and voluntary sector, the health authority and the local authority. The initial policy rhetoric on this implied 'equal partnership'. However, the HAZ that I researched created a partnership that was dominated by health professionals and elected local County and District Council[8] councillors. The feeling in the community was therefore that the governance arrangements had excluded local people. What was clear was that the arrangement had deviated from the original plan submitted in the application for HAZ status to the Department of Health. The original proposal was to build on a network of community forums. The forums were to link to local Health Alliance groups that existed in each of the four district authority areas and provide an opportunity for communities to engage with statutory agencies on local health issues. The plan was for the Health Alliance groups in turn to feed up to a Partnership Board and to a County-wide Strategic Alliance led by the health authority. The County-wide Strategic Alliance would have representation from agencies and local organisations interested in participating in the HAZ. The arrangements that later transpired, however, differed substantially from this. The resulting arrangement had two tiers: the Partnership Board and the Executive Team, serviced by a HAZ office. The most significant was the change from the proposal to base the organisation on a network of community forums to one which located statutory agencies and officers from the Health Authority, the District and County councils in a central position and with greater control of the HAZ. The community forums suggested in the initial proposal, and which would have provided an avenue for community involvement in influencing decisions, had disappeared from the structure.

At the time I began my research, therefore, there was detectable tension and mistrust between the professionals in the HAZ and sections of the community. Some of the voluntary sector organisations that usually represented community interests felt that they had been excluded from the HAZ decision-making arrangements, contrary to what had been agreed with them earlier. An example they cited was the way in which the original plan for the HAZ to fund the employment of four community workers to co-ordinate the work of Health Activists was changed. Another was the decision to introduce new criteria for who could become a Health Activist. The existing Health Activists interpreted this as an attempt by the professionals to transform the Health Activists' scheme to fit their own priorities. These decisions created mistrust and caused tension between the professionals and the Health Activists, and in turn created obstacles for me as a researcher in recruiting people to participate in my research.

---

[8] The local government structure in the area the HAZ covered was made up of several District Authorities within a single County.

The Health Activists' origins and problem of identity transformation

Several years before the HAZ was introduced, the Workers' Education Association, a voluntary group that promotes life-long learning, had already developed a Health Activists' scheme. The aim of the scheme at that time was to help women look after their own health and that of people in their community. This explained why most of the Health Activists were women. When the HAZ took over the scheme, it transformed the identity and role of the Health Activists. A new condition was that the Health Activists must undergo certain training and that they should undertake health promotion activities that addressed health priorities set by the HAZ. The existing Health Activists protested by pointing out that, for many years prior to the HAZ, they operated as 'community activists' working on local problems without the requirement to conform to externally set priorities. This added to the dissatisfaction with the earlier HAZ decisions to reverse a previously agreed plan to employ workers to support the Health Activists. Furthermore, these decisions were made through a governance structure that was widely viewed as having excluded local people's participation. These concerns became the focus of intense exchanges between the Health Activists and the professionals in the HAZ, to the extent that it involved the local press and the Member of Parliament for the area.

The Health Activists' scheme as originally conceived could be described in Rothman's terms (Rothman, 2001) as based on a locality development community intervention mode. However, when the Health Activists became part of the HAZ programme the scheme was transformed into one that assumed more of the characteristics of a social planning mode of community intervention. Furthermore, as the Health Activists increasingly challenged this change, their approach drifted towards direct action which is typical of a social action community intervention mode as opposed to the consensus approach that marked the locality development mode the scheme was originally based on. These were clearly fundamental changes that no doubt strained the relations between the Health Activists and the professionals in the HAZ.

Researcher identity and its impact on access to research participants

The tension and mistrust that the transformation of the Health Activists' scheme generated affected my efforts to gain access to both the Health Activists and the health professionals in the HAZ. Another factor that contributed to my access difficulties was the fact that the local health authority had sponsored my study. I was therefore initially perceived by some of the Health Activists as being on the side of the 'authorities' and coming to 'spy' on their activities. Voluntary sector organisations with interest in the Health Activists were also concerned that the perception of my research as 'surveillance' of Health Activists' activities would discourage local people from participating as Health Activists. Amidst all this, another problem was my identity. I was clearly seen as an 'outsider' because I stood out as a Black African male. This was an obstacle in involving the Health Activists in my research. A particular problem was that the Health Activists were white and of a different gender to me. On one occasion one of the Health Activists told me that if she were in my position she would find it difficult to work with the Health Activists, as she knew that many of them would prefer talking to a female researcher or someone indigenous to the area.

Turning the researcher identity 'problem' into a solution

In searching for ways to facilitate my access to the research participants, I was aware of the dangers of reinforcing any inherent tension and power imbalance that had developed between the professionals and the Health Activists. I also wanted to avoid reinforcing the perception that I was an 'outsider'. Instead, I wanted to use my ethnic origin as an African to enrich the exchange of experiences with the research participants.

The challenge of overcoming the obstacles to accessing the Health Activists inspired me to reflect on my childhood and upbringing. I recalled growing up as a child in the Acholi community of Northern Uganda. For example, I was constantly reminded by the older people about the importance of *'Pwonyo gwoko gang'*, which means learning the skills to look after the home or community. Among the Acholi, it is traditional that young people are expected at an early age to learn skills which they can use to provide food, housing, and other services for their families and the community (Girling, 1959). The learning of such skills is undertaken as an apprenticeship while, at the same time, the learner is helping to provide a service to family and community. Furthermore, relations between the same household are firmly grounded in their contribution to activities that support daily needs and ensure the survival of all members of the household. I recall observing *'awak'*. This is a practice where work parties including members of several different households help each other by collectively contributing their labour to till the fields, plant, weed and harvest crops belonging to a particular household that needs help. This to me was no different from the concept of social capital that, according to Putnam (1993), is about community organisation, social trust, norms and networks of reciprocity. Therefore, as my mind turned to the social practices of the Acholi, I related these to some of the ideas about community participation and health, as well as participatory research approaches to understanding social practices.

Researching with the participants

The reflection on my own cultural experiences had a very significant influence on my research strategy. I wanted very much to research with the participants in a way that offered an opportunity for mutual exchange and learning from each other's experiences. In other words, I sought an approach that would facilitate the generation of knowledge not only from me as the researcher but the Health Activists as those being researched. This is an approach that has been described by writers such as de Koning and Martin (1996), and

Tandon (1996) as participatory research. The Brazilian adult educator, Paolo Freire had a major influence on participatory research. Freire argued that the process of study is not neutral and that people are not passive objects of investigation but can use it for their liberation by challenging the often oppressive power relations involved. In other words, humans are not empty vessels into which ideas are 'thrown', but have the capacity to reflect on such ideas and positively contribute their own views on them. His work, particularly in the 1960s and 1970s, on alternative pedagogy had a major influence on the ideas and practice of participatory research and emphasised learning in a dialogical way (Freire, 1972). Freire considered the process of study or research as a part of transforming the world and emphasised the importance of subjectivity, which implied that both the researcher and the researched were integral parts of the research process. He rejected what is often described as 'objective' study and analyses, which consider people as the passive objects of investigation. According to Freire, studying is the task of the 'subject' and not the 'object' and that it is a way of reinventing, recreating, and rewriting reality. Studying or research is therefore not about consuming ideas but creating and recreating them (Freire, 1985).

Empowerment as a strategy for access to participants

Influenced by Freire's notion of using the process of study as a tool for liberation, I turned to some of the values I held. One such value was my commitment to empowering people with whom I worked. I was therefore committed to the empowerment of the research participants and concerned about the processes that oppressed and constrained them from exercising power over the issues they faced. Recognising the political nature of the research and the need for careful preparation, I familiarised myself with the local issues and the individuals involved in these. I made the Health Activists and the staff from the voluntary organisations who were working with them aware that I understood the problems they were facing. A number of staff from some of the voluntary organisations, for example, shared the Health Activists' opposition to the HAZ for reversing the decision to employ community workers to help the Health Activists. Although I shared their concerns, I explained that I also understood the difficult position in which central government had put the HAZ. I was on a number of occasions invited to attend staff and Health Activists' meetings. I used these meetings to share my thoughts on these concerns. In my view, the underlying problem was that the government had changed the focus of all HAZs from the original priority of tackling broader health determinants to that of addressing medical and treatment targets related to heart disease, cancer and mental health. This had made community development less of a priority, hence the cutting back of resources originally earmarked for community workers. Sharing this analysis with the Health Activists helped broaden their understanding of the origin of the tension that had emerged between them and the HAZ. In this way I helped empower the Health Activists to seek redress not just by confronting the professionals in the HAZ, who were largely just 'messengers', but by focusing on decision makers at the political level.

Beginning where people are

In order to translate my commitment to empowerment into practice, and further aid my access to the research participants, I had to apply what some participatory researchers such as Meulenberg-Busken (1996) described as starting from where people are. This requires patience and familiarisation with the research setting. I therefore ensured that I familiarised myself with the various HAZ activities that related to the Health Activists. This enabled me to appropriately time and identify my points of entry and engagement with the relevant participants. As is often the case in participatory research, this meant eliciting the support of key organisations and individuals or 'informants' trusted and respected by the prospective research participants. An organisation that was already closely involved with the Health Activists was the Workers' Education Association. The workers and tutors from this organisation were already training and helping the Health Activists. I identified key individuals in the organisation and cultivated relationships with them. This developed into a relationship with the Workers' Education Association as an organisation. For example, I was allowed to attend their staff meetings as an observer. I used the opportunity to explain my research, and also to learn about the work the organisation was undertaking with the Health Activists. Over a period of four months, I gained the confidence of a number of the workers who in turn introduced me to the Health Activists.

From an outsider to becoming an insider

Stoecker (2005) has pointed out the difficulty for a researcher to establish their own legitimacy, particularly when they enter a community without invitation. In my case, gaining the confidence of the Workers' Education Association staff was an important first step in accessing the Health Activists. The second step was to consolidate this by showing that I had something to offer which could help the staff in their role of supporting the Health Activists. I helped by facilitating some of the Health Activists community development training sessions. The trade-off was that I got to know the Health Activists and managed to recruit a total of 36 to participate in my research.

As Meulenberg-Busken (1996) has highlighted, one of the advantages of participatory research is the flexibility that allows for the use of more than one technique to gather information, an aspect I found useful in my study. Stoecker (2005) has made a further point that participatory approaches to research need to use methods that make sense to people if they are to be useful. In my research, I negotiated and obtained the agreement of the Health Activists on the methods that I eventually used to explore their participation in HAZ community activities. The methods included focus group discussions to explore the Health Activists' understanding of health and the factors that had most influence on their health; what they would look for if asked to judge whether their health had improved; how they defined their community and how they related participation in community activities to health; how and why they participated in community activities; and what activities they had benefited most from. I followed up the focus group discussions with individual in-depth interviews. The interviews explored in more depth issues that had emerged from the focus group discussions. To gain more insight into the Health Activists' involvement in health activities, I also conducted observation studies of activities in which the Health Activists participated. Depending on the nature of the activities, my role varied from being that of a participant, where I took an active part, to being a non-participant where I was a passive observer.

My experience and knowledge of some of the cultural practices in Africa came in useful, particularly in the participant observation studies. Reflecting on some of the communal practices of the Acholi in looking after a newborn child, for instance, came in useful in my observation of a group of Health Activists involved in a series of baby massage workshops. It was a challenge to gain the trust of both the tutor and the participants so that, as a male, I could take part as a participant observer and positively contribute to the group. I was eventually allowed to join the group having drawn on my past experience of life in Uganda where, as a child growing up, baby massage was a daily morning ritual in which various family members took part, even if it was just to observe and admire the newborn. It was a way of collective learning and the beginning of what could be a lifetime communal interest in the welfare of the new family member. Using a baby doll, I joined in the baby massage exercises and narrated how the Acholi of Uganda used freshly extracted sesame oil to massage babies, something which both the tutor and participants found very interesting. This contributed immensely to my gaining acceptance in the group and I was able to conduct my participant observation without any objections from the mothers. The contact with the group snowballed into invitations to a number of meetings and activities that the Health Activists held.

A final word

In researching complex social interventions such as the HAZ, there are often limitations in using experimental and randomised control trial types of approaches often considered more 'scientific'. This makes the type of emergent qualitative approach that I used the more important. However, as Millward et al. (2003) have reported, very little published research from which public health evidence is drawn is based on qualitative methodologies. This is despite situations such as that of the HAZ being well suited for such methodologies that can enable deeper understanding of the research setting characteristics, such as changing organisational structures, tensions between research participants, and the influence of the researcher. By applying a flexible approach that took account of these characteristics, I was able to transform 'problems' into opportunities for sharing and generating knowledge. This showed that in community health research, it is essential for the approach to fit the context. The challenge therefore is that of recognising the type of flexible and emergent methodology that I used as being valid ways of researching that could contribute to improving public health practice. The involvement of those being researched is central to this. This is consistent with the dialogical approach to learning which Freire (1972), and more recently Stoecker (2005) have advocated. This means that a two way learning process needs to be entered into with the intended beneficiaries of any public health interventions in order to assess and work with what is meaningful to them and in ways that can contribute to their capacity to look after their health and that of others.

References

Beck, U. (1992). Risk Society: Towards a New Modernity. London: Sage.

Crawshaw, P., Bunton, R., & Gillen, K. (2003). Health Action Zones and the problem of community. Health and Social Care in the Community. 11(1), 36-44.

Department of Health. (1999). Saving Lives: Our Healthier Nation. London: Stationery Office Ltd.

Freire, P. (1985). The Politics of Education: Culture, Power and Liberation. London: Macmillan.

Freire, P. (1972). Pedagogy of the Oppressed. London: Harmondsworth.

Giddens, A. (1991). Modernity and Self-Identity: Self and Society in the late Modern Age. Cambridge: Polity Press.

Girling, F.K. (1959). The Acholi of Uganda. London: HMSO.

de Koning, K., & Martin, M. (Eds.). (1996). Participatory Research in Health. London: Zed Books Ltd.

Meulenberg-Buskens, I. (1996). Critical awareness in participatory research: an approach towards teaching and learning. London: Zed Books.

Millward, L.M., Kelly, M.P., & Nutbeam, D. (2003) Public health intervention research – the evidence. London: Health Development Unit.

Petersen A., & Lupton, D. (1996). The New Public Health: health and self in the age of risk. London: Sage.

Putnam, R. (1993). Making Democracy Work: Civic traditions in modern Italy. New Jersey: Princetown University Press.

Rothman, R. (2001). Approaches to Community Intervention. In J. Rothman, J.L. Erlich, J.E. Tropman (Eds.), Strategies of Community Intervention (pp.27-64). Itasca, Illinois: F.E. Peacock.

Stoecker, R. (2005). Research Methods for Community Change. London: Sage.

Tandon, R. (1996). The historical roots and contemporary tendencies in participatory research: implications for health care. In K. de Koning & M. Martin (Eds.), Participatory Research in Health. London: Zed Books Ltd.

Williams, G., & Popay, J. (1997). Social science and the future of population health. In L. Jones & M. Sidell (Eds.), The Challenge of Promoting Health: Exploration and Action. London: Macmillan.

Community network analysis: Communications, neighbourhood and action (CNA²)

A community engagement strategy and research methodology

Peter Day and Clair Farenden

> CNA² is presented as both community engagement strategy and community research methodology. Promoting the need for a relationship between community technology researchers and community development practitioners, the authors outline the rationale of the Community Network Analysis (CNA) and ICT project, which investigates community communication relationships, the influence of ICT and their potential for supporting and sustaining social capital in the community networks of the Poets Corner neighbourhood in Brighton and Hove, UK. Having outlined the CNA community engagement strategy within the broader context of social cohesion, social capital and community networking, a methodology for community technology research, grounded in partnerships and participation, is introduced. Illustrating, through examples, how the CNA community engagement strategy and research methodology are interwoven into the fabric of community learning in Poets Corner, the chapter concludes by reflecting on 2 propositions that the CNA team believe to be fundamental to community networking.

Communications and communication media/technologies have been instrumental in developing and sustaining community infrastructures down the ages. From rock paintings in the Stone Age to Town Criers in the 16th century; from simple community newsletters produced on mechanical duplicating machines to web-based community networks and community media initiatives, people have always utilised forms of Information Communication Technology (ICT) or media to communicate, and share knowledge, with others in their communities. Communication is the bedrock upon which the diversity of social networks, groups, clubs, organisations, activities and actions that constitute the community environment are formed, developed and sustained. In essence, communication is the life-blood of community existence.

Effective communication is also crucial to researchers wishing to engage in community network research. The generation of academic knowledge and knowledge that assists communities to define their own problems, set their own goals and find their own solutions – a dual goal for academics engaged in community research – requires communicative dialogue between researcher and community. Building and sustaining this dialogue requires a strategy for engaging the community and building relationships of trust and reciprocity.

In this chapter, we introduce and reflect on the engagement strategy of the Community Network Analysis (CNA) and ICT project, an Economic and Social Research Council (ESRC) funded community communication technology research project. Funded for 3 years as part of the People at the Centre of Communication and Information Technology (PACCIT) programme, the project aimed to investigate the potential of ICT in building social capital and strengthening and sustaining social ties and cohesion in the community infrastructure. The CNA team comprised 3 academics from the University of Brighton – a project manager, a technical advisor and a research officer – working on a part-time basis, and a part-time worker from the Sussex Community Internet Project (SCIP) a community sector organisation, and our partners in the funding bid, that provides IT services and support for charities and community groups.

Unfortunately, the research was severely hampered by the withdrawal, 15 months into the project life-cycle, of our initial community partners, the Community of Interest Network (COIN). COIN was a network of over 200 community groups representing socially excluded and marginalised people in Brighton and Hove, UK. Changes to national government funding mechanisms resulted in a major shake-up of the city-wide structure and organisation of the community and voluntary sector. Fears for the future of the network's existence, the loss of a key worker and a structural division of the network, which ultimately led to its collapse, meant that COIN was unable to continue as CNA partners. This meant that the project effectively had to start again from scratch! After some critical discussions and a lot of soul searching[9], the CNA team set about identifying a geographic community to develop a community communications research partnership with. SCIP informed us that they had been approached by the Poets Corner Residents Society (PCRS)[10] – who were looking to develop their ICT suite, the services it provided, whilst improving communications within the community – but were unable to help them at that time. After an introduction through SCIP, PCRS invited the CNA team to visit them and the project was up and running again.

---

[9] The team was considering calling a halt to the project.
[10] Now the Poets Corner Community Society (PCCS).

In the following section we introduce the theoretical grounding of the project in order to provide the conceptual context for a subsequent reflection of the engagement strategy and methodology in later sections.

Engaging with community networks

> Community-type organisation is a feature of all human societies and studies of humans and other higher primates suggest that we share an inherent sociability, a willingness to connect and to cooperate (Gilchrist, 2004, p.1).

Pointing to relationships between social networks and their role in structuring modern community life, Gilchrist's statement is a reinforcement, if needed, that the world over, people socialise, develop relationships, plan events and organise activities in the name of community. Behaviour such as this forms the glue or social cohesion that forms and sustains community. Connected in this way, community activists give human purpose to social capital – i.e. they influence community norms; develop trust and sustain networks. Of course, community life is not always so harmonious. The diversity of values, cultures and beliefs found in community environments means that community life often harbours dispute, tension and conflict as well as cooperation and collaboration and often at the same time. In short, community comprises sets of contested spaces. In order to understand the way in which people connect and engage with one another in communities, it is important to develop an understanding of the diverse and multi-cultural nature of the community environment or network. Before turning to this however, it is also important to clarify what we mean by community engagement.

Community engagement

A quick trawl through the literatures of community engagement theory and practice reveals a number of interpretations. For some, community engagement describes a formal set of relationships existing between government and the public. It is often found nearer the 'local' end of the spectrum of government and usually relates to mechanisms involving the public in decision making processes (Johnson, 2005). An example of such an interpretation is provided by a Local Strategic Partnership (LSP) comprising representatives from public, private, and community and voluntary sectors in Middlesbrough, UK. The LSP suggests that "community engagement complements representative democracy within Middlesbrough, and in particular helps organisations to understand the wants and needs of citizens and to plan and deliver their services accordingly" (Middlesbrough Partnership, 2005, p.4).

This somewhat top-down perception of community engagement is countered by a more participative form of democracy, where deliberation by citizens forms a central component of engagement (Hartz-Karp, 2005). Here, engagement takes place through innovative forms of public deliberation such as, citizen's juries, consensus forums, 21st century town meetings, etc and seeks to improve decision making quality through the participation of diverse social groupings and cultures, and a recognition of shared meanings (Pollard & Stoker, 2005).

Whilst these interpretations focus on increasing the influence of local people in the decision making process, there is a sense of formality about many of the processes. Even in the most innovative approach people are required to go to government (Cavaye, 2005). An alternative is to take engagement to the spaces that form hubs or agora in local communities, such as schools, local clubs, parks or community groups. That is to say that the deliberative processes of community engagement should fit the reality and shared meanings of community environments as experienced by local people rather than vice versa.

At the community development level, community engagement seeks to empower local communities to make decisions that shape local action and activities. However, community development and neighbourhood renewal agencies are at risk of working with community representatives they know, which results in the same voices being heard time and time again. A consequence of this is that a process intended to be inclusive becomes exclusive (Skidmore, Bound & Lownsbrough, 2006). Similarly, research into community problems can tend to present 'solutions' from the perspective of the 'researcher' rather than those being 'researched', resulting in the community being excluded from influencing the 'community' research processes (Pollard & Stoker, 2005).

For the purposes of this chapter, community engagement refers to the processes by which the community engaged in shaping the planning and evolution of the CNA project, and the processes by which the research team engaged with and maintained dialogic partnerships within the community networks of Poets Corner (and latterly, the extended Neighbourhood Renewal Area of Portland Road & Clarendon).

Social cohesion and social capital

Of course, making and sustaining social network relationships can be problematic. From a human-centred perspective, the diverse and contested nature of community is understood as a strength not a weakness. It facilitates an environment in which social creativity and innovation can be nurtured in ways that stimulate and promote community learning. Healthy communities celebrate and respect diversity; building community connections and coherence through the promotion of a culture of shared communication, values and knowledge – a process known as social cohesion (Gill, 1997). Establishing and maintaining social connectivity can be challenging, and achieving social cohesion requires "stocks of social trust, norms, and networks that people can draw upon to solve common problems" (Sirianni & Friedland, 1997, p.14). Succinctly, achieving social cohesion requires social capital.

According to Putnam, "social capital calls attention to the fact that civic virtue is most powerful when embedded in a sense network of reciprocal social relations" (2000, p.19). The value of these social relations, as with any other form of capital, is the capacity to use them for a specific purpose. In the context of community networking that purpose is the collaborative, communal problem-solving of community building activities achieved through dialogue, i.e. communicative exchanges between social actors. "Dialogue and debate within networks transform information so that it becomes intelligence (about the current situation) and knowledge (about the wider context)" (Gilchrist, 2004, p.30). The capacity of people connected in community networks to identify problems, plan agenda, agree and execute actions, and evaluate outcomes is what Schuler calls 'civic intelligence' (Schuler, 2001). Civic intelligence "describes the capacity that organizations and society use to 'make sense' of information and events and craft responses to environmental and other challenges collectively" (Day & Schuler, 2006, p.34).

Democratic community networks

As a social construct, community networks have contributed to community life for as long as communities have existed. In a seminal text on the emergence of 'new', i.e. ICT based community networks, Schuler explains how the term 'community networks' was a sociological concept referring to community communication patterns and relationships (1996) long before the emergence of the community bulletin boards of the late 1970s (Morino, 1994) – forerunners of the web-based community networks we know today (Kubicek & Wagner, 1998). Despite that however, community networks are increasingly referred to as technological artefacts and appear to be understood in terms of the connectivity they give to ICT rather than the links they enable to be built within communities.

Establishing what lies at the heart of community networking, i.e. the purpose and nature of the social relationships within communities and their attendant processes of communication, is central to understanding community (Day, 2008). It provides a starting point for addressing the challenges accompanying the design, development and sustainability of technology mediated community networks. To put it simply, knowledge of what shapes and energizes community life is pivotal to developing effective community networks.

By expanding opportunities for people to engage in decision making through ICT mediated processes, a knowledge democracy can begin to be shaped (Smyre & Cohill, 2002). Actions supporting democratic knowledge sharing within community network research include:

1. community engagement;
2. democratic community research processes (Stoecker, 2005);
3. use of the Internet (especially social networking applications) to support citizen dialogue and community communications; and

4. a community learning infrastructure and resources.

It is within this context that we now turn our attention to the CNA community engagement strategy, its research methodology and partnership processes.

The CNA rationale – (Community) engagement, networking and partnerships

Engaging with a community or communities in order to create a partnership can be problematic and is hard work. CNA's involvement in Poets Corner followed a fortuitous invitation to visit PCRS at their self-renovated community centre in Stoneham Park – the Talkshop. The initial meeting provided a platform for the CNA team and PCRS members to discuss and consider mutual needs. As we exchanged stories about ourselves and our activities, the potential for a collaborative partnership of mutual benefit began to emerge. With the contact details of people the PCRS group felt we should talk to we used snowball sampling to contact and interview the majority of people involved in establishing and developing PCRS. This approach enabled us to describe and raise awareness of the project throughout the Poets Corner community infrastructure. In this way we not only collected socially rich qualitative data, which informed the development of the profiling exercise to come, but also identified the first cluster of people interested in participating in and shaping the project.

From these early community meetings we identified that despite ongoing Neighbourhood Renewal activities, Poets Corner, which makes up about half of the Portland Road & Clarendon Neighbourhood Renewal Area, was fragmenting as a network of community relationships. Large scale community activities, such as the annual summer festival and the family fun day, were well supported each year but the resources of social capital evident during the organising and running of these events appeared to diminish dramatically during the rest of the year.

Having cemented our relationship with PCRS and its affiliated groups, the CNA team sought to extend the partnership to other groups, clubs, organisation, agencies and individuals interested in community networking and community communication technology. Our initial strategy was to attend and support as many community meetings and events as possible. This enabled us to introduce ourselves, raise awareness of the project and listen to the needs and views of those we met. Eventually, we were placed on the mailing lists for meetings of the community forum, as well as various community associations, centres and action groups. Other invitations came through informal community communication channels – telephone, email, serendipitous meetings, etc. Slowly but surely, the project team earned the trust of increasing numbers of groups and individuals within the community infrastructure.

Immersion in the community in this way afforded us a privileged position as partners in community life, often with access to personal, private and public details about life and relationships in the community network. With the advantages of this position came great responsibility and we were mindful to remember the power and influence we wielded during the dialogic exchanges of the research processes in the community, especially during the early stages when confidence and trust were not as well developed among community participants as they are now. Similarly, perceptions of us as experts in the field put us in a very strong position to influence community decision making regarding the introduction of ICT. It would have been all too easy to have exerted that influence and power, effectively making decisions on the community's behalf – pulling them along in our wake. At times the temptation to do this was great. Frustrations emerged, not only for us but also among our community partners, who were often used to 'experts' or service providers doing things 'for' or 'to' them. This was not the purpose of the project however, and although it might have been a lot easier simply to have built a website and then trained local people to use it, that ran counter to the purpose of the project. Previous research shows us that the 'build it and they will come' approach does not work in the context of community adoption of technologies (Day & Harris, 1997). Regular dialogue both within the CNA team and within the research partnership to address these frustrations as they arose formed an important and ongoing part of our research and development strategy. Especially when the project was taking longer to develop than we had planned for, and the research programme committee[11] were getting 'feisty'!

At this point we note that the community services approaches of 'doing to' or 'doing for' have an important role to play in community practice (Glen, 1993). However, CNA's approach was influenced more by community development and community action perspectives than community service. Despite this, there were inevitably times when we did, and still do, provide some services for our community partners. Nothing is ever simply black or white in community life! However, it is important to recognise that doing things 'for' or 'to' the community can change the dynamics of the power relationships within and beyond the community network. With this in mind we resolved early on in the project that, wherever possible, our community engagement strategy should be implemented at the community's pace and in the way they wanted regardless of the pressure that this put us under in terms of our accountability to the PACCIT programme committee and/or ESRC.

For community researchers/developers, community engagement involves a great deal more than simply finding ways of engaging in dialogue with the community, as important as this is. Community engagement also concerns itself with identifying ways of supporting the community to engage with community research/development processes. Within the CNA

---

[11] CNA was funded by ESRC as part of the People at the Centre of Communication and Information Technologies (PACCIT) programme.

context, this involved processes of iterative interaction between inclusive partnership building; community empowerment and encouraging community ownership.

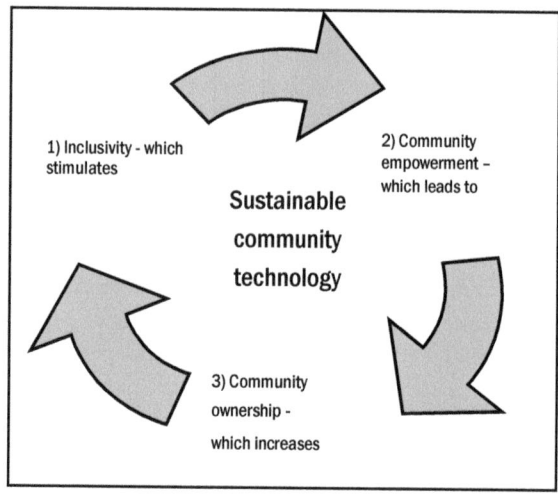

Figure 1: Community engagement for sustainable community technology research.

The CNA team adopted a 3 stage cyclical approach to community engagement, as illustrated in Fig. 1. Stage 1 required us to promote the project as widely and inclusively as possible. Working in partnership, providing support and exchanging knowledge with and between individuals, groups and organisations in the community enabled us to identify local needs, harness local ideas and facilitate community innovation. As the community engaged with technologies and started to develop new skills and knowledgebases we encouraged them to reflect and engage in critical discussions in order to stimulate community learning (See PLW section). Step by step individuals and groups were empowered (stage 2) to shape community communication research and development priorities for themselves. Community knowledgebases become more accessible and community communications networks and networking improved and developed. As empowerment grew so the community infrastructure identified more with the project, its outputs and outcomes and a sense of ownership started to emerge.

This was not without its problems as tensions emerged for a short while. As the project funding ran out a few people at PCRS believed that the CCS, which was being launched as a prototype only, should belong to them rather than the community at a whole. This caused a period of conflict and distrust among some groups for a while, which needed to be resolved. A series of discussions taking into account the sensitivities of the situation in a frank and realistic manner were enough to resolve matters and deflate the tensions.

The truth of the matter is that the community as a whole is still some distance from being able to sustain, and therefore own, the CCS, let alone a small but significant cluster of community groups such as PCRS. The technical knowledge and resources required to run and support a community server, populate the CCS with community generated content and ensure that the content reflects the social and cultural diversity and needs of the community is still some way. It does however remain the goal of the partnership, which has identified a number of collaborative community communication projects since the CNA project's funding ran out. The cyclical nature of the engagement processes means that as more people participate in the activities, CCS diffusion occurs in the community and its potential sustainability is strengthened as goodwill and a willingness to succeed are generated.

Since our first day in Poets Corner, CNA has sought to develop a community research partnership grounded in mutuality and reciprocity. Mutuality because it aims to be beneficial to all participants and reciprocity because it is founded on principles of trust, openness, accessibility, honesty and knowledge exchange.

The next section of the chapter introduces the project's methodological approach underpinning the CNA community research engagement strategy through descriptive example.

The CNA Methodology

CNA was a project with a dual focus. On the one hand it investigated the potential influence of ICT on the capacity to build social capital and facilitate social cohesion in community networks. On the other hand it prioritised the generation of knowledge to facilitate community development processes within the community. For some the unique selling point of the project was the opportunity to participate in the design and development of a community communication space (CCS). However, a good proportion of participants were also interested in developing their knowledge and understanding of community communication networks. Generating such knowledge required a deep understanding of the community and to achieve this we developed a range of participatory techniques. Inspired by ethnographic action research (EAR) we were able to work in partnership with the community, tapping into local knowledge, much of it tacit, whilst retaining the academic rigour (Tacchi, Slater & Hearn, 2003).

EAR – like its relation participatory action research (PAR) (Wadsworth, 1998) – works with community participants to plan, action, observe and reflect on all stages of the project lifecycle. The project itself comprised 4 inter-related yet distinct phases of investigation and community network development:

1. community profiling;
2. social network analysis (SNA);
3. participatory learning workshops (PLWs); and
4. community communication space (CCS) prototype development.

Each phase adopted the plan, action, observe and reflect approach identified in the UNESCO EAR methodology.

The nature of community as a set of diverse often contested social spaces required us to adopt an interpretevist approach to our work in Poets Corner. The mixed methods design of the research permitted us to develop understanding of the complexities of the social phenomenon existing in Poets Corner (Byrne & Humble, 2006). Our intention was to capture diversity by capturing differing ways of how the community infrastructure perceives and understands its environment.

> [This] means that instead of ultimately producing one integrated account or explanation of whatever is being researched (integrative logic), or a series of parallel accounts (parallel logic), one imagines instead 'multi-nodal' and 'dialogic' explanations which are based on the dynamic relation of more than one way of seeing and researching (Mason, 2006, p.10).

The four phases (see above) of the project were sequentially designed so as to enable the gradual building and interlinking of nodes of understanding within the research partnership. Community profiling enabled us to develop rich, detailed pictures of community life and the relationships existing in the community infrastructure. The social network analysis survey instruments provided insights into communication behaviour and patterns, and communication media preferences. From this we were able to develop detailed pictures of the relationships and ties within and beyond the community infrastructure networks. Both profiling and network analysis informed the shaping of the participatory learning workshops that provided data on addressing community communication needs and observational date on community learning and processes. This in turn informed and shaped the design and iterative development of the prototype community communication space.

Each phase of research and development contributed something to the overall understanding of communications and networking in the community infrastructure and the dialectical relationship that existed between the project's conceptual frameworks of community development and community informatics; the data generated during the project; and the analysis strategy necessitated a strategy that addresses the needs of both community and academic audiences. Analysis varied across project phases, in keeping with a mixed methods approach. Qualitative data analysis was thematic in nature, and variable analysis was adopted for the SNA data. In keeping with the principles of PAR and EAR, both data collection and analysis was conducted in partnership with community partners in order to ensure it reflected the experiences of participants.

Experiences of a mixed method PAR project

This section reflects on the experiences of a mixed method participatory approach and how these support the CNA community engagement strategy.

The CNA community profile

Community profiles, or community audits as they are also known, are community development tools (Hawtin, Hughes & Percy-Smith, 1994) used to describe a process or processes of community knowledge generation about a specific area or community. Particular emphasis is placed on community perceptions in order to identify and address problems in the community.

> A comprehensive description of the needs of a population that is defined, or defines itself, as a community, and the resources that exist within that community, carried out with the active involvement of the community itself, for the purpose of developing an action plan or other means of improving the quality of life of the community (Hawtin, Hughes & Percy-Smith, 1994. p.13).

The CNA community profile intended to map Poets Corner in order to identify and understand the information and communication needs, resources and assets (Kretzmann & McKnight, 1997), whilst providing context and content for the planning and participatory design of the CCS.

Throughout the profiling exercise we sought the active involvement of the community using a multi-faceted and multi-levelled approach that drew on a range of research tools and techniques designed to create co-ownership of the research processes with the community. The approach included:

1. exploiting existing information sources;
2. in-depth interviews;
3. mapping;
4. story-telling interviews;
5. reflective and scenario workshops;
6. transect walks; and
7. observation.

Encouraging community involvement in the project provided access to insights into the social fabric of community life that would otherwise have been hidden from researchers from outside the community.

Spread over 31 small, tightly packed streets Poets Corner forms a significant part of the Portland Road and Clarendon Neighbourhood Renewal Area (Social Exclusion Unit, 2001). Population sizes are 5,000 and 11,000 respectively of which circa 54% are women and 46 are men. 56% of the local housing stock is owner-occupied – much of which has been bought by London-based commuters, forcing house prices beyond the reach of many locals – ironical in an area where the majority of accommodation was originally built for artisans and factory workers! However, recent construction of 'social housing' (with more imminent) and a fairly large sector of privately rented accommodation (29%) means that the socio-economic profile of Poets Corner ranges from comfortable affluence to social exclusion and poverty. The area also has a mixed socio-cultural demographic, with resident population of a number ethnic groupings above the city average (ONS, 2001). All of which, once connected to the local social networks, makes Poets Corner an interesting and vibrant place to be.

Growing numbers of community organisations – e.g. Poets Corner Residents Society (PCRS), the Poet's Corner Multicultural group and the Vallance Community Centre, have begun questioning the value of their activities and services, wondering whether their assets and resources couldn't be put to better use in the community. An example of this is PCRS which, although operating for 7 years, has not had the resources to identify what the community really wants from a residents' society in terms of services, activities and support for local projects. The society has undertaken a significant number of activities – often attracting local volunteers, e.g. reclaiming Stoneham Park and organising annual summer festivals and family fun days. However, community priorities were often unclear and some local residents and community groups have been critical of their work – perceiving them as a 'closed group'. PCRS, naturally enough, are keen to change this perception and want to engage in dialogue with the community in a more effective and representative manner.

Despite the best efforts of community development agencies, the grass-roots community and voluntary sector has witnessed a weakening of social relationships between organizations and an apparent growth in territorial tensions. Communications within the community infrastructure are relatively poor and shrinking resources have meant that dialogue with the community at large is at times almost non-existent and community organizations are often inward looking and inimical to new ideas and new people. Organizations and networks that should collaborate with one another often regard themselves as competitors for resources and evidence was found of a culture of distrust emerging between some groups, where perceptions of power, often encouraged by stagnation in community communications and activities, lead to personal conflicts to the detriment of the community as a whole. However, there are also positives in this local story. The old community forum (West Hove Forum) which stagnated and became moribund due to political infighting and factionalism was re-established as the Portland Road and Clarendon Forum under the auspices of a community development agency—the Trust for Developing Communities. Evidence from the first few meetings points to a desire to bridge division within the community infrastructure and collaborate for the collective good. Similarly, a recent community workshop, facilitated by the CNA team, acknowledged the problem of local distrust and tribalism and expressed a desire to find ways of working together and improving community communications.

Indeed, there is growing interest in establishing cross-community relationships and ties. Groups who hitherto have felt excluded from the community infrastructure, e.g. the 'Bluebird Society for the Disabled' and the 'Switched On' club, which helps teenagers with special educational needs gain IT and creative skills, together with a growing number of ethnic and cultural groups, are now expressing an interest, in some cases no more than that, in engaging in dialogic communications and community networking. The community profiling exercise conducted by CNA has illustrated the necessity for an effective and more wide ranging community needs analysis to be undertaken in order to facilitate effective intra community communications across the entire Portland Road and Clarendon Neighbourhood Renewal area.

Social network analysis (SNA)

A major motivation in using SNA was to introduce our partners to the concept of social networks and the significance of communications to community organising and community building activities. The project's SNA activities involved surveying two significant areas of community communication activity – organisation of the family fun day and summer festival, and communication patterns within the community infrastructure.

The first survey focussed on developing a picture of communication within the summer festival and family fun day organising committee – who they spoke to in the broader community infrastructure, why and how. Our main objective was to use network data to illustrate the communication patterns in the community infrastructure. Because social network analysis uses graphical images to represent social realities we were able to use these visualisations as aids for critical reflection of communication processes. Providing the opportunity for community groups to reflect on and discuss their community communication behaviour proved to be an essential element in the community network learning process. For example, we were able to show members of the organising committee how effective their internal communication behaviour was, with almost everyone in regular contact with everyone else. However, a different picture emerged for communication patterns between the committee and the community infrastructure as a whole. Here, only one or two 'champions' were effective in maintaining contact across the community infrastructure. If anything happened to incapacitate them, as it did, communications collapsed and major organisational problems occurred. Letters were relied upon as the prime means of inviting volunteer helpers, even though the committee expressed a preference for face-to-face communications or telephones (landline and/or mobile [cell]) themselves. When potential helpers didn't reply to these letters no attempts were made to chase them up and contact was lost. Since discussing the survey, the committee reviewed its communication processes and now utilises a wide range of media, including face to face contacts. As a result, it has a more vibrant committee and network of helpers and all the indicators are that this year, weather permitting, will be a great success.

The second survey collected data on formal network relationships within the community infrastructure, where the transactional exchange connecting each network element and node (Csermely, 2006) is communication. A detailed analysis of these relations is beyond the scope and space of this chapter but the 104 groups, clubs, associations, etc that made up the community infrastructure, at the time of the survey, were organised into 8 main clusters and 5 smaller clusters. These clusters, or affiliation networks, organised around a parent organisation, e.g. the YMCA, community centres or places of worship and affiliation tends to be based on organisational support mechanisms and/or the availability of physical space to support activities. A number of isolated nodes or dyadic networks, such as the infant and junior schools and various ethnic groups were also identified.

Although not an intended component of the social network analysis surveys, we were able to develop a picture of the kind of informal, social networks that exist within the community, from the observational, story-telling and interview activities of the community profiling. This illustrates an interesting relationship between our approaches to community profiling and SNA, both of which are predominately qualitative and inform and are informed by the other. Our insights into 'informal' networks are by no means complete but we can say that their structures in the community tend to be more open and dynamic than their 'formal' counterparts but they are also more transient. Networking often occurs in public spaces, e.g. Stoneham Park, local pubs and coffee shops, or serendipitous street meetings. This agora 'effect' provides opportunity for knowledge exchange and for comfort and support contacts to be made. Communication transactions tend to be both self-organising and mutually reinforcing, especially where familial and/or friendship ties predominate.

The organisation of informal networks falls into one of two categories:

1. spontaneous; and
2. planned.

Spontaneous informal networks tend to be unstructured and spur-of-the-moment in nature. During the collection of personal narratives we discovered that a person's cat had gone missing and neighbours immediately organised a search of the locality. In another story, learning of the arrival of a new family, neighbours collectively left bags of clothes/toys on door steps as a welcoming gesture. Groups of people popping in to each other's houses for coffee and a chat – reinforcing and developing social bonds – is another example of spontaneous informal community networks. Planned informal networks are more structured and preconceived but have no formal membership. For example, a curry club – where participants experiment with new curry recipes – is organised at irregular intervals by email. Similarly, a book club – run along much the same lines as the curry club – is organised by mobile phone. Circles of baby-sitters and parents requiring 'sitters' evolved through the local grapevine, as did a number of key holder groups. Formed by neighbours in the same street, spare keys are cut and distributed in case of key loss, accident or unannounced absence (especially among the elderly).

Our study revealed that both network types play a significant role in developing relationships of trust and social cohesion in the community. In addition, the examples of the curry and book clubs, illustrate that people are increasingly comfortable in using communication technologies such as email and mobile telephony to support their network structures and facilitate communicative exchanges.

If technology mediated community networks are to support the diversity of social realities in communities, then community practitioners and researchers must focus on the design and development of safe and welcoming spaces that encourage and facilitate participation and engagement. Enabling people to interact with one another by constructing narratives and sharing meaning in convivial environments is central to effective community networking.

Participatory learning workshops (PLWs)

Originally, PLWs were intended as interactive ICT learning spaces designed to provide and share knowledge of and skills in the use of network technologies. The CNA team believed that traditional community ICT training courses often lack social or community contextualisation and are typically driven by performance indicators and targets. Training tends to be task based, aimed at users as individuals rather than as members or participants in a community network. Although such sessions assist in learning how to perform specific IT tasks they are often not situated, providing no consideration of how acquired skills might be applied in community contexts. PLWs were intended to provide fora for community discussion of communication technology applications and influence, through participatory design, the community communication space

Identification of the technologies that formed the learning focus of PLWs was determined by community interest – underlining the importance of ongoing dialogue between researchers and community in order to identify community learning needs. Workshops were designed to stimulate critical reflection of the social appropriation of technologies and encourage community networking. To achieve this we:

1. employed more participatory and interactive techniques than the didactic approach of traditional training;
2. worked at a pace set by the community themselves;
3. worked with technologies and applications that the community wanted to learn; and
4. wherever possible, used content generated by workshop participants as learning materials.

At this point workshops tended to be tied to a particular location, often the Talkshop ICT suite, but as learning developed, community groups became eager to apply their new found skills to group activities. These often took place away from the Talkshop and, reflecting the portability of many of the technologies being used, a suite of mobile workshops began to emerge. Again, mobile PLWs reflected interests identified by the community and included digital photography, video and podcasting. Content from these sessions was often used in the static workshops at the Talkshop, where people wanted to learn to use the CCS.

Wireless internet (wifi) networks enabled us to take laptops to locations suitable to community group activities or resources. As skills developed participants were encouraged to engage in active consideration of how the knowledge they were acquiring could be applied to building and sustaining the groups and networks of Poets Corner. This approach focussed people's minds on community networks as a way of structuring the community, and networking as a means of organising it.

Mobile PLWs formed an increasingly significant element of our engagement strategy. They were developed to provide support for community learning across a diverse range of community events and activities. These included community memory activities, e.g. the use of mobile (cell) phones to record annual family fun-day events, uploading the video clips and photos to a laptop, editing and packaging them as video podcasts; or creating family fun-day photo and video montages on CD or DVD to support community funding application and social events.

We worked with a range of community groups to develop their skills in recording and archiving their activities during the summer festival and other community events e.g. local history walks, holistic health days, tai chi in the park, poetry, art and music. Digital video, photography and podcasting have proved popular activities in the community and we will soon work with interested parties to create digital community story maps for the CCS. As our community learning strategies developed so did our approach to PLWs. Scenario PLWs were developed whilst working with community forums from socially excluded communities in Cape Town and were subsequently adopted in Poets Corner.

Scenario PLWs were originally intended to introduce participants to the concept of social networks and the role communication plays in effective networking but we have subsequently used them to address other forms of community needs, e.g. how to set-up and sustain a community newsletter. In the social network workshops, participants work as individuals, and later in groups, to identify the social networks that they feel part of in a community. A picture or map of the community network emerges as groups share their information. Groups then list and prioritise the communications media they use within their different networks, reflecting critically on their selections. At this stage a community communication scenario is given to participants, usually in the form of a problem or a need. Participants collaborate in their groups to solve the problem or address the need. Solutions are then presented in plenary session and further dialogue and learning takes place.

Using this technique in Poets Corner, community groups expressed concern at an emerging tribalism and territorialism within the community infrastructure. They were anxious that this situation was encouraging suspicion and mistrust. Having articulated a community problem they then expressed a collective desire to address it by improving relationships within the community. They identified the need for a building or space to act as 'neutral ground' for intra-community activities and networking. They also expressed a need for an online forum to facilitate dialogue within the community infrastructure. The results from the workshop were shared with a subsequent Community Forum meeting, being addressed by the developers of a social housing project in the area. A condition of planning permission for this project was the provision of a community space built into the complex. We were able to get the developers to agree to facilitate a participatory design workshop for community stakeholders as part of the public consultation they are obliged to undertake. Whilst there is still a long way to go, progress so far illustrates the significance of effective community networking and dialogue in community development processes.

Whichever format workshops took, we sought to ensure they provided space for community discussion of CCS design considerations and needs. These insights contribute to the planning, design, implementation and ongoing development of the CCS prototype. During our work with the community we have discovered a strong desire to share stories and meaning. More than that, we have also discovered an enthusiasm to learn how communication technologies can assist them in doing this. Now, as the CCS component of the project moves into a community diffusion phase we are exploring innovative and creative pathways in support of both community voice and memory.

Community communications space (CCS) – A prototype

If ICT are to support community networks then the platforms must provide spaces for community voices to be heard and needs to be met. Enabling people to tell their stories and interact in ways meaningful to them, and in environments in which they feel comfortable is an important part of effective community networking. The CCS provides ICT based support for community networking activities through the creation of public and private communication spaces for the Poets Corner community.

The CCS supports video and audio podcasting, digital story-telling, digital art, poetry and music. Local communication forums are being established to support community development/building processes currently underway. It is anticipated that the diversity of forum subjects will require new forums to emerge as the community learns to use them. The CCS also facilitates blogging and provides spaces for local web pages, notice boards, local diaries and visitor pages. A growing range of social networking applications are also being considered.

The exciting developments outlined above indicate how ICT are beginning to be utilised in support of a wide range of community activities in Poets Corner but this should not deflect from the significance of developing effective community engagement strategies in non-digital environments. At the beginning of the CNA project we resolved to operate using the Community Development Foundation's (CDF) 'involvement ready' model (Chanan, Garratt & West, 2000). In the CNA context, the rationale behind this model was to start the project by working with those in the community ready, willing and able to work with the project. As community development occurred and news of the activities spread through the community, more participants would emerge. Translating this in terms of CNA activities we can say that as awareness of the CCS increases so community interest in participating increases, although at this stage most interest lies within the community infrastructure, however, some individual residents are now beginning to join up as members of the CCS. All of which draws interesting parallels between community development and diffusion of innovation (Rogers, 2003) theories.

Conclusion

Throughout the project life-cycle CNA was guided by two propositions that we believed were fundamental to effective community networking:

1. Healthy communities are founded on the 'connectivity' existing within and between diverse social networks and social actors; and
2. Community participation in the planning, implementation and ongoing development of community ICT initiatives designed to underpin/support such 'connectivity' is pivotal to the strengthening of internal and external social network ties.

The use of PAR methods in a community technology context, depended on achieving common ground between partners so that the iterative cycles of planning, action, observation and reflection would be effective in meeting common goals. Such an approach to community engagement takes time, resources and patience but does enable relationships of trust and mutual respect to develop with partners in the community in a way that enriches the knowledge generated.

By engaging with the community and grounding our research in community life the project team developed knowledge of the history, structures, organisation and cultures of the Poets Corner community. The ethos of knowledge sharing that underpins our participatory and collaborative approach to research has facilitated better community understanding of the richness and diversity of social capital, talent and community generated content that exists within their own neighbourhood environment. It has also equipped them with skills that will be of use in various community contexts.

An interesting consequence of these developments is that as the community research network has grown within the community so have other relationships within the community infrastructure network. Illustrating that not only can ICT be utilised to support community building processes and social capital but the processes of community research and the partnerships that evolve can also. All of which places enormous ethical responsibility on the shoulders of academic researchers and their funding agencies.

References

Byrne, J., and Humble, A.M. (2006). An Introduction to Mixed Methods Research. Halifax, Nova Scotia: Atlantic Research Centre. Available online: www.msvu.ca/ARCFamilyWork/pdf_files/MixedMethodologyHandout.pdf

Cavaye, J. (2005). Community Engagement – New Insights and Learnings from Practice. In Gardiner, D. and Scott, K. (2005). Proceedings of International Conference on Engaging Communities. Aug. 15th – 17th. Brisbane, Australia: Queensland Department of Main Roads. Available online: www.engagingcommunities2005.org/abstracts/Cavaye-Jim-final.pdf

Chanan, G., Garratt, C. and West, A. (2000). The New Community Strategies: How to Involve Local People. London: Community Development Foundation.

Csermely, P. (2006). Weak Link: Stabilizers of Complex Systems from Proteins to Social Networks. Berlin: Springer

Day, P. (2008). Community Networks: Building and Sustaining Community Relationships. In Schuler, D. (Ed.) Liberating Voices! A Pattern Language for Communication Revolution. Cambridge, MA: MIT Press [forthcoming]

Day, P., & Harris, K. (1997). Down-to-Earth Vision: Community Based IT Initiatives and Social Inclusion, [The Commit Report]. London: IBM/CDF.

Day, P.and Schuler, D. (2006). Community Practice in the Network Society: Pathways Toward Civic Intelligence. In Purcell, P.(Ed.) Networked Neighbourhoods: The Connected Community in Context. London: Springer-Verlag.19-46.

Gilchrist, A. (2004). The Well-Connected Community: A networking approach to community development. Bristol: The Policy Press

Gill, K.S. (1997). Knowledge Networking and Social Cohesion in the Information Society. A Study for the European Commission. Brighton: SEAKE Centre, University of Brighton

Glen, A. (1993). Methods and themes in community practice. In Butcher, H. et al (eds.) Community and Public Policy. London: Pluto. Pp.22-40

Hartz-Karp, J. (2005). Deliberation as a Key to Community Engagement. In Gardiner, D. & Scott, K. (2005). Proceedings of International Conference on Engaging Communities. Aug. 15th – 17th. Brisbane, Australia: Queensland Department of Main Roads. Available online: www.engagingcommunities2005.org/abstracts/HartzKarp-Janette-final.pdf

Hawtin, M., Hughes, G., and Percy-Smith, J. (1994). Community Profiling: auditing social needs. Buckingham: Open University Press.

Johnson, A.L. (2005). Evaluating Community Engagement: Experiences from Queensland, Australia. In Gardiner, D. and Scott, K. (2005). Proceedings of International Conference on Engaging Communities. Aug. 15th – 17th. Brisbane, Australia: Queensland Department of Main Roads. Available online: www.engagingcommunities2005.org/abstracts/Williams-Rick-final.pdf

Kretzmann, J.P.and McKnight, J.L. (1997). Building Communities from the Inside Out: A Path

Toward Finding and Mobilizing a Community's Assets. Skokie, IL: ACTA Publications

Kubicek, H., and Wagner, R.M.M. (1998). Community Networks in a Generational Perspective. Paper presented to the 'Designing Across Borders: The Community Design of Community Networks' workshop at the Participatory Design Conference (PDC), Seattle, WA, USA, Nov. 12-14 1998. Available online: www.scn.org/tech/the_network/Projects/CSCW-PDC-ws-98/kubicek-wagner-pp.html

Mason, J. (2006). Six Strategies for Mixing Methods and Linking Data in Social Science Research. Manchester: Real Life Methods, University of Manchester. Available online: www.reallifemethods.ac.uk/research/wps/2006-07-rlm-mason.pdf

Middlesbrough Partnership. (2005). Community Engagement Framework. Available online: www.middlesbroughpartnership.org.uk/

Morino Institute. (1994). Assessment and Evolution of Community Networking. Paper presented to Apple Conference on Building Community Computing Networks - 'The Ties that Bind'. Cupertino, California, May 5, 1994. Available online: www.morino.org/under_sp_asse.asp

ONS (2001). Census. London: HMSO. Available online: www.statistics.gov.uk/census2001/census2001.asp

Pollard, L. and Stocker, L. (2005). Making Meaning Together – New Approaches to Governance and Community in Modern Democracies. In Gardiner, D. & Scott, K. (2005). Proceedings of International Conference on Engaging Communities. Aug. 15th – 17th. Brisbane, Australia: Queensland Department of Main Roads. Available online: www.engagingcommunities2005.org/abstracts/Pollard-Lisa-final.pdf

Putnam, R. D. (2000). Bowling Alone. The collapse and revival of American community, New York: Simon and Schuster.

Rogers, E.M. (2003). Diffusion of Innovation. 5th Edition. New York, NY: Free Press

Schuler, D. (1996). New Community Networks: Wired for Change. Harlow, UK: Addison-Wesley

Schuler, D. (2001). Cultivating society's civic intelligence: patterns for a new "world brain". Journal of Society, Information and Communication, 4, (2), 157-181

Social Exclusion Unit (2001). A New Commitment to Neighbourhood Renewal: A National Strategy Action Plan. London: Cabinet Office.

Sirianni, C. and Friedland, L. (1997). Civic Innovation and American Democracy. Change. 29 (1) January-February. Available online: www.cpn.org/crm/essays/innovation.html (Accessed 21/9/06)

Skidmore, P., Bound, K. and Lownsbrough, H. (2006). Community Participation: Who benefits? York, UK: Joseph Rowntree Foundation

Smyre, R. and Cohill, A. (2002). COTF System for Community Transformation. The Knowledge Democracy Centre. Available online: www.designnine.com/library/docs/cotf_sys_all.pdf#search=%22COTF%20System%20for%20Community%20Transformation%22

Stoecker, R. (2005). Research Methods for Community Change. London: Sage

Tacchi, J., Slater, D., and Hearn, G. (2003). Ethnographic Action Research. New Delhi: UNESCO. Available online: cirac.qut.edu.au/ictpr/downloads/handbook.pdf#search=%22Ethnographic%20Action%20Research%22

Wadsworth, Y. (1998). What is Participatory Action Research? Action Research International. Available online: www.scu.edu.au/schools/gcm/ar/ari/p-ywadsworth98.html

Children in communities affected by conflict and natural disaster in north and east Sri Lanka

A qualitative case study to determine vulnerability

Jaya Earnest and Robert P. Finger

> The 20-year-old civil war between the Government of Sri Lanka and the Liberation Tigers of Tamil Eelam (LTTE) has seriously undermined the country's enormous development potential. Approximately 800,000 people, 1/3rd of who are children, have been displaced. On 22 February 2002, the United National Front Government entered into a formal ceasefire agreement with the LTTE. The commencement of peace negotiations has increased humanitarian access to many areas in the conflict-affected North and East regions of the country. The impact of the Tsunami of December 2004 has added yet another dimension of complexity to the conflict areas of the East and North.
>
> This research was conceptualised using a psychosocial framework consisting of three interlocking domains of human capacity, social ecology and culture and values. Twelve Focus Group Discussions with 212 participants and 73 key informant interviews were carried out in two Eastern and four Northern districts affected by civil war and tsunami in Sri Lanka in early 2006. Data gathered was subjected to qualitative thematic analysis. Vulnerability factors were identified using a participatory qualitative approach in communities affected by protracted conflict and the tsunami. This chapter details the phases of the participatory rapid ethnographic assessment used in the field by the researchers in early 2006.

Nearly 900,000 children live in areas most affected by the ethnic conflict; in addition there are 300,000 displaced children and 2,500 child recruits. The majority of the children in the North East have known nothing but conflict (Save the Children, n.d.). The situation of many communities has been further deteriorated by the December 2004 Tsunami. This study attempted to identify vulnerability factors in communities in North and East Sri Lanka using participatory rapid ethnographic techniques.

The chapter commences with a geopolitical and historical background to the conflict t in Sri Lanka and an overview of children in North and East Sri Lanka. The chapter then introduces the psychosocial framework that underpins the study and outlines the methodology used in the field research and its implementation. The dimensions of vulnerability and the Sri Lankan context of vulnerability are documented before phases of the rapid participatory approach are detailed. Sections on data analysis and issues of rigour are included as well.

The discussion section provides a short analysis of literature on children in Sri Lanka and the impact of the Tsunami, explains the development of indicators and the vulnerability framework from the analysis of the rapid participatory assessment. A short reflective section discusses challenges encountered during the research process in this specific setting of a region affected by protracted conflict.

Background to the study

Geopolitical and Historical Perspectives

The island nation of Sri Lanka is a Democratic Socialist republic situated in the Indian Ocean, off the south-eastern tip of the subcontinent of India. A 22-mile stretch of shallow water known as the Palk straight separates Sri Lanka from India. Sri Lanka is a small, multi-racial, multi-ethnic and multi-religious country. Nearly 75% of its population of 19.5 million is Sinhalese who speak Sinhalese and are mainly Buddhist. Sri Lankan Tamils account for 18% of the population. The majority of them are Hindus with a substantial Christian minority, living in the North and East of the country. About 4% of the population is Muslim or Moors and are concentrated in the eastern province and Colombo. There are also small groups of Burghers (Eurasians of mixed decent), Malays and Veddahs (The Virtual Library of Sri Lanka, n.d.). The vast majority of the population lives in the rural sector (80%), only 15% live in urban areas, with another 5% living in the estate sector. Geographical disparities exist within districts between urban and rural and tea-estate populations. Traditionally however, poverty has been a largely rural phenomenon. Ninety percent of the total poor in Sri Lanka reside in rural areas (Jabbar & Sennayake, 2004).

History of the conflict

A former Portuguese, Dutch and British colony, Sri Lanka gained independence in 1948. From the 1950s tension between Tamils and Sinhalese grew, considerably so after Sinhalese was made the only official language (instead of both Sinhalese and Tamil) in 1956. Following ongoing tensions, the Tamil United Liberation Front who demanded a separate Tamil state was formed in 1976. Tensions increased further and escalated in 1977 into ethnic riots in which 128 people died.

A further escalation of tensions led to civil war between the Government of Sri Lanka (GoSL) and the Liberation Tigers of Tamil Eelam (LTTE) in 1983, which continued with short interruptions and changing intensity until 2002. Lead by Vellupillai Prabhakaran, the LTTE fought for a separate state, 'Tamil Eelam' in the North and East of Sri Lanka for the Tamil minority. Talks to negotiate a settlement in 1995 broke down when the LTTE unilaterally withdrew from talks and resumed fighting. It has been estimated that 60,000 people have died in the protracted conflict prior to the peace agreement in 2002 (Korf, 2006).

During 2004, a faction of the LTTE predominantly from the East (the Karuna faction) split from the LTTE, and added further uncertainty with regards to the continuation of the peace process, destabilizing the situation mainly in the North-East. In Sri Lanka, the consequences of this long period of conflict are felt in every sphere of life. There is a widespread sense of insecurity and vulnerability especially among the Tamil population. A large civilian population has been displaced several times. A major refugee problem has developed and large numbers of Sri Lankan Tamils have sought refuge overseas (Arunatilkae, Jayasuriya, & Kelegama, 2001).

Children in Sri Lanka

Sri Lanka is committed to its children, and has been for some time, as can be seen in the National Plan of Action for the Children of Sri Lanka, to be implemented from 2004-2008, and the recent declaration of the year 2006 as the Year of the child in Sri Lanka by President Mahinda Rajapakse. Services provided by the government to all children are free education and health care, a subsidized minimum food basket and subsidized transport (Department of National Planning, 2004).

However, women and children throughout the world today bear the brunt of poverty, disease, conflict and displacement (UNICEF, 2006). In the wake of the ongoing conflict in the Northern and Eastern provinces, children have suffered losses, displacement, disruption of their education, food insecurity and increased morbidity and mortality. All these multiple problems and complexities have been exacerbated by the tsunami, with massive losses and destruction of infrastructure and private assets. Further problems and adversities faced by children in Sri Lanka are a high rate of institutionalization in children's homes, sexual exploitation and child labour (UNICEF, 2003).

In order to address the needs of children affected by war in Sri Lanka, the Government of Sri Lanka, LTTE, UN and NGO partners are collaborating on a multi-sectoral, holistic programme designed to improve the living conditions for children affected by war in all eight districts of the North East of Sri Lanka . Children are supported through a range of services that include opportunities to access education, skills training, income generation and improved health care. In 2004, a recommendation was made that the implementation of activities should move away from an individual referral mechanism to a community-based approach, in order to more effectively reach the most vulnerable children. This recommendation proposed a vulnerability assessment in the North East to identify priority geographic areas for community-based activities. This research study is an outcome of the multi-sectoral recommendation

The Conceptual Framework used for the Study

The availability of resources and vulnerability among individuals in a community are strongly related. Figure 1 shows the interlocking circles of human capacity, social ecology and culture and values (Psychosocial Working Group, 2003). This framework encourages the exploration of the goals and priorities of existing programmes that deal with vulnerable populations. Understanding the interdependency between the domains enables barriers to be identified and to promote planning and implementation of interventions/action plans. The framework guided the Resource and Vulnerability Assessment Mapping (RVAM) Process. These domains map the human, social and cultural capital available to people responding to the challenges of prevailing events. The interlocking domains of human capacity, social ecology and culture/values in figure 1 were explored in relation to the current situation in the North-Eastern communities and their understanding and perceptions of the met and unmet needs of children.

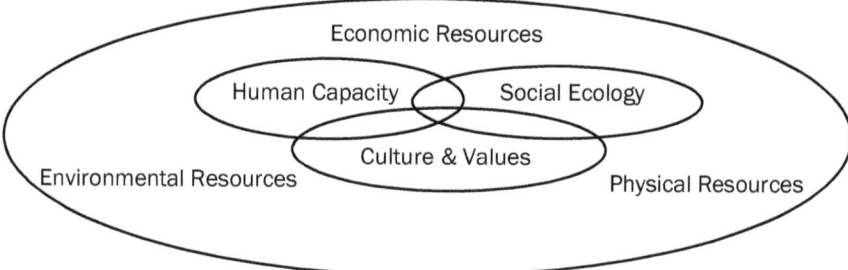

Figure 1: The interlocking circles of human capacity, social ecology and values Psychosocial Working group, 2003).

Dimensions of Vulnerability

There are social, generational, geographic, economic and political dimensions that impact people in various ways. Changing social, economic, environmental and political factors usually alters power balances in a society. Vulnerability can be increased through powerlessness, exploitation and discrimination. Vulnerability defines the characteristics of a person or group and their situation that influences their capacity to anticipate, cope, resist and recover from a hazard. Vulnerability involves a combination of factors that determine the degree to which someone's life, livelihood, property and other assets are put at risk by a discrete and identifiable event or a cascade or series of such events in nature and society (Actionaid, 2003).

Programmatic, Personal & Societal Vulnerability

In various contexts, vulnerability results from personal, programmatic and societal factors that affect one's ability to exert control over one's health or well-being. These factors influence a person's decision and choice on their own livelihoods:

- **Programmatic vulnerability** includes information and education services, health and social services, and human rights programmes. This aspect can be further divided into support structures based on the 3As (availability, accessibility and awareness) of resources.
- **Personal vulnerability** focuses on factors in the individual's development or environment that render him or her more or less vulnerable; such as physical and emotional development, socio-cultural factors and knowledge and skills.
- **Societal vulnerability** includes issues such as political structures, gender relationships, attitudes to sexuality, religious beliefs, violence, and cultural values/norms/expectations. These are contextual factors that influence personal and programmatic vulnerability (UNDP, 2004).

The Vulnerability Context

The vulnerability context affects different people in different ways. Natural disasters often have a more adverse effect on livelihoods and assets. Different types of conflicts can have profound effects on the poor. In areas of protracted conflict people suffer from multiple displacements, lawlessness, asset loss, emotional effects. Often conflicts further marginalize poor communities. Understanding the nature of vulnerability is a key step of any needs, sustainability or livelihoods analysis. The concept and context of vulnerability and the related terms of coping, resilience and adaptation are used in different ways by different disciplines and communities (Moench & Dixit, 2004).

The Approaches to defining Vulnerability

- **Natural Disasters Approach:** This approach focuses on hazards and the close exposure of affected communities to identify hazard-related vulnerabilities. This view focuses on factors such as frequency, intensity and nature of the physical hazard as the key components of vulnerability. A clear significance is attached to infrequent but extreme events.
- **Social Vulnerability Approach:** In this approach, vulnerabilities are embedded in the social and political order. Vulnerabilities exist prior to and independent of natural hazards. This approach treats the vulnerability environment as given. In this approach, policy attention is toward more micro-level processes and people may be seen as 'victims' trying to cope with multiple problems.
- **Integrative Approach:** The integrative approach is set out in the Hyogo Framework 2005-2015 adopted by the UN in 2005. Vulnerability is defined as: The conditions determined by physical, social, economic and environmental factors or processes which increase the susceptibility of a community to a hazard.

Hazards include latent conditions, future threats and can have natural origins or are induced by human processes (Yamin, Rahman, & Huq, 2005).

The Sri Lankan Vulnerability Context and Children's Needs

The concepts highlighted above and various dimensions of vulnerability to the specific needs of the task ahead in Sri Lanka was discussed with key informants and based on a thorough review of the available literature. It has been well documented, that there is widespread damage to the physical and social infrastructure in North East Sri Lanka and in most cases; even the basic facilities do not exist. Due to the intensity of war there is also devastation of social fabric and multiple displacements, resulting in the destruction of family units.

Women and children are the worst affected having endured severe mental and physical problems due to war. Children of the North East have endured experiences ranging from seeing death, disappearance and injury of family members. Artillery or aerial bombardments, torture, imprisonment and harassment have all been part of their daily lives. Other children have witnessed systematic destruction of properties and village infrastructure, including schools, health facilities and places of worship. These experiences have left deep and lasting scars in the minds of children and any measures to redress this should be comprehensive in its approach while acknowledging the inherent coping capacities of children (Human Rights Watch, 2004).

Methods of Data Collection

The research used a pre-dominantly qualitative rapid participatory assessment approach. Data collection took place in Colombo, and six districts of the North and East [Ampara, Batticaloa, Vavunia, Mannar, Kilinochchi and Mullaitivu]. The culturally sensitive nature of the present study led to a multi-method rapid ethnographic, case study approach to allow triangulation of the methods and cross validation of the data. Using qualitative methodologies, the data collected complemented each other and together formed a more coherent and complete picture of the issues being studied (Denzin, & Lincoln, 2000).

The study had a conceptual structure organized around a small number of research aims that sought information (Merriam, 1998). The research was underpinned by the constructive and critical theory perspective. The critical theory perspective implied that reality is shaped over time by social, political, cultural, ethnic and gender factors (Guba, & Lincoln, 1994). This study also drew on a constructive perspective, which assumed that there are multiple realities in which the researchers and their subjects create their own understanding (von Glasersfeld, 1993).

The methods of data collection included Focus Group Discussions (FGDs), semi-structured and key informant interviews, school visits, and a systematic review of documents (Punch, 2003). Data from the FGDs and interviews was compared and compiled together with identified secondary data (desk review). Women from conflict villages, workers from community organisations, secondary school students, district education officers, community youth, and officials working in child protection participated in thematic focus group discussions and interviews pertaining to their experience of living in an area of protracted conflict and the impact the conflict has had on their lives. Focus group discussions (FGDs) enabled the researchers to explore perceptions and experiences and provided a rich and detailed set of data about thoughts, feelings and impressions.

Broad topics and themes raised for discussion explored: the socio-cultural contexts of the lives of the adolescents; the sense of belonging, security and community cohesion experienced; cultural and social identities and how these link to perceptions and anxieties about the future; and the mediating influence of the community. In interviews specific issues relating to their ties with their villages, perceptions of their future security in their country and changing access to resources were explored.

Participants & communities were approached through the local UNICEF offices. Collaborations with local NGOs were used to recruit key informants, mothers and children were recruited at schools or through women's groups with the help of local NGOs. The project was introduced as a UNICEF sponsored project, which was conducted with the approval of the GoSL and LTTE respectively. The researchers felt that this did not impact participation.

As one of the researchers was of South Asian origin, most FGDs and interviews with locals were conducted by her assisted by local NGO or UNICEF staff speaking the local language. The researchers felt that this facilitated a more open discussion. However, the presence of the second researcher, who is Caucasian, did not impede motivated participation by locals. The research team consisted of the two main researchers, helped by many local and international NGO, UN and government staff.

The Resource and Vulnerability Assessment Phases: A Rapid Ethnographic Assessment

The RVAM used a pre-dominantly qualitative rapid ethnographic assessment approach employing focus group discussions; extensive field visits to schools, resettlement villages, Internally Displaced Persons (IDP) camps, and communities; semi-structured interviews and key informant interviews (FHI, 2005).

During the pre-country **Phase 1** the researchers collected relevant available information and identified possible key stakeholders at a national, district and community level with help of the sponsoring organization (UNICEF). An in-depth literature search and review was also carried out at this stage.

Relevant consultancy, government and inter-agency reports, ethnographic studies, research reports on children in armed conflicts and prolonged conflicts and the most recent Sri Lanka National Census were systematically analysed. Preliminary analysis of recent reports from Ministry of Social Welfare, Education and Health data and local newspaper articles for 2002-5 was also carried out.

In **Phase 2**, after dialogue with government, international agencies and local NGOs, various at-risk groups of children and their care providers were identified. Opportunistic, snowball and purposive sampling was used to build the sample for the focus groups.

Field visits of approximately three to five days were undertaken in **Phase 3**, in certain pre-selected sites of the North and East (where safety and security of researchers could be ensured). Focus group discussions, consultations, meetings and interviews were carried out to identify community resources and locations of programmatic vulnerability. These were arranged by UNICEF field offices and NGOs working in the area. The researchers found that participants were open and keen to share their experiences of the conflict and how it impacts their lives.

A key challenge to the researchers were the contested borders within North and East Sri Lanka. In the political economy of the war in Sri Lanka, these contested borders are zones of control. The areas under full control of the LTTE are called '*uncleared*' areas and those under the control of the Sri Lankan Army (SLA) are called '*cleared*' areas. These terms have been coined by the GoSL and often do not reflect the reality on the ground which remains more complex and fluid. It is well known in the conflict areas, that the LTTE has a firm control of areas during the night, whereas the SLA attempts to keep control of the major roads and towns during the day. This contested space makes mobility a daily challenge for communities (Korf, 2006). In these contested spaces are '*grey areas*' these are areas of disputed territory (Goodhand & Lewer, 1999). Wheatley (1998) described the so-called grey areas in the East of the country as areas with minimal GoSL control and a strong LTTE presence. These areas are ethnically mixed and susceptible to sporadic upsurges in fighting, making these areas extremely vulnerable. Thus while the GOSL retains formal territorial control, in the contested border of the North and East, the regulation of Tamil populations is transferred to non-state actors, in this case the LTTE.

This rapid assessment was undertaken in these contested border zones of conflict. The researchers experienced the constant border checks, the 'demining' activities undertaken by the SLA along the major highways and the LTTE cadres in the contested border zones, and the controls at the juncture of the contested borders within a nation state. The resource analysis provided information on community resources, and contributed to the development of a preliminary list of key socio-economic indicators for monitoring and evaluating programmatic vulnerability.

The Programmatic vulnerability assessment in **Phase 4** provided information on the availability of resources; identify challenges in implementing services and the possible constraints in accessing services. The Personal and Societal Vulnerability Assessment will identify and prioritize communities with the highest concentration of vulnerable children and identify particularly vulnerable groups (eg; orphaned children, displaced children, child soldiers, disabled children).

The FGDs elicited programmatic and societal/personal vulnerability themes and identified the contextual factors that influence vulnerability and explored a family's/child's capacity to use the resources and cope with the current situation. Some of the contextual factors have been listed below:

- Displacement and loss (material and personal);
- Impediments to access of education and health services;
- Increase in the number of children who drop out of school;
- Increase in child morbidity and mortality;
- Impacts on physical and psycho-social well-being;
- depletion of resources to mitigate adverse events/developments by households and communities;
- Natural disasters like the Tsunami further worsen the situation.

The above mentioned contextual issues lead to children becoming soft targets for military recruitment, child labour and other forms of abuse. These contextual issues have a long lasting negative impact and in turn deplete children of essential resources and life skills (physical, emotional, social) necessary for future parenting and often lead to cyclic vulnerability.

Analysis and Rigour

A continuous, cyclic approach to the thematic, qualitative analysis of the collected data was chosen. Analysis occurred throughout the data collection phase to enable early information gathered to inform later parts of the research (Thomas, 2003). A preliminary presentation took place during the assessment to allow for input into the final version of the framework developed. Guided by framework analysis, common themes were sought which reflected the range of experiences that were presented and allowed for constant generation, comparison and development of themes during the whole research process.

The qualitative data collected during the workshops was coded and categorized in different stages. The first stage contained categorization – where possible – separated by district and workshop session, where session one included programmatic vulnerability and mobility and session two personal and societal vulnerability. Once this had been finished, the data was categorized into the previously identified categories for all the workshops done. The continuous feedback provided by the key informants aided to focus on reviewing the chosen categories and the results in light of existing programme strengths and resources and strengthened validity by providing a form of member checking (Lacey & Luff, 2001).

Steps were taken throughout the data collection and analysis to establish trustworthiness of the method and findings. Multiple methods provided varying perspectives on the subject enabling the development of a more holistic and contextual portrayal of real-life situations. Multiple research methods also served to 'triangulate' resulting themes as they evolved during analysis (Denzin & Lincoln, 2000). Verification strategies such as systematic checking of data to eliminate errors and ongoing monitoring and interpretation of data to modify direction of research were used to achieve reliability and validity. Constant analysis of incoming data guided future sampling and questioning strategies to ensure confirmation of newly formed conjectures (Patton, 1990).

An audit trail, as discussed, was also established, ensuring methods and data were documented so that the analysis of the data could be confirmed and replicated by other researchers. It is widely accepted that multiple methods in any study are useful in achieving greater understanding. This research was carried out in accordance with the Australian National Health and Medical Research Council guidelines. The Human Research Ethics Committee of the Office of Research and Development of Curtin University of Technology approved the project. Approval was also obtained from UNICEF, Sri Lanka.

Development of the Definition of Vulnerability, the Set of Indicators and the Final Framework

The information gained was used to develop a comprehensive definition of 'vulnerability' as perceived by the participants, identify and prioritize communities with the highest concentration of vulnerable children, establish a set of indicators, which will be operationalised within the conceptual framework. The framework and indicators allow a community's vulnerability to be assessed, identify available and needed resources, help allocate resources accordingly and help empower communities to initiate action plans.

A comprehensive definition of 'vulnerability' as perceived by the researchers & participants was developed and shared with stakeholders. The developed definition, framework and indicators will allow a community's vulnerability to be assessed, will help identify/include available and needed resources, help allocate resources accordingly and help empower communities to initiate action plans.

Systematic analysis of literature

State of Children in the North-East

Children in the Northern and Eastern provinces are among the most vulnerable children in Sri Lanka. A multitude of adversities affects them, of which the single biggest one is the prolonged conflict. Every conflict forces children to live through some terrible experiences. The protracted Sri Lankan conflict is no exception. Often described as a 'no mercy war' it has affected the lives of children for more than two decades. Both the Government of Sri Lanka and the LTTE have violated the principals of Humanitarian Law and children are among of the most affected (United Nations, n.d).

War, especially civil war, destroys homes, fragments communities and breaks down trust between people, undermining the very foundation of children's lives. Children in the North-East have been excluded, for differing periods of time, from essential goods and services, such as schools, health care facilities, water and sanitation, and have been denied the protection from exploitation, military recruitment, violence, abuse, neglect, and the ability to participate fully in their society (International Save the Children Alliance, 1996).

Along with rapid social change, war and conflict leads to a breakdown of family support systems which are essential to a child's survival and development. Death, displacement and poverty also increase tensions within the family and the likelihood of domestic violence. Destruction of physical infrastructure, strains on health care and education systems, workers and supplies and increased insecurity because of the remnants of landmines and unexploded ordnances are further risks to children's lives. Children face a heightened risk of rape, sexual assault, prostitution and other forms of gender based violence in the Northern and Eastern provinces of Sri Lanka (United Nations, n.d).

The armed conflict has led to the displacement of as many as 380,000 children. The ongoing conflict has led to the recruitment of children as soldiers by the LTTE. Releases of child soldiers have been reported sporadically. However, the majority of recruited children are not released. Fear and intimidation perpetrated by the recruiting agencies lead to under-reported numbers of children recruited (Human Rights Watch, 2006).

Access to Health Care and Educational Services

An assessment of the health care system in the Northern and Eastern Provinces by the World Health Organization (WHO) in 2002 documented vast rebuilding and reconstruction needs and the lack of human resources in 65% of the facilities. The destruction and heavy damage to health infrastructure and the non-availability of human and other resources are major constraints to the delivery of health services to children in most districts in the North-East. The incidence of vaccine preventable diseases, other communicable diseases such as TB, respiratory tract infections, diarrhoeal diseases, vector borne diseases and infectious diseases such as hepatitis showed an upward trend in the region over the past few years compared to the rest of Sri Lanka. A reliance on unsafe drinking water, poor sanitation and poor personal and domestic hygiene are some of the environmental and public health challenges more pronounced in the North-East. An environmental survey by WHO revealed a high level of water contamination (World Health Organization, 2004).

Most children's education has been disrupted by the civil war. Detailed information of school enrolment and the infrastructure of schools in the North-East are limited. While registration rates may give an indication of the number of children enrolled, they do not reflect the quality of education nor the actual attendance patterns. Where children in conflict areas do go to school, their learning is often hindered by trauma, hunger, untrained or ill-prepared teachers and a lack of sufficient school materials. Survival pressures may also force parents or care-givers to withdraw their children from school to engage in income earning activities, or exclude one child from school to look after the household while the parents are working (Nicolai & Triplehorn, 2003).

While education generally adds a measure of stability to children in conflict areas, conflict can distort its benefits and introduce additional risks. The LTTE is known to have positioned recruitment booths near schools and used street theatre to induce children to join. The education systems of countries in conflict can also easily be politicized to the detriment of children. Education systems can be manipulated into instruments to distort history for political purposes, encouraging hate and segregate, repress and condition a population to accept ethnic differences while propagating fear and pre-emptive self defence (Human Rights Watch, 2006).

The 2004 Tsunami and its Impact

On December 26, 2004, an earthquake off the western coast of Sumatra created tsunamis that washed over the Eastern and Southern coasts of Sri Lanka. The Tsunami created an 'emergency within an emergency' as it hit Sri Lanka's coastal areas affected by 20 years of conflict (Save the Children Fund, 2006). Thousands of children lost their lives and many more were separated from parents or orphaned by the tsunami. Almost 1,000 children lost both parents and almost 4,000 lost one. Children, especially those living in poverty and in regions affected by the 20 year civil war, are among the most vulnerable victims of the tsunami and its aftermath. Children survivors face significant issues of loss, bereavement, separation from parents and family, fear, helplessness and the possible downward spiral of poverty and food insecurity that accompanies loss of homes, family support and livelihood (Wessels, & Kostelny, 2002). Large numbers of children and families still reside in transitional accommodation today. Many poor families living in these camps see few other alternatives than sending children out to work or to live and work with wealthier relatives or families. The tsunami also broke down existing social structures of protection and increased IDP communities' vulnerability to violence and harassment (TNS Lanka, 2006).

Discussion

In all six districts of the field visits [Ampara, Batticaloa, Vavuniya, Mannar, Kilinochchi and Mullaitivu] the underlying sense of insecurity, fear of war, a sense of hopelessness and uncertainty was very prevalent. All participants wanted peace and security, the opportunity to improve their lives, educate themselves, have jobs and improve their economic condition. The study identified that education and health of children was valued highly amongst all interviewed mothers and children, although access to educational and health services were severely limited in the conflict affected areas. Discussions in the field centred on the post-tsunami context as most of the areas of conflict were also affected by the Tsunami in December 2004. Most key informants, school head teachers and district education officers informed the researchers that several UN and international aid organisations had provided much needed help and assistance in the forms of latrines, water and sanitation projects, and rehabilitation of schools and hospitals.

Recurrent themes while talking about children, health, education and vulnerability were: the increase in the number of children dropping out of school after the tsunami due to displacement and loss, the need to supervise younger children while parents were at work as daily wage earners, evidence of community resilience and support. In rural areas, people talked about lack of access to health and education facilities and an acute lack of transport facilities.

Most children, especially under-age recruits who have been child soldiers, undergo catch-up education (CUE) for a year before being integrated into mainstream school. Key-informant interviews with officials revealed that 90% of underage recruits had not been forcibly recruited. Girls and boys recruited often come from families with problems and were therefore soft targets for recruitment. Sometimes villages felt that they had to give a child to the LTTE cause. Many of the under-age recruits often joined if friends and older siblings had joined the LTTE cadres.

Living in single female-headed households, often led to worse long-term outcomes in terms of poverty, income and support. Women were empowered by access to micro-credit facilities and establishment of small grassroots businesses. Communities who had returned to their village after displacement displayed less dysfunctionalism, better educational and health indicators as compared to those living in IDP camps or those that had been relocated. 'Peace' was cited by all participants as an absolute prerequisite for further development.

Reflections on the field research

- Challenges encountered during the data collection and in-field research were often related to the very polarized society and the political economy of war in Sri Lanka.
- Data gathered from the Government of Sri Lanka would be accepted only hesitantly by the LTTE and vice versa.
- Several times the credibility of sources of information was questioned due to the difficult, complicated and complex relations between the GOSL and LTTE.
- There was an undercurrent of fear from children, women and other key informants living in the LTTE controlled areas. The researchers felt that this may have led to underreporting by participants.
- There was the need to create secure surroundings for interviews and focus group discussions, which would guarantee that confidentiality of participants was ensured.
- All information that could lead to identification of participants in the project such as photos taken, names and locations were either not collected or removed prior to publication of any data.
- As the political situation was comparatively stable at the time of in-field data collection, almost all areas of the North and East could be accessed. Since then, the political situation has deteriorated considerably in the North and East, which would make another project along these lines impossible to implement at the moment.
- The publication of the final report occurred during the time of deterioration of security situation in the North and East of Sri Lanka, thus the report could only be published as an in-house report which limited the dissemination of findings.

Conclusion

Researching topics which are highly political or have the potential to be politicized are critical in terms of needing to balance multiple views of the actual situation. It is very easy to over represent the leading opinion and to comply with what is expected by those in power. Publishing findings which do not represent the official line of thought can often be detrimental to the researchers as sources of information might be discredited and the researchers' integrity doubted. The sponsoring organization preferred not to publish the study's findings due to the rapid and escalating deterioration in the security situation in the North and East. Experiences gained by the researchers from this project highlighted the fine line between scientific and academic research and political agenda and the need to maintain a sensitive and professional balance between the two. The study has shown that the rapid participatory ethnographic assessment is a useful approach that can be effectively used by researchers and communities especially in areas affected by conflict.

References

Actionaid (2003). Participatory Vulnerability Analysis: A step-by-step-guide for field staff. Actionaid International, UK.

Arunatilkae, N., Jayasuriya, S., & Kelegama, S. (2001). The economic cost of war in Sri Lanka. World Development, Vol 29, 9, 1483-1500

Denzin, N. & Lincoln, Y. (2000). Handbook of qualitative research (2nd Ed.). California: Sage Publishers.

Department of National Planning (2004a). National Plan of Action for the Children of Sri Lanka. Department of National Planning, Colombo, Sri Lanka.

FHI. (2005). Rapid ethnographic guide. Retrieved 20-November-2005 from www.fhi.org/en/HIVAIDS/pub/guide/RapidAssessmentGuide/rag5.htm

Goodhand, J., & Lewer, N. (1999). NGOs and peacebuilding in complex emergencies. Third World Quarterly, 20, 13-26

Guba, E. G., & Lincoln, Y. S. (1994). Competing paradigms in qualitative research. In N. K. Denzin & Y. S. Lincoln (Eds.), Handbook of qualitative research (pp.105-117). Thousand Oaks, CA: Sage Publications.

Human Rights Watch. (2006). Living in fear: child soldiers and the Tamil tigers in Sri Lanka. Report 16 (13 C). Retrieved 20-February-2006 from www.hrw.org/reports/2004/srilanka1104

International Save the Children Alliance. (1996). Educational content and methodology: promoting psychosocial well-being among children affected by armed conflict and displacement: principles and approaches. Retrieved 23-March-2006 from www.ineesite.org/edcon/promoting.asp

Jabbar, S. & Sennayake, D. (2004). Overview of Poverty in Sri Lanka. Centre for Poverty Analysis, Colombo, Sri Lanka.

Korf, B. (2006). Dining with the devils? Ethnographic enquiries into the conflict-development nexus in Sri Lanka. Oxford Development Studies. Vol 34, 1, 47-64

Lacey, A. & Luff, D. (2001). Trent focus for research and development in primary health care: An introduction to qualitative analysis. Trent Focus, United Kingdom.

Merriam, S. (1998). Qualitative research and case study applications in education. San Francisco, CA: Jossey-Bass.

Moench, M. & Dixit, A. (2004). Adaptive capacity and livelihood resilience: Adaptive strategies for responding to floods and droughts in South Asia. Kathmandu Institute for Social and Environmental Transition, Nepal.

Nicolai, S. & Triplehorn, C. (2003). The role of education in protecting children in armed conflict. Human Practice Network, New York.

Patton, M.Q. (1990). Qualitative evaluation and research methods. Newbury Park, CA: Sage Publications.

Psychosocial Working Group (2003). Psychosocial interventions in complex emergencies: A conceptual framework. Refugee Studies Centre, Queen Margaret University College, Edinburgh, UK.

Punch, K. (2003). Introduction to social research. London: Sage publications.

Save the Children Fund (n.d.). Where we work: Sri Lanka. Retrieved 27-October-2005 www.savethechildren.ca/wherewework/southasia/srilanka.html.

Save the Children Fund (2006). 1-year progress report: Rebuilding lives after the Tsunami through the eyes of children. SCF, UK.

The Virtual Library of Sri Lanka. (n.d.) People and ethnic groups. Retrieved 23-March-2006 from www.lankalibrary.com/cul.html

Thomas, D. (2003). A general inductive approach for qualitative data analysis. School of Population Health, University of Auckland.

TNS Lanka (2006). Report on the assessment of the water supply, sanitation and hygiene status, education needs and social protection services in transitional shelters, camps and settlements: Tsunami affected areas in Sri Lanka. UNICEF, Sri Lanka

UNDP (2004). Human Development Report 2003: Sri Lanka. UNDP, Colombo.

UNICEF (2006). The State of the World's Children 2006. Retrieved 20-February-2006 from www.unicef.org

UNICEF (2003). Action Plan: Addressing the needs and care for the children in the North East affected by war. UNICEF- Sri Lanka. Unicef, Sri Lanka.

United Nations (n.d). Special concerns: impact of armed conflict on children. Retrieved 23-March-2006 from www.un.org/rights/concerns.htm

von Glasersfeld, E. (1993). Questions and answers about radical constructivism. In K Tobin (Ed.), The practice of constructivism in science and mathematics education (pp.23-38). Hillsdale, NJ: Lawrence Erlbaum.

Wessels, M. & Kostelny, K. (2002). After the Taliban: A child-focused assessment in the Northern Afghan provinces of Kunduz and Badakshan. Christian Children's Fund International, Afghanistan.

Wheatley, A. (1998). Situation Report: Children affected by armed conflict in North and East Sri Lanka. Save the Children Fund, Colombo, Sri Lanka.

World Health Organization (2004). North-East emergency reconstruction project (NEERP): Recovery of the health system in the North-East of Sri Lanka final report (2003-2004). WHO, Sri Lanka.

Yamin, F,. Rahman, A. & Huq, S. (2005). Vulnerability, adaptation and climate disasters: A conceptual overview. IDS Bulletin, 36, 4, 1-14.

Hearing the voices of service users: Reflections on researching the views of people from South Asian backgrounds

Cathy Lloyd, Mark Johnson, Jackie Sturt, Gary Collins and Anthony Barnett

Across the world, the prevalence of diabetes is increasing rapidly, and in the UK this is of particular concern in South Asian groups. Given the centrality of diabetes self-management to both policy and practice, it follows that research in this area, in particular to identify optimal ways of supporting those with diabetes in this regard, is required. However in groups whose main language is not English, such as those from South Asian communities, there are serious limitations to the research that has been carried out to date. In this chapter the difficulties of researching the views and life experiences of people with diabetes, with particular reference to issues around diabetes self-management, in those whose main language is not English, will be discussed and reflected upon.

An on-going study, the UK Asian Diabetes (UKAD) project, initially utilised self-complete measures to elicit views around self-care and knowledge of diabetes. This proved extremely challenging, in particular with regard to the authenticity or quality of the collected data. Hearing the concerns of those researchers who collected the data has led to the design and subsequent funding of a new study to investigate these issues further. This chapter will outline the UKAD study and discuss how that research experience led directly to the design of a further study to address those difficulties identified in the UKAD project.

A research team are currently developing alternative modes of data collection in groups of South Asians with diabetes. This research is led by a multidisciplinary group of academics and health care professionals and uses qualitative methods to develop new ways of collecting data in groups who cannot read or write any language and whose main language does not have an agreed written form; namely Sylheti and Mirpuri. A key principle of this research is that service users are involved from the outset and play a pivotal role in the development of these data collection methods. This chapter will outline this research and will discuss the process of working in a multidisciplinary team alongside lay involvement in the project. It will debate the key issues of 'authentic' and 'valid' knowledge and consider the implications for collecting information and seeking out the views of those people from South Asian backgrounds who currently utilise health care services in the UK. The chapter will consider how 'success' is measured in research and the validity of the experiences of the 'researched' or service users, whose input into the research process is increasingly being considered as vital to the success of any project.

Diabetes is a major health concern of the 21st century, with the incidence and prevalence of this condition increasing rapidly, particularly in South Asian groups in the UK (Department of Health, 2002; Chowdhury, 2002). Given the centrality of diabetes self-management to health and well-being, it follows that research in this area, in particular with regard to identifying optimal ways of supporting those with diabetes, is urgently required. However in groups whose main language is not English, such as many from South Asian communities, there are serious limitations to the research that has been carried out to date. In order to build upon and improve research it helps to learn lessons from past experiences in this field. In this chapter the difficulties of researching the views and life experiences of people with diabetes, in those whose main language is not English, will be discussed and reflected upon. Two pieces of research that led on from each other will be considered and our experiences in carrying out these studies used to inform the debate around how we hear the voices of services users.

Health research in minority ethnic groups in the UK is a relatively new phenomenon, and is most often carried out within biomedical settings, often by medically trained health care professionals. One such study is the UK Asian Diabetes (UKAD) Study, which was set up to identify the most cost-effective and acceptable risk reducing strategies in the South Asian population with Type 2 diabetes (O'Hare, 2004). Individuals from South Asian backgrounds in the UK have a greater risk of developing diabetes compared to white Caucasians; it is over four times more common and age of onset is earlier (Department of Health, 2002; Chowdhury, 2002). Individuals with diabetes run the risk of developing further conditions such as heart disease, kidney problems and sight problems. It has been shown conclusively that strict management of blood glucose levels, blood pressure and cholesterol can prevent or at least delay the development of these conditions (The Diabetes Control and Complications Trial Research Group, 1993; UKPDS group, 1998). The UKAD study was designed to test out a protocol for managing these three risk factors within primary care in Birmingham and Coventry, in the UK. The idea was for diabetes specialist nurses, practice nurses and support workers (known as Asian Link Workers) to work together to implement this protocol (O'Hare, 2004). Prior to attending general practice sessions, the Asian Link workers contacted patients to encourage attendance at the clinics and to organise educational sessions. The remit of the Link Workers was to work alongside the practice nurses and the diabetes specialist nurses in order to promote greater understanding and compliance with self-management recommendations (O'Hare, 2004). During their clinic visits, participants underwent a series of clinical investigations, and were invited to attend subsequent educational sessions.

Most of the research in diabetes is biomedical in nature, and when it includes non-medical data collection, utilises self-completed questionnaires. Along with questionnaires to record biomedical data on family history of diabetes and presence of other conditions, the UKAD Study researchers used self-completed psychosocial measures to elicit views around self-care and knowledge of diabetes, seen as important aspects of this intervention. The two questionnaires, the Diabetes Management Self-Efficacy Scale (DMSES) (Bilj, 1999; Sturt, 2003; McDowell, 2005) and the revised Diabetes Knowledge Scale (DKS-R) (Fitzgerald, 1998) were thus translated and back translated according to accepted methods (Bradley, 1994) and a conciliation meeting took place between the two different translators and one of the researchers. The two self-complete questionnaires were translated into Urdu and Bengali, as these were the two main languages written by the South Asian population under investigation. The two questionnaires were then given to the Link Workers to implement during the participants' clinic visits.

In much survey research a copy of the questionnaire is handed to the consenting person and they are invited to complete the form over a certain time-period. In this research even before the questionnaires were offered to participants challenges arose. Immediately during the translation process it became clear that some English words had a very different meaning (or did not exist) in Bengali or Urdu. This meant that the final version of the questionnaires differed in some respects compared to the original English versions. Furthermore, although an agreed written translation of the questionnaires was finally made, these were frequently unusable in this particular study population. The majority of the study participants were unable to read or write either Urdu or Bengali and used a spoken-only language (Mirpuri or Sylheti). The majority of the participants asked for the Link Worker to complete the questionnaires for them, so further (verbal) translations were then made on an ad hoc basis. As three Link Workers were involved in this study this meant that three different translations were being performed. As the Link Workers reported later, there were often several words that could be used when translating an English word into Mirpuri and they did not always use the same one. On-going consultation with the Link Workers during the research process proved to be vital and the Link Workers subsequently agreed a version in Mirpuri that could be used during data collection, with the responses to the questions recorded on the Urdu translation of the questionnaires. As none of the Link Workers spoke Sylheti only the Bengali written questionnaire could be used in the study with people of Bangladeshi origin (many of whom in the UK come from the Sylhet region of North-East Bangladesh). This meant that those potential study participants who spoke only Sylheti and did not read/write Bengali were effectively excluded from this study.

In survey research generally, questionnaires are usually pre-tested to ensure that their meaning is understood by the respondents. In the UKAD study it became apparent that the meaning of some of the words in the questionnaires may not have been the same for all respondents let alone the Link Workers. These meanings also differed from those understood by the research team in some cases. This had serious implications with regard to the authenticity or quality of the collected data. Indeed our concerns were so strong that a decision was eventually made not to analyse the data.

Experienced researchers often take for granted the process of research, having performed certain procedures time and time again according to accepted methods. However we decided to take a step back and think about what we had been doing from the initial design of the questionnaire, through to the process of data collection. Standard methods of collecting data were questioned and as a first step the Link Workers were interviewed in order to gain insight into what might have impacted on the data collection process. Detailed results of this part of the study have been reported elsewhere (Lloyd, 2006).

Apart from the immense translation difficulties, the most common problem reported by the Link Workers was the time required to complete the two questionnaires. Each study participant was allocated 30 minutes in which to have all their medical history, personal details and various clinical measures collected as well as to complete several questionnaires. Even explaining the rationale behind the questionnaires took up valuable time. A further common problem reported by the Link Workers were the frequent negative reactions they received from the participants, who were often uncomfortable about their [own] perceived lack of knowledge and were concerned about giving incorrect answers to the questions. Previous research has also demonstrated that poor knowledge of diabetes, fear of the condition and its complications, and the stigma attached to diabetes, are common in South Asian people with diabetes (Curtis, 2003; Greenhalgh, 1998). Rankin and Bhopal (2001) have reported in their research in South Asian populations, that there is often a misunderstanding of the term 'diabetes', with many individuals being unable to provide a description of diabetes or suggest any risk factors for developing this condition.

It is important to note that for a small minority of participants the completion of these questionnaires was a positive experience. This was evident for those individuals who wanted to know more about their diabetes and was influenced by their understanding that identifying the gaps in their knowledge could lead to more diabetes education in that area and thus improve their knowledge and could lead to changes in self-care. However for most of them being asked questions about their knowledge of diabetes and their self-care practices was an uncomfortable experience they would not wish to repeat. Vyas (2003) has suggested that, even when interpreters are used to collect data, the way information is collected is still a crucial issue. Whilst the translations were seen to have been technically accurate, and also culturally sensitive, the content of the questionnaires and the actual mode of data collection were often seen as inappropriate by both those collecting the data as well as those providing the data (i.e. the study participants).

In our study the Link Worker's role was of pivotal importance, although not without its limitations. They did not, between them, speak all the languages that were required in order to encourage full participation in the study. This raises questions with regard to whether the sample recruited could be said to represent the South Asian community, or even part of that community. When assisting those who required help in completing the questionnaires, they had to rely on their memories of the agreed words to be used in Mirpuri. Maximising the chances of meeting standardised data collection procedures meant reliance was also placed on the Link Worker's skills in accurately recording responses, avoiding the use of leading questions or answering for the respondent.

A recent systematic review of the process of translation and adaptation of health-related quality of life measures (Bowden, 2003) suggested that there is currently a misguided preoccupation with the scales being used rather than a focus on the actual concepts being scaled, with too much reliance on unsubstantiated claims of conceptual equivalence. When questionnaires are translated, it is frequently the case that any cultural differences are not accounted for (Greenhalgh, 1998; Hunt, 1994, 2003; Froman, 2003). One might argue that both the content and the design of the scale are equally important, although success in either aspect cannot be fully achieved if the specific needs of the target population are not addressed. In this case the need for assisted completion or finding other ways of collecting data which does not involve having to complete questionnaires in a written form appears to be crucial. A further consideration must surely be who should be involved in research and how members of minority ethnic communities can participate more fully in research in order to prevent excluding certain sections of the population.

Not only must the needs of the potential study participants be considered however, the needs of those who are charged with the task of collecting the data must also be taken into account if success is to be achieved. The Link Workers who attempted to collect this data were all highly trained in working with people with diabetes and using standard forms for the collection of personal and medical information. However none of them had used verbally translated questionnaires before and this could have impacted on how they worked. If the Link Workers were unsure how to use these questionnaires this may well have influenced patients' willingness to take part and so may have impacted on response rates. Training and experience in the administration of translated questionnaires is thus critical for studies such as these. This, alongside greater involvement in all other aspects of the research process may well influence the success (or otherwise) or the research, not just the response rate. Healthcare professionals' communication with patients has been seen as crucial in previous research in this area (Rhodes, 2003; Curtis, 2003). The use of interpreters can be difficult, lead to role conflict and relies heavily on communication skills (Hanna, 2006). In this research, the Link Workers agreed that the time taken to work with them to develop an agreed form of Mirpuri to be used when required was invaluable and gave them a chance to voice their concerns with regard to the data collection methods.

Hearing the concerns of the Link Workers and being confronted with these difficulties in collecting data from minority ethnic groups led to the design and subsequent funding of a new study to investigate these issues further. At the time of writing a research team are developing alternative modes of data collection in groups of South Asians with diabetes. This research is led by a multidisciplinary group of academics and health care professionals and has used qualitative methods to develop new ways of collecting data in groups who can not read or write any language and whose main language does not have an agreed written form; namely Sylheti and Mirpuri. A key principle of this research is that both the Link Workers and service users will be involved from the outset and play a pivotal role in the development of these data collection methods. This is sometimes termed a 'participatory' approach, where professionals and lay people work together towards common aims or goals. Community empowerment is seen as central to the process, enabling people to have a greater say and more control over their lives and local health care decisions (Bandesha, 2005; Singh and Johnson, 1998; Johnson 2006). The experiences of lay people, the 'researched' or the service users, is considered as vital to the success of our project as the skills and knowledge of the professionals involved.

Participatory research is not without its difficulties however, and its use in studies of community participation in health has sometimes been problematic. Although the principles of community participation have long been operationalised in the developing world as part of the movement for social justice (Ansari, 2002), in the UK the discrepancies between perceived levels of skill, knowledge or expertise between professional groups and lay members of the community can lead to difficulties in research (Bandesha, 2005). Johnson is clear when he describes the only real involvement of lay members of (ethnic minority) user groups is often as being in the role of fieldworkers or research staff, employed because of their ability to speak a particular language or to gain access to certain groups (Johnson, 2006). Real partnerships between health researchers and members of minority ethnic groups in research are rarely cited and seem to be few.

The design of the new study was based on an action research model. The definition of action research suggested by Rapoport (1970) describes it as a research method for the solution of practical problems within a real work environment whilst concurrently satisfying the goals of social science by engaging in mutual collaboration with research participants within an ethical framework. This method has enabled the researchers and the study participants the time and opportunity to reflect upon, and evaluate, the findings of the research as it progresses, and to make changes in the study protocol when required. At the same time, this action research remains within a participatory research framework.

The study had two aims:

1. to engage in a qualitative assessment of the cultural adaptation of the two questionnaires for use in people with diabetes from particular minority ethnic populations, so that accurate and culturally sensitive translations can be developed; and
2. to identify the most appropriate method of instrument administration and data collection in groups with ethnic origin from the Indian subcontinent whose first language is not English, or where a written language may or may not exist, and where levels of literacy are an influential factor when self-report instruments are used.

The new study involved recruiting research workers who could gain access to people with diabetes by virtue of their language skills. The Link Workers from the original study were also closely involved. People with Type 2 diabetes who spoke either Urdu/Mirpuri or Bengali/Sylheti were recruited to take part in focus groups to discuss both the content of the questionnaires as well as the mode of delivery. Two researchers (one male and one female), one who spoke Bengali and Sylheti and one who spoke Urdu and Mirpuri were employed to work on the study. Almost immediately some of the assumptions about gender and access to minority ethnic communities were challenged as it became clear that it was not unacceptable to have a male researcher recruiting female diabetes patients, although it was slightly more difficult. A female presence or 'chaperone' for the male researcher when facilitating the all-female focus group was seen as vital however. Traditional boundaries between the roles of 'principal investigator' or senior/ professional researcher/academic and research assistants were also challenged as the aim was to work within a participatory, facilitative and empowering framework. Reliance on the two research assistants to translate the audio recordings of the focus groups for example, and to report back to the investigative team has been a key issue and a new experience for some.

It has been argued elsewhere that service users may be involved at a number of different points in the research process (Johnson, 2006). The level of involvement may be associated with different types of impact on the research. In the new study we aimed to recruit people from the community to participate in focus groups to consider alternative modes of data collection. The focus groups were planned to consider both the content of questionnaires as well as the mode of delivery. Both the research assistants and the study participants have had a strong impact on this research. Involvement of the investigators in the actual running of the focus groups has been extremely limited given that they were conducted in either Mirpuri or Sylheti, and none of the principal investigators spoke (or indeed still speaks!) these languages.

Our experiences with the UKAD study, as well as our current work, have challenged our ideas of what is considered to be 'valid' or 'authentic' knowledge. In the UKAD study we had serious concerns with regards the data we collected using the Link Workers to complete the questionnaire on behalf of the participants and translating on an ad hoc basis. In retrospect, there might be questions around why we considered this process to be 'invalid' – which was probably on the basis of (our) ideas around science and 'hard data' and the use of standard, structured questionnaires. Our concerns were based on our traditional research training in quantitative methods of data collection and standardised methods of research. Currently accepted standards for research in health are largely the use of quantitative studies such as those included in systematic reviews, and involve methods which measure or count things or people (Collins, 2006). At this point in our research we might wonder whether validity criteria should be applied to a study such as this and if so what these might be. The most recently accepted evaluation criteria recommended by leading researchers and academics for clinical trials and systematic reviews are based upon traditional notions of biomedicine, the importance of hypothesis testing and numerical data (Needleman, 2001). However, Im and colleagues (2004) have argued that there are criteria that can be applied to both quantitative and qualitative cross-cultural research. These include not only cultural relevance, contextuality and appropriateness, but also mutual respect and flexibility. The use of two or more different data collection methods (often termed 'triangulation'), where the findings are compared has also served this study well. Being able to compare the information gained from the Link Workers with that from the focus group participants has given further support to our findings.

Authenticity of data or information relates to the accuracy and applicability of the measurement especially in qualitative research. This is often seen in relation to the study population and whether those studied 'represent' the wider population. Given the diversity of experiences between but also within particular cultural and ethnic groups, it might be suggested that this is difficult to achieve to say the least. We would argue however, that this does not invalidate our research, but rather, instead of generalising, strengthens what we can say about particular sections of the South Asian community.

Conclusions

This chapter has outlined some of the key issues when researching with the South Asian communities in the UK. We have only worked alongside small sections of this community, but already it is clear that there are important implications. Collecting information from and seeking out the views of those people from South Asian backgrounds who currently utilise health care services in the UK is not easy. Using a participatory approach to research we would argue can only help to inform those attempting to improve both health and health services. Listening to the voices of those involved in researching on our behalf, as well as those being researched is critical and can go some way towards building an accurate picture of the needs and views of local communities.

References

Bandesha, G. & Litva, A. (2005). Perceptions of community participation and health gain in a community project for the South Asian population: A qualitative study. Journal of Public Health, 27, 241-245.

Bilj, J.J. van der, Poelgeest-Eeltink, A. van & Shortridge-Baggett, L. (1999). The psychometric properties of the diabetes management self-efficacy scale for patients with type 2 diabetes mellitus. Journal of Advanced Nursing, 30, 352-359

Bowden, A. & Fox-Rushby, J.A. (2003). A systematic and critical review of the process of translation and adaptation of generic health-related quality of life measures in Africa, Asia, Eastern Europe, the Middle East, South America. Social Science and Medicine, 57, 1289-1306.

Bradley, C. (1994). Translation of questionnaires for use in different languages and cultures. In: C. Bradley (ed.), Handbook of psychology and diabetes (pp.43-55). Switzerland, Harwood.

Chowdhury, T.A. & Lasker, S.A. (2002). Complications and cardiovascular risk factors in South Asian and Europeans with early onset type 2 diabetes. Quarterly Journal of Medicine, 95(4), 241-6.

Collins, G.S. & Johnson, M.R.D (2006). Addressing ethnic diversity in health outcome measures. Health Technology Assessment.

Curtis, S., Beirne, J. & Jude, E. (2003). Advantages of training Asian diabetes support workers for Asian families and diabetes health care professionals. Practical Diabetes International, 20(6), 215-218.

Department of Health (2002). NSF for Diabetes Standards of Care Document 2002. www.dh.gov.uk/en/Publicationsandstatistics/Publications/PublicationsPolicyAndGuidance/DH_4002951. Accessed 7th June 2007.

Fitzgerald, J.T., Anderson, R.M., Funnell, M.M., Hiss, R.G., Hess, G.E., Davis, W.K. & Barr, P.A. (1998). The reliability and validity of a brief diabetes knowledge test. Diabetes Care, 21(5), 706-710.

Greenhalgh, T., Helman, C. & Chowdhury, A.M.(1998). Health beliefs and folk models of diabetes in British Bangladeshis: a qualitative study. British Medical Journal, 316, 978-983.

Hanna, L., Hunt, S. & Bhopal, R. (2006). Cross-cultural adaptation of a tobacco questionnaire for Punjabi, Cantonese, Urdu and Sylheti speakers: qualitative research for better clinical practice, cessation services and research. Journal of Epidemiology and Community Health, 60, 1034-1039.

Hunt, S.M. (1994). Cross-cultural comparability of quality of life measures. International Symposium on Quality of Life and Health (pp.25-27). Berlin, Blackwell Verlag.

Hunt, S.M. & Bhopal, R. (2004). Self report in clinical and epidemiological studies with non-English speakers: the challenge of language and culture. Journal of Epidemiology and Community Health, 58, 618-622.

Im, E-O., Page, R.., Lin, L-C., Tsai, H. & Cheng, C-Y. (2004). Rigor in cross-cultural nursing research. International Journal of Nursing Studies, 41, 891-899.

Johnson, M.R.D. & Singh, G. (2001). Research with ethnic minority groups in health and social welfare. In H. Goulbourne (Ed.), Race and Ethnicity: Critical Concepts (pp.250-266). London, Routledge.

Johnson, M.R.D. & Collins, G.S. (2004). Getting it right in multi-cultural research. British Medical Journal, 328, 7431.

Johnson, M.R.D. (2006). Engaging Communities and Users: Health and Social Care Research with Ethnic Minority Communities. In J.Y. Nazroo (Ed.) Health and Social Research in Multi-ethnic Societies (pp.48-64). London, Routledge.

Lloyd, C.E., Mughal, S., Sturt, J., O'Hare, P.& Barnett, A.H. (2006). Using self-complete questionnaires in a South Asian population with diabetes: problems and solutions. Diversity in Health & Social Care, 3(4), 245-51.

McDowell, J., Courtney, M., Edwards, H., & Shortridge-Baggett, L. (2005). Validation of the Australian/English version of the Diabetes Management Self-Efficacy Scale. International Journal of Nursing Practice, 11, 177-184.

Needleman, I. (2000). Is this good for research? Look for CONSORT and QUORUM. Evidence-Based Dentistry, 2, 61-62.

O'Hare, P., Raymond, N.T., Mughal, S., Dodd, L., Hanif, W., Ahmed, Y. et al. (2004). Evaluation of enhanced diabetes care to patients of South Asian Ethnicity: The United Kingdom Asian Diabetes Study (UKADS). Diabetic Medicine, 21, 1357-65.

Rankin, J. & Bhopal, R. (2001). Understanding of heart disease and diabetes in a South Asian community: cross-sectional study testing the 'snowball' sample method. Public Health, 115, 253-260.

Sturt, J. & Hearnshaw, H. (2003). Measuring Outcomes: self-management, empowerment and self-efficacy. Diabetic Medicine, 20(Supp 2), 78.

The Diabetes Control and Complications Trial Research Group.(1993). The effect of intensive treatment of diabetes on the development and progression of long-term complications in insulin-dependent diabetes mellitus. New England Journal of Medicine, 329, 977-986.

UKPDS group.(1998). Intensive blood glucose control with sulphonylureas or insulin compared with conventional treatment and risk of complications in patients with type 2 diabetes. Lancet, 352, 837-853.

Vyas, A., Haidery, A.Z., Wiles, P.G., Gill, S., Roberts, C. & Cruickshank, J.K. (2003). A pilot randomized trial in primary care to investigate and improve knowledge, awareness and self-management among South Asians with diabetes in Manchester. Diabetic Medicine, 20, 1022-1026.

The doors to Aleut orthodoxy

Don Wren

The Aleuts of the Pribilof Islands are Russian Orthodox and members of the Church from the time of their baptism until their death. Pribilovian social relationships derive in part from the activities and doctrines of the Church. The Aleut were brought from the Aleutian chain to provide the labour for the Northern Fur seal harvest. The Russian Orthodox faith came to the islands with the Aleut and their Russian overseers.

I was welcomed to St. Paul Island in part because my research received the blessing of the Bishop of Alaska. People knew my consultant and I were coming to the Island. One of the managers of the Village Corporation met us and offered names of people best able to describe the Church. I spent two semesters doing documentary research at the Arctic and Polar Regions Archives at the University of Alaska Fairbanks in order to understand the history of the Islands.

During interviews with the Elders, I showed them historical photos from the Archives. The photos put the interviewees at ease. My consultant, who was born on Saint Paul, ensured the community's involvement in the knowledge gathering process. We were on St. Paul during the Paschal season, a time of great importance to the Orthodox faithful. I conducted participant observation in the Church and many homes, and talked with people about their icon walls, the practice of the faith and their feelings about the Church.

This research has special significance to the Pribilovians because it has helped document an aspect of their culture that the Elders are concerned is disappearing.

The Path

I am writing to describe my experiences with the Russian Orthodox Church in Alaska. My studies began nearly 20 years ago when I went to visit a friend of mine, a person who became my consultant and eventually my spiritual brother. When I walked into his house, I saw what is known as a pretty wall, a wall filled with icons. I had seen icons before but had never experienced them in this context.

My friend is an Aleut… was an Aleut. My brother passed on last year and left me to carry on this work, work that he took up towards the end of his life. He saw my studies as validation of the importance of the Orthodox faith to his people.

After I began my studies, I thought it would be important to visit each of the major centers of Orthodoxy in Alaska. My first trip, with studies in mind, was to St. Paul Island in the Pribilof Island group. While I was there, I went to the Church of Saints Peter and Paul. July is typically a festive time. July 12 is the feast of Saints Peter and Paul, a feast known as 'PetroPavel'. The Fourth of July is a very big day for celebrating as well. It was a good time for me to be on the island. I visited the church, like most of the other people touring the island, for an interpretive tour conducted by one of the church trustees. Once he finished the standard tour, I stayed after and asked him a number of questions about the faith on the island, the church and the icons.

That discussion demonstrated to me the need for a systematic exploration of the faith. The Aleut (also known as Unangan – a term translated as 'the people') know their own faith. However, to someone from outside the faith and outside the Unangan culture, it might be difficult to understand. When I returned to Anchorage from St. Paul, I began to gather documentation on the church.

The final paper for my history degree was entitled, 'Orthodoxy in South Central Alaska'. Many of the materials I gathered in that study are part of my current study because of the similarities of the manifestation of the faith amongst the different native peoples of Alaska. The Athabascans live in South Central Alaska. The Unangan people live in the place of my current studies. The studies led me to a number of people who are expert in the church. There was always my brother to whom I could turn with questions. I talked with many of the priests in the area: Father Nicholas Molodyko-Harris, Father Paul Merculieff and Father Simeon Oskolkoff were but a few. The people from whom I learned the most were the Aleut members of the St. Innocent Orthodox parish. The ethnic makeup of Anchorage includes a number of various Alaska native groups: Yupik, Aleut, Athabascans, and Tlingit. All of these different groups were the subjects of evangelization by the Russian Orthodox missionaries who arrived in North America in 1794. However, the first people to encounter the missionaries were the Aleut. Their exposure to the faith has been the longest of any of the Alaska native groups. This exposure has led to a firm entrenchment among the Unangan. The next to be contacted were the Yupik, followed by the Athabaskans on the Kenai Peninsula, the Sugpiaq in Kodiak and the Tlingit in southeast Alaska.

The ethnic makeup of St. Innocent's parish is predominantly Alaska native, a number of Russians (not at the time I began my study) and Orthodox faithful from outside the state of Alaska who moved to Alaska from other places: Pennsylvania, Florida, California and across the lower 48. However, the church is still very much an Alaska Native institution. It is a remnant of the Russian period in Alaska and one to which the Alaska Native people are strongly committed.

Once I decided on a topic for my studies, the people who were most accessible to me were the Aleut faithful from the congregation of St. Innocent's Bicentennial Orthodox

Cathedral. It was there that I made a number of contacts with whom I continue to talk today. The process I followed when I was beginning my formal studies of the faith was to immerse myself in the ceremonies and the activities of the church. I participated in a number of momentous occasions at St. Innocent's. One of the most significant is the canonization of St. Yakov Netsvetov. He was a Creole, a person of mixed descent, half-Aleut and half-Russian. Metropolitan Theodosius, then Metropolitan of All America and Canada, presided over the ceremony. I was chrismated by him. During that ceremony, the name of St. Yakov joined the list of saints in the Orthodox faith. There were over 1000 people at the ceremony. A second highly significant event in which I participated was the personal blessing of His Holiness Patriarch Alexei II, Metropolitan of Moscow and All Russia. The Patriarch came to Anchorage to celebrate the bicentennial of Orthodoxy in Alaska. Over 3000 people attended his personal blessing service. It was a highly momentous occasion for the church. His was the first visit of a Patriarch of the Russian Orthodox Church to Alaska. It was a validation of the faith of not only the church, St. Innocent's, but the faith of the Alaska Native people.

In the church, services are sung in a mix of languages. Hymns are sung in English, but with a mix of Church Slavonic, which is very widely used, as well as hymns sung in Aleut, Yupik, Tlingit and Athabascan. This mix of languages is a unique phenomenon not found anywhere else. The church is a reflection of its members.

The Doors

The church is the physical manifestation of Heaven on earth. Behind the royal doors, at the front of the altar, is a window on the kingdom of heaven. The symbology in the church is very intricate. On the icons, the use of colour, the symbology and artifacts represented on the icons, the gestures of the hands, looks on the faces, and the very makeup and construction of the icon have meaning. The people understand these meanings. People know the stories behind the icons because that is part of the faith. They understand the origin of a particular icon and the depiction of the saint. The icons are a conduit through which the people petition the particular person represented in the icon, saint or otherwise. It benefits the people to have this knowledge of the true symbology on the icon. It puts them in mind of the saints and provides the concentration required to say prayers properly by focusing on the object of your petition.

When I visited Aleut homes, every home had an icon wall. Each icon had its own particular story: its origin, the reason it occupies a particular part of the wall, and the person who brought the icon to the home. The icons in the church have the same significance as those found in the home. The icons are a part of the belief system and play a role in the individual's daily prayer ritual.

The family is the basic unit of Aleut social structure. Within the family, the young are socialized and taught the right way to do things. However, another component of that socialization process takes place in the church. The church becomes the purveyor of worldview. The Aleut concept of hell is a place where there is no land, no sanctuary, only open water. It is a place with no safe harbour. In the baptism ceremony in the church, the young are immersed in water. This symbolizes Christ's descent into hell after his death and his subsequent resurrection. When the baby is raised from the water, the baby has had his or her sins washed away. The child is born anew.

There is a correlation between the traditional worldview of the Aleut and the worldview represented in the church. It was not a big step for the Aleut to embrace Orthodoxy because many of the tenets of the faith closely corresponded with their traditional beliefs. The Aleut lived in natural structures constructed from natural materials found on the beach, wood, skins from hunting sea lions, and whalebone for the frame of their barabaras. They used seal oil for their lamps. Natural materials are used in the church as well. The decorations in the church, in particular the Church of Saints Peter and Paul, willows decorate the altar. The royal doors are made from wood. Construction using natural materials was easily understood. The idea of a creator was not foreign to the Aleut. They believed in a creator, an all-powerful spirit. There is one story of a shaman who went and communed with spirits in a cave in the side of mountain. He fasted and saw a vision in which there were beings that came to him and told him of things to come and ways to live. When he came down, he recounted this to one of the missionaries who in turn wrote to one of his superiors in Russia and said, "What is this? The shaman related this story to me. What do you think it means?" The reply he received was that these were emissaries of the Lord, angels.

The ease with which the Aleut adopted the faith was facilitated by the approach of the missionaries. In their work, one of the first things they did was learn the local language. When the Bible was translated into the local language, the people understood the similarities between their pre-contact beliefs and those of the newcomers.

My entrance into the church was facilitated by my friendship and brotherhood with a dear person. It was his guidance and determination that helped me get to this point and that kept me going. Our meeting changed both our lives. He and I both became a different people from our interactions. Knowing that someone was so interested in what he believed and thought, led him to open himself to me. He opened both his heart and his home. There is no way I could have completed this work without his help.

During my field trip to St. Paul, my second trip, I brought my brother with me. My intention was that I would be in the background as a participant observer. I set up the equipment, made sure we kept to a schedule, and took notes. He was very glad to come along because he had not been home in a number of years. We stayed at his mother's house so I had a chance to see firsthand what it was like to live in an Aleut household. I am not saying that their household was typical. It was unique and, more importantly, it was a place where my brother was at home.

Leading up to the research, I wrote a letter asking permission from both the village corporation and the traditional council. I felt it was important that the people in charge of the governance structures on the island were aware of what I intended to do with my research. They were told the scope and nature of my work. I received responses from the village council and the corporation granting me permission to come to do the research. The factor that played the biggest part in my receiving permission from the council and the corporation was that I had obtained permission from Bishop Innocent, then Bishop of Sitka and all Alaska, the hierarch of the church in Alaska.

When I wrote to the Bishop and described my work, he said, "There is one person with whom you must talk. That person is MB." MB was the same person I had talked to the first time I was on the island inside the church. When we arrived on the island, he was one of the first people we saw. He gave us a list of all the people he thought we should talk to in the course of our study.

This research is part of the body of work for my Master's thesis. I have recorded the voices of the Elders as a contemporary record to inform my study which spans the period of the American occupation of the Islands. The documentary record has been an essential part of my investigation. While completing my course work at the University of Alaska Fairbanks, I had open access to the resources at the Arctic and Polar Regions Archives. Of all the documentary records I found there, the most important was a photo album compiled by a nurse who lived on St. Paul prior to the Second World War. This photo album contains pictures of many people who are still alive. Prior to leaving for the field, I assembled a binder full of copies of the photos. The binder is a visual reminder of what the island was like when, from what some people told me, the church was at its height. The photo album was the key to triggering memories from the people we were interviewing.

As part of traditional culture, it is customary for someone seeking information to present a gift in recognition of the time that the Elder is spending with you. As part of my gift to the Elders for doing the interviews, I asked them if there were photos in the album of relatives or friends of which they would like copies. On my return to Anchorage, I ordered prints from the album and sent them out to the Elders. I felt it was part of my responsibility as a researcher coming into the community and gathering information. The people with whom we talked were very happy that someone was there to help them document something that was so important to them.

This research has now become part of the history of the island. Some of the Elders I talked with are gone now. There is now a record of what they think/thought about the church and their role in the church. This record is now accessible to future generations at the Arctic and Polar Regions Archive at the University of Alaska Fairbanks. Many of the people we interviewed talked about their joy in seeing someone coming to gather their memories and feelings about their church, something that was so important to them that they would take time from their day to talk to someone who knew about the church but was in essence a stranger.

Many times when I would visit with my brother, he would have relatives by. I remember one particular instance where his niece and nephew were over and he made a joke. He called me *vladiska*, which means priest. Both of them stiffened visibly. They did not know what to think of me but then my brother told them he was joking and they relaxed. That shows the reverence, the depth to which the people hold the clergy in esteem. There are a number of priests who were born and raised on the Pribilofs. The faith is strongest, as far as I can see, on the islands. The Aleut are the most devout and dedicated to their church. The church has been a part of the people's lives for over two centuries. When a church becomes a people's own, the attachment becomes that much stronger. The church in Alaska is not Russian anymore. It is a native church where the true faith manifests itself most strongly.

I need to talk about some of the other things I have done in and around the different churches in Alaska. Some of the reasons that people there on the island recognize my understanding of how the church works. After my trip to Saint Paul, a few years later I made a trip to Unalaska. While there, I attended service at Holy Ascension Cathedral. Reader Perfinia Pletnikof was serving that day. While on Unalaska, I talked with Matushka Gromoff, wife of Father Ismail (Smiley) Gromoff. My brother told me that she was one of the people with whom I should talk. Father Smiley was one of the priests who was born and raised on St. Paul. When I got to the church, I did not know who I was looking for. After services, I called Matushka Gromoff on the phone and we wound up talking for a long time. She had an appointment that kept us from visiting in person, but we talked for a long time. I told her about my studies and my intentions. We had a nice talk. She talked to me about the history of the church there and some of the things that took place there during the war.

I visited the church in Sitka, St. Michael the Archangel Cathedral. The priest who was serving there at the time was also born and raised on St. Paul. He is the father of a very dear friend and a cousin of my brother. I talked with him and told him about my studies. He showed me the church and talked about its history.

In 1996, I went on pilgrimage to Spruce Island, the location of the hermitage of Saint Herman of Alaska. There is an annual pilgrimage right around Saint Herman's feast day on Aug. 9. I flew to Kodiak, attended services at Holy Resurrection Cathedral, and joined the dozens of others who were making the pilgrimage. It had been cloudy on Kodiak the week prior to the pilgrimage. On the morning when we loaded on the fishing boats, the skies cleared and the seas calmed. We spent a beautiful day on Spruce Island. I talked with some monks who had set up residence on the island (they have now left because of a dispute over the land). Saint Herman was the first North American saint in the Orthodox Church. He was canonized in 1970. Saint Herman was beloved by the people of that area. There were a number of miracles performed while he lived on Spruce Island. The people adored Saint

Herman. They thought that he was a compassionate man, but also a man with extraordinary power. There is another similarity between Orthodoxy and traditional culture. There are people who spend their lives seeking spirituality. They have access to the spirit world. St. Herman demonstrated his abilities to the people on Spruce Island. He showed them that he was humble. He lived with very few things. He could communicate with the animals. On the night of his repose, people who lived near there said they saw glowing lights off in the distance. Kodiak is one of the centres of orthodoxy. Holy Resurrection Cathedral houses Saint Herman's reliquary. Part of the pilgrimage is the veneration of the relics. This experience, when related to the people of St. Paul, was met with respect.

It has been a long process. It has taken me decades to come to the depths of understanding that I have about the church. It is important that the information I gathered, these experiences, this knowledge be relayed back to the people of the community. It is crucial that they know that this is what has come from their investment of time, effort and caring. None of this would have been possible without the help of my brother. He was instrumental in my choice of this topic and in the execution of the research. He is gone now. He fell asleep in the Lord on Saint Herman's day, August 9 last year. I miss him a lot. He changed my life with his friendship and by showing me the light of the church.

The title of this chapter is 'The Doors to Aleut Orthodoxy'. There is a point in the orthodox service where catechumens are to leave the nave and excuse themselves to the vestibule. When this point in the service comes, the priest shouts out, 'The doors, the doors'. At that time, the doors to the nave are closed and the catechumens are isolated from the mysteries of the faith. They do this until the catechumens are received into the church through chrismation. I can say that I have passed through those doors. It was not easy. The community, and most instrumentally, my brother brought me through those doors. Now I am a part of the community. Moreover, that community is a part of me and always will be. There are people who know me there, think highly of me and would welcome me back. I think the main reason I would be welcomed back is the fact that I was respectful. I showed an interest in their lives and in something highly significant to them, their faith.

Acknowledgement

The research for this chapter was funded in part by a Philips Fund Grant for Native American Studies from the American Philosophical Society and an Arctic Institute of North America Grant in Aid.

Don Wren

Research as a living partnership

Soulful research: Using an arts-based methodology to authentically engage with local communities

Victoria Foster

This chapter focuses on a participatory research project that was carried out at a Sure Start programme in the north west of England, UK. Sure Start, a government initiative working with young children and their families in areas of social and economic disadvantage, holds as its ultimate goal the ending of child poverty. The project has applied an innovative, arts-based methodology to the research in order to engage more authentically with the local community. The necessity of turning to alternative, emancipatory means of knowledge creation, particularly in the current political climate, has been discussed.

The challenges of applying such an approach have been explored, including the perhaps inevitable clash between participatory research and bureaucracy. Each step of the research process has been addressed, from recruiting participants and providing training, through to the design of the questions and collecting, analyzing and disseminating data. The chapter considers the success stories that have emerged from the project and the subsequent changes made to people's lives as a result.

The author has suggested that it is the process of carrying out participatory research, with its focus on building relationships and enjoyment of the work, that makes this approach so beneficial, as well as the fact that the findings produced are rich and authentic. The inclusion of creative writing, short-film making and visual art as methods of collecting data has encouraged self-reflection in research participants. Moreover, turning to the arts and humanities has vivified the dissemination of findings, impacting emotionally upon an audience which included professionals, academics and members of the local community.

This chapter, concerned with alternative ways of knowing the social world, examines the process of carrying out a participatory, arts-based research project at a Sure Start[12] programme in North West England, UK. The project's innovative methodology draws from a number of different areas – feminist epistemology, emancipatory, participatory research, postmodern ethnography and performance studies. The notion of such an approach to knowledge creation being a holistic, life-enhancing practice is a theme of this

---

[12] See: www.surestart.gov.uk.

chapter and, as such, the emotional and spiritual dimensions of research practice are considered.

Sure Start is a government initiative working with young children and their families in socially and economically disadvantaged communities with the ultimate goal of ending child poverty. The area where the programme concerned is situated is a 'run-down', ex-mining community with particularly high levels of unemployment. Inhabitants are predominantly white and working-class, cut off from surrounding areas by lack of their own vehicles and poor public transport links. There are much higher than average instances of poor health in the area, amongst both adults and children, and almost half the population of 16-74 year olds have no qualifications (Office for National Statistics, 2001).

At the time that the research was carried out, there were around five hundred Sure Start programmes across the country, each being required to produce an evaluation of an aspect of its services. These 'local' research projects fed into a large-scale national evaluation of the initiative. Whilst a sizeable number of the Sure Start programmes elected to carry out research themselves, others employed local universities or independent researchers to conduct projects for them. This particular project was funded by the Economic and Social Research Council (ESRC) and was a collaboration between the University of Liverpool, where I was a doctoral student, myself and the Sure Start programme.

The project, negotiated with the manager of the programme, looked at families' experiences of living in the local area and raising children there. It considered their involvement with the Sure Start programme, looking at if, and how, it had impacted upon their lives. Particular emphasis was given to the emotions and feelings involved in this, understanding, in line with a feminist methodology, that the world of emotion is not only acceptable as data but also as an important part of a holistic knowing.

One of the underlying ambitions of the project was that the local community created knowledge about itself, thus contrasting with the established ritual of having an external, professional researcher making assumptions and judgements on a community's behalf. Hence, the project involved recruiting a team of women, all working-class mothers of young children attending the Sure Start programme, and providing them with training to enable them to carry out the research themselves.

As well as using more traditional methods of collecting data – such as in-depth interviews and questionnaire surveys –the research encouraged Sure Start parents and carers to express themselves and to describe their life experiences through poetry, visual art and short-film. This was important in a number of ways, not least in that it added another dimension to the research findings. It allowed a greater range of participants to become involved in the research project and for them to develop new skills and to think a little more deeply about their lives and experiences. In addition, it offered them an element of control over how these thoughts were communicated to a wider audience. This is a very different process from that of research interviews, where, in analysis, professionals inevitably have to dissect what was said, often quoting snippets out of context, sometimes deliberately to fit a particular thesis or political agenda.

Both participatory research and feminist approaches to research recognise that there are many ways of knowing the world, and that this knowledge must be put into practice to change the world – not merely on a local level, but on a much wider, even spiritual level. Heron and Reason (2001, p.179) agree that a problem with traditional academic research is that the kind of thinking done by researchers is often theoretical rather than practical. Ideally it should be about both: "revisioning our understanding of our world, as well as transforming practices within it".

Dissemination of research findings is thus a crucial part of the participatory research process. For knowledge production to meet its aim of contributing to 'progress', it is crucial that the community – as well as academics and practitioners - has access to the research findings. In addition to a conventional written report presented to the Sure Start programme, we used drama as a novel and engaging means of communicating the research findings to the wider community. In an area where literacy levels are particularly low, this was a particularly apt means of dissemination.

A major aim of this project was for its audience to understand the lives of the families involved and to empathise with them. Through the drama as well as poetry, short-film and art work, we offered up a glimpse of the lived reality of raising children in such an unequal society. I see this as being particularly important at the present time in the UK when current government policy is focusing intently on the family, encouraging parents into paid employment and ensuring that they are 'responsible'.

Because we rarely, if ever, get to hear the stories of the working-class poor, there are many misconceptions about their lives. Recent Fabian Commission/MORI research revealed people's attitudes towards poverty to be grossly distorted. One prevalent view displayed was that "'hard-up' parents are feckless and irresponsible, wasting their money on drinking and gambling – on 'dog-racing and scratch cards'" (cited in Bamfield, 2005, p.6).

Of course, most parents are acutely aware of their responsibilities to their children and the findings from our research demonstrate that working-class, impoverished parents are as committed to raising their children well as any other section of society. The means by which they do this may differ to some extent and everything is so much harder when one is struggling to make ends meet. Particularly demonstrable through the arts-based projects, mothers' absolute love and devotion to their children is unquestionable. The knowledge produced by the local community is thus a world apart from the popular media and public opinions that the government draws upon in justifying its punitive policy in the area of child and family welfare.

This chapter also aims to demonstrate that participatory inquiry can be understood as being greater than the sum of its parts. Importantly, it provides a means of understanding and challenging the wider structural and social inequalities which conventional research often simply reproduces. For Dockery (2000, p.95), "participation as a basic principle is important – not just a concept relevant to research". It is about working together with other people in order to make sense of the world. If we are able to do so with compassion, humility and love, then social justice is within our grasp:

> If social activism is ever to be transformative in any lasting way then qualities such as compassion and humility must be understood not as feelings or even ideas but as actual practices; practices that are a necessary component of this transformative social activism (Fernandes, 2003, p.59).

Beginnings

Participatory research is, as Hall asserts, "an integrated three-pronged process of social investigation, education and action designed to support those with less power in their organizational or community settings" (2001, p.171). A democratic and transformative approach, its goals range from building skills with, and 'giving voice' to, those involved in the process - hence improving the lives of individuals - through to ameliorating communities and, ultimately, liberating the oppressed, thus impacting on social reality. A major criticism of participatory research is that it has, until recently, for the most part remained gender-blind and has thus failed to assist women in creating knowledge which has the potential to transform their lives (George, 1996). It is argued here that an emancipatory practice should draw from both of these fields.

The project involved a reciprocal relationship between the university and the community, a relationship which, I believe, should be nurtured. Separating academic knowledge from practical, applied knowledge results in institutions "ostensibly devoted to knowledge creation, critical reflection and training of new societal elites" having a depressingly "poor connection to their surrounding environment" (Levin & Greenwood, 2001, p.104). This argument supports this chapter's premise that a more holistic approach to knowing the world is necessary to create understanding and social change.

It should be acknowledged that there can be enormous differences between conducting research with community groups and conducting research with statutory organisations. Hilary Rose (in Dockery, 2000, p.96) makes the distinction between those government programmes which want to encourage public participation based on the objectives of the powerful from those groups which are spontaneous social movements from below.

The project was complicated by the fact that Sure Start's lead agency is the local Primary Care Trust (part of the National Health Service (NHS) – a bureaucratic, hierarchical institution). Dockery (2000, p.99) queries whether such an institution can, politically, economically and professionally, "afford to support the participatory research approach which is grounded in empowering and accountable processes". A host of barriers was put in place that had to be negotiated before the research could begin, including an extremely lengthy application process for approval from the NHS Research Ethics Committee culminating in a board meeting of senior hospital officials.

My own experiences are mirrored by those of Barrett (2001) in her research with a project in a hospital setting working with new mothers. This is no coincidence, according to Maguire (2001, p.63-4):

> Socially constructed and maintained, active and complex silencing mechanisms include censorship, suppression, intimidation, marginalization, trivialization, ghettoization, other forms of discounting and gatekeeping... gatekeepers who can give or withhold permission to speak with women. Historic, hidden, taken-for-granted male control of local institutions, public forums and development processes has often silenced or marginalized women in action research.

Yet, in spite of these initial difficulties, the project proceeded to run according to plan. It was, however, a lengthy two-year process. The first task was to recruit a team of 'community researchers'. I was greatly advantaged in this respect in that I had, for some two years prior to this, been involved in running a community art group as part of the Sure Start programme. This not only provided me with a host of insights into Sure Start and the local community which I was able to feed into the research, but also allowed me to build relationships with participants and to become known and trusted by local people. I visited Sure Start's various groups to talk to participants about the research and managed to gather together an initial group of eight parents, all women and each of them mothers of young children involved in Sure Start. The voluntary aspect of the project was stressed and for the most part, the appeal of the project lay in the fact that it was something 'interesting' to be involved in and offered a brief respite from the rigours of motherhood.

I established links with a tutor at the local Community College who agreed to deliver Basic English classes to those parents who were interested in embarking on the research. The classes were made open to everyone living in the community and proved to be extremely popular. Although no longer a part of the research project, they continue to be delivered at the Sure Start programme. Due to demand from parents and carers, maths classes also began to be delivered by the same tutor. Participants, including four of the community researchers, gained qualifications in both English and mathematics which they feel has boosted their confidence. One community researcher who, after taking part in the research training and data collection, left the project to begin a full-time college course reports:

> If I hadn't gone to the maths and English there's no way that I'd have been going now, going on to this course. 'Cause when I actually went on the interview, I had to do this written test.... And if I hadn't done that course there's no way I'd have [been able to do it] - 'cause it refreshes you, reminds you.

Having a background in research herself, the basic skills tutor was also able to deliver sessions on 'Interpersonal Skills and Ethics', with issues around confidentiality being particularly highlighted. I delivered sessions on interview techniques as well as questionnaire design.

The team of community researchers worked on designing the research questions. This was considered a crucial aspect of the project since, as Bauer states, the interviewer imposes on the information produced in three ways: "by selecting the theme and topics; by ordering the questions and by wording questions in his or her language" (cited in Holloway & Jefferson, 2000, p.31). A member of the community research team talks about why she feels the parents' involvement in posing the questions was important:

> I think if I've done research before, it's always when I'm filling out forms. I always think, "That's a daft question to ask", or "What am I supposed to put there?" But because we've developed and designed 'em, the feedback we've had from the people we've done the research with, I think it's a lot – better. Yeah, it's a lot better. Because being parents ourselves, we know what questions to ask and what output we want from the questions.

The research training was always informal and flexible with crèches provided and meetings arranged around participants' needs. If participants missed a session for any reason, then it would be repeated at a suitable time. Whilst this appeared to be the only way of ensuring the success of the project, it was an incredibly time-consuming means of conducting the training – arranging crèches was by no means straightforward and sessions were repeated up to three times. Yet, as one community researcher says, "informal's better for me."

Arts-based techniques were incorporated into the methodology in part as a result of my own background in Fine Art, but also in keeping with my passion for exploring alternative ways of knowing the social world. I felt it appropriate to build in to the research from the outset projects which would allow for more creative and engaging approaches to collecting data and disseminating findings. However, the fact that this approach proved so fitting was not least due to the fact that the Sure Start programme already had a history of successful community arts ventures working with local parents and carers.

Making links with a local arts centre, I set up weekly creative writing and drama groups. I arranged for a local artist to run workshops within the community art group and the University of Liverpool offered to provide a short-film making course for Sure Start parents and carers. Whilst, again, recruiting local people to take part in these activities was greatly aided by my being known in the community, the groups were slow to get off the ground. Word-of-mouth proved the most effective way of encouraging participants and the groups eventually attracted a range of local people including mothers, fathers and grandmothers.

Data collection and analysis

Once approval from the NHS was finally granted to the project, community researchers had to undergo police checks for relevant criminal records. Again, this took considerable time, especially since members of the team did not always have the required documentation. It was a testament to the loyalty of team members that they underwent this procedure and remained committed to the research. The community researchers were acting as volunteers for the programme and did not receive any payment for the hard work and valuable time they gave to the project. Whilst the barriers we encountered were frustrating, they also served to strengthen our resolve to complete the project, engendering a sense of 'us' and 'them'.

In participatory research, the initiating researcher is never a detached observer. In fact, as Dockery points out (2000, p.95), in order for it to be a radical process, researchers must form an alliance with those being researched. Should this not be the case, then the process can amount to mere tokenism or manipulation by researchers. What is needed, Fernandes (2003, p.57) proposes, is the development of a feminist approach to leadership "which is based more centrally on qualities such as humility and tolerance; where visibility is a tactic rather than an end; where leadership is understood more appropriately as a form of labour and service rather than in terms of achievement". Only by appropriating a "radical humility" can we "really manifest social justice in this world" (Fernandes, 2003, p.44).

It was never my intention to keep a 'professional distance' from the Sure Start parents and carers and I believe that this stance contributed overwhelmingly to the success of the research and the arts-based work as well as enhancing my life and the lives of others. My son (who was three years old when the research began) also found his life revolving around this community as he was invited to, and attended, a considerable number of birthday parties and other local events. The friendships we formed during the course of the research continue to date, two years after the completion of the project.

The first aspect of the project to be embarked upon was a door-to-door survey, at the behest of the Sure Start programme, questioning the significant number of the poorest, most 'socially excluded' families that were eligible to access Sure Start but were not doing so. These families who had not taken up the services on offer were considered 'hard-to-reach' by Sure Start's staff and thus we were surprised to find ourselves made welcome in virtually every household we did approach, more often than not invited into the home. Nobody objected to any of the questions posed, which focused on attitudes towards Sure

Start, and interviewees often seemed glad to have someone to talk to. One member of the research team tells how she "knocked on one house and could smell the tea cooking. I apologised - felt awful - but she seemed glad of the break".

We were convinced that this reaction to the survey was because the researchers were clearly members of the local community. Outsiders, or professionals, would very likely have faced a much different response. A community researcher reports that a parent she visited during the survey told her, "I don't mind you coming back [with leaflets about Sure Start], but not someone official." She thinks that if a member of staff conducted these visits then families would be, "more paranoid, wary." She continues:

> If I went they'd think oh, she wouldn't be nosy. If I knew one of them [a Sure Start worker] was coming I'd clean up like mad, but if it was [a parent] coming I wouldn't bother. I'd feel more comfy.

The research findings themselves demonstrate much scepticism of the Sure Start initiative and a widespread lack of trust in professionals generally. After several months spent on the questionnaire survey, the second aspect of the project, in-depth interviews with parents and carers attending the Sure Start programme as well as members of its staff, began. Here the aim was to elicit people's experiences of Sure Start and to evaluate its impact. The interviews, conducted by members of the research team, were tape recorded and I typed up their content. The resultant transcripts were distributed to the team for comment and analysis. Together, we drew out themes from the data and, as was also the case with the door-to-door survey, supplemented the data with our own observations and discussions, adding richness to the findings.

The team members improved their interviewing techniques over the data collection period with the resultant data being exceptionally rich and evocative. Participants spoke candidly about experiencing post-natal depression and intense isolation before engaging with Sure Start through which they had made friends, improved their confidence in their parenting abilities, and increased their self-esteem. I would often be moved to tears and laughter as I transcribed the interviews. Asked whether she thinks that having parents conducting the interviews has benefited the research, a community researcher answers:

> Yeah, a lot better. 'Cause like we're on the same wavelength as the parents who we're asking the questions. They're more likely for t' open up as well, do you know like, I mean like if they've had like bad experiences or anything within Sure Start, then I think they're more likely for t' tell a normal parent than an actual worker.

The interview data was enhanced by the art work simultaneously being produced by parents and carers in the various groups (see Foster 2007a; 2007b for further details). The creative writing was particularly successful with participants creating incredibly intimate poetry about their lives and experiences of motherhood. Through learning a new means of expressing themselves, those involved reported an improvement in their emotional wellbeing, as the following quotation demonstrates:

> The creative writing is something I really enjoy. I'm now creative with my feelings. I love writing poems as it helps me to deal with certain issues that's happened in my life.

This participant carried on writing after the completion of the research and subsequently won a prize in a regional poetry competition.

The short-film making course yielded impressive results. The films that parents and carers have made about their lives are extremely candid and moving; two tell the stories of overcoming drug use and emphasise how the local Sure Start programme has become an integral part of the women's lives. Yet as much emphasis was placed upon the process itself as on the completed work. Learning to handle recording and editing equipment, which previously had been unavailable to participants, proved most effective in building confidence. Using the computer itself was a new experience for some participants, as one parent comments:

> I didn't have a clue – I couldn't even turn on a video camera at the beginning. So to do what I've done, it's been a real personal achievement, it really has.

She goes on to say of the finished films: "I'm proud because it shows how we all are now. What we've come through".

The visual art element of the project involved participants recording a visual diary of their day-to-day lives. To begin with, participants in the art group – eight mothers and two grandmothers – were given a disposable camera to enable them to take images of meaningful objects, people and situations in their lives. Using a variety of techniques including photograph transfer, collage and painting, parents and carers each then worked on a canvas to express these aspects of their daily lives, namely their role as mothers/grandmothers.

Participants were struck by the authenticity of the work: "When you look at adverts on TV.... These pictures are real – they're about real lives, real families". This is very much a theme of the research: the data and the art-works produced are continually described as 'real', as 'true'. Yoland Wadsworth (2001, p.430) writes of irony of the repeated criticism of participatory action research as 'easy', 'lacking rigour' and 'unscientific', given that it "drew on every store of knowledge, experience, logic evidence-based reasoning, recordkeeping and retrieval, writing capacities and emotional intelligence that I had, not to mention stretched me to almost indescribable limits of personal endurance."

I feel similarly that the research project at the Sure Start programme, imbued with our combined energies and passion, not only has depth and integrity, but has produced findings that are incredibly rich and valid.

Dissemination of research findings

The findings from the project included themes such as negative experiences of statutory services, experiences of parenting, friendship and mental health and were disseminated in a number of ways. An in-depth report was submitted to the Sure Start programme, written by myself but verified by members of the research team who read and commented on the various drafts I produced. We delivered presentations at a number of academic institutions as well as to Sure Start's staff and partnership board. This was a new experience for the parents and carers involved, who found their confidence growing with each delivery; one woman has subsequently begun a university degree. It also made for a much more engaging presentation for the audience, with the issues that we raised being discussed enthusiastically.

It was an arts-based presentation of research findings to an audience predominantly consisting of members of the local community, but also practitioners, academics and policy makers, that was considered the most crucial means of dissemination. This comprised two short plays, three films, poetry readings and a display of visual images. The plays were performed by members of the drama group, all Sure Start parents and carers. The first, *The Bus Stop*, an 'ethno-drama' (Mienczakowski, 2000) involved scripting from the interview transcripts and honouring the speakers' words as closely as possible. It focuses on three women waiting at a bus stop, talking about their lives, their families and their experiences of Sure Start. The realism of the work prompted the women involved to comment that the script could very well be a conversation they had had.

Drawing on our collective imaginations, after much deliberating, we came up with a second short play based on the story of the *Wizard of Oz* which we re-titled the *Wizard of Us* to fit with our tale. The stories told in the play are all based on those that we were told in the course of the research. Dorothy is a young mother who has experienced postnatal depression since the birth of baby Toto. She is unhappy with things and is searching for a new life for her and her daughter. On her journey she meets Scarecrow. Scarecrow has always been told she's stupid, by her parents and her teachers, and that her life would never amount to anything. Lion lacks confidence and stays indoors all day watching daytime television. Tinman is rusty after taking time off work to raise his son.

Whilst we did not include children in the actual production, we did play video clips of participants' children singing *Somewhere Over the Rainbow* and *Follow the Yellow Brick Road*. Thus the project involved whole families. It was a huge amount of fun to put together and it aimed to actually give something *to* the community rather than just take data *from* them.

The day was a great success with feedback from the spectators overwhelmingly positive. One of the parents watching the presentation comments:

> Very enjoyable, the girls did very well. The girls' stories made tears come to my eyes when I heard their stories about their past lives. But all they said and did was the truth about [the local area].

Once again, this underlined the authenticity of the work. Any work, whether in the field of the arts or the social sciences, that professes to explore and enhance our understandings of the world we live in needs to engage not only with the intellect of its audience but also with emotion and spirit. It must therefore be presented in a form which can allow for this. As Wolf (1992, p.119) asserts, if our work is "not easily accessible to those who share our goals, we have failed.... Our readership must not be confined to intellectual elites".

A member of staff tells of the impact that the presentation had on her:

> I found the presentation today very moving (can't believe I couldn't stop crying!) I've been a member of staff in the programme virtually from the beginning and am so happy to see the parents who helped me settle in on that stage today with loads of confidence, etc etc. The videos were excellent as others maybe do not fully understand their lives. I've known [member of the research team who also took part in the drama and short-film] for ages and am made up for her. The *Wizard of Us* play was excellent and got loads of messages across. I feel really valued and somehow made me feel I had a hand through Sure Start to improve lives.

Conclusion

Whilst the results of the project are rich, multi-layered and often startling, ultimately the process of the research was not merely about producing these results. The relationships formed, the learning experiences gained and the understanding gleaned were very much the stuff of life itself.

As well as discussing the fun and friendship the project provided, one community researcher, when asked what she had gained from the research project, answered:

"confidence, definitely". Another agreed: "I'm more confident talking to [my son's] teachers, and that, 'cause I'm mixing with people and talking to them".

The community researchers were also aware of the benefits to the Sure Start programme:

> Well, obviously you've got to have improvements to make things better. If people won't come because there's certain things happening, then if you don't change 'em, then you're never gonna get them, are you. You can't capture 'em. So you've got to try and improve services all the time.

The programme manager did take on board a number of our suggestions to improve services, including employing local parents and carers to carry out outreach work. However, she was preoccupied much of the time by the government's shifting of Sure Start's goals and targets and at times it was frustrating when, despite our meticulous attention to means of dissemination, our findings were not always listened to by those with the authority to make changes.

There is, without doubt, little scope for marginalised groups to set the agenda in research about themselves; the project at Sure Start provided the opportunity for a group of poor, working-class women to do just that. Whereas traditional research is a product of the researcher's "individual relevances and concerns" (Aldridge, 1993, p.56), employing participatory methodology allows for a much more democratic process. It also, I argue, produces more authentic results. Moreover, "If human inquiry is not exciting, life enhancing, even pleasurable, then what is it worth?" (Reason, 2000, p.6).

The competency of this group of women is evident: they are able to bring their local knowledge to the project as well as to develop their critical thinking. Moreover, the tenacity they displayed, seeing the lengthy project through to the end, conducting the survey often in dreadful weather conditions, involving themselves in dramatic performances and giving presentations at academic institutions is remarkable. I attribute this to the relationships we formed with each other, particularly since the women were anxious not to let me down. Friendship is a concept rarely explored in debates surrounding the research process, yet building up trusting relationships offers the potential for more authentic data to be collected, and a commitment to analyzing and representing this as faithfully as is possible.

This energy and commitment required from the researchers underlines the fact that participatory research shares with feminism Du Bois' (1983) idea of 'passionate scholarship'. When spirituality is defined in terms of "practices of compassion, love, ethics and truth" (Fernandes, 2003, p.10), then participatory research can even be viewed as a spiritual act. Certainly, at the heart of the project at Sure Start is the understanding that any one woman is as worthy as any other, "a political, moral and also spiritual assumption" (Stacey, 1994, p.88).

The following poem, *Superhero*, written by a young mother during the course of the research about her son, illustrates how such a methodology can bring real humanity and feeling to a policy area which is plagued with misapprehensions and negative responses towards impoverished young mothers. It is a startling reminder of the intense love and raw emotion that transcends boundaries of class and culture in relation to childbirth and childrearing.

Superhero

He saved me with his presence:
fluttering knowledge that he had come
to love and be loved.

He saved me with his eyes.
Wise twin almond orbs absorbing
the dim night: all I had dreamed of.

He saved me with his need:
As helpless as I had been hopeless,
his graceful crane-leg fingers clinging on.

He saved me with his silence,
which bore such acceptance,
and stirred the courage I thought had gone.

He saved me with his contentment.
That unworthy I could draw out his smile
tested my belief.

He saved me from the lane I led.
As he turned his head to consider his first day,
I saw hope for our family.

References

Aldridge, J. (1993). The textual disembodiment of knowledge in research account writing. Sociology, 27 (1), 53-66.

Bamfield, L. (2005). Making the public case for tackling poverty and inequality. Poverty (Journal of the Child Poverty Action Group), 121 (Summer), 5-8.

Barrett, P.A. (2001). The early mothering project: what happened when the words 'action research' came to life for a group of midwives. In P.Reason and H. Bradbury, Hilary (Eds.), Handbook of action research (pp 294-300). London: Sage.

Dockery, G. (2000). Participatory research: whose roles, whose responsibilities? In C. Truman, D.M. Mertens, and B. Humphries (Eds.), Research and inequality (pp 95-110). London: UCL Press.

Du Bois, B. (1983). Passionate scholarship. In G. Bowles and R. Duelli Klein (Eds.), Theories of women's studies (pp 105-116). London: Routledge and Kegan Paul.

Fernandes, L. (2003). Transforming feminist practice: non-violence, social justice and the possibilities of a spiritualized feminism. San Fransisco: Aunt Lute Books.

Foster, V. (2007a). The Art of Empathy: Employing the arts in social inquiry with poor working-class women. Social Justice, 34 (1).

Foster, V. (2007b). Ways of Knowing and Showing: Imagination and representation in feminist participatory social research. Journal of Social Work Practice.

George, A. (1996). Methodological issues in the ethnographic study of sexuality: experiences from Bombay. In K. De Koning and M. Martin (Eds.), Participatory research in health: issues and experiences (pp 119-129). London: Zed Books.

Hall, B. L. (2001). I wish this were a poem of practices of participatory research. In P.Reason and H. Bradbury (Eds.), Handbook of action research (pp 171-178). London: Sage.

Heron, J. and Reason, P.(2001). The practice of co-operative inquiry: research "with" rather than "on" people. In P.Reason and H. Bradbury (Eds.), Handbook of action research (pp 179-188). London: Sage.

Holloway, W. and Jefferson, T. (2000). Doing qualitative research differently. London: Sage.

Levin, M. and Greenwood, D. (2001). Pragmatic action research and the struggle to transform universities into learning communities. In P.Reason and H. Bradbury (Eds.), Handbook of action research (pp 103-113). London: Sage.

Maguire, P.(1996). Proposing a more feminist participatory research: knowing and being embraced openly. In K. De Koning and M. Martin (Eds.), Participatory research in health: issues and experiences (pp 27-39). London: Zed Books.

Maguire, P.(2001). Uneven Ground: Feminisms and Action Research. In P.Reason and H. Bradbury (Eds.), Handbook of action research (pp 59-69). London: Sage.

Mienczakowski, J. (2000). Ethnography in the form of theatre with emancipatory intentions. In C. Truman, D. M. Mertens and B. Humphries (Eds.), Research and inequality (pp 126-142). London: UCL Press.

Office for National Statistics (2001). 2001 Census: Census area statistics. Retrieved 20-July-2003 from www.neighbourhood.statistics.gov.uk/dissemination.

Reason, P.(2000). Action research as spiritual practice. Learning Community Conference, University of Surrey, UK. May 4th-5th.

Wadsworth, Y. (2001). The mirror, the magnifying glass, the compass and the map: facilitating participatory action research. In P.Reason and H. Bradbury (Eds.), Handbook of Action Research (pp 420-432). London: Sage.

Wolf, M. (1992). A thrice told tale: feminism, postmodernism and ethnographic responsibility. Stanford, Cal: Stanford University Press.

Issues in researching the health of Irish people in the UK

Paula McGee

> This chapter draws on the author's experiences of researching the mental health of Irish people in one UK city. The main focus is on the collaborative nature of a project in which representatives from Irish welfare and community organisations, statutory mental health services and researchers worked together. Researching with communities in this way requires researchers to adopt new ways of working that can greatly enhance an investigation. In this instance collaboration was particularly helpful in creating appropriate information for potential participants, communicating effectively with them and in promoting awareness of the project. This was particularly important in a project that concerned one of the UK's most severely marginalised minority ethnic groups whose members frequently live in very poor circumstances. However, as this chapter shows, a collaborative approach to research can easily be subverted by bureaucratic approaches to research governance and those responsible for administering governance procedures must be better prepared to accommodate this type of research.

The health of Irish people in the UK is a source of increasing concern. Evidence to date suggests that they experience higher levels of morbidity and mortality than other immigrant groups (Abbots et al. 2001a; Bracken, 1998). In the 2001 census 17.4% of white, middle-aged Irish people (aged 50-64 years) reported poor health and life limiting illness compared with 12.4% of white British respondents. This picture was repeated among younger people (aged 16-49 years) with 5.4% of Irish adults reporting poor health and life-limiting illness compared with 3.9% of the white British population (Walter, 2004). In both age groups, Irish men reported poorer health than Irish women whose health was in turn worse than that of their white British counterparts (Walter, 2004). Further analysis of census data confirms that the percentage of Irish people who experience long-term illness is higher than in any other minority ethnic group (see, for example, Dudley Metropolitan Borough Council Census, 2001).

Various reasons have been put forward to explain the poor level of health experienced by Irish people. These include poverty, homelessness, social isolation, religion, problems with alcohol and other risky behaviour and the ease of migration from Ireland to the UK (Department of Health Social Services and Public Safety, 2003; Abbots, Williams and Ford, 2001b; Clarke, 1998; Kelleher &Hillier, 1996). The ease and affordability of travel between the two countries, the common language and other apparent similarities may contribute to Irish people regarding the UK as an appropriate destination for those who want to migrate (O'Meachair, 1996). However, those perceived similarities, coupled with the legacy of colonialism and the political issues surrounding Northern Ireland have militated against the formation of a positive Irish identity in the UK (Aspinall, 2002; Walsh & McGrath, 2000; O'Meachair, 1996). Moreover, the apparent similarities may mask differing understandings of health and illness. Little has been done to critically examine any of these ideas (O'Sullivan, 2001).

This chapter is based on a study about Irish people and mental health. It begins by setting the scene, explaining the background to and aims of the project. It then goes on to address two important factors: developing a collaborative approach and recruiting participants. Key elements in each of these factors are examined. The chapter closes by emphasising the need for research governance procedures to take more account of the ways in which collaborative projects function if culturally competent research into the health needs of Irish people is to develop into a robust source of evidence from which to lobby for improvements.

Background to the project

The Irish Health Summit held in Manchester in 2004 highlighted concerns about the health and well being of Irish people in Britain and called for more to be done to bring about improvements. Mental health was of particular concern because Irish people, particularly men, are twice as likely as their white British counterparts to be admitted to psychiatric hospitals (Bracken *et al*, 1998; Commander *et al*, 1999; Healthcare Commission, 2005). Irish people are also more likely than their white British counterparts to commit suicide possibly because living abroad, particularly in the UK, is stressful and does not contribute to the development of a positive ethnic identity (Leavey, 1999). A longitudinal study in the west of Scotland found that older adults of Irish Catholic descent were more likely than white Scottish people to suffer from depression (Abbotts *et al*, 2001a; 2001b; Abbotts, Williams & Ford,1999). Stillwell *et al*. (2004) found that Irish girls in the UK are more likely to engage in alcohol abuse than young people from other backgrounds.

Alongside these findings are reports about the changing nature of life in the Irish Republic. Membership of the European Union has brought an uneven distribution of prosperity in a previously very poor country. This has had a marked effect particularly in rural areas where traditional male roles have been eroded or abandoned (Clarke, 1998). The rate of suicide in Ireland has risen, especially amongst young men (Lynch *et al*, 2004). In Northern Ireland one in four people consult their GP because of mental ill health and an estimated 83,000 people suffer from some form of mental illness (Eastern Health and Social Services Board, 2003).

Mental health is, therefore, clearly an area of concern for Irish people but there are other factors to consider, most notably the long history of racism and discrimination, extending over hundreds of years and directed by the British against Irish people. Until the introduction of legislation about race relations in the early 1970s employers and landlords could advertise vacancies and, at the same time, openly state that Irish people were not welcome. The introduction of anti-terrorist legislation meant that all Irish people in Britain were viewed with suspicion as potential terrorists and ostracised from the mainstream society (Hillyard, 2005; Scally, 2004; Keneally, 1999). Irish people found themselves shunned at work, spat at in the streets, barred from shops and excluded from every aspect of society. Attitudes towards the Irish in Britain have improved in recent years. Indeed some aspects of Irish culture such as dance and music have been re-evaluated to become almost chic but the prominence of this *Irish culture lite* masks the legacy of oppression and the continuance of prejudice and discrimination in more subtle forms; both of which serve to create a sense of distrust that may prevent Irish people from seeking help early (see, for example, Whitmore, 1994).

Such distrust afflicts also afflicts other minority groups. For instance, black people's negative experiences of mental health services have created a well- documented sense of distrust and even fear (see for example, The Sainsbury Centre for Mental Health, 2002; Keating &Robertson, 2004; Norfolk, Suffolk and Cambridgeshire Health Authority, 2003). Current health policy is directed towards addressing the causes of such experiences by making services more accessible and appropriate, improving working practices and reducing hospital admissions by developing better primary care especially for those with long term conditions (Department of Health, 1997, 2000, 2004a, 2005b). In the context of mental health, the achievement of this policy requires consideration of the multiple social, psychological and economic factors that contribute to patients' well being and the various statutory and voluntary services that work to assist them. Inter-agency cooperation and collaborative approaches to care form an essential part of helping people to maintain their mental health and provide much needed support during exacerbations of their conditions or when crises arise.

Current health policy places a high priority on race and equality issues (Department of Health, 2005a, 2004b, 2003a, 2003b). This, coupled with increasing white immigration from Poland, and other former eastern block countries, has created an opportunity for an already established but severely marginalised white minority, such as the Irish, to renegotiate its position vis à vis the dominant majority. Thus Irish people in the UK have begun asking questions about their health and health services and are seeking ways of addressing the social inequalities from which many suffer.

Aims of the project

The project referred to in this chapter is one of several instigated by Irish community welfare organisations in different cities in the UK. Many of these projects are still in progress but examples include Lillis, Afford and Byrne (2006), Ryan *et al.* (2006), Cant and Taket (2005) and Walls (2004).

Following the Irish health summit in 2004, a series of meetings were held, at the instigation of an Irish welfare organisation, in one UK city, to discuss what could be done to improve Irish health locally. Contact was made through the mailing list provided for those attending the summit and word of mouth. Those who attended represented the Irish community welfare organisations in the area as well as health and social care professionals from practice and university settings both in the city and the surrounding area. Those people were, for the most part, either first or second generation Irish people, the author herself being second generation. The meetings focused on what it was like to be an Irish person living in Britain, what factors, including health, influenced daily life and how these might be changed; for some members this was the first time they had had the opportunity for such discussion. Some individuals came only once, others dipped in and out but gradually a core group emerged with some clear ideas for a way forward. This group included representatives of the Irish welfare organisation, a counselling service for Irish people, the Federation of Irish Societies, general practice and statutory mental health services in the National Health Service and university-based nurse researchers. All were based in the city and the group continued to meet regularly during the following year to develop a collaborative project.

The aims of this project were threefold: to map the nature and accessibility of statutory and voluntary primary care mental health services available to Irish people; explore the views and experiences of Irish people who used mental health services; examine if and how practitioners adapted their practice to meet the needs of Irish clients. Funding was raised by the Irish welfare organisation which instigated the initial meetings. The long-term intention was to utilise the findings to develop practical guidelines for culturally-competent best practice in working with Irish users of mental health services.

Issues in collaborative working

In designing this project, a number of issues arose and this chapter presents a discussion of two of these: *developing a collaborative approach* and *recruiting participants*. These factors are discussed below.

Developing a collaborative approach

All health and social care research in the UK has to conform to the requirements of the Research Governance Framework. This states that, wherever possible, participants or their representatives must be involved in the design, conduct, analysis and reporting of projects (Department of Health, 2001, 2005c). This requirement indicates a philosophical shift from doing research *on* to undertaking research *with* those being investigated (McGee, 2007). This is particularly important in researching minority ethnic communities and especially when addressing sensitive topics such as mental health which carries a high degree of social stigma. A collaborative approach that involves potential participants or their representatives requires researchers to adapt their skills and to learn new ones. Participants are no longer the objects of study, specimens to be investigated; rather they are people, equal to the researcher, who have contributions to make to the development of mutual understanding of a problem and the ways in which it might be addressed.

However, developing sound working relationships that will sustain the conduct of this type of project require considerable investment of time and energy. In the project discussed here, it took a year for the project team to learn to work together and design the project. One of the difficulties was that all the members were very busy people with limited time available and so meetings were not as frequent as, with hindsight, they ought to have been; sometimes two or three months elapsed between meetings.

A second difficulty was the conflict between developing a collaborative approach and meeting the demands of research governance. Reason (1994) argues that research can only be conducted *with* people if the researcher engages with them as people because while *"understanding and action are logically separate, they cannot be separated in life: so a science of persons must be an action science"* (Reason, 1994, p.10). Researchers can only achieve understanding of the world if they accept that they are part of it. Participatory approaches to research can integrate scientific ideas with being open to people as fellow human beings and thus contribute to a deeper understanding of human existence (Reason, 1994). Applying such approaches requires researchers to adopt new ways of working becoming members of a group on an equal footing with other members. This allows every member to be a resource for the group, sharing differing perspectives and expertise on a cooperative basis rather receiving instructions from a designated leader. Such an approach can make for slow progress and things do not always develop in a streamlined, linear fashion but it does mean that researchers are no longer working alone; instead there is a much richer research team in which many different perspectives and sources of expertise are brought to bear on the investigation.

Unfortunately, this collaborative approach is out of step with the demands of official bodies. The Research Governance Framework may claim to espouse the values of collaborative research but those charged with administering it continue to look for project leaders, identifiable people with whom to communicate and whom they regard as responsible for the research (Department of Health, 2001, 2005c). Adherence to the Framework required that the proposed study be reviewed by an NHS Research Ethics Committee and that permission be obtained from the University sponsorship committee and the various NHS research and development departments concerned; all of these bodies required that a named individual take the role of chief *investigator*. This role first requires the completion of a considerable amount of paperwork; three different application forms in which the project must be explained in detail, the ethical, safety, data management and costing details clearly set out without cutting and pasting from the research protocol. All research tools and participant information material; written permission for access to patients and staff, as research subjects, must be included. In addition, formal police checks must be carried out on the *chief investigator* and anyone else in the team who will have contact with patients. More importantly, the *chief investigator* is required to sign legally binding agreements regarding the conduct of the research. Failure to identify a *chief investigator* means that the applications for ethical review and permissions to conduct the research will be deemed invalid.

Whilst it is right and proper that all proposed research involving people should be subject to scrutiny, the necessity of having a *chief investigator* contradicts the ethos of collaborative working and makes it difficult to maintain. It is not simply that filling out forms and assembling the paperwork takes quite a long of time but that it was inevitable that one person (the author) had to take assume the *chief investigator's* responsibility for steering the project through this series of reviews. Thus, the author found herself separated from the team, in danger of slipping back into traditional ways of working. Comments from team members questioning whether the project would ever begin, absences from team meetings all suggested to her that the team was beginning to lose cohesion.

This situation demonstrates the importance of reflexivity in qualitative investigations. By maintaining a reflective diary throughout the project the author was able to examine events and develop an awareness of their implications at an early stage (Koch, 1994). In this diary she recorded events as they arose, the circumstances in which they occurred, what she thought about them, what actions were taken and why. This diary formed part of an audit the trail for the project, the rest being made up of minutes from team meetings and email communications between team members. Thus, the author was able to maintain self-awareness, recognising the significance of her isolation from the team and the ways in which exterior demands can alter the dynamics of the team (Lipson, 1991). She was then able to make a conscious effort to offset this by regularly emailing members about what she was doing, why, the deadlines for submissions to the various committees and when she expected to receive the outcomes of the reviews. This helped to keep the team informed about what was happening and reduce unease about the length of time involved but it did not alter the fact that disruption had occurred.

Recruiting participants

Discussion and research within the project team informed the view that Irish people born and raised in the UK might have different perspectives and experiences from those who came to work in the 1950s and 1960s. Consequently, a decision was made to focus on three subgroups of Irish people:

- 1st generation – those born in Ireland who made a decision to come to the UK as adults;
- 2nd generation – those born in the UK but who had one or both parents born in Ireland; and

- 3rd generation – those born in Britain, who had one or more grandparents born in Ireland.

An important concern was how to identify members of these three groups. Patient lists were unlikely be useful in identifying Irish people; women in particular might prove impossible to trace if they had married, the spelling of some names could mean that some Irish people were mistakenly thought to be Scottish, others might have changed or altered the spelling of their names. The Irish welfare and counselling organisations provided services for all Irish people but it was felt that some of the second and third generations might not regard these as particularly suited to their needs.

Consequently, it was agreed that multiple strategies should be used to recruit participants and encourage those using mental health services to get involved with and contribute to the project. This had the advantage of attracting people, from a wide range of backgrounds across the city, who could be self-selecting in terms of their involvement. Consequently multiple strategies were employed and strengthened by the multidisciplinary nature of the project team. Members were able to use their own networks to promote the project thus reaching as many people as possible. Posters and leaflets were placed in Irish welfare organisations, public libraries, leisure centres, clinics and health centres; the St Patrick's Day parade provided a particularly good opportunity to reach a very large number of people through the different organisations taking part. Feature articles were published in local and Irish newspapers. However, those members of the project team who worked in Irish welfare advised that, in their experience, many older Irish people could not read and write very well. Consequently, arrangements were made for interviews at local radio stations and oral presentations were made at Irish luncheon clubs around the city.

An important element of this recruitment campaign was to convey, to members of a community marginalised because of ethnicity and the stigma of mental health problems, that the Irish welfare and counselling organisations and the statutory services were part of and actively supported the project. One strategy employed to achieve this was to ensure that all promotional material carried the logos of the organisations involved and a statement about their support. Oral presentations were also made to community psychiatric nursing teams around the city to ensure that, if their clients asked about the project, they would be able to discuss it with them. The medical director ensured that all the consultant psychiatrists were also informed about the project.

The project team held several discussions about the low levels of literacy among older, first generation, Irish people. The Research Governance Framework provides detailed guidelines about the information which all researchers must present to those they seek to recruit as participants (National Research Ethics Service, 2007). These guidelines stipulate all the topic areas to be covered and what must be conveyed. Failure to comply with these guidelines means that projects will not be approved by the Research Ethics Committee. For the project team these guidelines were helpful in identifying what had to be conveyed to potential participants but distinctly unhelpful in terms of the level and type of language that was used. Two main problems were identified by the team: the complexity of language used; language and communication styles among Irish people.

There were several points to consider in relation to these problems. Whilst the majority of Irish people speak English as a first language, some may prefer to speak Gaelic, particularly those who are first generation immigrants to the UK from the west of Ireland. In addition, when Irish people speak in English, their idiomatic use of the language differs from that of other English speakers in the same way that English spoken in the US, New Zealand, India and European countries may differ subtly from that spoken in the UK. Even within the UK, local variations and dialects can militate against effective communication (Crystal, 1997; McGee, 2000).

It was, therefore, essential to find appropriate ways of communicating what the project was about. Information materials went through several drafts which were the focal point of several consecutive team meetings in which the discussions focused on the suitability and readability of the language used so that those with limited literacy would not be disadvantaged (see appendix). Readability is an attempt to match the reading level of written material to the reading with understanding level of the reader; in other words someone may be able to read complicated material, recognise the words, but not understand it (McLaughlin, 1969). For example, buyers may be able to read the assembly instructions that accompany flat pack furniture but still not understand how to put together what they have bought. The combination of expertise from first generation Irish people of differing ages in the project team and the concept of readability enabled the research team to produce information that was meaningful for potential participants. This information was then recorded onto CD, using the voices of first generation Irish men and women. Recordings were made in English and in Gaelic to ensure that as many people as possible had the opportunity to find out about the project (see appendix).

Allied to language is the matter of communication style, culturally-based ideas about not only what can be said, when and to whom but also how. It is important for researchers to be aware of and understand their own communication styles and how these may differ from those of participants; this is part of the researcher's self awareness within the context of a project; developing self awareness is an essential step in becoming culturally competent (McGee &Johnson, 2005). Incompatibility in communication styles hinders effective communication and undermines interactions. People do not feel at ease and consequently do not feel they can trust the person to whom they are speaking (Campinha Bacote, 2003, 1991). In this project, developing self-awareness about communication style was an important step.It meant articulating what was taken for granted in daily interaction and how this might affect the research. This led to the realisation that the group would need help in collecting and analysing data. The second generation Irish people in the project team had English accents and manners and some first generation Irish people might well have mistaken them for English people and not want to discuss certain matters with them. Consequently, the team decided to recruit help with data collection from among the linkworkers in the Irish welfare organisation. These linkworkers worked with Irish people who were often in dire social and financial straits; they were known and trusted by their clients. The author and a colleague from the university provided training for six volunteer linkworkers who were then able to participate in data collection as co-researchers. As the project got underway their help was invaluable in accessing the views and experiences of some of the poorest, most socially excluded people in the city; individuals whose stories and voices would not otherwise have featured in the research.

Conclusion

Researchers need to move beyond traditional ways of conducting projects, developing the self-awareness, knowledge and skills required to collaborate *with* others rather than researching *about* them. In particular, researchers have to learn ways of building trust, particularly when working with marginalised people. Building relationships takes time. Those who have been hurt or damaged in the past, or who carry the legacy of oppression with them, are unlikely to welcome strangers. Even the organisations that provide services and care may initially be sceptical of invitations to collaborate. Attempting to speed things up does not help because it puts people under pressure. True collaboration requires mutual respect which will not occur if one party feels forced or rushed. However, if truly collaborative research is to become a reality those responsible for administering research governance must be prepared to accommodate new ways of working. This chapter marks the beginning of a long uphill journey to achieve this and in doing so develop a knowledge base through which a population, that has long maintained invisibility on the margins of UK society, can make clear to service providers how they can best meet the needs of Irish patients.

References

Abbotts, J., Williams, R., Sweeting, H. and West, P. (2001a). Poor but healthy? The youngest generation of Irish Catholics in west Scotland Health Bulletin 59 (6) pp.373-80

Abbotts, J., Williams, R. and Ford, G. (2001b). Morbidity and Irish Catholic descent in Britain. Relating health disadvantage to socio-economic position. Social Science and Medicine 52 pp.599-1005

Abbotts, J., Williams, R. and Ford, G. (1999). Morbidity and Irish Catholic descent in Britain: relating health disadvantage to behaviour. Ethnicity and Health 4 (4) pp.221-30

Aspinall, P.(2002) Suicide among Irish migrants in Britain: a review of the identity and integration hypothesis. International Journal of Social Psychiatry 48 (4) pp.290-304

Bracken, P.Greenslade, L. Griffin, B. and Smyth, M. (1998). Mental health and ethnicity: an Irish dimension, British Journal of Psychiatry 172 (2) pp.103-5

Campinha Bacote, J. (2003). The Process of Cultural Competence in the Delivery of Healthcare Services: A Culturally Competent Model of Care. Ohio, Transcultural Care Associates.

Campinha Bacote, J. (1991). Community mental health services for the underserved: a culturally specific model. Archives of Psychiatric Nursing 5(4) pp.229-35.

Cant, B. and Taket, A. (2005). Promoting social support and social networks among Irish pensioners in South London, UK Diversity in Health and Social Care 2 (4) pp.263-70

Clarke, L. (1998). Constructing mental illness in Irish people: race, culture and retreat. European Nurse 3 (1) pp.22-32

Commander, M., Odell, S. Sashisdharan, S. and Surtees, R. E. (1999). Psychiatric morbidity in people born in Ireland. Social and Psychiatric Epidemiology 34 (11) pp.565-9

Commander, M., Odell, S., Surtees, P.and Sahsidharan, S. (2003). Characteristics of patients and patterns of psychiatric service use in ethnic minorities International Journal of Social Psychiatry 49 (3) pp.216-224

Crystal, D. (1997). The Cambridge Encyclopaedia of Language. 2nd edn. Cambridge, Cambridge University Press.

Department of Health (1997). The New NHS Modern. Dependable London, DoH

Department of Health (2000). The NHS Plan. A plan for Investment. A plan for Reform. London. DoH

Department of Health (2001). Research Governance Framework. London, DoH.

Department of Health (2003a). Delivering Race Equality: A Framework for Action. Mental Health Services. Consultation Document. London, DoH

Department of Health (2003b). Inside Outside. Improving Mental Health Services for Black and Minority Ethnic Communities in England. London, DoH

Department of Health (2004a). The NHS Improvement Plan: Putting People at the Heart of Public Services, London DoH

Department of Health (2004b). The NHS Knowledge and Skills Framework and the Development Review Process. London DoH

Department of Health (2005a). Delivering Race Equality in Mental Health Care: An Action Plan for Reform Inside and Outside and the Government's Response to the Independent Inquiry in the Death of David Bennett, London DoH

Department of Health (2005b). Supporting People with Long Term Conditions: Liberating the Talents of Nurses who Care for People with Long Term Conditions, London, DOH

Department of Health (2005c). Research Governance Framework for Health and Social Care, London, DoH, 2nd edn.

Department of Health, Social Services and Public Safety (2003). Promoting Mental Health. Strategy and Action Plan 2003-8 Belfast, DoHSSPS

Dudley Metropolitan Borough Council Census (2001). Strategic Research and Intelligence Team Publication No 3 Dudley Borough Ethnicity Statistics

Eastern Health and Social Services Board (2003). A Strategy for Adult Mental Health Services in EHSSB Draft Consultation, Belfast EHSSB

Healthcare Commission (2005). Count Me In. Results of a National Census of Inpatients in Mental Health Hospitals and Facilities in England and Wales, London, Mental Health Act Commission, National Institute for Mental Health in England, Healthcare Commission and Care Services Improvement Partnership

Hillyard, P. (2005). The "War on Terror": lessons from Ireland. Essay published by the European Civil Liberties Network, retrieved 6.8.07 from www.ecln.org/essays.

Keating, F. and Robertson, D. (2004). Fear, Black People and Mental Illness: A Vicious Circle? Health and Social Care in the Community 12 (5) pp.439-447

Kelleher, D. and Hillier, S. (1996). The health of the Irish in England Chapter 6 in Researching Cultural Differences in Health, eds. D. Kelleher and S. Hillier, pp103-123. London: Routledge.

Keneally, T. (1999). The Great Shame: A Story of the Irish in the Old World and the New. London,

Chatto and Windus

Leavey, G. (1999). Suicide and Irish migrants in Britain: identity and integration. International Review of Psychiatry, 11 (2-3) pp.168-172

Koch, T. (1994). Establishing rigour in qualitative research: the decision trail. Journal of Advanced Nursing, 19 (5) pp.976-86

Lillis, J., Afford, B. and Byrne, C. (2006). Count Us In. A report on the 1st generation Irish community in Northampton and their experiences of mental health and mental health services. Northampton, Northampton Irish Support Group.

Lipson, J. (1991). The use of self in ethnographic research. Chapter 5 in Qualitative Nursing Research. A Contemporary Dialogue, ed. J. Morse, pp73- 89. Newbury Park, California, Sage Publications.

Lynch, F., Mills, C., Daly, I. and Fitzpatrick, C. (2004). Challenging times: a study to detect Irish adolescents at risk of psychiatric disorders and suicidal ideation. Journal of Adolescence 27 (4) pp.441-51

McGee, P. (2000). Culturally-sensitive Care: A Critique. Unpublished PhD thesis, University of Central England.

McGee, P. and Johnson, M. (2005). Cultural competence. Editorial. Diversity in Health and Social Care 1 (2) pp.75-9

McGee, P. (2007). Ethical considerations in planning a research project. Journal of Heath, Social and Environmental Issues 8 (1) pp.5-9

McLaughlin, G. H. (1969). Smog grading – a new readability formula. Journal of Reading, May, pp.639-46.

O'Meachair, G. (1996). Irish health issues: myths and realities. Paper presented at the Health of the Irish in Britain conference and published in Federation of Irish Societies (1996) The Health of the Irish in Britain. The Report of the Community Conference pp21-8 London, Federation of Irish Societies

National Research Ethics Service. (2007). Information sheets and consent forms. Guidance for researchers and reviewers. Version 3.2. London, NORSE

Norfolk, Suffolk and Cambridgeshire Strategic Health Authority. (2003). Independent Inquiry into the Death of David Bennett. Report of an inquiry set up under HAG (94) 27 Chaired by Sir John Bluffed, Cambridge SASHA.

O'Sullivan, P. (2001). The Irish and Mental Health Issues. Report to the Bradford Irish Mental Health Project. Bradford, Unpublished paper.

Reason, P. (1994). Inquiry and alienation. Chapter 1 in Participation in Human Inquiry, ed. P.Reason, pp.9-15. London, Sage Publications.

Ryan, L., Leavey, G., Golden, A., Blizard, R. and King, M. (2006). Depression in Irish migrants living in London: case–control study. British Journal of Psychiatry 188 pp.560-66.

The Sainsbury Centre for Mental Health .(2002). Breaking the Circles of Fear. A Review of the Relationship Between Mental Health Services and African and Caribbean Communities. London, The Sainsbury Centre for Mental Health, London.

Scally, G. (2004). The very pests of society: the Irish and 150 years of public health in England. Clinical Medicine 4 (1) pp.77- 81.

Stillwell, G., Boys, A. and Mardsen, J. (2004). Alcohol use by young people from different ethnic groups: consumption, intoxication and negative consequences, Ethnicity and Health 9 (2) pp.171-87

Walls, P. (2004). Consulting the Irish community on Inside Outside: Improving mental health services for black and minority ethnic communities in England – the community response and its evaluation. London, Federation of Irish Societies

Walsh, J. and McGrath. (2000). Ethnicity, coping style and health behaviour among first generation Irish immigrants in England. Psychology and Health 15 pp.467-82.

Walter, B. (2004). Mapping Irish health and the 2001 census. Unpublished paper presented at the Irish Health Summit, Manchester, 2004.

Whitmore, E. (1994). To tell the truth: working with oppressed groups in participatory approaches to inquiry. In Participation in Human Inquiry, ed. P.Reason, pp.82-98. London, Sage Publications.

Appendix: Extracts from information for participants

First draft of the beginning of the information for participants

You are being invited to take part in a research study. Before you decide it is important for you to understand why the research is being done and what it will involve. Please take time to read the following information carefully. Talk to others about the study if you wish.

- Part 1 tells you the purpose of this study and what will happen to you if you take part.
- Part 2 gives you more detailed information about the conduct of the study.

Please contact us if there is anything that is not clear or if you would like more information. Take time to decide whether or not you wish to take part. (NRES May 2007)

Final version

What is this about?

We are trying to find out whether mental health services in Birmingham meet the needs of Irish people. We are asking for you help in this matter. Please take a few minutes to read this leaflet and talk to other people about it if you wish.

SMOG score 6.87 – With the help of potential participants the development of information about the project becomes a process that is integral to the research rather than something of an afterthought when all the other work has been completed.

Participation in health research: The need for a second mirror

Gaby Jacobs

> In a participatory action research (PAR) project in The Netherlands, the 'Aspiring to Healthy Living' project, it turned out that the so-called participatory-dialogic approach involved several dilemmas and problems. First of all, participation was seen in different and competing ways: as an intrinsic value or goal in itself (the strong ideological position); as a strategy or instrument to improve the scientific validity of the results or the effectiveness of a program (the scientific position); or as a way to create a practicable program (the pragmatic position). Frustrations arose within the project team because these differences were not topic of an explicit dialogue between the participants. Another important pitfall was the lack of openness and equality out of a protective stance towards the community members in the research. The conclusion is that PAR, if not reflected on and spoken about, can become a frustrating process. Double and triple loop learning are both a precondition for realizing dialogue and participation, as an outcome of dialogic relationships. Collaboration with communities therefore requires researchers to be 'dialogic professionals'.

How, on the one hand, the complex agenda for participation is achieved when, on the other, the pushes and pulls of traditional research appear to mitigate against genuine participation, remains open to question (Ray, 2007, p.86).

In this chapter I address the problems that arose in working on empowerment of the elderly in a participatory action research (PAR). I do this by means of a case study: the Dutch project 'Aspiring to Healthy Living'. In this chapter I will focus on the process of collaboration and on the different values involved. Especially interesting is the fact that problems not only arose between the different stakeholders (the community members, researchers, project manager and health professionals), but also *within* the academic research group. I present this particular case study because I believe that researchers working with communities will recognize the tensions inherent in this particular project and because I hope we can learn from each other in dealing with these tensions.

I will start with a brief outline of the aims and methods in the 'Aspiring to Healthy Living' project. Then I will discuss the collaborative process in the project and the different positions taken in relation to participation. I will conclude with some suggestions for dealing with the tensions that arose from this clash of positions.

The project 'Aspiring to Healthy Living'

The percentage of older people in the Dutch population, like in most developed nations, is now about 20 per cent and still on the increase and so is the population of older immigrants, such as the Moroccan guest workers who immigrated to the Netherlands in the 1960s and 70s. In 2004, there were 22,953 Moroccan people aged 55 and over (the entire Dutch population is approximately 16 million people). Although this number seems to be small, it is expected to increase sharply in the next decade. The majority of these Moroccans live in one of the four big cities: Amsterdam, Rotterdam, The Hague and Utrecht. Moreover, there are some important differences in actual and experienced health between elderly native Dutch and elderly immigrant groups; the lower socio-economic status of immigrant elderly is an important factor in this. Knowledge of older people's (different) experiences and meanings of health is important when developing a multicultural health policy and health promotion practice.

The Aspiring to Healthy Living project strived to develop insight into healthy living among elderly Dutch and Moroccan men and women with a lower socio-economic status, and to develop activities to promote their health. In order to reach this goal, a PAR approach was taken. In this approach the focus is on bringing forward (personal and social) change processes, not so much on obtaining theoretical insights (Reason & Bradbury, 2001). PAR begins with a research topic that "matters to, and ideally comes from, the community itself, and involves members of the community – in our case older people – in the research process. They are not simply objects of study but co-contributors to knowledge and understanding" (Holstein & Minkler, 2007, p.23).

In this project, we were particularly interested in the stories of the elderly. The involvement of older people in research, policy and practice – not only to understand their lives but also to change them - lies at the heart of critical gerontology (Bernard & Scharf, 2007). This project can be situated in this tradition and also in the paradigm of the New Health Promotion with its focus on social justice, equality in health, and empowerment (Laverack, 2004; Minkler & Wallerstein, 2003). It radically differs from mainstream 'top-down' approaches, in which professionals define the problems and needs of communities and take control over actions. We wanted to 'move out of the comfort zone' (Ray, 2007) and create partnerships with communities of older people and practitioners, to work together on health promotion.

The project consisted of two phases: a 'narrative' and an 'action' phase. In the first year of the project, we collected stories of elderly Dutch and Moroccan people on healthy living. The study of narratives is both a means to understand personal meaning as well as to promote social change (Murray, 2004; Ray, 2007). Central questions were: What does healthy living mean to the elderly? How do they 'practice' healthy living? Following the World Health Organization's definition (WHO, 1986), a broad and positive definition of healthy living was the starting point, in which health is not limited to physical and mental health but also involves social, cultural, economic and political factors, and in which health is not only the absence or prevention of disease but a state of well-being and vitality. In the stories, the meanings and practices of healthy living were contextualized in the participants' individual life histories and social and cultural positioning regarding to age, ethnicity, gender and class.

In the second year, the knowledge, experiences and needs of the elderly were used as input to develop a program for healthy living for the Dutch and Moroccan community of lower-class elderly in Rotterdam, the second largest city in The Netherlands. Four pilot programs were conducted and evaluated with different gender and ethnic groups of elderly in Rotterdam.

In both the narrative and action phase the aim was to involve the elderly as much as possible, thereby contributing to their empowerment. Four Dutch and four Moroccan lower-class older people were involved in the project team as co-researchers, co-developers and co-educators. Besides them, the project team consisted of two health practitioners, three researchers from the university and the project manager (a university professor). The two basic principles in the collaboration process were participation and dialogue, and hierarchical research relations were avoided to enhance the empowerment of the elderly. Data about the process have been collected partly prospectively (with minutes) and partly retrospectively (by interviews) and have been compared with the qualities claimed for PAR. Before discussing the collaboration process, I will introduce some theoretical insights on participation and dialogue, as a framework to understand the tensions that arose in the project.

Participation and dialogue

Participation is "so widely and so loosely used, like many other catchwords in development jargon, that the meaning of the concept has become rather blurred" (Mikkelsen, 1995, p.62 cited in Chiweza, 2005, p.1). The same is true for empowerment (Jacobs, Braakman & Houweling, 2005). Both concepts raise many questions, such as:

- Is participation a necessary precondition for empowerment?
- Is participation a means or an end in itself?
- Participation by whom, for whom, in what and how?

In the project we used the concept of community participation, which is defined as "a process whereby community members take part in the identification of their needs, setting priorities, identifying and obtaining means to meet those priorities, including the development, implementation and evaluation of those means in terms of their outcomes" (Koelen & Van der Ban, 2004, p.138). Although at first reading this could seem a pretty forward description, there are different orientations to participation, in which different levels and meanings of participation are involved, with different outcomes for the communities involved. One way to address these differences in participation is a continuum with different stages. A well-known continuum is the ladder of Pretty (1995)[13]. Pretty describes seven stages in participation, shown in Figure 1.

---

7. Self-mobilization
Community members set their own agenda and organize for action. Professionals have a role in the background, are facilitative and supportive but only if asked.

6. Interactive participation
Professionals and community members work as equal partners in defining the problems or needs and the strategies for change. There is a sharing of knowledge and valuing of 'local' or 'lay' knowledge. Professionals facilitate and support the process.

5. Functional participation
Community members are involved in decision making and the development and execution of programmes or activities. Professionals are in control and take responsibility for the process.

4. Participation by consultation
Community members are asked to give their opinions on the program plans. The professionals decide what to do.

3. Participation by information
Community members are informed in an early stage about the program plans and are given the opportunity to ask questions.

2. Passive participation
Professionals are in control of the program; community members are informed about the program.

1. No participation
Community members are not informed about the program, only about the activities for which they have been recruited.

Figure 1: The Ladder of Pretty: Seven stages of participation.

Mo Ray (2007) has distinguished traditional, consumerist and democratic participatory approaches. By traditional approaches she refers to the 'shallow' participation we often

---

[13] Similar typologies exist, such as the ladder of Hart (1995; in Shier, 2001) and the ladder of Arnstein (1969).

find in mainstream research and which is limited to the involvement of community members as sources of information. This sort of participation is generally located at the lowest steps of the ladder of participation, steps 1 to 3. Consumerist approaches are based on a market ideology and often treat participants as 'instruments' to achieve predefined goals. These approaches are characterized by an instrumental rationality (Habermas, 1984) and levels of participation of community members that do not exceed levels 4 and 5, i.e. consultation and functional participation. Democratic approaches, by contrast, emphasize the empowering potential of collaboration and collective action: traditional power arrangements in health research, policy or practice are changed. These so-called transformational approaches are characterized by a communicative rationality (Habermas, 1984) and high levels of participation, i.e. levels 6 and 7 on the ladder of Pretty.

In transformational approaches, participation involves dialogue, the orientation at reaching shared understandings out of a feeling of commitment and interdependency with others: 'Dialogue, in particular, looms large as an important methodological link among the activities pursued because of its existential significance for human life. More than a technical means to an end, it is an expression of the human condition that impels people to come together as thinking and feeling beings to form a common entity that is larger than its constituent parts (Freire, 1970). Dialogue occupies a central position [..] by making it possible for participants to create a social space in which they can share experiences and information, create common meanings and forge concerted actions together' (Park, 2001, p.82).

However, dialogue is not a harmonious process. According to Benhabib it is "a continuous process of conversation in which understanding and misunderstanding, agreement as well as disagreement are intertwined and always at work" (1992, p.198). The task of the dialogue is recognizing differences and similarities in things seen and done, starting from one's own knowledge, but never remaining in or accepting the immediate situation uncritically as it appears. These processes of inquiry involve wondering, questioning and doubting, in critical reflection with self and others, seeking to hold tensions in ways that lead to multiple paths of exploration.

Closely connected to this democratic conception of participation and dialogue are the values of 'openness' and 'equality'. 'Openness' means: transparency of motives, considerations and choices. It also denotes the open-endedness of the dialogue. 'Equality' means equal access to participation in the dialogue. Both values play an important role in the participatory-dialogical method used in the 'Aspiring to Healthy Living' project. They are the guiding principles in the relationships between and within the different subgroups involved (researchers, health practitioners, community members).

However, participation in this project is fraught with difficulties and tensions. In the next section, I will discuss two of them, but first, I will briefly describe the levels of participation in the project, using the ladder of Pretty as a tool.

Participation in the 'Aspiring to Healthy Living' project

In the project we can distinguish three phases: phase 'zero' (before the project actually had started); the 'narrative' phase (the first year of collecting stories from the elderly); and the 'action' phase, i.e. the second year of developing an intervention program.

Phase zero is the phase of looking for funding, collaboration opportunities and writing the project proposal. Ideally, participation of the community starts (or is already existent!) in this phase. However, in this project, the goals were defined and the methods determined before the participation of the elderly was actually sought.

Once the project was financed, the recruiting of community members for (paid) participation in the project group started. In this first stage, knowledge building on healthy living of Moroccan and Dutch older women and men was the central goal. The project group met monthly to exchange views and experiences. In reality, the community members dominated the discussions, because the researchers and practitioners felt a bit wary of enforcing their views on them and leaving too little room for their contributions.

In the course of the first year, the elderly were trained to interview and learned how to recruit interviewees from their communities: older Moroccan and Dutch women from a lower socio-economic background. The interviews were allocated to the researchers and professionals as well as the community members. Filled with dismay, the researchers found that the first interviews conducted by the community members were of very poor methodological quality (i.e. reliability and validity), in fact they did not serve the purpose of knowledge-building. Some transcripts covered only a few pages and the answers remained superficial. In other interviews the interviewer did the talking instead of the interviewee. Fortunately, in the second round and after additional interview training things got better. However, the project had lost much time by then.

The researchers started to analyze the interview material, each taking a different perspective as a framework. Important results and findings that were hard to interpret were submitted to the project group, including the elderly. This method enhanced connection with the experiences of the elderly and improved the quality of the interpretation. Moreover, the feedback meetings were the link between the knowledge building phase and the program development in the next stage (the 'action' phase), because they threw light on important topics and strategies for working with the elderly. In this stage, researchers, professionals, and community members worked together, exchanging views and learning from each other.

However, during the action phase of the project, the participation of the community members and the close teamwork diminished. The mutual exchange of information and opinions gave way to consultation and interviews with the elderly as representatives of their community. The project group met less frequently, i.e. bimonthly instead of monthly, and in the last six months of the project the team met only twice. The researchers and professionals now worked more individually, each focusing on their own task. The researchers worked on the analysis of the interview material and passed the results and conclusions on to the professionals who were working on the program. Two community members were involved as peer educators in the program and were interviewed about their experiences by an outside researcher who was hired to evaluate the program.

The development of participation of the elderly in the project can be illustrated by the Ladder of Pretty. Participation of the community in the project rose sharply and then declined. In the preparation phase, participation was almost absent (level 2 in Figure 1). In the research phase, the level of participation was high: functional participation (level 5) combined with elements of collaboration and co-learning (level 6). However, in the 'action' phase of the project the participation level dropped and moved to somewhere between levels 2, 3 and 4. In other words: the elderly started as active members of the project group in the first year but in the course of the project they turned into a feedback group. Why did this happen?

Dilemmas and tensions

Reflecting on the project, I see three major but related problems. First, project members held different positions regarding participation. Second, there was a tendency to 'protect' the community members within the project. Thirdly and most importantly, these issues and tensions were not subject of dialogue; therefore learning became obstructed.

Empowerment, academic quality or practical usefulness?

At the start of the project, before the community was involved, there seemed to be consensus about the project aims and means to realize them. All researchers and health practitioners subscribed to the importance of community participation. However, in the course of the project it turned out that participation did not mean the same for everyone. The analysis of minutes of meetings makes it possible to reconstruct three different positions in relation to participation.

First of all, there is the strong ideological position. In this view, empowerment of the (marginalized) communities of older people in Dutch society is the aim of the project and participation is an important means to realize this. The focus is not so much on results, but on the empowering capacity of the process. A slightly modified version of this ideological position is the ideal to give voice to communities who are unable to speak up for themselves in academic discourse, unless someone mediates for them. This view dominated with two researchers, but was in a lesser degree also present with the health practitioners and the project manager.

The second position is the scholarly one. In this view, participation is important because it can contribute to the methodological quality of the research (the so-called 'member check'). Neither a specific ideal, nor the creation of a social relevant outcome (in this case a health education program) is important, but the academic status of the project and publications resulting from it. The focus is on the conventional methodological questions and technical norms for 'good research' and not so much on moral considerations. This view dominated with one researcher, but it was also present with the other researchers and the project manager.

In the third position, that I have called the pragmatic position, high value is attached to the practical usefulness of the project. Members who prioritize this value focus on the practical outcomes and its contribution to health promotion policy and practice, and the community. This pragmatic view dominated with the health professionals, the project manager and the community members; in a lesser degree it was also present with some of the researchers.

Whereas for the second and third position a low degree of participation (level 1 to 4) suffices, empowerment only can be realized by participation on level 5 or higher (Khanna, 1996). Although the PAR project was explicitly aiming at empowerment, in the course of the project it turned out that the project members, in line with their value priorities, had different opinions about the desirable form and degree of participation in each phase. Some project members strove for as much community participation as possible, or for giving as much voice as possible within this project to the community. They advocated the active participation of the elderly as co-researchers, co-developers and co-workers in the project. They adhered to a form of participatory action research, directed at empowerment and characterized by a bottom-up approach, the so-called empowering action research (Hart & Bond, 1995).

The goals of empowering action research are consciousness raising and increasing the participants' control, and ultimately changing the structural power relations in society. In this project the focus was on personal empowerment (understood as critical consciousness-raising, self-efficacy and capacity building) by a high level of participation of the elderly in all phases[14]. The community members felt indeed empowered at the end of the project: they told the external evaluator that they had achieved more understanding of different perspectives on health, their self-esteem and communication skills had improved, as well as their way of coping with uncertain situations. Although their reason for participation was mainly pragmatic (contributing to the health of their communities and earn some money), they nevertheless were very critical of the way participation was 'done' in the project. As set

---

[14] To read more about the concept of empowerment in health promotion, see Jacobs (2006).

out before, in the second year of the project the active participation of the communities fell back to consultation. For the researchers and health practitioners that took a strong ideological position, this was not a desirable form and degree of participation, but also for the 'pragmatic' elderly, consultation was not enough. As they told the external evaluator:

> the researchers did listen to us, but they didn't do anything with it; and
>
> we could offer our opinions, but it didn't really matter... the decisions were made elsewhere and often it was not clear what was decided.

Two community members were quite explicit in saying that they had wanted to be involved more in the project, e.g. in developing an interview schedule:

> I wanted to make a contribution.

However, other project members (who adhered to an academic or pragmatic position) advocated exactly this feedback function. For them participation was not an intrinsic value (or at least not the most important value) but an instrument for improving the quality of the research (by means of the so-called 'member check') or the effectiveness and usefulness of a program for healthy living by involving the community as a feedback group. Participation also took a strategic form: to inform the community as a strategy to smooth the path for the planned health activities (levels 2 or 3) or mobilizing community members to get access to the broader community (level 5). For these project members, not participation but methodological quality or effectiveness (the realization of change) were the main values. Participation was the strategy or instrument to help realize these values[15].

To sum up, different priorities were presented. The ideological position, aimed at empowerment, collided with other values of achieving a product of high academic standard or working towards a practical program – both of which possibly did not have to involve a high level of participation. However, the clash between these positions was not only a clash between different stakeholders, it also took place within the researcher group and even within one and the same person. An example was the project manager, a professor who struggled to keep the academic standards and empowerment ideals while conforming to the demands of the financing institution to develop a practicable program. The result of this clash of values became manifest in problems like periodical dropout, tensions between the project manager and the researchers and between the researchers and the health

---

[15] In the typology of Hart & Bond (1995) this is the so-called 'experimental' respectively 'professionalizing' type of participatory action research. The experimental type of action research is more theoretically oriented compared to the other types: the researcher and his or her research question are central. In the professionalizing type, the problem to be solved is defined by and in the interest of the health professionals, but there is some interaction with the users.

professionals, and frustrations about poor academic quality or the lost ideal of empowerment.

However, these different priorities should not necessarily have caused problems. Professionals, and academic researchers in particular, are generally very capable of dealing with different opinions, provided that there is an opportunity for exchange. So what happened in this project?

Before elaborating on these problems, I will present a second dilemma that became manifest in the relationship between researchers and health professionals on the one hand and the community on the other hand.

Openness or 'protection'?

In participatory action research, researchers not only need knowledge and expertise in research methodology, but also competencies for dealing adequately with the interpersonal and political dynamics of the research process (Nelson et al., 2004). At the outset of the project, the researchers and health professionals had little or no experience in participatory approaches. Many aspects of the project were completely new and posed questions regarding their professional performance and actions. The researchers and health professionals felt particularly insecure in collaborating with the community members as equal partners in the project. An example is the poor quality of the interviews held by the community members in the first round. Looking back, it is difficult to reconstruct how and why the decision was made not to speak openly about this poor quality and its implications for the analysis. Was it caused by fear of demoralizing the community members or of hurting their feelings? Was it difficult for the researchers to admit that they made a mistake by expecting to cram lay people in four workshops into 'co-researchers'? Was it the effect of trying to prevent losing more time by avoiding discussion in the project group? Whatever the reason(s), the community members felt that something was wrong with their interviews, but initially they did not get straightforward answers to their questions. In the evaluation at the end of the project, the elderly criticized the lack of clarity and feedback, actually they were still searching for answers:

1. Was the quality of our interviews all right?
2. Why did the researchers do interviews as well?
3. What have the interviews contributed to the health promotion program?

By having separate meetings, the 'professional' members tried to avoid overburdening the community members or bothering them unnecessarily with problems of time management, logistical procedures, decisions or illness of co-workers, for fear of 'losing them'. But this also meant that the tensions, problems (e.g. with the interviews) and uncertainties within the project were not openly discussed, at least not in the whole project team.

A similar reticence was seen in the contact between the project manager on the one hand and the researchers and health professionals on the other hand. The project manager correctly took primary responsibility for the progress of the project and meeting the demands of the financier. Consequently, she stressed the importance of sticking to deadlines and producing output. As a consequence, in the researchers' and professionals' view she did not pay much attention to the scientific quality and participatory values of the project. The researchers' reaction to the project manager's pressure was to ask for more time. Consequently, the project manager took action to relieve them of their tasks and ease the schedule. However, she did all these things without consulting the other researchers in order to avoid burdening them with administrative matters. The researchers for their part felt left out and not taken seriously as equal partners in the project.

These forms of 'protection' may take place with the best of intentions, but they interfere with an open and equal dialogue. Such a dialogue is not only important from a methodological or technical viewpoint (it improves the validity and usability of results in a participatory approach), but also from a moral professional viewpoint. Realizing dialogical relationships with the community is an intrinsic value or goal in participatory action research. In addition, an open and equal dialogue is a breeding ground for professional development, because it creates a space for reflection and double or triple loop learning (Brockbank & McGill, 1998).

Two mirrors

In the 'Aspiring to Healthy Living' project, the main 'problem' was that there was no open and shared discussion on participation. Admittedly, there was a lot of discussion in the meetings as well as corridor chatting about the activities and division of roles, but the basic values and viewpoints on participation were not part of this dialogue. Moreover, by having separate meetings, the community members were unwittingly excluded from this dialogue. And by limiting this dialogue, shared learning has also been obstructed. I will explain this by referring to the distinction between single, double and triple loop learning (see e.g. Brockbank & McGill, 1998).

PAR stands within a critical scientific paradigm that requires researchers to accept "that research cannot occupy a value-free realm: it means acknowledging that we all view the world – and do our research – with a view from somewhere… our standpoint affects our thinking" (Holstein & Minkler, 2007, p.19). This standpoint is morally and politically relevant because we act upon what we see; therefore, it should be part of reflection and dialogue as 'normative' professionals. In reflecting on this project, I have become aware of the importance of exactly this dialogue for so-called double and triple loop learning processes in collaborative research.

In single-loop learning, the (implicit) frame of reference (including one's theories and models of action, opinions and values) guides the actions and decisions taken. Reflection is restricted to technical-methodical questions: are we doing the right things to achieve the goals of the project? This was the dominant way of learning in the project. In the dialogue, the goals and frames themselves and the differences and similarities within the project team were not subject to discussion. The result was that the clash of positions within and between project members took place almost unnoticed.

Double-loop learning on the other hand, is characterized by reflection on the action and frames underlying the action. The guiding questions are: what am I doing? What are my motives for acting like I do? What presuppositions, models, theories and values underlie my actions? Learning then means to put to question ones basic assumptions, reflection. "Reflection means showing ourselves to ourselves or holding up a mirror to ourselves" (Ray, 2007, p.69), which means that the frames and goals can change. This kind of reflection and learning thrives in an open and equal dialogue. In the 'Aspiring to Healthy Living' project, the 'protective' stance (instead of openness) and the time pressure obstructed the dialogue and thereby reflection-on-action and double-loop learning.

Double-loop learning is a precondition for triple-loop learning, which is characterized by reflection on the reflection and learning process itself, which means taking a meta-position towards the collaborative process. The guiding question is: how do learn from each other? What kind of learning processes (e.g. the dialogue) do we need to develop our capacity to learn from each other? This requires "a second mirror: we… look at ourselves looking at ourselves. The important distinction here is that someone or something else – an older person, a reminiscence group, a nursing home – holds up the second mirror. To be reflexive, we need an Other to show ourselves to ourselves" (Ray, 2007, p.69).

The participatory inquiry process itself is deconstructed by critically reflecting on ones openness for and capacity to deal with multiple perspectives. In the project, there was no triple-loop learning, only in reflecting on the project afterwards, double and triple loop learning processes finally took place.[16] Not only did the team find out the different positions involved regarding participation, they also became aware that the community members (as the Other) were systematically but unwittingly excluded from the dialogue and that this was reflected in distancing ourselves from questioning our own identities as 'ageing people'. In other words, it became clear how structural, symbolic, interpersonal and intrapersonal factors intermingled to produce a quite explosive stuff and in being not reflected upon, led to disappointment, frustration and disturbed relationships.

Conclusion

Conducting PAR means dealing with a highly contested and difficult concept: participation. Participation has different meanings in different discourses: ideological and

---

[16] The study by Tonja van den Ende on 'normative professionalism' (Van den Ende & Jacobs, 2006), was an important factor in this learning process, as was the evaluation with the health professionals and the community members.

communicative in the empowerment tradition; instrumental in the traditional scientific paradigm, and pragmatic in professional and lay views. Also the relationship between participation and empowerment is complex and multilayered. In this project, the elderly felt empowered, although they were not participating in the goal setting or decision making processes. This raises the question whether participation on a high level is a necessary condition to achieve empowerment.

On the other hand, this project makes it clear that the involvement of the elderly as researchers in fieldwork does not in itself make a change in power structures between academic researchers and communities, as is also stated by Mo Ray (2007). Instead, in its instrumental use, it points to the danger that participation can become part of a 'ticking the box approach' to show that the requirements of research grant-awarding bodies are met. Therefore, reflexivity should be part and parcel of the PAR process; we should ask ourselves:

1. What do we mean by participation?
2. Why do we think participation is important?
3. Who should benefit from the research and in what way?
4. What criteria and methods can we use to judge the success of participation and how is participation involved in these?

My conclusion is that participatory (action) research, if not reflected on and spoken about, can become a frustrating process. In order to realize dialogic relationships the frames of reference and the reflection and learning processes themselves need to become the subject of discussion. An open dialogue requires 'rooting and shifting': recognition of one's own position and the unique positioning of each member of the project (Yuval-Davis, 1994). It also requires taking a meta-reflexive stand, to see what voices are heard and what voices are not; to see what procedures, what language or images, what behavior or communication patterns and what personal needs and longings are inhibiting or supporting an open and equal dialogue.

The rhetoric of empowerment, equality and reflection on power relations in PAR often does not correspond with reality. In mainstream health (research) practice we find not much thought about the conflict or suppression of values, about differing interests and goals or about the resistance and emotions accompanying these clashes and the ways the different parties involved deal with them (cf. Wallerstein, 1999). In this sense, the 'Aspiring to Healthy Living' project is not unique. Sharing the experience of working within the tension between the ideal and sticky reality, between the desirable and the possible, and between technical and moral considerations could have fostered a sense of connection, vitality and empowerment between the project members. However, whereas the project failed to take this meta-position, this book is a second chance to share and learn from each other stories, meanings and experiences.

References

Arnstein, S. (1969). Ladder of citizen participation in the USA. Journal of the American Institute of Planners, July, 216-26.

Benhabib, S. (1992). Situating the Self: Gender, Community and Postmodernism in Contemporary Ethics. Oxford: Polity Press.

Bernard, M. & Scharf, T. (eds.) (2007). Critical Perspectives on Ageing Societies. Bristol: Policy Press.

Brockbank, A. & I. McGill (1998). Facilitating Reflective Learning in Higher Education. Buckingham: Open University Press.

Chiweza, A. L. (2005). Participation: Reality or Rhetoric in Rural Communities of Malawi? Tanzanet Journal, 5(1): 1-8. Available online: www.tanzanet.org/int/journal/tznetjournal_07_2005_partic_reality_rural_comm.pdf.

Freire, P.(1970). Pedagogy of the Oppressed. London: Zed Books.

Habermas, J. (1984). The Theory of Communicative Action. Boston: Beacon Press.

Hart, E. & M. Bond (1995). Action research for health and social care. Philadelphia/ Buckingham: Open University Press.

Holstein, M.B. & Minkler, M. (2007). Critical gerontology: reflections for the 21st century. In M. Bernard & T. Scharf (eds.), Critical Perspectives on Ageing Societies (pp.13-26). Bristol: Policy Press.

Jacobs, G., Braakman, M. & J. Houweling (2005). Op eigen kracht naar gezond leven. Empowerment in de gezondheidsbevordering: concepten, werkwijzen en onderzoeksmethoden. Utrecht: UvH.

Jacobs, G. (2006). Imagining the flowers, but working the rich and heavy clay: participation and empowerment in action research for health. Educational Action Research, 14(4), 569-581.

Khanna, R. (1996). Participatory action research in women's health: SARTHI, India. In K. de Koning & M. Martin (eds), Participatory Research in Health (pp.62-77). London: Zed Books.

Koelen, M. & Van der Ban, A. (2004). Health education and health promotion. Wageningen: Wageningen Academic Publishers.

Minkler, M. & N. Wallerstein (eds.) (2003). Community-Based Participatory Research for Health. San Francisco: Jossey-Bass.

Murray, M. (2004). Challenging Narratives and Social Representation of Health, Illness and Injury. In M. Murray (ed.), Critical Health Psychology (pp.173-186). New York: Palgrave MacMillan.

Nelson, G., Pancer, M., Hayward, K. & R. Kelly (2004). Partnerships and participation of community residents in Health Promotion and Prevention: Experiences of the Highfield Community Enrichment Project (Better Beginnings, Better Futures), Journal of Health Psychology, 9 (2), 213-227.

Park, P.(2001). Knowledge and Participatory Research. In P.Reason & H. Bradbury (eds.), Handbook of Action Research. Participative Inquiry & Practice (pp.81-90). London: Sage.

Pretty, J., Guijt, I., Thompson, J. & I. Scoones (1995). Participatory Learning and Action. A trainers' Guide. London: Institute for Environment and Development.

Ray, M. (2007). Redressing the balance? The participation of older people in research. In M. Bernard & T. Scharf (eds.) Critical Perspectives on Ageing Societies (pp.73-87). Bristol: Policy Press.

Ray, R.E. (2007). Narratives as agents of social change: a new direction for narrative gerontologists. In M. Bernard & T. Scharf (eds.), Critical Perspectives on Ageing Societies (pp.59-72). Bristol: Policy Press.

Reason, P.& H. Bradbury (eds.) (2001). Handbook of Action Research. Participative Inquiry & Practice. London: Sage.

Shier, H. (2001). Pathways to Participation: Openings, Opportunities and Obligations. Children & Society, 15, 107-117.

Yuval-Davis, N. (1994). Women, Ethnicity and Empowerment. Feminism & Psychology, 4(1), 179-197.

Wallerstein, N. (1999). Power between evaluator and community: research relationships within New Mexico's healthier communities. Social Science & Medicine, 49, 39-53.

WHO (1986). Ottawa Charter for Health Promotion. Geneva: World Health Organization.

Involving refugees in focus group research

Maria Higgins and Catherine O'Donnell

This chapter describes the process of conducting a study, funded by the Scottish Executive, exploring the health care use and needs of asylum seekers living in Glasgow. As part of this, we conducted five focus groups facilitated by asylum seekers and refugees in participants' own language. These were Swahili, French, Russian, Farsi and English. The experience showed that seeking the views of asylum seekers and refugees about their use of and need for health care was problematic due to the heterogeneity of the population, language barriers, lack of trust in the research process and fear that involvement would be linked, and possibly damaging to, asylum applications. Thus, our original vision for how the project would be conducted turned out, in reality, to be simplistic and required a flexible process-driven approach to working with the refugee community.

We focus on how the design and process of the study itself offered solutions to a research design based on prior identification of the 'research problem/questions' and in particular on the iterative interplay of data generated across the facilitator training sessions, the analysis sessions and the focus groups themselves. This ensured that the research process was grounded in the experience of asylum seekers themselves and also highlighted the importance of researcher reflexivity and awareness that any such project is an interactive process that is constitutive of the data, and cannot be separated from it.

Asylum seekers and refugees are a marginal group in all societies, often experiencing hardship and difficulties in access to services, including health care (Burnett & Peel, 2001). This is due in part to language barriers, but also to cultural dissimilarities and lack of knowledge both within the asylum seeking community and within the communities of professionals providing care. However, seeking the views of asylum seekers and refugees regarding their use and needs for health care is problematic, not only for the aforementioned reasons, but also due to a lack of trust in the research process and the fear that involvement will be linked, and possibly damaging to, their asylum application.

Over the past 5 years, the UK has instigated a policy of dispersal, with asylum seekers housed in major urban conurbations, usually in areas of socio-economic deprivation. Although free health care within the UK National Health Service is available, asylum seekers often do not access health care or experience difficulties in accessing care as and when required (Williams, 2005; Feldman, 2006). As part of a larger study funded by the Scottish Executive in 2003, which explored the health care use and needs of asylum seekers living in Glasgow, we conducted a series of five focus groups with asylum seekers. These were conducted in participants' own language, facilitated by asylum seekers and refugees, and covered Swahili, French, Russian, Farsi and English.

This chapter will explore the unfolding of the project given the difficult circumstances and the need for a flexible process-driven approach when working with the refugee community. We will focus on how the design and process of the study itself offered solutions to a research design based on prior identification of the 'research problem/questions' and in particular on the iterative interplay of data generated across the facilitator training sessions, the analysis sessions and the focus groups themselves. In addition we address some important ethical issues and, in the light of a post project evaluation focus group with facilitators, explore their experience of having been involved as researchers.

The Rationale for Focus Groups

Focus groups can be useful when little is known about subject matter (Morgan, 1997) and have been described as effective in establishing trust and rapport with hard-to-reach populations. (Krueger, 1993) These considerations informed the original design of the project, particularly when the aim was to seek the views of the asylum seeker/refugee community, many of whom may have limited English. However, in reality this was simplistic and our experiences during the project demonstrate that the focus group method alone is sometimes not enough to address such challenges. In fact the focus groups proved in some ways counter to establishing trust and it was only through 'informal' observational work, recording of field notes, extensive visits to local refugee groups and dogged determination not to let the project collapse that the focus groups actually happened. This also revealed the limitations and possibilities of focus groups in such research.

Accessing people seeking asylum and refugees

The initial phase of the work involved gaining access to asylum seekers and refugees (ASR). We contacted key people across a range of settings including voluntary sector groups who provided services to ASR, statutory sector community development projects, church groups and local colleges where ASR attended English classes.

Initially, gatekeepers seemed reluctant to engage with us and facilitate access. They explained that there were frequent requests to research this group of people which were often a waste of time with projects failing to get off the ground. This was seen to be largely due to researchers' lack of understanding of the fragile circumstances and level of anxiety within the community. Their sceptical and protective reaction served to emphasise just how insecure this community appeared to be and consequently how ambitious our plans were in comparison!

We managed to arrange face-to-face meetings with some of the gatekeepers. These were critical in developing a sense of trust, understanding about the purpose of the study and that we were prepared to devote adequate time and resources to the project. Key to this was the role of the principal researcher, MH, who subsequently secured invitations to attend ASR drop in groups run by the voluntary sector. In addition, she negotiated access to the wider ASR community via college classes and community development projects. At these, information leaflets about the proposed project were distributed in various languages, with stamped addressed envelopes to facilitate replies back to the researcher.

Recruitment of Facilitators

The first phase of recruitment involved identifying suitable candidates within the communities to conduct the focus groups. This required a reasonable grasp of English and an ability to commit to a training programme. This was one of the most challenging phases of the project and, after several months, we were still unsuccessful. A second mailing of information via all of our contacts generated no replies from possible facilitators. Things were beginning to look as bleak as had been predicted!

MH continued to visit various drop in groups and organisations on a weekly basis establishing a relaxed, informal presence and becoming a familiar face to both ASRs and voluntary workers. Field notes were kept during this to document the process.

This phase of the project, although not factored into our initial plan, was hugely time consuming but instrumental in paving the way for positive human interactions with people in the face of considerable power relations. To become a 'familiar face' also signalled to key gatekeepers that MH was committed to the project and allowed them to assess her on a personal level as someone they could trust and indeed wanted to help. Eventually, as relationships developed with community organisations, several of our contacts presented us directly with details of particular people who they thought would fulfil the facilitators' role. It is doubtful that the project could have progressed much further without gaining the trust of our contacts and their subsequent active input. MH talked to the seven people who had been recommended on the telephone to secure their interest and invited them to an initial 'training session' at the burgh hall, a familiar location close to where the majority of the asylum seeking community lived.

Training and Collaboration

At the first session another colleague presented a generic 'Introduction to Focus Groups' talk followed by an open discussion about our plans for the project. There was a strong feeling amongst the volunteers that people would be unwilling to come out to a focus group to discuss health and most volunteers felt uncertain about going ahead given the uneasy climate of the community. Also, despite the fact that most volunteers held skilled jobs previous to migration and were proficient in English, they expressed low confidence in their personal ability to lead focus groups. It seemed clear that, rather than developing a training package for facilitators, there was a more urgent need for us to listen and learn from the volunteers about the community we were attempting to research.

The project was subsequently taken forward by MH working alone and a further two open agenda meetings were held giving a further opportunity to air thoughts and feelings around the topic of health and the proposed design of the project. After these meetings a core group of volunteer facilitators was formed. These were four men: two from Democratic Republic of Congo (LB, JK), one from Somalia (NS), one from Afghanistan (AR); and one female from Kenya (MK). A process of preparation, mutual training and recruitment began in earnest.

MH conducted a focus group using the devised topic guide with the facilitators as participants as a way of providing an example of what it might be like both to run a focus group and to be a participant. This part of the process became extremely important in generating preliminary data and subsequently adapting our topic guide to ask better questions grounded in the experience of those from within the community. For example it became clear in the discussion after the focus group that there was a widely held assumption within the ASR community that registering with a GP was an essential part of their asylum claim. This was linked to the fact that information about registering with a GP was included in an information pack, together with instructions about the asylum application process, distributed by the council to orientate newly arrived asylum seekers. Hence it was regarded as a possibly punitive element of surveillance rather than a beneficial service. Consequently our questions around this topic were adapted to be less direct and designed instead to probe deeper into how opinions around this were formed, and how this could be addressed, rather than unwittingly push buttons that activated people's defences.

It also became apparent that the use of the term 'asylum seekers', which we had used in our recruitment material, was felt to be an insult. This highlighted our blind spot as to how the term was being used in the wider media and the effect this had on that community. We decided as a group to change our paperwork accordingly simply referring to 'people seeking asylum' where necessary. Facilitators were also concerned that they would be unable to keep people on the topic of health when other things were much more pressing such as racism, housing and poverty. Thus, we decided to prepare a list of contact information where people could access further help about these issues to distribute at the end of the session as a way of managing this.

Throughout these six 2-hour preparatory sessions several new people turned up through word of mouth but did not return. MH subsequently met one of these people at the drop in centre and was able to discover a possible reason for this:

Field Notes 28: Saw **** today who confided that he had not returned to the group because other volunteers had been criticising the healthcare they had received and he felt that he did not want to become involved with something where people were criticising health provision while he was going through an asylum application. He seemed afraid and said "They should be very careful what they are doing and saying."

This was important in many ways. First, it contradicted Krueger's (1993) view that focus groups can be used to build trust, particularly in a climate where there is real fear of exploitation and misrepresentation. Second, it demonstrated that the tendency of policy and other programme development to simplistically locate local minority groups as a homogenised 'other' is flawed. The use of informal observation and field notes produced data here about the experience of being one refugee amongst others, which would not have emerged via our original research protocol.

Recruitment of participants

Researchers recommend developing partnerships with community agencies to facilitate recruitment (MacDougall, 2001) and these links were important to the project. However, the personal networks of our facilitators were also critical, yielding over half of the overall participants.

Importance has also been attached to focus group composition in terms of sociodemographic characteristics (Madriz, 1998). Indeed, group composition should have been a specific concern given that the experience of forced departure from homelands impacts disproportionately on women, and that policy and programmes in the receiving country can militate to impact further on the already disadvantaged. However, in reality our most lofty aim was getting enough participants to enable focus groups to actually happen across the five language groups. Recruitment covered a wide range of avenues as previously described and mushroomed as the process continued and our networks expanded. We visited a college project where asylum seekers who were trained health professionals were completing a retraining course; a satellite class provided by a local college at the burgh hall where women with families who were unable to travel to local colleges, could attend a basic English class with childcare provided; and a men's health drop-in clinic run by a much trusted asylum seeker liaison nurse. This vast amount of work often resulted in just one person from each source. So to a certain degree we achieved a reasonable reflection of diversity, but importantly, although women were recruited, there were none from services designed to target the most marginalised and hardest to reach of this section of the community. We were not resourced to pursue inroads to this section of the community further but other projects would be well advised to plan in advance to address this issue.

The tome of the recruitment material was also important. Facilitators pointed out that the professionally translated recruitment invitation letters were flawed in various ways either being inaccurate or written in a formal style of language that would be impossible for someone with basic literacy to read. They subsequently worked on improving these to make them more accessible and inviting.

Another important factor, highlighted by the facilitators own experience, was the absence of nursery provision for ASR families and the fact that people do not have access to extended family networks. In addition to this there was particular anxiety around separation for both parents and children and so we stated clearly on the invitation that professional crèche facilities would be available on site.

Both of these issues themselves addressed our research questions by identifying issues concerning interpreting/translation services and lack of childcare as barriers to access to health services information and attending appointments.

Pilot Focus Group

One focus group, conducted in Farsi, got off the ground relatively quickly due to availability of premises and help with recruitment at Homestart, a trusted voluntary project which offers help to ASR with young families. One facilitator, AR, felt confident to take the plunge and drew on his personal network to secure a few participants. We set the date one week in advance and MH telephoned those who had expressed an interest and given contact details on the day before the group. This resulted in four participants.

This group functioned as a pilot focus group and important lessons were learnt which we used as the basis for three further training and planning sessions. The main difficulties were lack of time and practical support. The focus group was scheduled to last one hour and the room and crèche had been booked for an hour and a half to enable time to set up the buffet and reimburse travel expenses. However, there was a staggered arrival of people arriving late with children which was disruptive as AR had to interrupt the group several times to direct them to the crèche. Language limited the extent to which MH could help with these practical issues. Two facilitators speaking the language in which the focus group was being run would have allowed smoother running and thus a better group dynamic. More time for a debriefing session immediately after the group would have been supportive to the facilitator and allowed MH to produce field notes valuable to the analysis. Subsequently we decided that LB and JK would co-facilitate a focus group in French, MH and MK would conduct a female only group in English, and AR and NS would conduct the Russian and Swahili groups alone with the project secretary arranging food and travel expenses. We adapted our recruitment invitations to make it clear that it was important to arrive at the stated time and also extended the time we booked local premises for the groups.

Successfully running a focus group was energising for the team and further training sessions focused on AR feeding back to the other facilitators his positive and negative experiences of conducting the group. We used excerpts from the transcript to illustrate particular difficulties and skills with facilitating such as getting group discussion flowing, avoiding a 'going round the circle in turn' dynamic and allowing silences and uncertainty. This form of experiential learning was very useful in helping facilitators to fully understand the method in a way that it would not have been possible to convey through talks or handout material. The process of training promoted confidence in the group in that they believed that the study was worthwhile and subsequently the facilitators' skills promoted confidence within the focus groups.

Issues from the Focus Groups

Insider or Outsider?

Focus groups were carried out over a period of a few weeks with 6-8 participants attending each one. Contrary to the recommendation that Morgan (1997) makes regarding the desirability for anonymity, about half of the participants were known personally to the facilitator and each other. This helped considerably to authenticate the facilitators' insider status and promoted a comfortable group dynamic. The exception to this was the women's English focus group led by MH and co-facilitated by MK where none of the participants, who were mostly African and all recruited via gatekeepers, were known to the facilitators. This group was characterised by a noticeably tense dynamic. Participants had attended group prepared to meet an outsider, but there was a strong sense that MK's presence generated confusion and suspicion as people were unable to judge her 'identity'. MH observed apparent hostility extended towards MK and dialogue during the group was occasionally halting and punctuated by some tense non-verbal behaviour suggesting that her presence was a block to frank discussion. MH took the following field note immediately after the group.

> **Field notes 47:** I was anxious to check M was okay as I was aware of tension throughout the group. But she thought it went really well and said she had very strong feelings of being "the professional" which she enjoyed.

This confirmed for me that, as a result of the complex interaction dynamic involving MK's anonymity and position working with the university and personal feelings of wishing to be aligned with the outsider as a professional, that insider status for MK had not been established. Previous researchers (Acker, 2000) have found that where there is compromised 'insider' status the researcher is not regarded as neutral and certain information is not divulged that would be to an outsider who wished to learn about the community. Again this says something very important about the assumption that people who are 'asylum seekers', are a community per se within any location that they can be found and even within similar groups of origin. The heterogeneity of this group of people and endemic fear and suspicion can do more to set people apart than draw them together.

From a theoretical perspective, our experience concurs with recent findings which understand the insider/outsider stance as an interactive phenomenon dependant on the particular context in which fieldwork takes place and not from the status characteristics of the researcher/volunteer (Kusow, 2004).

Both of these factors reveal that our plan to use 'insiders' in this context was simplistic and it is wise to be mindful of the fluidity of insider/outsider status and plan and predict what the dynamic may be in any given situation depending on the context and people involved.

Researchers or educators?

There was some blurred territory between volunteers as researchers or community educators which challenged traditional notions of research objectivity. This turned out to be an interesting 'blur' which facilitators enjoyed and which resulted in some positive outcomes. As part of the training process facilitators became knowledgeable about which services were available and how to access them. Often their own misconceptions were challenged and they subsequently changed their views. This inevitably led to an ability to pass on knowledge within the focus groups, which occurred on several occasions. Information given verbally by a known member of the community proved to be a very effective way of giving information to people who reported having either ignored information packs due to being unable to read them or assuming they were not for their benefit but part of Government surveillance. Informal feedback some time after the focus groups revealed that some people had registered with a GP or gained access to services that they did not previously know about.

Public/Private Opinions

The fact that people knew each other, led to an interesting interplay between public and private faces. The Swahili focus group was particularly characterised by a desire to present a positive picture with many declarations of being happy and grateful for the services provided. However, in a discussion about interpreters several women challenged another participant who claimed she was happy with the interpreting service;

      P   "Oh come on you are always complaining about this!"
      M   "How can you say this!" (Laughter in the group).

This highlights the critical importance of recognising the possible dangers of presenting focus group data as an accurate assessment of need rather a particular angle on a complex issue, especially where there are significant power relations and participants feel vulnerable. Thus focus groups should not be used in isolation to assess needs of this population and should not be analysed in a way which assumes pure data.

Researcher Effect

MH attended all groups and sat within the circle, introduced by the facilitator. This seemed less obtrusive than sitting on the outside which could have created an atmosphere of being observed. This appeared to be successful in that I did feel 'invisible' once the focus groups got underway. The fact that I did not speak the language, therefore could not interact or respond within the group, seemed to successfully exclude me from the dynamic. Facilitators, in later analysis sessions, described the benchmark of 'honest' data to be the extent to which people said negative things. The following field note was taken after the pilot focus group:

> **Field note 16:** I was aware that the participant had mentioned something about me. I asked AR and he told me that she said "Is it okay to tell the truth?" He was laughing and said; "I told her yes. It seemed funny to me because I know you but in my country most of the time it's not okay to tell the truth."

The establishment of this trust was subsequently planned for and actively facilitated throughout the process. It was interesting that people in most groups were not afraid to talk frankly about experiencing racism, despite the presence of the researcher who represented the 'other' in terms of race, contradicting the emphasis placed on this in much minority ethnic research.

Translation and Analysis

The recorded focus group sessions were translated and transcribed by MH and the facilitators working together. Initially facilitators tended to convert the spoken words into better English or provide a summary of what was said in their own words instead of translating accurately word for word. We had to work hard to maintain the integrity of the transcripts, but facilitators quickly adapted to what was required. Some interesting issues arose during this process for example one facilitator found it difficult not to translate what the person was describing as 'stress' but explained that there is no word in Swahili for stress. This suggested at least a possible reason for the lack of understanding and communication within consultations that some people reported.

After transcriptions were completed several analysis sessions were held with the facilitators, MH and COD. These sessions allowed different perspectives on the interpretation of data and were rich in insights which the researchers alone could not have had access to. A common opinion was that many people believed that if they were found to be in poor health, this would jeopardise their asylum claim. This belief contradicted a common narrative presented in the media regarding people falsifying stories of illness and injury in order to stay in the country. Parents who believed their children could possibly have been infected with HIV refused to have them tested for fear they would be further stigmatised or expelled from the country.

An extremely valuable element of these sessions was the facilitator's in-depth background information on participant's countries of origin, the economic factors and health care systems provided there. Differences and similarities in how people experienced healthcare here were clearly based on these historical factors.

These sessions also functioned as a longitudinal focus group generating further data as people discussed in more depth issues which were raised or indeed not raised. For example, one facilitator shared a very personal and deeply traumatic experience within the confines of the group which shed light on why people would not discuss certain issues in focus groups. It was a difficult element of the session for all but was treated with sensitivity and respect from fellow co-facilitators. This was something that the researcher could not guarantee or have any real control over other than a mindful facilitation of group development to make it as emotionally 'safe' as possible.

The facilitators evaluate the project

MH conducted a post project focus group with facilitators to explore their experiences of participation. Overall they reported a positive experience in which their aims of gaining skills and doing something for their community were mostly compatible with the aims of the project.

However most had experienced a subsequent 'new' position within their communities where there was mistrust from some due to their involvement with the project. Some people who did not participate in the groups due to fear and suspicion maintained these opinions and consequently directed their mistrust onto facilitators. One facilitator was asked to leave a weekly support group for women that she had been attending due to the women's fears that things they were discussing were being passed on through her to the 'authorities'. Another facilitator confided that he had experienced similar negativity but it had not occurred to him that it could be something to do with his involvement in the project. However, despite this, all agreed that in retrospect they would make the same decision to be involved in the project and that the gains superseded any negative reactions from the 'community'. People were particularly happy with the certificate we provided from the university which recognised their training and achievement and hoped that this would be useful for the future in applying for jobs and courses.

Discussion

Considerably more time had to be invested in the initial stages of the project than initially intended. This was essential to establish strong ownership of the project and a team identity in order to inspire confidence in the volunteers. Also developing relationships with community organisations over a period of time was critical to our efforts. Without recognition of these factors there would have been a high risk of drop out, difficulties in recruiting participants and potential collapse of the entire project. The 'training sessions' necessarily became a mutual and collaborative process which necessitated that we loosen our grip of control of the project, accept uncertainty and be open and responsive to what arose from the volunteers at every stage of the project. These are factors which any researcher who has undertaken Participatory Action Research (PAR) (Reason, 1994) might be familiar with. This was not set up to be a PAR project but circumstances dictated that we move further along the continuum of methods towards a participative research approach. This could almost be described as a form of 'grounded process'. The subsequent interplay of data between training groups and the focus groups was critical and generated far more robust data than if the data gathering and analysis had been separated as is the case in many projects. The research process itself demonstrated one of the most important outcomes of the project, that community participation is a good model for effectively informing the refugee community. Further to this, the complexity of information which became apparent throughout the process served to emphasise the dangers of presenting data from focus groups alone, for example, as a needs assessment of a particular population, without exploring and analysing what issues do not come up and why.

An important element of this project was the attempt to allow the community to define the issues addressed. Many research projects do not obtain good data simply because they have not been able to get a sense of what the relevant issues might be for a particular community. Hence there is a danger that a tick box mentality is applied in which communities are 'given a voice' but in reality are not facilitated to express what is important to them. The facilitators' personal experiences as asylum seekers were invaluable here and resulted in a natural ability to ask pertinent questions with a sensitivity that would have been beyond the capabilities of the researcher.

The practical issue of getting people to attend on time was considerable especially with the African groups where temporal organisation is culturally divergent. However this loss of focus group discussion time could have been mitigated if more time and thought had gone into tapping the rich resource of naturalistic talk which happened around the sharing of food after the group was over. Krueger (1993) recommends that food is provided as a way of relaxing people and promoting frank discussions and we certainly found this to be the case but had not provided the time or space to capitalise on this. Other researchers working with refugees have used informal methods of data collection such as individual chats at social events and in participants own homes successfully after being unable to set up focus groups. (Lipson, 2003) Although we succeeded in setting up focus groups to good effect, our experiences of their limitations, and the importance of our informal observational work would support this as an effective and appropriate way to conduct research in this field.

It is important to emphasise, to those who are starting out on refugee research, that diversity in working with such groups is huge. So don't be surprised if you experience similar issues to those described here and indeed be on the look-out for them, but don't assume they will all happen either.

Some ethical issues are raised around the level of support which should be provided for volunteers and researchers in projects of this nature. Volunteers should be made aware of the possible pitfalls of becoming involved in projects, which are held in suspicion by the wider community. Also, the task of setting up and running focus groups, although enjoyable, was stressful especially for volunteers who were in extremely difficult and uncertain circumstances either as refugees or going through an asylum application. Likewise these are difficult conditions for a lone researcher and support and debriefing time from colleagues is essential. Hence, it is important to ensure from the writing of the proposal stage, to its evaluation and beyond, that all participants' interests, including researchers, are respected and ensured through the careful anticipation of adequate resourcing. The consequences of failing to attend to this are broken morale, mistrust and a waste of potential.

The project suffered from a lack of follow on funding to promote sufficient dissemination of the results of the project within the community. This could have mitigated to a certain extent the after effects that facilitators experienced within the community. However, links were made informally with the local Public Involvement Officer whose task was to involve marginalised sections of community in information gathering and activities. Several facilitators became involved with projects in which they were able to use their skills and knowledge gained from the focus groups to good effect feeding back both results of groups and the successful format for gathering information and educating community about important matters such as health. Another facilitator became inspired to campaign for nursery provision for ASR families. These activities were arguably more effective than the official submission of a research report to the Scottish Executive and hence similar research projects should have both the funding and intention to harness energy and explore the potential of mobilising the community and enabling them to put into action possible changes suggested by results.

Conclusion

Although entry to this group of people was difficult it is important not to underestimate the dynamic energy and motivation that can exist particularly within asylum seeker/refugee 'communities' which make it an ideal setting for a fully funded PAR approach using either focus groups or more informal methods. However, this comes with a strong caveat that, whichever method is used, a creative and flexible approach where process is closely related to outcomes is the basis for success and should remind us as researchers that there is no such thing as pure data 'out there' to be found or a pure 'community' to be engaged with.

Acknowledgement

We wish to thank Allah Na Waz Rustankhil, Londi Beketch, Mercy Kamanja, Jean Kabongo, Nasa Saad, Rev. Moyna McGlynn and Angela King for their invaluable participation in this project and also to Catherine McNeil, project secretary for her support. Thanks also to Professor Debra Hopkins for her helpful feedback on initial drafts of this chapter.

References

Acker, S. (2000). In/out/side: positioning the researcher in feminist qualitative research. Resources for Feminist Research 28 (1/2): 189-208, 2000

Burnett, A. and Peel, M. (2001). Asylum seekers and refugees in Britain: health needs of asylum seekers and refugees. British Medical Journal, vol.322, issue 7285, pp.544-547

Feldman, R. (2006). Health care for refugees and asylum seekers: A review of the literature and a framework for services. Public Health.

Krueger, R. (1994). Focus Groups: A Practical Guide for Applied Research (2nd ed). Thousand Oaks, CA: Sage.

Krueger, R. (1993). Quality control in focus group research, in D.L. Morgan (ed.), Successful Focus Groups: Advancing the State of the Art. London: Sage

Kusow, A. (2004). Contesting stigma: On Goffman's assumptions of normative order. Symbolic Interaction, 27; 2, 179-197.

Lipson, J. (2003). Bosnian and soviet refugees' experiences with health care. Western Journal of Nursing Research, 25(7), 854-871

Madriz, E. (1998). Using focus groups with lower socioeconomic status Latina women. Qualitative Inquiry, 4, 114-128.

MacDougall, C. (2001). Planning and recruiting the sample for focus groups and in-depth interviews. Qualitative Health Research, 11, 117-126.

Morgan, D. (1997). Focus Groups as Qualitative Research. 2nd edition. London and New Delhi: Sage (Qualitative Research Methods, vol. 16).

Reason, P. (1994). Three approaches to participative enquiry. In Norman K. Denzin & Yvonna S. Lincoln (eds) Handbook of Qualitative Research. Thousand Oaks, CA: Sage

Williams, P.(2005). Failed asylum seekers and access to free health care in the UK. Lancet, 365:1767

The Gudaga Project: Researching with our local Aboriginal community

Jennifer Knight, Elizabeth Comino, Elizabeth Harris, Lisa Jackson Pulver, Cheryl Anderson and Pippa Craig

> This chapter tells the story of working with the indigenous Aboriginal community of south west Sydney to establish a birth cohort study of Indigenous infants. It is known as the Gudaga project. The cohort is made up of 159 Indigenous babies and their mothers. The project aims to describe the infants' health, development and use of health services during the first twelve months of their lives. This work cannot be done without the support and active participation of the local Indigenous community. In identifying and working with the Indigenous community at least seven groups were identified with key interest in this work. This chapter describes the range of strategies that the research team used to work with, engage, and maintain involvement over time.
>
> There are two take home lessons from the Gudaga project that are relevant to community based indigenous health research. The first is time. Researchers first became involved in the local Indigenous community in 1997. The first results from Gudaga will start coming through in 2007 – ten years later. None of that time has been wasted. It has been spent embedding the research in the community resulting in a strong sense of ownership. The second lesson relates to the values that underpin and sustain the project: trust, respect, reciprocity, open communication and staying connected. These values can only be established over time and, once established, cannot be taken for granted. As researchers, our challenge is to nurture and enhance these values as we work with the Gudaga mothers and babies.

It isn't often that public health research within a tertiary, academic setting can profess a direct link with the sale of frozen chickens but such is the 'claim to fame' of the Gudaga project. It is a long story spanning ten years but one which has led to the establishment of an Aboriginal home visiting team in the Campbelltown area (a large satellite city on the urban fringe of south west Sydney, Australia) and the recruitment of a cohort of almost 160 Indigenous[17] babies whose health and access to health services is being studied in the first longitudinal study of Indigenous infants undertaken on the east coast of Australia. The study is known as the Gudaga project.

---

[17] The word 'Indigenous' is used to refer to those with either an Aboriginal or Torres Strait Islander background.

This chapter tells the Gudaga story: yarns on the veranda; early dreams and schemes; initial short term funding for home visiting and finally, a successful proposal which led to NHMRC (National Health and Medical Research Council) funding. Pivotal to the story is the way we have worked in partnership with the local Indigenous community which includes a number of groups - all of which play a very important part in the success of our research project. These stakeholder groups, and our strategies for working with each of them to ensure robust results and a successful study, are identified and described in the following discussion.

Background

The story began in 1997. At that time, researchers from the University of New South Wales (UNSW) sat with Aboriginal health workers (AHWs) on the veranda of Campbelltown's Aboriginal Community Controlled Health Service, Tharawal Aboriginal Corporation. Over many months they talked about the health problems faced by the area's Indigenous families and about ways to improve the health of Indigenous children in the area. The AHWs were concerned at the difficulties in providing access to culturally appropriate, outreach services to mothers with babies once they had left hospital. They were concerned about the impact of *otitis media*[18] on the health, development and capacity to learn of local Indigenous children. The researchers and AHWs also realized that the origins of *otitis media* needed to be addressed early in life and not as children entered school. We all dreamed of establishing a home visiting service to provide support to Indigenous families with young children.

> An Aboriginal community controlled health service (ACCHS) is a primary health care service initiated by local Indigenous communities to deliver holistic and culturally appropriate care to people within their communities. Indigenous communities around Australia have been establishing such services since the early 1970s in response to a range of barriers limiting access by Indigenous people to mainstream primary health care services and, as an expression of self-determination. There is currently a network of approximately one hundred ACCHS across Australia providing culturally and clinically appropriate health care to Indigenous clients. Board members are elected from the local Indigenous community (National Aboriginal Community Controlled Health Organisation).

It is one thing to talk and dream: it is quite another to turn those dreams into reality. As we spoke to members of the Tharawal Board, local elders, mother with young children and the AHWs it was obvious that there was a great deal of concern that a home visiting program funded by the state government may not be welcome in the community. Many feared it to be a potential vehicle for allowing welfare officers to take their children. This was a major issue with strong historical precedence. To assess the feasibility of the idea researchers from the Centre for Health Equity, Training, Research, and Evaluation (CHETRE), in

---

[18] *Otitis media* is an inflammation of the middle ear.

collaboration with the AHWs, applied to the Ingham Foundation[19] for a small research grant to conduct a feasibility study of a home visiting program. This funding provided the impetus and motivation to start a pilot project – and so locally we spoke of it as 'what the chicken money bought'. In November 2000, a pilot Aboriginal home visiting team was established and the first home visit was made. Fears that families wouldn't welcome team members into their homes were allayed as mothers opened their doors and readily invited in team members. The Aboriginal Home Visiting Service has continued although there have been ongoing problems including organizational issues, inadequate funding, staff vacancies and difficulties in seeing all the mothers.

The Gudaga study

A barrier to extending the Aboriginal Home Visiting Service has been the lack of epidemiological data on the health and health service needs of the area's Indigenous infants. Without this empirical evidence it has been difficult to advocate effectively for services for Indigenous families in the area.

Demographically, the area is unique in a number of ways. The Campbelltown region has, for example, one of the largest Indigenous populations in NSW comprising 3,602 people: 2.4% of the regional population of 150,000 and 5.1% of the state Indigenous population (Sydney South West Area Health Service, 2005). The area's Indigenous population has a number of defining characteristics. It is a relatively young population. In 2001, 47% of the area's Indigenous population was aged less than 15 years compared to 27.0% of the area's population (Sydney South West Area Health Service, 2005). The Indigenous population has a generally lower socioeconomic status than the non-Indigenous population. This is reflected in report of lower household incomes, higher unemployment, higher rates of incomplete schooling, and public housing tenancy than the non-Indigenous population (Sydney South West Area Health Service, 2005). For example, close to four out of ten of the region's Indigenous population live in public housing compared to one in ten of the area's general population (Sydney South West Area Health Service, 2005).

In eastern Australia, there is little information on the health status of Indigenous babies in an urban setting. Research published elsewhere has repeatedly demonstrated poorer health for Indigenous people compared to the general Australian population. This is reflected in a lower life expectancy, a greater burden of disease and a higher hospital separation rate (Australian Bureau of Statistics and Australian Institute of Health and Welfare, 2001; Read, Gibbins, Stanley, Morich, 1994). Compared with non-Indigenous children of the same age, Indigenous children aged less than 12 months have lower birth weights (Australian Institute of Health and Welfare, 2002), slower growth (National Health

---

[19] The Ingham Foundation was established by a local businessman/philanthroper who made his fortune from the commercial sale of frozen chickens. The Foundation supports research activities within region's health services.

Strategy, 1992; Cousham, Gracey, 1997), greater mortality (Alessandri, Chambers, Garfield, Vukovich, Read, 1999), higher hospital admission rates (Read, Gibbins, Stanley, Morich, 1994; Gracey, Gee, 1994) and are more frequently born prematurely (NSW Department of Health, 2002). These differences in health commence prenatally (National Health and Medical Research Council, 2000) and often continue across the lifespan. Adverse social and environmental conditions such as overcrowding, poor hygiene, environmental smoke and parental skills (Leach, Boswell, Asche, Nienhuys, Mathews, 1994; Wigg, Tong, McMichael, Baghurst, Vimpani, Roberts, 1998) are also common. These factors contribute to the exposure of infants to infectious diseases and cross-infection, resulting in the early onset, high prevalence and chronic of *otitis media* among Indigenous children (Boswell, Nienhuys, 1995; Torzillo, Pholeros, 2002; Harris, Kemien, 1990).

It is against this demographic profile that CHETRE based researchers determined to redress the shortfall in data on the health needs of the area's Indigenous children. In collaboration with the local Indigenous community and two Indigenous researchers from the UNSW funding was sought to undertake a birth cohort study of Indigenous children in the Campbelltown area and to follow them for one year. Funding was sourced in 2003. The next two years were spent identifying and engaging the various groups within the local Indigenous community with whom we would work. As will be discussed this was a lengthy process but well worth the time invested. We began the recruitment process in mid October 2005 and finished in early May 2007. We successfully recruited 159 babies from 152 mothers into the project (seven mothers gave birth to two babies within the 18 month recruitment period and both infants were included).

The aims of the Gudaga study are:

1. to establish how well Indigenous infants are identified through health services;
2. to describe the obstetric outcomes and health service use for mothers of Indigenous infants;
3. to describe the health, development and health service use of Indigenous infants aged 0-12 months; and
4. to identify issues participating mothers would like addressed to improve the health and wellbeing of themselves and their families.

These aims are operationalised in three ways. Firstly, we survey all mothers admitted to the maternity ward of Campbelltown Hospital following the birth of their child to identify babies with an Indigenous mother or father. This information will be used to extract routine antenatal data to compare mothers of Indigenous babies with mothers of non-Indigenous babies (Aims 1 and 2). Mothers of Indigenous babies are invited to participate in the study. Secondly, we visit the mothers and their babies at 2-3 weeks, six and twelve months, to complete a number of anthropometric measures (length, head circumference and weight) and a questionnaire on health status and health service use (drawn primarily from the NSW Child Health Survey and the WA Aboriginal Child Health Survey). At 12 months all participating babies are examined by a paediatric registrar (Aim 3). Finally we are documenting the stories of mothers' experiences using available health services (Aim 4). Collecting the stories will provide a qualitative component to the research and capture a richness so often lost in hard numbers.

Grounding the research in the community

Whether the researchers were aware of it or not, the years spent talking and dreaming on Tharawal's veranda built a spirit of equality, respect and reciprocity between themselves and the community's mothers, elders and health workers. It was imperative these values remained in place as we moved through every step of the research process including the building of the research team, identifying the community we would work with and then working with the various groups that make up that community. We continued to stay involved in the community and invest time during the establishment and implementation of the project.

Building the research team

In keeping with the project's ethos it was important the research team include Indigenous academics, with strong research backgrounds and the necessary technical expertise, as well as members of the local community. Unfortunately neither was readily available. In contrast to countries such as New Zealand and Canada there is a shortage of skilled Indigenous health researchers in Australia as has been recognised by, for example, Henderson, Simmons, Bourke, Muir (2002). At the time of instigating this project there were no Indigenous health researchers at UNSW with an interest in public health. Fortunately, during the early days of the establishing the project, two academics joined UNSW and established Muru Marri Indigenous Health Unit and both were invited to join the research team. Neither of these researchers were from the local Indigenous community. They, like the other (non-Indigenous) researchers, had to earn the respect of those with whom we were working. CHETRE's longstanding relationship with the local community helped this process but it was not enough. The Indigenous researchers actively sought to earn the respect in little ways – by travelling long distances to attend community meetings, and by spending time talking with and engaging key Indigenous leaders.

Formalising community input was equally problematic and at times fraught. Even so, a major factor that facilitated this input was the active interest taken by several of the research team in concerns of the community and advocating for services over several years. In addition, considerable time was invested in negotiating and talking with local AHWs and managers encouraging them to become involved in the research. The negotiations were successful and, as will be discussed, Tharawal's CEO, and two of the most senior Indigenous health workers from the local Area Health Service agreed to be part of the research team. The research team is committed to working with each of these health workers to ensure their engagement is ongoing.

Identifying the Gudaga community

A basic premise of the study is that every facet of the research needed to be owned by the Indigenous community. That ownership cannot be an abstract concept. It has to be real. When determining what such involvement would mean in reality we realised we had to ask ourselves a rather basic question: "what is the Indigenous community?" We knew there are many different groups that make up the Indigenous community in south west Sydney and that involving this community would mean identifying and working across a spectrum of organisations and individuals. We also knew we could not assume any of the groups would want to be involved in our work.

We have identified at least four groups from the Indigenous community with whom we work. They include:

1. the Gudaga mothers and their babies;
2. the local Indigenous community of Campbelltown;
3. the local Indigenous healthcare workers; and
4. Indigenous health organisations.

There is also strong Indigenous representation on three other groups that are part of the Gudaga project. These three groups are:

1. project management groups;
2. mainstream academic and health organisations; and
3. other research activities in the region that have similar aims.

The relationship of these seven groups with the Gudaga project is depicted in Figure One below. As the following discussion will demonstrate, different strategies are required to work and maintain contact with each of these groups.

Figure 1shows the extent to which we define 'community'. The term is, obviously, not limited to the geographical boundaries that are the Campbelltown Indigenous community. Rather we have looked to community-based participatory research and defined 'community' broadly as all those who will be affected by the research results which includes lay residents of the local area as well as practitioners, service agencies and policymakers (Green and Mercer, 2001).

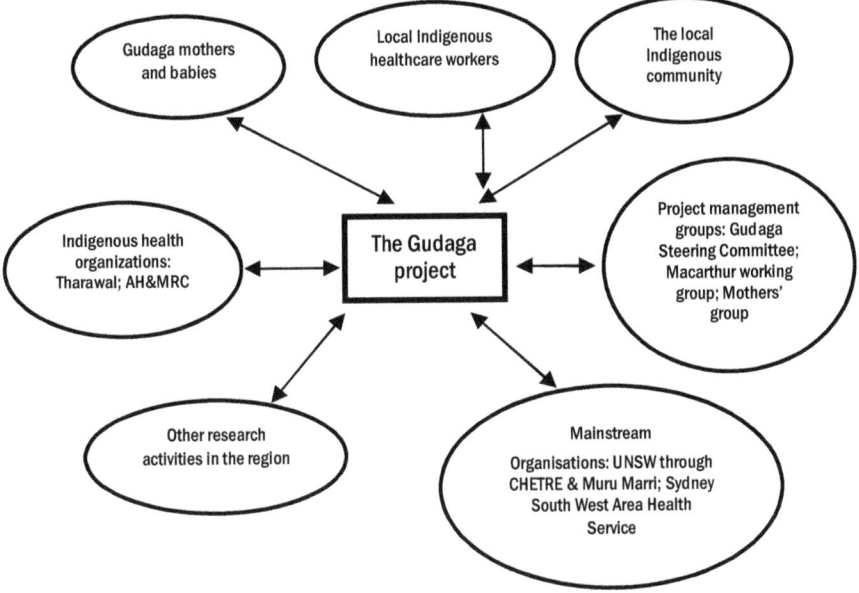

Figure 1: The Gudaga Community.

Working with the Gudaga community

The scope and nature of these seven groups is exceptionally broad. Each requires different strategies for them to be engaged fully in the project. We have spent considerable time and energy identifying innovative strategies to work with each group.

Gudaga mothers and their babies

The Gudaga mothers are the lynchpin of this project. Without them, and their long term commitment to the project, it would be impossible to maintain the cohort over time. Not surprisingly, the women come from a very diverse cross-section of the community. Some of them are young teenagers with their first baby, others are older women who already have three or four children. Some live in extreme poverty while others are financially secure. A few live in refuges and have a different address every time we visit them while others live in very stable and comfortable homes. Some have a history of domestic violence, regular contact with illicit drugs and/or mental health concerns and vulnerable lifestyles.

We have been working with the mothers for almost two years now and over this time we have observed a growing commitment toward the project. This is evident in a number of ways. Quite regularly, mothers who move away make contact and let us know their new contact details or visit the Project Officers when they come back to the area visiting friends and relatives. This initiative of the mothers is ensuring that attrition is minimal. There is also a sense of enthusiasm amongst the mothers. Many appreciate the potential use of the project's results and findings on the future provision of health services. They see themselves as making a positive contribution to the research and take pride in this. Opportunities for the mothers to be actively involved in the study vary. There is, for example, limited opportunity for them to be involved in the actual design of the study as we are using well established instruments that have been validated over time. We anticipate a greater role for the mothers as we move into the data analysis stage. We will actively seek their input as results start to come through. We are planning to present the results to the mothers in a variety of ways: small group meetings, easy to read printed material and large community fora.

Over time our Project Officers are building strong links with the Gudaga mothers. The strength of these links was obvious at, for example, the death of one of the babies. One of the Project Officers had visited the mother and baby just a few weeks before the death and had taken several photos. She went to the funeral and was able to give the photos to the mother – a simple gesture which meant a lot to the family.

The issue of trust is pivotal to Indigenous health research (Pyett, 2002). Some Indigenous researchers have contended trust has been "forever violated" by past research of indigenous communities (McKendrick & Bennett, 2003, p.22). This has not been our experience. We are constantly astounded at the level to which participating mothers will confide in the Project Officers; the level to which they will disclose information over and above that which is sought through the structured survey questions asked of each mother. We originally decided against asking the mothers about their drug taking habits fearing this would be seen as too intrusive and we may not obtain accurate information. During the first few months of conducting the first round of interviews we found many mothers volunteered the information. On the basis of this experience we decided to include some questions on illicit drug use in the interview conducted at six months. Similarly mothers freely talk to the Project Officers of their experiences with domestic violence and financial stress.

We have always been very conscious of the importance of making the project a 'win-win' for not only for the research team, but the mothers as well. Each time we make a home visit we leave a health pack with the mother as a thank you for her time. These packs include small token gifts for both mother and baby as well as information on age appropriate health issues such as SIDS (first home visit), transition to solids and immunisation (six month visit), and dental care (12 month visit). The packs also include a small contact telephone directory fridge magnet we have designed which includes local phone numbers of frequently used health services as well as a photo of the baby. The Project Officer takes a photo of the baby at each home visit and it is given to the mother at the following visit. The photos are always well received as both the mothers and the research team delight in watching the babies grow and develop.

Many of the small gifts included in the health packs have been specifically designed to engender a sense of involvement in the project. At six months all babies receive a screen printed "I'm a Gudaga baby" t-shirt and at 12 months we give the babies a sunhat with the same wording. At this time the mothers receive a Gudaga coffee mug.

The local Indigenous community

A strength of cohort study design is the ability to promote the research within the Indigenous community. We have put in place a number of strategies to encourage visibility of the project. These include the choice of local Indigenous mothers to work on the project, opportunities to join a 'mothers' group' that is kept informed about the project, and the use of a project name and logo that are recognizable within the community.

We considered it imperative that the Project Officer positions be filled by local Indigenous mothers. We have employed two Project Officers. Both have young children and are very well known within the community. We are certain their strong links to the community are making a significant contribution to the success of the project. The recruitment of the project officers placed a high priority on Indigeniety, being a mother and being part of the local Indigenous community. Strong research experience was not considered essential. We have trained each project officer in a number of specific areas including interviewing techniques, conflict resolution, the importance for confidentiality, communication skills, and data management to assist them in their work. We have a capacity building program in place to build their project skills.

The project's name is 'Gudaga' which means 'healthy baby'. The name, suggested by local AHWs, comes from the local Tharawal language. Once we had a name we were keen to have a logo designed for us. Finding someone proficient in Indigenous art and logo design wasn't easy but we eventually found a young man who put together some art work for us. When we showed his work to a group of mothers they immediately asked if the work had been designed by a woman. For these women, it was imperative any artwork concerning mothers and babies be designed by a woman. The search continued. After a number of weeks our Project Officer finally found a local Indigenous mum who created a wonderful logo featuring Indigenous art that is rich in maternal/child symbolism (figure 2). This time the mothers were delighted with her work and endorsed it as the project logo.

Figure 2: The 'Gudaga' project logo.

We were particularly keen to incorporate Indigenous art into the project. The idea is in keeping with our attempts to work with the community. But it is much more than that. For us, the inclusion of Indigenous art is recognition of the cultural distinctiveness of Indigenous peoples and their right to enjoy that distinctiveness (National Health and Medical Research Council, 2006).

The logo is used extensively throughout the project. It is, for example, featured on all promotional material including posters and brochures that inform the community of the project. The posters are prominently displayed at the local hospital and Tharawal and brochures are distributed at the offices of local general practitioners, Tharawal, and given out by members of the Aboriginal Home Visiting Service. The logo is also featured on the shirts worn by staff and the gifts we give the mothers and babies. We anticipate measures such as these will engender a sense of project ownership within the community. The Gudaga mothers in particular already identify strongly with the logo and have pride in it and the project it symbolizes.

Local Indigenous healthcare professionals

Within the region there are a number of Indigenous healthcare professionals who are responsible for the health and welfare of Indigenous babies and their families. Some are employed by Tharawal while others work for the local area health service, either in Aboriginal Health or as part of the Aboriginal Home Visiting Service. We have attempted to involve these healthcare professionals in the project on a regular basis. All the healthcare professionals receive the project's monthly newsletter and a number are members of the Macarthur Working Group which meets monthly.

Our experience is that multiple communication strategies are needed to ensure Indigenous healthcare professionals, in particular, are aware of and understand what the project is doing and the implications of various constraints on what the project can and cannot do. Early on in the life of the project we found ourselves repeatedly reminding the local Indigenous healthcare professionals of what we could and could not do. There were times when possible misunderstandings could have arisen as they attempted to understand that the project was not able to actively support and promote their work, nor could we provide them with the names of participating mothers. We spent a lot of time working with the healthcare workers, explaining why we couldn't undertake specific requests. Open communication and time resulted in a resolution of the issue and it has not been problem as the project has progressed.

Another issue related to the non-interventionist nature of the project, and coming to understand what this actually meant. As the project seeks to describe use of health care, we cannot actively intervene in the provision of health care for the project's mothers and babies. There have been times when the project officers have been asked questions of a medical nature during home visits. The project officers don't answer questions of this nature. There are several reasons for this strategy. Neither of the project officers are medically trained and are not in a position to provide any advice. Even if the project officers were healthcare professionals it is outside the scope of this style of study for them to provide advice. Our strategy is to refer the mother to Tharawal Medical Service or the Aboriginal home visiting team and for the mother to work with other Indigenous healthcare workers to obtain the care needed.

Indigenous health organisations

Formal contact with Indigenous health organisations early in the research design process is recommended both internationally (World Health Organisation) and nationally (National Health and Medical Research Council, 2002; National Health and Medical Research Council, 2006). For us, this has meant engaging and working with two Indigenous health organisations.

For consultation on health matters affecting Indigenous peoples, representative bodies in Australia have established that the primary point of contact should be the local Aboriginal Community Controlled Health Service (ACCHS) (National Aboriginal and Islander Health Organisation, 1989). Our local ACCHS is Tharawal Aboriginal Corporation which includes the local Aboriginal Health Service. It is, of course, a focal point of the area's local Indigenous community. It has a high profile within the community and its involvement in Gudaga is fundamental to the project's success.

From the outset the staff at Tharawal has played a key role in the project. The Corporation's CEO is an associate investigator to the project. The project's monthly bulletins are tabled at each Board meeting and members of the research team meet with the Board on a semi-regular basis to keep them informed of the project's progress. Wherever possible, project staff attend events hosted by Tharawal.

The second Indigenous health organisation we work with is the Aboriginal Health and Medical Research Council. This involvement is in line with all Australian based research projects working with Indigenous communities. Ethics approval was sought from the Council at the very outset of the project and we adhere strictly to the Council's annual reporting requirements.

Project management groups

Three groups have been established to assist in managing the project. These include a steering committee, a working group as well as a grassroots group made up of mothers and grandmothers from the local community.

The mothers' group meets on an *ad hoc* basis at Tharawal. It is a very informal gathering of mothers involved in the project as well as older women who have an interest in the work we are doing. We provide a light lunch for the mothers and spend time chatting casually with them about the project: the sorts of things we are noticing, any difficulties we are experiencing in accessing and retaining mothers. While the idea of such a group sounds helpful the group has, unfortunately, somewhat of a chequered history. We have had difficulty organising it to meet regularly as well as enthusing sufficient numbers of mothers to be actively involved. We remain committed to this idea for we consider this group to be very important. We are looking for ways to generate enthusiasm for the idea and plan to try combining our meeting time around opportunities for the women to interact and socialise as a group with the project providing tea/coffee and biscuits or a light lunch for all those attending. As the findings begin to emerge we want to discuss them first with the mothers and to listen to their thoughts and ideas of the implications of the findings for themselves, the broader Indigenous community and the provision of health services.

In addition to the mothers' group two committees have been established to provide direction and advice to the project: the Gudaga steering committee (made up of the project's chief and associate investigators) and the Macarthur working group (made up of local healthcare professionals directly involved in the project such as the hospital's maternity ward director of nursing, members of the Aboriginal home visiting team and the paediatrician conducting the developmental assessments). These two provide the best opportunity for local Indigenous healthcare professionals to be actively involved in the project. We have ensured all relevant Indigenous healthcare professionals in the region are on one or other of these committees. These committees also give them an opportunity to meet together to discuss the research and issues of common concern.

The Gudaga steering committee, made up of the study's chief and associate investigators, meets quarterly. The academic researchers are joined by the providers of Indigenous health services from the local area health service. This group gives overall direction, advice and support to the project. The steering committee meets at Tharawal and is chaired by Tharawal's CEO.

The Macarthur working group meets monthly. This group provides a venue for information exchange about various activities in the region of relevance to the Gudaga project. The group comprises a number of relevant Indigenous healthcare professionals including representatives from the Aboriginal Home Visiting Service, Tharawal, maternity ward staff and a hospital paediatrician. It is very operational in terms of the issues it considers and advice it provides.

Other research activities in the region

When the planning for this project began ten years ago there was little, if any Indigenous child health research activity in the region. Fortunately this is no longer the case and there are now two other research projects underway in the region. The Safe Koori Kids project is a three year project run by The George Institute and Yooroang Garang: School of Health Studies at the University of Sydney. It aims to develop a school, family and community based intervention around Indigenous child safety (The George Institute, 2005). A second project is statewide in nature though will recruit some participants through Tharawal. The Study of Environment of Aboriginal Resilience and Child Health (SEARCH) is based at the Sax Institute and plans to follow approximately 2000 urban Indigenous children from 800 families across NSW to explore the determinants of health and to trial strategies to improve health outcomes (The Sax Institute, 2006).

The Western Australia Child Health Study (Zubrick, Lawrence, Silburn, Blair, Milroy, Wilkes, Eades, D'Antoine, Read, Ishiguchi, Doyle, 2004) and the National Longitudinal Study of Indigenous Children (Penman, 2006) are two additional studies which, though not locally based, inform our research.

We are developing strategies to interact with these projects and have ongoing plans to share our experiences and study findings.

Mainstream organisations

Finally, we work with two organisations: one academic in focus, the other health. The project's academic base is UNSW which includes CHETRE and the Muru Marri Indigenous Health Unit. CHETRE, which is part of the University's Centre for Primary Health Care and Equity, is a research and evaluation centre located in south west Sydney with a focus on disadvantaged communities. As has been discussed, CHETRE researchers have a long association with local AHWs and Tharawal staff and have long advocated for better health services for the area's Indigenous families. As the project's auspicing body CHETRE is Gudaga's 'home'.

The project has also drawn upon Muru Marri's professional staff with two of the Unit's members working as chief investigators on the project. They bring to the project, not only the professional rigour expected of academic staff, but Indigenous heritage and culture which adds authenticity and credibility to the project.

Our local area health service (Sydney South West Area Health Service) has been exceptional in the support it has provided the project: office space at Campbelltown hospital, the use of a car for the home visits and access to the paediatricians for the 12 month health and development assessments. Without this 'in kind' support the project would struggle financially.

The take home lessons

The Gudaga project has begun well. We finished recruiting in April 2007 with 159 babies in the cohort, attrition has been minimal and the mothers are keen to participate. There is a strong sense of ownership of the project amongst the Gudaga mothers as well as within the local Indigenous community and considerable interest from academics and Indigenous health researchers further afield.

There are at least two take home lessons from the Gudaga project. Both are relevant to community based indigenous health research. The first relates to time. CHETRE first became involved in the Indigenous community of south west Sydney in 1997. The first results from Gudaga will start coming through in 2007 – ten years later. The ten years has been spent developing and nurturing respect, trust and reciprocity. The past decade has enabled the non-indigenous researchers to demonstrate to the local Indigenous community that they are prepared to make a commitment over a long period and they are not 'fly-by-nighters': that they will advocate for the local Indigenous community; work with the community's agenda (rather than a pre-determined research agenda); and, if necessary, stand up to the bureaucracy on their behalf.

The second lesson relates to the values that underpin and sustain the project: trust, respect, reciprocity, a commitment to open communication and staying connected. None of these concepts are new. They lie "at the heart" (National Health and Medical Research Council, 2006, p.8) of two key Australian based documents produced by the country's peak research body, the NHMRC: *Strategic framework for improving Aboriginal and Torres Strait Islander health through research* (National Health and Medical Research Council, 2002), known as *The Road Map*; and *Values and Ethics: Guidelines for Ethical Conduct in Aboriginal and Torres Strait Islander Health Research* (National Health and Medical Research Council, 2006). These two documents are foundational to those working in the area of Indigenous health research. Gudaga is demonstrating, in a very practical way, what it means to translate the values espoused in these documents into day to day reality.

In working with these values there is a tension with which we must attempt to reconcile regularly. We balance the need for robust descriptive, non-interventionist research of health issues with the ideals of action research including the timely feedback of findings. We are not prepared to compromise the scientific integrity of the study.

What began as a yarn on the veranda almost ten years ago has led to an environment of mutual trust and respect which in turn has led to a ready acceptance of the Gudaga project by the Indigenous community. But none of this can be taken for granted. The project needs to continue to involve every facet of the Indigenous community. The strategies identified and employed are essential to maintain trust and respect. The project remains committed to long term sustainability, the ongoing need for open communication, staying connected with all our stakeholders and feeding results back to the local Indigenous community in ways that are accessible and appropriate. This is the challenge that lies ahead for all of us involved in Gudaga as we work to ensure all infants within the Indigenous community of south west Sydney are indeed, healthy babies.

Acknowledgement

The Gudaga project wishes to acknowledge the Darug and Tharawal people of south west Sydney. Without the cooperation and enthusiasm of these traditional land owners this research project would not be possible. The authors also wish to acknowledge the input of the Gudaga research team including Prof Mark Harris, Prof Richard Henry and Dr Lynn Kemp. We would also like to acknowledge the support Gudaga receives from our local Area Health Service, Sydney South West Area Health Service. The study was funded by the National Health and Medical Research Council.

References

Alessandri, L.M., Chambers, H.M., Garfield, C., Vukovich, S., Read, A.W., (1999). Cumulative Mortality in children aged 1 to 6 years born in Western Australia from 1980-89. Archives of Diseases of Childhood, 80,15-20.

Australian Bureau of Statistics and Australian Institute of Health and Welfare (2001). The health and welfare of Australia's Aboriginal and Torres Strait Islander peoples. Canberra: Australian Bureau of Statistics.

Australian Institute of Health and Welfare (2002). Australia's Health 2002. Canberra: Australian Institute of Health and Welfare.

Boswell, J., & Nienhuys, T. (1995). Onset of otitis media in the first eight weeks of life in Aboriginal and non-Aboriginal infants. Ann Oto Rhin Laryngol, 104, 542-9.

Cousham, E.K. & Gracey, M. (1997). Persistent growth faltering among Aboriginal infants and young children in north-west Australia: a retrospective study from 1969 to 1993. Acta Paediatrica, 86, 26-50.

Green, L.W. & Mercer, S.L. (2001). Can public health researchers and agencies reconcile the push from funding bodies and the pull from communities? American Journal of Public Health, 91, 1926-1929.

Harris, M.F. & Kamien, M. (1990). Change in Aboriginal childhood morbidity and mortality in Bourke 1971-84. Journal of Paediatrics & Child Health, 26, 80-4. Henderson, R., Simmons, D.S., Bourke, L., Muir, J. (2002). Development of guidelines for non-Indigenous people undertaking research among the Indigenous population of north-east Victoria. Medical Journal of Australia, 176, 482-5.

Gracey, M., Gee, V. (1994). Hospitalization of infants for infections in Western Australia, 1980-91. Journal of Paediatrics and Child Health, 30, 502-5.

Leach, A.J., Boswell, J.B., Asche, V., Nienhuys, T.G., Mathews, J.D. (1994). Bacterial colonization of the nasopharynx predicts very early onset and persistence of otitis media in Australian Aboriginal infants. Paediatric Infectious Diseases Journal, 13, 983-9.

McKendrick, J., Bennett, P.A. (2003). The ethics of health research and Indigenous peoples. Monash Bioethics Review, 22, 20-5.

National Aboriginal Community Controlled Health Organisation website (undated). www.atns.net.au/agreement.asp?EntityID=1792. Accessed 23 July 2007.

National Aboriginal and Islander Health Organisation (1991). Report of the national workshop on ethics of research in Aboriginal health, Camden, NSW, 29 July 1989, in NHMRC Guidelines on Ethical Matters in Aboriginal and Torres Strait Islander Health Research. Canberra: Commonwealth of Australia.

National Health and Medical Research Council (2002). Nutrition in Aboriginal and Torres Strait Islander Peoples. Canberra: National Health and Medical Research Council.

National Health and Medical Research Council (2002). The NHMRC Roadmap. A strategic framework for improving Aboriginal and Torres Strait Islander health through research. Canberra: Commonwealth of Australia.

National Health and Medical Research Council (2006). Values and Ethics: guidelines for ethical conduct in Aboriginal and Torres Strait Islander health research. Canberra: Commonwealth of Australia.

National Health Strategy (1992). Enough to make you sick: How income and environment affect health. Canberra: National Health Strategy.

NSW Department of Health (2002). The Health of the people of NSW: Report of the Chief Health Officer. Sydney: NSW Department of Health.

Penman, R. (2006). The "growing up" of Aboriginal and Torres Strait Islander children: a literature review. Occasional Paper No 15. Department of Families, Community Services and Indigenous Affairs. Canberra: Australian Government.

Pyett, P. (2002). Working together to reduce health inequalities: reflections on a collaborative participatory approach to health research. Australian and New Zealand Journal of Public Health, 26, 332-6.

Read, A.W., Gibbins, J., Stanley, F.J., Morich, P.(1994). Hospital admissions before the age of 2 years in Western Australia. Archives of Dis Childhood, 70, 205-10.

Sydney South West Area Health Service (2005). A health profile of Sydney South West: a status report describing the population, their health and the services provided for Sydney South West Area Health Service. Sydney: NSW Health.

The George Institute (2005). Safe Koori Kids promotional brochure. University of Sydney: Yooroang Garang: School of Health Studies.

The Sax Institute (2006). Available at www.saxinstitute.org.au/researchassetsprograms/ImprovingAboriginalHealththroughResearch/SEARCH.cfm?objid=410 (accessed 22 December 2006).

Torzillo, P.J., Pholeros, P. (2002). Household infrastructure in Aboriginal communities and the implications for health improvement. Medical Journal of Australia, 176, 502-3.

Wigg, N.R., Tong, S., McMichael, A.J., Baghurst, P.A., Vimpani, G., Roberts, R. (1998). Does breastfeeding at six months predict cognitive development? Australian & New Zealand Journal of Public Health, 22, 232-6.

World Health Organization. Indigenous peoples and participatory health research. Available at www.who.int/ethics/indigenous_peoples/en/index7.html (accessed 22 December 2006).

Zubrick, S.R., Lawrence, D.M., Silburn, S.R., Blair, E., Milroy, H., Wilkes, T., Eades, S., D'Antoine, H., Read, A., Ishiguchi, P., Doyle, S. (2004). The Western Australian Aboriginal child health survey: the health of Aboriginal children and young people. Perth: Telethon Institute for Child Research.

NGO-University partnerships: Practicing what we preach

Claudette Legault and Madine VanderPlaat

> This chapter explores the successes, challenges and tensions emerging from a pan-Canadian community-university-government partnership created to produce policy relevant research on immigration, integration and diversity. Specifically, the authors examined the extent to which the promise of equal partnership and a collaborative research ethic can ever truly be achieved in research relationships driven by an academic paradigm.
>
> The Metropolis Project is an international forum for comparative research and public policy development about population migration, cultural diversity and the challenges of immigrant integration in Canada and around the world. Committed to on-going assessment of its activities and events to ensure that the project constantly improves and is of maximum utility to its partners, the Canadian Metropolis Project commissioned a study in March 2004 to systematically elicit community partner feedback on the sector's engagement in the Project to date and identify successes, challenges and areas which require further discussion.
>
> The main conclusion reached is that most of the challenges experienced by the NGO community relate to the lack of structural support and the intercultural aspects of working with two distinctly different organizational cultures. The examples highlight the differences in ways of working, thinking, organizing and communicating and the impacts these have for successful partnership and collaboration.

The Metropolis Project is an academic research forum engaged in comparative research and public policy development about population migration, cultural diversity and the challenges of immigrant integration in Canada and around the world. In Canada, the Metropolis Project is built upon partnerships between all levels of government, academic researchers and community organizations in five university-based Centres of Excellence.

This chapter explores the successes, challenges and tensions emerging from this pan-Canadian community-university-government initiative. Specifically, the authors, one of whom is located in the NGO sector and the other in academia, examine the extent to which the promise of equal partnership and a collaborative research ethic can ever truly be achieved in research relationships driven by an academic paradigm.

The Metropolis Project is reflective of a more general trend toward intersectoral collaborations. Decreases in government spending, decentralization policies and an increased demand for citizen participation have necessitated the emergence of strategic alliances across the sectors (Walsh and Annis, 2003). Likewise, a growing demand for the applied relevance of academic research, evidence based service delivery and community capacity to maximize scarce resources has resulted in a proliferation of networks and communities of practice (Provan and Milward, 2001; Wenger, 1998; Wenger et al., 2002.) The challenges presented by these prevailing organizational models are being increasingly identified and documented (Cox, 2000; Rubin, 2000; Levesque and Chopyak, 2001; Suarez-Balcazar, et al., 2005). Competing normative discourses, conflicting interests, and power imbalances, all contribute to the dynamic tension emerging from such collaborations (Baum, 2000; Eccles, 1996). The Metropolis Project both exemplifies some of the tensions already identified in the literature and introduces new complexities.

The chapter begins with a brief history of the Metropolis Project and sets the context within which NGO-government-university interactions take place. The second section outlines the issues that emerged from an NGO Scan designed to measure NGO satisfaction with the Metropolis Project along with the response from academia and possible solutions.

Background

The Metropolis Project in Canada was initiated in 1996 in response to increased local and global challenges emerging from the migration, settlement and integration of ethnic and religious minorities in cities around the world. The Metropolis Project seeks to increase the amount of academic research done in the fields of immigration and diversity; to create opportunities for significant interchange among decision-makers, researchers and NGOs; to encourage discussions that go well beyond the mere stating of positions, descriptions, and advocacy; and to provide settings for problem solving using the best information and analysis. The commitment to intersectoral collaboration comes from the recognition that successful migration and integration policies require input from and knowledge transfer between all sectors.

The Project is funded by a consortium of federal government departments and agencies and monies are administered through the Social Science and Humanities Research Council of Canada (an academic granting agency and one of the primary funders). Activities are coordinated through five Centres of Excellence across the country each of which may receive additional funding from their partner universities. At each Centre research is conducted through thematic 'domains' led by university based researchers and intended to reflect the interests of all sectors. A Metropolis Secretariat coordinates Centre activities at the national level and serves as a liaison between the Centres and federal government Departments.

In their commitment to on-going assessment of its activities and events to ensure that the project constantly improves and provides the maximum utility to its partners, the Metropolis Secretariat commissioned a study in March 2004 to systematically consult the NGO partners on their involvement in the project. Through a national survey, four focus groups, and a conference workshop, the researchers sought to elicit community partner feedback on the sector's engagement in the Metropolis Project to date and identify successes, challenges and areas which require further discussion. In each case the number of respondents was relatively small and they are in no way representative of the total NGO sector or even that portion that does have or has had a working relationship with the Metropolis Project. However, consistently the same themes emerged across the country indicating that concerns and issues were not Centre specific but more germane to the project as a whole.

NGO partners did identify a number of achievements and successes resulting from their collaboration. In particular, the Metropolis initiative is seen by NGO representatives as having made a significant contribution to the field of immigration by increasing the knowledge available to policy makers and the public regarding immigrant issues. This increased research attention is bringing a greater focus and respect to the immigration field, which ultimately benefits and supports the work of the NGO community. The enhanced networks created by Metropolis bring new people into contact with immigrant settlement agencies, ensuring a broader presentation of relevant issues. Metropolis is seen to have made good attempts to ensure appropriate input and involvement of NGO partners across Canada. However, the NGO community also presented a number of thoughtful critiques and significant challenges. This latter response is the focus of our discussions in the following sections.

Issues

Most of the challenges experienced by the NGO community relate to aspects of working with two distinctly different organizational cultures, namely the academic and government cultures. The tensions identified below highlight the differences in ways of working, thinking, organizing and communicating. These differences often have not been addressed overtly within the initiative, or in any systematic manner thereby limiting the extent to which they are understood, shared and considered when planning and interacting within the Metropolis context.

In general, tensions emerge from and revolve around three primary areas – the partnership/collaboration process; the nature and purpose of research; and, academic privilege. We discuss these below in order of their perceived complexity and the extent to which we feel they can be resolved. In each area we first present the critiques derived from the NGO data followed by our response to the issues raised.

Partnership/Collaborative Process: Critique

One of the main challenges for any collaborative relationship is ensuring that the collaboration is indeed genuine. The Metropolis NGO partners pointed to a number of areas where they felt they were being treated as less than equal partners. The first of these is in the actual governance of the Project. While each Centre ensures NGO representation throughout their committee structure there are limited venues to engage in meaningful dialogue. Committee meetings are perceived by the NGO community as sign-off opportunities rather than opportunities for dialogue and increasing understanding between stakeholders. This limits the involvement of community partners who are accustomed to more participatory processes. In addition, national Metropolis conferences are often designed to accommodate academic interests, creating a forum within which scholars can receive academic credit for the papers presented (see discussion on academic privilege below). The workshop agendas at the conferences are set by academic researchers, and while the NGO sector participates, their capacity for organizing and creating workshops is limited, thus undermining their ability to help construct a conference agenda more reflective of their own interests. Because of this there is little opportunity for NGO driven research to be included in the conferences. Likewise, the annual regional/local consultations (retreats) sponsored by Metropolis were perceived with great enthusiasm when they were initiated but are now seen as academic mini-conferences where individual academics present their research. There is little exchange or dialogue about the research findings and their applicability to service delivery. This is immensely frustrating for people from community agencies who are unaccustomed to this approach and feel thwarted by the academic, peer-review, 'power point'-only approach to conferencing.

The NGO sector also expressed frustration with the inability of the Metropolis Centres to be genuinely and consistently collaborative in their research efforts. While recognizing that Metropolis was not intended to help the NGO sector directly in service provision to the immigrant population the sector feels not enough attention has been given to the role of NGOs in the research process, resulting in an ad hoc approach to their involvement. At best, they are partners with academic researchers based on previous relationships of respect established with individual researchers. (Although there is concern that the informal relationship that had previously existed between the academic and NGO communities is becoming increasingly formalized under Metropolis, consequently further limiting community involvement in the research process.) At worse, the NGO community feels it is seen and treated as a conduit to harvest immigrant participants for interviews and focus groups.

In terms of their overall participation, the NGO sector does readily acknowledge that their ability to participate actively in Metropolis as strong partners is constrained by their lack of resources and the limited budget lines dedicated to research allowed by their funders. It was also noted that some NGOs can participate more fully than others because they are larger and better funded. These differentials are not well recognized by the Centres and not taken into consideration in terms of representation and access to funding.

Finally, there was some consternation among the NGO partners regarding the lack of appropriate recognition for those NGOs involved in research projects. It is perceived by the community agency representatives that the primary objective of Metropolis is to strengthen the quality of academic research through involvement of community organizations. However, stories are told of agency people who are fully involved in a research project as co-researchers only to find the agency's name mentioned in the acknowledgements section of the final report, rather than listed as a co-researcher. Likewise, there have been instances where the NGO partners are not acknowledged as rightful co-authors of conference presentations. This raises the issues of ownership of research findings and integrity of research data as it is presented in a variety of fora by the academic researcher. It is difficult to monitor if research is being appropriated as the research is ultimately 'owned' by the academic researcher. Without due recognition as co-producers of the research, the level of professionalism inherent in the NGO sector is unacknowledged.

Partnership/Collaborative Process: Response

In terms of the limited NGO participation in the governance and day-to-day decision making of the Centres the criticism is legitimate because the Directors and lead researchers are all university based and receive compensation/incentives for their involvement with Metropolis. Hence, they are expected to spend their time on Metropolis related activities. For many NGO partners Metropolis is an add-on to their existing workload which, as many domain leaders have noted, makes it difficult to participate on the domain committees where most of the research/conferencing decision making takes place. Ensuring meaningful participation of NGOs will require broadening the current mandates of settlement organizations to include a research/collaboration role. In Canada it should be possible to negotiate this as a legitimate activity within some NGO contracts, especially with the funding partners of the Metropolis initiative who are also the principle funders of the settlement organizations. Without this type of structural support the NGO sector is unlikely to be able to participate at the same level as the academic and government sectors.

The lack of adequate discussion time at conferences, workshops and retreats has plagued the Metropolis Project since its inception. Part of the problem is the need to provide a venue within which to accommodate the perspectives of the various partners and stakeholders and to ensure sectoral, institutional and jurisdictional representation. For example, in Atlantic Canada the AMC covers four provinces, three levels of government, and multiple universities. It is also true that the conferences and retreats tend to be dominated by academic interests. Part of the reason for this is discussed below under academic privilege. However, the issue is exacerbated by the fact that Centres and universities will not usually provide travel funds unless the applicant is presenting a paper or organizing a workshop. Again, because it is an integral part of their employment and reward system university-based researchers are much more likely to do so. A reframing of the 'dissemination paradigm' to include the NGO sector's interest in more discussion of implementation strategies is required. This could lead to the creation of other fora or possible expansion of traditional academic based conferences to include pre or post conferences focussed on exploring implications and action components of the research. If this consideration was a criteria of initial requests for funding then financial considerations would not be an issue.

The issue of meaningful research collaboration is a complex one and revolves around the utility and efficacy of establishing formal protocols. Without a formalized process community groups run the risk of potential exploitation, lack of meaningful participation and an increased burden of demand. However, adherence to protocols can also be time consuming and, at times, in conflict with academic deadlines. As a number of Centres have found, the creation of formal protocols can also stifle previously healthy and vibrant collaborations between university based researchers and the NGO sector. For example, at the Atlantic Metropolis Centre an initial attempt to develop protocols was put on hold when the process recommended by the community partners was perceived to be too cumbersome by the academic researchers and threatened to undermine, rather than enhance, the commitment to collaborative research. Equitable consideration for community, agency and academic processes at the outset of a collaboration is a must if difficulties are to be avoided. Respect for individual partner differences and limitations as well as building in sufficient flexibility in timelines, where possible, can strengthen the chances of a successful collaboration which meets each partner's needs. The challenge is to develop protocols that respect and reflect the interests of all parties without being overly prescriptive or alternatively, so vague they are meaningless.

Finally, issues of authorship and ownership are not uncommon in collaborative relationships. The problem usually occurs when data collected by all partners is presented in an article or conference paper authored by a single partner and embedded in a theoretical framework that may not have been part of the original research project. Likewise, individuals who put the work into crafting a paper may feel reluctant to assign authorship to individuals who did not contribute to the writing process. In one of the author's experience, an effective rule of thumb was for the team to agree that the first article published would bear the names of everyone who participated but that subsequent papers would only carry the names of those who contributed to the writing process in some manner AND who were willing to assume responsibility for its content. Protocols pertaining to authorship and ownership should be established at the outset of any collaborative endeavour.

Nature and Purpose of Research: Critique

Tensions also exist as to the focus, content and use of the research conducted through the Metropolis Centres. The academic researchers involved with Metropolis are perceived by the NGO sector to be driven by the need to publish. When this demand is satisfied their engagement with members of the community can end. NGO organizations, on the other hand, continue to work with the community being studied. If the research process has stepped on toes, or has been perceived as disrespectful in any way to the community, it is the NGOs credibility that is questioned, as they have an ongoing interest in the community and a well developed relationship to maintain. Sometimes there are promises made through the research process that are subsequently unrealized and the NGO is perceived as the betrayer of trust, having enabled access to the community only to have the academic researcher move away and onto the next research project leaving the NGO to implement the research findings. Creating a sustainable and respectful relationship with the community and potential research participants is a shared responsibility, particularly in smaller jurisdictions. Accountability and compliance with protocols must be formalized and reflected in the collective practice of the partners.

The NGO representatives also questioned the relevance of the research being conducted through Metropolis. Broad research priorities are established by the federal funders. Specific projects are decided by individual university-based researchers and NGOs are then invited to offer feedback or input about the chosen research projects, making their involvement reactive not proactive. There is no mechanism within the NGO sector to identify or convey research themes to Metropolis, ensuring the topics are relevant and applicable for their purposes. Because of this, NGOs often do not feel they benefit directly from the research, and that the research themes have little direct relevance to practice or service delivery. Community agencies also feel that the research topics chosen are too government focused and reinforce current government policy concerns and security issues such as 9/11 whereas NGO groups are more interested in studying issues relating to service delivery and social integration.

NGO representatives also expressed concern with existing knowledge translation practices. There is a sense that there is an inadequate focus on getting the research results out to the community and that this activity is often left until the last minute when funds are already spent, leaving little resources for dissemination. There is often no appropriate dissemination strategy obvious to community agencies and there appears to be little conversation about the practical benefit of research or how it could be applied.. From the NGO perspective academic knowledge dissemination seems to be equated with the presentation of a paper at a conference. For the NGO dissemination means bringing the research findings back to the community with the intention of considering the practical implications. NGOs have knowledge and experience to be able to assist with diffusion but no funds or time to assume responsibility for the process. In addition, from the NGO perspective, the research themes appear to lack a coherent framework. There is no mechanism for coordinating the research focus to link individual research projects. The NGO community considers it important to knit the research themes together, ensuring a greater impact on policy and programming.

Nature and Purpose of Research: Response

The issue of a researcher withdrawing from a community is an ethical dilemma well recognized among researchers especially those who operate within a critical/feminist framework. It is important that expectations/obligations are discussed early on in the research process. The question of respect is one of academic integrity and one would hope not a recurring problem. However, what does on occasion occur is disagreement between the researchers and community members as to how the data is analyzed and/or theorized. What happens when the data disseminated presents the community in a negative light? The problem is not easily addressed. At minimum we feel the nature of the disagreement should be acknowledged in publications and conference papers. Another possible solution is for researchers to ensure that submissions for publication include a community rebuttal.

The problem of research relevance is in part due to the funding structure – major funders do set the federal priorities for how internal research funds should be used. Researchers are free to obtain outside funding but ultimately the success of the Metropolis Project itself, and its continued viability is determined by the extent to which research is being produced in the priority areas and the extent to which the knowledge needs of the primary funders are met. It is also true that service delivery is not an interest area for many academics associated with the Metropolis Project, nor is it the primary objective of the initiative. There is a growing although somewhat reluctant acceptance by many NGOs that research will inevitably be linked in large part to individual "academic researcher" interests. However this is also accompanied by a realization that some of the responsibility and the impetus to identify relevant research themes and present viable research projects lies with the NGO sector. As NGOs mature and gain internal expertise more NGO generated research will likely follow. Graduate students who do not yet have a particular focus for their research are also seen as potential sources for collaboration.

The problem of knowledge translation is not restricted to the Metropolis Project and is a major concern throughout the public and private sector. There is a general agreement that the presentation of academic papers at conferences and the publishing of articles is no longer seen as adequate, especially if the research project includes government and NGO partners or collaborators. Even the language is in a state of flux in the struggle to define the difference between 'knowledge dissemination', 'knowledge translation' and 'knowledge mobilization' and how best to put these concepts into practice (Landry, Amara and Lamari, 2001; Schryer-Roy, 2005). Just recently the major academic funders, in particular SSHRC, have allocated funds specifically for knowledge mobilization purposes. Involvement of the NGO sector in this debate will help broaden the concept of knowledge transfer and applicability.

Privileging of Academic Culture: Critique

Community organizations are familiar with and adept at using a participatory action research model in their own research initiatives. Community groups contend that the prevailing research methodology within Metropolis excludes participatory action research methods and the inherent inclusion and respect of community groups as equal partners in the research methodology. In addition, academic schedules and priorities prevail when determining research project timelines. Limitations imposed by the formal academic review process, required by all Canadian universities, also potentially limits community engagement by forcing a timeline that ignores the realities of the NGO sector.

Representatives of the community agencies also contend that Metropolis related research is driven by academic researcher interests and tenure/promotion criteria. The pressure on academics to publish produces research that is not immediately relevant to the community and forces attention on individual research priorities rather than a focus on local solutions and needs. It is understood by the NGO community that it is not in the best interests of an individual academic to be seen as a community researcher. There are no additional career points to be gained by doing community based research, in fact the general perception is that this type of commitment to community interests may be a career-limiting move for an individual academic. The NGOs would prefer research that continues to live in programming choices, but recognize that academics are often forced to pursue their own individual career interests.

The community representatives also felt that not enough attention is paid to the expertise and knowledge existing in the NGO sector. There is a great deal of respect within the NGO community for academic rigor and an appreciation that the knowledge generated must be based on 'good science'. However, there is also a great deal of knowledge and expertise within the NGO sector that serves the immigrant population and it is felt that this expertise is not well recognized, appreciated or used in the development of research questions. Community-based action research that is conducted without an academic researcher's involvement is perceived not to be rigorous enough. Likewise, academic researchers typically seek direct involvement with recent immigrants, but are less likely to view NGO staff as valid data sources. This perception is aggravated by funding agencies such as SSHRC which limit the eligibility criteria for principal investigators.

Privileging of Academic Culture: Response

It is true that the Metropolis Project privileges the academic research paradigm. However, the paradigm does not, by definition, exclude participatory action research nor is participatory action research necessarily always the best approach to a research problem. The tension here is between an individual scholar's area of expertise and right to work within her/his paradigm of choice and the Project's general commitment to working with the community. However, this is not to say that there are not numerous research projects where there is extensive overlap between the interests of the community and those of university-based researchers. In addition, many scholars, especially those who operate within a feminist/critical framework are genuinely committed to participatory practices although this commitment is frequently challenged by the dictates of successful grant crafting and the disciplinary leanings of institutional Research Ethics Boards.

While community-based research is considered legitimate within academia the standard notions of what constitutes 'scholarship' still prevails. Although articles written by multiple authors are acceptable they still do not carry the same weight as single authored papers. Likewise, the academically determined quality of the journal or publisher is considered important. Women scholars tend to be disproportionately affected by these traditional standards as they are more likely to engage in collaborative community work. Recently, there has been some movement on this front. For example, the Canadian Health Services Research Foundation (CHSRF) has implemented a project to encourage universities to better assess and reward the activities of applied scholarship.

It is also true that the federal funding agencies' focus on collaborative partnerships has not been accompanied by a restructuring of eligibility criteria and grant evaluation processes. This is slowly starting to change as is evidenced by the introduction of more community friendly CV forms. However, there is still considerable need for process and policy changes to adequately support collaborative funding.

Conclusion

It is evident that many of the intersectoral challenges and tensions within the Metropolis Project require external structural changes. For example, to be genuine partners in collaborative projects requires that the NGO sector be provided with an enabling mandate by their funders along with the resources to fully participate.[20] Likewise, the notion of equal partnership needs to be better reflected in the criteria and evaluation processes used by major granting agencies. In addition, the changing role of the university in modern society requires an accompanying recognition of the changing role of the scholar which in turn needs to be acknowledged in the value systems governing hiring, tenure and promotion. While these changes are outside of the purview of the Metropolis Project, there is room for optimism. The creation of more supportive environments for networks and communities of practice is neither unrealistic, nor at odds with current trends and emerging discourses (Dewar, 1998; Edwards, 2000). The experience of Metropolis could be highly informative for this transformation.

---

[20] The primary funders for the settlement and multicultural organizations are also the primary funders of the Metropolis Project. On the one hand this exacerbates the frustration felt by the NGO sector. On the other, it should facilitate the possibility for negotiation.

Other issues can be addressed within the Metropolis Project itself. For example, the struggle to define protocols for ensuring respectful working relationships, including authorship and ownership and acknowledgement of expertise, may be difficult to move from principle to practice but experience, dialogue and the assumption of good will can all facilitate this process. Issues related to knowledge translation/mobilization have been identified as a priority for the Metropolis Secretariat as it has for the major funding agencies and much can be gained by being attentive to the emergence of best practices and new learnings. It may be within this context that we also start to envision new and innovative formats for national conferences and regional retreats.

Finally, there will always be tensions created by the fundamental and often irreconcilable differences in cultures. Perhaps most profound is the fact that academia and NGOs exist for very different reasons, have different priorities and play to very different audiences. Academic freedom is as fundamental to the scholar as integrity in service delivery is to the community worker. The two can and will clash. Perhaps the best we can hope for and work towards is a commitment to fostering collaborative relationships that acknowledge and respect difference while at the same time mutually reinforcing our capacity to do our respective jobs well.

Acknowledgement

The authors gratefully acknowledge the work of Judy Johnson who conducted the focus groups for this project and prepared the original report.

References

Baum, H.S. (2000). Fantasies and Realities in University-Community Partnerships. Journal of Planning Education and Research, 20, 2, 234-246.

Cox, D.N. (2000). Developing a Framework for Understanding University-Community Partnerships. Cityscape: A Journal of Policy Development and Research, 5(1), 9-26.

Dewar, M. (1998). Learning From Difference: The potential transforming Experience of Community-University Collaboration. Journal of Planning, Education and Research, 17, 4 334-337.

Eccles, J.S. (1996). The Power and Difficulty of University-Community Collaboration. Journal of Research on Adolescence, 6, 1, 71-79.

Landry, R., Amara, N., & Lamari, M. (2001). Utilization of Social Science Research Knowledge in Canada. Research Policy, 30, 333-349.

Levesque, P.N. & Chopyak, J. M. (2001). Managing Multi-sector Research projects: Developing Models for Effective Movement from Problem Identification to Problem Solving. Presented at the Fifth International Research Symposium in Public Management. Barcelona, Spain.

Marullo, S. & Edwards, B. (2000). From Charity to Justice: The Potential of University-Community Collaboration for Social Change. American Behavioral Scientist, 43, 5, 895-912.

Provan, K. G. and Milward, H.B. (2001). Do Networks really Work? A Framework for Evaluating Public-Sector organizational Networks. Public administration review. 16:414-423.

Rubin, V. (2000). Evaluating University-Community Partnerships: An examination of the

Evolution of Questions and Approaches. Cityscape: A Journal of Policy Development and Research, 5(1), 219-230.

Schryer-Roy, A. (2005). Knowledge Translation: Basic Theories, Approaches and Applications. IDRC: Research Matters. Available on-line: www.crdi.org/uploads/user-S/11552210541Basic_Theories__KT.pdf.

Suarez-Balcazar, Y. Harper, G. & Lewis, R. (2005). An Interactive and Contextual Model of Community-University Collaborations for Research and Action. Health Education and Behavior, 32(1), 84-101.

Walsh, D. & Annis, R. (2003). Exploring University-Community relations: The Case of Brandon University's Community Outreach Service. Paper presented at: The Future of Rural Peoples: Rural Economy, healthy people, Environment, Rural Communities., University of Saskatchewan.

Wenger, E. (1998) Communities of Practice: Learning, Meaning and Identity. Cambridge: Cambridge University Press.

Wenger, E., McDermott and Snyder, W. (2002). Cultivating Communities of Practice: A Guide to Managing Knowledge. Cambridge: Harvard Business School Press.

The stranger within: Rethinking distance and proximity of the researcher as community member

Uzma Jamil

> This chapter focuses on my subjective positioning as a researcher and community member and the challenges involved in doing research with the Pakistani community in Montreal, in the context of a 2005 pilot study that examined the meaning systems evoked around '9/11' in the Pakistani immigrant community. Three main issues emerged from this experience. The first was the impact of age and gender as status markers in defining my role and creating an alliance with the Montreal Pakistani community. The second was the transformation of my sense of Self as an insider/outsider in the research team and the Pakistani community. The third was my ethical and political responsibility as a researcher who gained access to the community by virtue of being Pakistani. The chapter concludes with a positive recommendation for doing similar research projects with culturally-mixed research teams and a greater awareness at the outset of the tensions inherent in negotiating identity and representation as a researcher.

In 2005, our inter-disciplinary research team at the Montreal Children's Hospital, carried out a pilot study documenting the meaning system evoked around 9/11 – the September 11, 2001 terrorist attacks on New York and Washington DC – within two Pakistani groups, one an immigrant community in Parc Extension, Montreal and the other, a group in Karachi, Pakistan. The study consisted of ethnographic fieldwork and semi-structured interviews with respondents in each city.

This chapter describes my subjective positioning as a researcher and community member and the challenges involved in doing research with the Pakistani community in Montreal. It is about my insider/outsider role in the research team and in the Pakistani community, and my negotiation between the two. On one level, my sense of professional identity and belonging came from being part of an academic environment, the research team at the hospital and working on this specific project. On another level, my personal identity as a Pakistani female in North America was also a part of how I perceived myself and how others perceived me as a Pakistani community member. This overlapping between two different worlds and my sense of belonging in each placed me in an ambiguous position as a simultaneous insider and outsider, depending on which group served as a reference point.

This chapter explores these themes of belonging, identity, and representation in describing my experiences as a researcher in this particular project in Montreal.

The chapter is divided into several parts. Following a brief look at the relevant literature on researchers as community members, the next section contextualizes the research team, the goal of the research project and our fieldwork site in Montreal. The next two sections describe the process of research and the challenges and learning experiences that came out of it. The last section focuses on the ongoing process of sharing research results with the community, and the ethical and political responsibility of the researcher who is also a community member. It concludes by looking at the positive impact of having a culturally mixed research team and the key points that I took away from this research experience.

Literature: From Objectivity to the Negotiation of Distance

As researchers, we are often the outsiders who observe and document and analyze what happens within society or within a particular community. There is an assumption of objectivity in this position as an outside observer, one which is often valued within academia. But, this so-called objectivity and distance between the researcher and the researched is relative. When the researcher is also a member of the same community, the boundaries between insider and outsider become blurred, calling into question these assumptions of distance and objectivity (Mekki-Berrada et al., 2001, p.43).

One way this blurring of boundaries is demonstrated is in the shared understandings of cultural meanings and markers. When the researcher is an outsider in the community under study, he/she has to take the time to learn and to understand the shared cultural realities of the community members. In cases where the researcher is from the same community, that first step is often eliminated because the shared reality is often taken for granted, whether rightly or wrongly. As Altorki and El-Solh (1988) note, the indigenous field worker is able to attach meanings to patterns much faster than a non-indigenous researcher and does not need as many markers to understand a particular social reality (Altorki and El-Solh, 1988, p.7). But, shared understandings of taboos and blind spots may often also be included in this common cultural ground. They may create an explicit or implicit sense of alliance and collusion between the researcher and the community which would not be present otherwise.

While this shared understanding of cultural behavior and patterns between the researcher and community may be present, it does not automatically eliminate all differences between the two. Lila Abu-Lughod (1988) uses the term "partial insider" because it captures the limitations inherent in being a cultural insider (Abu Lughod, 1988, p.143). The researcher is identified as belonging to a particular class, group, and way of life by others from within the community, and a set of assumptions and judgments are evoked around that identification. This internal dynamic is as significant as the fact that they share the same ethnic community identity. She and other female researchers in Arab and South Asian societies discuss having to deliberately fudge or misrepresent certain personal details about their lives in order to avoid being judged by the community members and therefore losing access or trust with the respondents (Abu Lughod, 1988; Naveed-i-rahat, 1991; Ahmed-Ghosh, 1991). The strain caused by this inauthentic representation of oneself to those who are, theoretically at least, 'one's own' is important to stress, because it is often overshadowed by the similarities between the researcher and the community.

The literature highlights two themes which also came to be reflected in my personal experiences during the research process. First, there is the issue of distance and closeness, and the fluid movement between these two poles when the researcher and the researched share a common cultural identity. Second, there is the negotiation of representation and identity, internally inside the researcher and externally in relation to the community. The following section describes the personal and professional contexts within which this research study was conceptualized and undertaken, before going on to subsequent sections which discuss how these two themes were illustrated in the fieldwork process.

Context: Identity and Location

My identity in this project was shaped by my location within the Pakistani community and within the research team. I am of Pakistani origin, the daughter of parents who emigrated from Pakistan thirty years ago. I grew up mostly in North America, and was educated in the mainstream American and Canadian educational systems. For several years after I first moved to Montreal to attend McGill, I hardly ever socialized with Pakistanis because I didn't meet very many of them. It was in the context of work that I came to know Pakistanis, and eventually built personal relationships with a few. Among them were members of the Pakistani Canadian Society of Quebec (PCSQ), a community organization. Now, I volunteer on their board, and write regularly for their magazine. Professionally, I am an academic researcher in the Transcultural research team at Montreal Children's Hospital and a doctoral student in sociology at University of Quebec at Montreal (UQAM).

Our research team on this project was interdisciplinary (psychology, anthropology and politics) and included both Québeçois and Pakistani researchers. It was part of the larger Transcultural research team at the Montreal Children's Hospital. The Transcultural team has been working with immigrant communities and children on issues around intercommunity relations for many years in Montreal. This particular pilot project was the introductory phase of a larger research project, which is currently ongoing. It examines the moral development and effects of terrorism on children from the South Asian Muslim communities in Montreal.

The Transcultural team is unique in several ways which replicate the 'in between' positioning already present in my position as a researcher and community member. First, it is a fairly large team, with about 25-30 members from diverse interdisciplinary academic and clinical backgrounds. With such a large number, the fluid dynamics of exit/entry and belonging are important in maintaining a harmonious team environment. Second, as a team, we occupy linguistically overlapping spaces of French and English. We are in a French-speaking province, but affiliated with an Anglophone university (McGill). Thus, we are situated in an ambiguous position in the highly political and sensitive French-English language divide in Canada and in Québec. Third, our team is part of both the academic milieu and the clinical one, because we are connected to a university research network and to the hospital. Thus, we represent both the theoretical domain of academia and the practice-oriented one of clinical work through the diversity of our team members and the projects we undertake. All of these characteristics formed the context for my role and identity in this particular research project.

Turning to the fieldwork site, we chose to work in the Parc Extension neighborhood in Montreal because it has a concentrated population of Pakistanis, in contrast to the rest of the Pakistani population in Montreal, which is more geographically dispersed throughout the city, and in the suburbs. Parc Extension is an ethnically diverse neighborhood in Montreal, inhabited primarily by South Asians and Greeks. Pakistanis make up about 5,000-6,000 of the total South Asian community in the area. It is a close-knit and socially conservative community of new immigrants and refugees. Education and income levels are both relatively low. Many people work in low-paying factory jobs, in local ethnic grocery stores or receive social assistance from the government.

Until I began working on this research project, I had only been to Parc Extension a handful of times to shop at Pakistani grocery stores there. Otherwise, I had almost no connection to that neighborhood, and my sense of belonging as a Pakistani was limited to a very small social circle of university-educated, more affluent Pakistanis who lived in other parts of Montreal. The research process made me reassess my sense of identity and location in Montreal, both as a Pakistani and as a researcher. The next two sections describe my personal and professional learning process in the course of the project.

Gender and Age as Status Markers

Gender and age were the two status markers which I felt had the most significant effect on my role and the perceptions related to my role as a researcher. As a member of the research team, although they defined me, my gender and my age did not change my position within it. The research director was also a woman, which made team dynamics more inclusive and less hierarchical. However, within the Pakistani community, these two markers had a different impact. In some cases, it meant that I had to negotiate my status internally within the community with other male authority figures because of my gender and age, in addition to being a researcher. In other cases, being a young female researcher facilitated access with respondents who might not have been as willing to open up to an older, male researcher.

I started networking in the community through a Pakistani community organization, whose support was my initial gateway into the Parc Ex community. But, while the director of that organization was extremely supportive of the pilot study and of my role in it, other community leaders, who were also Pakistani men over the age of 50, were less supportive and less willing to offer contacts. Thus, the authority present in my professional status and personal identity evoked a different response among different male figures. On one hand, the director offered me a protective male authority, as a young, Pakistani woman, in order to gain introductions and access within the community. On the other hand, I also came up against resistance from other men precisely because I was young, Pakistani and female. Apart from the personal aspect, negotiating my status within the community also shed light on the patriarchal, power and gendered implications of who speaks for and within the community (Bhopal, 1997).

In the field research phase, my gender and age operated as status markers in a different way. We began the data collection and interview phase without having any idea of the amount of resistance that we would encounter as we tried to find respondents within the Parc Ex Pakistani community. Initially, we thought that networking within the community, by using organizational contacts, would be sufficient. That turned out not to be the case, and we came across two challenges. The first was finding respondents who would be willing to participate in the study. The second was creating enough of a trust with them, so that they would be open in sharing their thoughts and experiences.

We tackled the first issue – the difficulty in finding respondents – by adapting our strategy to include 'street recruiting'. In other words, I went to Parc Extension, with a female friend to accompany me, and asked Pakistanis I met on the street, in the park, or in the grocery stores on Jean-Talon Street if they would be interested in participating in this pilot study. In this situation, my being a young woman probably helped minimize the sense of threat felt by some potential respondents. I fit into their perception of a student, and therefore asking them to participate in a research study made more sense in that context. Although most people we met said no to participation, a few agreed, and those interviews gave us valuable feedback in documenting the reasons for the resistance and avoidance we encountered throughout the networking and recruitment phase.

One young woman in particular, N., a 22-year-old, whom I met at the bus stop on Jean-Talon, was very open and helpful, inviting us to her house nearby. In the interview with her, she was very frank, the most that anyone had been with me in the entire process. Through her, I gained a unique insight to the community, in addition to access to her friends and their families in Parc Ex. In her case, my gender and age facilitated trust and sharing and helped overcome dual challenges of finding a respondent and having a detailed interview with the person.

N.'s role and the relationship I created with her – which was a combination of friend/mentor/older sister – were significant because they demonstrated the importance of creating a personal relationship with a local person who was enthusiastic about helping. She connected with me personally because I was a single, Pakistani female in a position of independence from my family, a quality which she admired because of the socially conservative and close-knit nature of her own family and local community. In return, she offered me her 'authority' and access, as a woman within the Parc Ex community, to other Pakistani women in order to help in this research project.

Ironically, while knowing her and connecting with her gave me greater access to the Pakistani community in Parc Ex, it also confirmed for me the extent of the resistance in the community's thinking. For example, she accompanied me to an interview at her friend's house, another girl who attended the same school with her, and the girl's mother and sister-in-law. The girl's mother was quite reticent in answering my questions, and when N. asked questions to help her open up a little bit more, the woman shut down her line of questioning very quickly. I had the impression that she didn't want to share her thoughts with a stranger, namely me, even if I was there with someone she knew very well.

These dichotomies in my interactions with Parc Ex Pakistanis highlighted the complexities of being a Pakistani woman engaged in research. In some cases, my gender and age facilitated access. In other cases, the same status markers were a source of resistance from other community members. For me, it exposed the variation in my own sense of vulnerability and security, depending on internal and external location and place within the community. These themes are discussed further in the next section.

Self and Other/Insider and Outsider

Working with the Pakistani community in Parc Extension as a researcher evoked a transformation in my self-image as a Pakistani and became a learning experience in unexpected ways, personally. The experience challenged me to face my Self and my own cultural history and assumptions and thoughts in every encounter with what I considered the Other, even if the person was a member of the same ethnic community. In truth, the Pakistanis in Parc Extension felt like foreigners to me. My upbringing and my life were very different from theirs. I have never lived in Pakistan, although I was born there. I am familiar with the culture and customs through what my parents transmitted to their children. But admittedly, I am more Westernized than Pakistani in some ways, ways which set me apart in my interactions with the recent immigrants and refugees from Pakistan in Parc Ex.

For a long time, as I was doing interviews and looking for respondents, I was conscious mostly of the things that made me different from the respondents, from my urban background, education, and socio-economic status to the way I dressed, the way I spoke Urdu and my tendency to switch back and forth between Urdu and English in the same sentence. The irony is that while I was extremely self-conscious about differences, the reason why I was doing this project in the first place was because of the *similarities*. I was of Pakistani origin. I spoke Urdu. I was a member of a Pakistani community organization and had access to a network within the community, which a non-Pakistani researcher would not. In essence, I was doing this project because I was a Pakistani.

Furthermore, like all Pakistani women, I was raised to be aware of the social codes that shape young women's dress and behavior in the South Asian community. As Handa (1997) documents in her work with South Asian-Canadian women, young women's bodies and their movement and conduct in public space are linked to constructions of gender identity, particularly notions of femininity and sexuality, within the South Asian community (Handa, 1997, pp.272-273). Regulating the physical female body through notions of 'culturally appropriate' dress and female presence in the public sphere are important concerns in maintaining the social identity of the South Asian community, especially in the diasporic setting.

Being aware of these social codes and the contradictions in my positioning as a Pakistani researcher did not help me feel more at ease every time I went up to Parc Extension. In the end, I tried to adjust as much as I could, trying to maintain a balance between being authentic inside myself while also trying to 'fit in' with the Parc Ex community enough to be able to do field research successfully. Externally, I modified my way of dressing whenever I went to Parc Ex, so that instead of wearing *shalwar kameez* like the other women in Parc Ex, I wore the *kameez* (long, loose tunic top) with jeans because it felt more socially comfortable than wearing my usual Western garb. Although I went alone to do interviews with respondents, I tried to take a female friend to Parc Ex with me to do 'street recruiting' whenever possible, both for my own sense of personal safety and also so that I wasn't perceived as a lone female on the street, with all the negative connotations associated with that in the Parc Ex community.

In small ways, ways which eventually accumulated into a larger sense of discomfort and unease, this research experience made me feel the dislocation inherent in my position as a Pakistani woman raised in North America. It exposed a feeling of being a stranger in a community that was supposed to be 'my own' by virtue of being Pakistani. Certainly, from the perspective of the research team, I was an insider in the Pakistani community. Yet, in practice, I felt differently. I became very aware of the inversion of the usual designations of Self and Other in my identity, and the limitations of being a cultural insider in the Parc Ex Pakistani community. I did not resolve my internal feeling of dislocation by the end of the project, and it still continues to come up when I go to Parc Ex now, a year later, in the context of another research project. I live with it as part of being a researcher working with this particular community.

However, as my level of familiarity with the area has increased over time, there has been a decrease in my degree of uneasiness, such that the latter does not feel so overwhelming anymore. I realized this unexpectedly when I went to Parc Extension recently with a new Pakistani interviewer. Hearing her comment about the differences of Parc Ex made me realize that I have stopped paying conscious attention to those same things, although I am aware that they are there. I just don't think about them as much anymore. I live with a sense of dislocation that is now a low hum in my internal background, instead of the central focus it used to be.

Responsibility of the Researcher

As Bhopal (2000) discusses in her work as a South Asian woman interviewing other women from the same community in East End London, the role of power in the researcher-researched relationship is very important to address. This issue of power is particularly significant when working with a community that is marginalized and in a neighborhood that is socio-economically disadvantaged. Parc Ex has a reputation of not being a 'good' area, with a history of gang violence and related problems. The Pakistani community there is very closed, since many residents do not know French, and therefore do not interact much with mainstream Montrealers. In addition, many occupy a precarious position in society by virtue of their refugee migration status and therefore feel particularly vulnerable.

As researchers in general, and as a researcher who was able to gain access to the community by virtue of being Pakistani, there was a responsibility upon the team, and on me, to make sure that we did not harm the community in doing our research. We all felt this ethical responsibility very strongly before beginning the project, because we knew we were broaching a topic that was very sensitive and politically-charged in a neighbourhood that was already historically marginalized for other reasons.

In the course of the field research, as we began to discover the resistance and fear felt by community members in speaking openly about the topic, this responsibility took on an added layer. Once we had gained the trust of the respondents, we had to balance the responsibility to represent their views and thoughts accurately with making sure that we did not cause any negative repercussions for the community. We did not want to contribute further to their marginalized status or to a negative portrayal of the community by appearing to exploit or to use them for our academic purposes.

This is an issue that we are still very much concerned with, as the team thinks about how to disseminate our research results now. For me, personally, I felt the responsibility of the trust that respondents gave me, in sharing their thoughts and opinions with me during interviews. Even those who engaged in avoiding overt discussion about the topic gave me, the researcher and the Pakistani, their trust in speaking with me in the first place. Since I continue to be involved with research projects in Parc Extension on the basis of being a Pakistani researcher, this is a responsibility I take seriously.

If not harming our respondents and the Parc Ex community is one of our concerns, the other is how to translate the research results into something that is useful and perceived as beneficial to the community itself. One of the common reasons why many people did not participate in the study was, according to them, the fact they didn't see the utility of research in their lives. Most people were concerned with day-to-day survival, getting by financially, making sure their families were safe and cared for, and in many cases, remaining under the radar of any official or governmental power. A vague, ambiguous answer of 'this research will help the community' did not register with most people as a priority, if it didn't help them with their practical and immediate concerns.

We addressed this situation in two ways. First, we offered small, local grocery store gift certificates to respondents, as a way to compensate them for taking the time to participate in the study. Second, whenever the director of the Pakistani community organization or I spoke with anyone from the Pakistani community, we stressed that we were doing this project to try to help the community in the long-term. This included helping those who lived outside Parc Ex to understand what the residents thought and how they felt about living in Canada, and also helping future Pakistani immigrants to adjust more smoothly. Our research team is now consulting with community organizations to determine the best way to share our results within the Pakistani and South Asian communities in Parc Ex.

Conclusion

This chapter has been focused around three main issues which emerged from my experiences in this research project. The first is the impact of age and gender as status markers in defining my role and creating an alliance with the Parc Ex Pakistani community. The second is the transformation of my sense of Self as an insider/outsider in the Pakistani community in the course of fieldwork. The third is my ethical and political responsibility as a researcher who gained access to the community by virtue of being Pakistani.

Out of all three themes, this research project pushed the insider/outsider dynamic to the forefront as part of the research process. It called into question the dichotomy of my role as a researcher and as a Pakistani female in a much more striking and unexpected way than I expected, and it demonstrated the dual sense of authority and fragility that stemmed from that identity. On one hand, when I was downtown at the hospital, meeting and discussing with the research team, my position as a cultural insider, as a Pakistani, was more authoritative, because I was in a context and location where I felt comfortable and secure. When I was in Parc Ex doing interviews, I felt more vulnerable and insecure as a Pakistani female, because the context and the location made me feel destabilized internally. As mentioned earlier in this chapter, I am still in the process of living out and negotiating the dislocation inherent in going back and forth between these two sites, internal and external, psychological and geographical, as I continue to work as a researcher in Parc Extension.

There are two points that are important to mention for future projects. First, in this project, having a culturally mixed team, one which included both Pakistani and Québeçois researchers, contributed greatly to the success of the study by adding nuances in perspectives. The combination of perspectives meant that we could avoid potential pitfalls of replicating certain biases inherent from long-term familiarity with each of our own respective communities. For example, in certain situations in the interviews, I did not pick up anything unusual in the assumptions that respondents made in talking about their self-image of the Pakistani community, because I was already familiar with hearing them, as a Pakistani. But, my Québeçois colleagues *did* notice them because they did not share the same cultural background and therefore the same unspoken assumptions.

As a researcher and a community member though, it would have been helpful to have had some idea of the subjectivity inherent in having to negotiate representation and identity as a 'partial insider' at the beginning of the project. Incorporating this awareness from the beginning would have been beneficial in shortening the learning curve while doing interviews in the field. While this awareness may not change the tensions inherent in the research and fieldwork process, it emphasizes the fact that research does not always take place in the distant, objective, purely academic kind of way that we imagine it will. Although as researchers, we are trained to stand at a distance and analyze our data, we are also still human beings and still connected to our communities of origin in multiple and multi-layered ways.

References

Abu-Lughod, L. (1988). Fieldwork of a Dutiful Daughter. In C. Altorki & C.F. El-Solh, (Eds). Arab Women in the Field: Studying Your Own Society (pp.139-161). New York: Syracuse University Press.

Ahmed-Ghosh, H. (1991). From Ivory Towers to Mud Huts: Trials and Acceptance of a Fieldworker. In M.N. Panini(Ed.) From the Female Eye: Accounts of Women Fieldworkers Studying their Own Communities (pp.11-19). Delhi: Hindustan Publishing Corporation.

Altorki, C. & El-Solh, C.F. (1988). Introduction. Arab Women in the Field: Studying Your Own Society. New York: Syracuse University Press.

Bhopal, K. (1997). Gender, 'Race' and Patriarchy: A Study of South Asian Women. Aldershot, England: Ashgate Publishing Ltd.

Bhopal, K. (2000). Gender, 'race' and power in the research process: South Asian women in East London. In C. Truman, D.M. Mertens, & B. Humphries(Eds.) Research and Inequality (pp.67-79). London: UCL Press.

Handa, A. (1997). Caught between Omissions: Exploring 'Culture Conflict' Among Second Generation South Asian Women in Canada. PhD dissertation. University of Toronto. Toronto, Ontario, Canada.

Mekki-Berrada, A., Rousseau, C. and J. Bertot (2001). Research on Refugees: Means of Transmitting Suffering and Forging Social Bonds. International Journal of Mental Health. 30: 2, 41-57.

Naveed-i-rahat (1991). "Participant Observation" and Identity Crisis. In In M.N. Panini(Ed.) From the Female Eye: Accounts of Women Fieldworkers Studying their Own Communities (pp.41-51). Delhi: Hindustan Publishing Corporation.

Recording oral memory: Views of Indigenous Victorians

Graeme Johanson, Kirsty Williamson and Don Schauder

The inter-relationships between researchers and the Indigenous community in the state of Victoria, Australia, are analysed in this chapter. In order to gain an understanding of the expectations of Indigenous Victorians of a planned process for the capture and preservation of their oral knowledge, researchers undertook an analysis of Indigenous views. Views were elicited by means of 72 interviews about what Indigenous communities may need by way of a trusted system to help to create, collate, and maintain stories in an online repository of their oral memory.

The research team included a liaison officer who, as an Indigenous Elder recruited participants and liaised with them during and after interviews. They agreed that the long-term value of oral memory has been overlooked by non-Indigenous historians and curators in the past, and that storytelling is fundamental to community identity, and essential for cultural continuity.

Responses to this project from Indigenous communities were generous and welcoming. The co-operation of Indigenous interviewees provided much useful data. The research was underpinned by interpretivist/constructivist research philosophy, with ethnographic method being used to analyse the needs of Indigenous communities.

The research team and Indigenous communities share some common goals. Researchers and researched were involved in a joint venture from the beginning. The interactions were open and frank, and deliberate effort has gone into the mutual contributions which will sustain a good working relationship into the future. The means for achieving collaboration are described.

> I guess if it was non-Indigenous persons who were trusted within the community, [they could] start to build a trust in the community, like going out and talking to people like you are. Maybe sitting down, have a coffee, just dropping in and getting to know the communities. That's how you get trust in our areas. You know, someone just coming up and saying, 'I'm going to fill out a form', that's too confronting. I know most people would like

someone to sit down with them have a cuppa, get to know them. That's more of the way that they like it (Participant 1).

This chapter describes a research project in progress. It begins by outlining the project aims, then describes how grounded theory was used to undertake data collection and analysis in its first phase. Initially there was a risk that researcher and researched might not find common ground. This chapter points out that the project began with a degree of hesitation among both researchers and researched, and describes how the research grew into a form of partnership over time, where the voice of the Indigenous community is elicited and in return the researcher has privileged access to special knowledge. The final section identifies a set of effects of the project, mostly constructive.

Research project aims

The Australian Research Council funded the project. Supported by the Public Record Office of Victoria (PROV), the Australian Society of Archivists Indigenous Issues Special Interest Group, the Koorie Heritage Trust, and the Victorian Koorie Records Taskforce, this university research involved an extensive analysis of Indigenous needs in 2004-2005. It aimed to develop trust and understanding of key issues which relate to whether government and other archival services might meet the needs of Indigenous people for preservation of and access to their oral memory, in ways that are better than those already in existence. One of the partners, the Koorie Heritage Trust has already established significant records of Indigenous life, in relation to 'Mission Voices'[21] and these provide invaluable lessons for the current project.

Before European settlement, Aboriginal culture was communicated orally in the main. It has to be acknowledged that there are a variety of other important forms of recorded knowledge which complement oral memory, including paintings, carvings, dance, and song, for example. It is impossible to separate the forms in practice. Yet story-telling of communal memories played an essential role in the transmission of community knowledge, and this continues to be the case. As Booth describes it, "to bear witness… is to illuminate, preserve, and transmit the trace, to resist the solvent-like powers of time and becoming, to attempt to ensure the persistence of a truth, of justice, of a person…" (Booth, 2006, p.91). Many valuable records about Indigenous communities reside in non-Indigenous cultural institutions – libraries, public record offices, archives, historical societies, museums, research centres, universities and galleries – and are very often provided from a non-Indigenous perspective. As Lynette Russell (2005, p.4) reminds us,

> many significant records about Indigenous communities … are the products and consequence of colonisation, dispossession, removal and relentless

---

[21] See www.abc.net.au/missionvoices/living_culture/stories_of_living_culture/default.htm

surveillance to which Indigenous people were subjected. These are virtually all written records and not oral.

The project began with some uncertainty. At the start the views of the Indigenous community were unexplored, and although the research method had been applied by the authors in other contexts, possible reactions in this context were untested. The researchers strongly hoped for collaboration. As we identified ways in which Indigenous communities would like their memories represented, kept and delivered, it seemed that the tide would turn. This chapter will follow the currents, by focusing on the interactions between the researchers and the interviewees primarily, but before that the whole project requires brief description.

In its gestation the project was divided into three phases. The first phase systematically discovered what the expectations and needs of Indigenous Victorians were, and what they understood about existing limited official provision for retention of their cultural memory. The second phase of the project now aims to model Indigenous community-oriented archival services, based on the described needs. The third phase could use the model guidelines to develop the Koorie Annotation System that enables Koorie communities, families and individuals to provide their perspectives, stories and contextual information alongside the official record.

The research team is at Monash University, in the Centre for Australian Indigenous Studies (CAIS) in the Arts Faculty, and in the Faculty of Information Technology[22], and is actively assisted by the partnering practitioners. One of the special strengths of this project is that it brings together a multidisciplinary team – Indigenous, technical, archival, historical and sociological approaches – and focuses them on a little-explored challenge: how to capture a fecund oral culture in perpetuity using computer technology? Another is that it has had the benefit of the advice and support of an Indigenous Elder, who acted as liaison officer from the outset. She helped to locate Indigenous interviewees from across the state. The research has been approved by the Monash University Standing Committee on Ethics in Research involving Humans (SCERH).

This chapter is about the first phase of the project – the stage where the needs of the Indigenous participants were elicited by interview. It used a semi-structured interview schedule, allowing for follow-up questions, or prompts, to be used for more detail or to explore related issues. The development of the interview questions is described in the next section of this chapter. Our questions related to three main topics:

1. the nature of storytelling and storytellers, the types of stories, and the use and abuse of the stories;

---

[22] See www.sims.monash.edu.au/research/eirg/trust/

2. desirable recording activities – what recording of stories has occurred already, by what means, and how satisfactory has it been; and into the future, whether there are reasons for not keeping stories, and who should control access to the stories; and
3. practical and ethical dilemmas surrounding use of archives – prior awareness of existing repositories of Indigenous documents; prior usage of official records; the morality of the retention of historical, personal information about 'protected' Indigenous individuals; the chance to add to the official record; potential restrictions on access to records; and ease of access to the repositories.

The 72 interviews lasted about 70 minutes each on average, and identified a rich variety of issues to be analysed by the research team. Issues emerging from phase one, and requiring consideration in phases two and three, include: access paths to the records; accessibility; archival description/metadata/indexing; contested memories; ownership, custody and control; preservation and security; links between oral memory and written records; rights management, including intellectual property; selection of content worthy of retention; and trust.

In the sections that follow, quotations from the project interviewees are identified as 'Participant 1', 'Participant 2', and so on, in order to protect their anonymity.

The role of technology

The relevance of technology is challenged by this project. For example, there is a glaring gap in the forms of knowledge presented by storytelling, created by face-to-face human interactions, which contrast with conventional documents, manufactured by mediating tools of some sort.

Respect for the value of spoken language is fundamental, because it plays a special role in the transmission of culture in Indigenous communities, which is vastly different from our machine-induced representations of knowledge, heavily relied on by the non-Indigenous to 'capture' ideas and events. Fortunately in recent decades historians have changed their narrow views about the virtues of the spoken word, having moved away

> from the conventional view that language was a passive, potentially transparent instrument for transmitting content, for organising, representing or expressing the truth of a reality outside of itself, and toward a view of language as the dense, fertile and autonomous site and through which the objective reality of the world as well as the subjective reality of language users [is] actively produced or constructed (Teows, 2001, p.8916).

A starting point for understanding Indigenous needs is that oral transmission plays an essential survival role among Indigenous communities, and proudly underlies their identity. It reaches out as it communicates, and it nourishes inwardly by means of self-affirmation. Walter Ong has reminded us of the significance of the relationships between the spoken word and all the forms of technologising it, whether by information technology or not:

> Intelligence is relentlessly reflexive, so that even the external tools that [intelligence] uses to implement its workings become 'internalised', that is, part of its own reflexive process (Ong, 1991, p.81).

Therefore one might expect that a heavy reliance on oral memory might create some different cultural shapes and features. Some of our interviewees asserted that the valuable essence of storytelling could never be replicated using any technology. Yet others believed that the prospect of keeping records online was a necessary and exciting prospect, even allowing for limitations of existing technological systems. As an example of internalised storytelling technology, one interviewee mentioned 'Dust Echoes', (Australian Broadcasting Corporation, 2006), television animations of traditional Indigenous stories.

Another reflexive process – around the redistribution of power – is also in play as part of the interview procedure, and can be explicated by the theory of structuration. Two loci of power interacted in the interviews: one locus was the records management system (still to be precisely delineated), suggested as a means to convert oral memory to a fixed form as a means to assist to perpetuate it, and another locus was the implicit power of oral memory itself within and beyond Indigenous culture. The discussion of the possibility of the transfer of oral knowledge to more formal records brought together the researchers' understandings of potential structures and uses of information technologies, alongside the special needs and concerns of the Indigenous interviewees. A dialectic between groups and systems is summed up by the sociologist Anthony Giddens in his theory of structuration:

> According to the notion of the duality of structure, the structural properties of social systems are both the medium and outcomes of the practices [which] they recursively organize (Giddens, 1984, p.25).

> All interaction involves (attempted) communication, the operation of power, and moral relations. The modalities whereby these are 'brought off' in interaction by participating actors can also be treated as the means whereby structures are reconstituted (Giddens, 1976, p.127).

For Giddens, structures are the sets of transforming rules which are organised as the properties of social systems and groups (Stillman, 2006). The expectations of the interviewers and interviewees changed as the interviews proceeded. Giddens argues that order is primarily created, communicated, and modified by means of language, "not as a system of signs or symbols, but as a medium of practical activity" (Giddens, 1976, p.154). At this point Giddens reinforces Ong's dictum that technologising of the spoken word is a form of internalising it. Both parties – the interviewers and interviewees – were seeking a common vision of how to internalise mutual needs in order to act practically to achieve the shared project goal of creating a workable system.

As Giddens suggests, instantiation of practical activity is not predicated on an even distribution of power or other resources, and in fact, asymmetry is part of the natural order. Factors which affect the nature of institutionalised practices include domination, legitimisation and sanction – all contextualised by different power relationships between actors and institutionalised social practices. This research project seeks to redress some of the imbalances that have been institutionalised in non-Indigenous recording mores in Victoria long ago. The use of technology artefacts in this project aims to further the development of liberating (rather than oppressive) structural principles. Our recorded interviews were a harbinger of planned technological preservation.

Analysis of the intersections between social groups (in our case, Indigenous Victorians and researchers) and information and communications technologies fits within 'community informatics,' an increasingly recognised area of practice, study and research:

> Thus 'communities', as people coming together in pursuit of their common aims or shared practices both physically and electronically enabled, proliferate even while their 'researched' reality remains in considerable dispute. Not surprisingly, there is growing interest in how different information and communication technologies can enable and empower these groups in relation to the achievement of their collective goal (Stillman, 2004, p.1).

At the start of this project we encountered three potent obstacles. First of all, Indigenous groups have been researched to the point where they are nauseated by perpetual external diagnosis and prognosis. Secondly, Indigenous knowledge does not encompass a Socratic tradition of challenging orthodoxy by questioning the truth of some stories. And thirdly, as is to be expected, we uncovered Indigenous anxiety about the use of communications technologies for several reasons. The first two obstacles were summed up by the one interviewee:

> I guess a lot of my trust is trusting the word of Indigenous people against that of academics. To me, Indigenous oral history should count more than some academic that flies into a community for two weeks and then writes a book about it.

> In Indigenous culture you are not really supposed to ask questions. You accept the information as a given. It is this society here that questions everything (Participant 2).

The second obstacle was linked to the third when developed further in another interview with an Elder. In his view European methods of perpetuating memory were inferior, placing an unnecessary barrier between storytelling participants. Traditional storytelling has survived for millennia without technical aids:

> Recording of stories is a European perception of history. It's a documentation of their history. I don't see recording from my perspective as a necessity because recording can be mishandled, can be mistreated, can be misplaced. Therefore the recording… should remain in the oral form so that people then participate… While there has been release of lots of sacred information as well as ordinary information, a lot has been retained and not told (Participant 3).

The beauty of the momentary context of storytelling was highly prized by another interviewee. An act of recording may be seen as a personal insult to the status of the storyteller. Spontaneity disappears:

> Maybe some of the Elders that have been entrusted with some of these stories might feel that the technology of trying to record them in such a way, might make them feel inferior in a way, because they've been entrusted with these stories. If they feel the role has been taken from them by just putting it on a recording and pressing 'play' whenever, then you've lost the context of how it is being delivered – the facial expressions of an Elder, the voice and tone (Participant 4).

Another interviewee enlarges on the paradox: the need to record, conflicts with the need to protect localised and personalised conversations. She would love more chit-chat to be recorded. Yet she is aware of the many inhibitions which people feel in social circles when confronted by recording equipment. She begins by talking of Indigenous get-togethers where reminiscences bloom:

> We just start talking. Someone could say, 'Oh remember… da da da,' and it just snowballs. And then everyone starts talking about whatever, and you cover all these subjects. It would be wonderful if we could just push a button and have a video going and hone in on everything like that. It would be great. But a lot of black-fellows, they don't want to be talking into mikes or being videoed. But if you just listen to it, they go on and on and on (Participant 5).

The ability of recorded stories to change social attitudes towards Indigenous communities was a prevailing reason for another interviewee to advocate middle ground, to countenance information and communications technologies as a means of achieving a greater good, the hope of 'some sort of connection'. She wanted to improve awareness among non-Indigenous people:

> Aboriginal people have always progressed over time. There's no reason why we can't progress to a time where we are recording things in a modern way, yet still keep the meaning of the stories.
>
> I think there are a lot of people who need to relate to what really happened to the Aboriginal people, because there was this impression by Westerners that Aboriginal people had no feelings. It didn't matter what they did to them because they would die out anyway. And I think it is very important that there is some sort of connection because that promotes more tolerance and more understanding... It is important to get the stories across (Participant 6).

Powerplay is inherent in all technologies. This section has outlined some perceived strengths and weaknesses of information and communications technologies, as used for this phase of the research, and as proposed as part of the project end-product.

Grounded perspectives on engaging communities

Fiction readers may be familiar with *The Poisonwood bible*, the novel by Barbara Kingsolver (1998), set in the Congo as Belgium withdrew as an imperial power, in which a family of six US immigrants experience challenges to their cultural roots. All the imaginary characters reacted to local communities differently, from the violently antagonistic to the fully tolerant. Although fiction, the novel illustrates well the different interpretations people make of their experiences, as well as investigating the challenges for those who are thrust into cultural contexts that are foreign to them.

This project adopted methods which aimed to integrate a range of Indigenous views into the research from the outset. At the start we were uncertain about how many participants would be willing to contribute. Because we wanted to gain proper understandings about Indigenous oral knowledge, we chose a qualitative, interpretivist/constructivist approach to our study, rather than the box-ticking processes of a positivist-style survey, which often results in superficial data lacking the 'rich picture' perceptions of interpretivist/constructivist studies.

'Interpretivism', which concerned with meaning, is an umbrella term under which various paradigms such as constructivism, phenomenography and critical theory fit (Williamson, 2002, p.30). Constructivist research is based upon the idea that "there is no unique 'real world' that pre-exists and is independent of human mental activity and human symbolic language" (Bruner, 1986, p.95). Knowledge and truth are therefore created rather than discovered, and there are often multiple, conflicting constructions of reality. Supporters of qualitative research (of the interpretivist/constructivist kind) argue that it allows greater flexibility and therefore results in the discovery of new insights (Sutton, 1997) and that "it can produce new and unexpected data, evidence we did not know was there" (Madjar & Walton, 2001, p.41). In other words it is the serendipity encouraged by this approach to research which is a major strength.

The present study is guided by constructivist paradigms, both personal constructivist and social constructionist. The former is explained by a range of theorists who have postulated that individual reality is determined by each person's perceptions of what is real, and the notion that the 'meanings' that each person makes may differ from those of others (Kelly, 1963; Lincoln & Guba, 1985; Hammersley, 1995; Saule, 2002). Social construct theory, which places emphasis on the ways people develop meanings together, emerges from philosophical roots similar to those of personal construct theory. Well-known proponents of social construct theory are Berger and Luckman (1967) who argue that meaning is developed through the interactions and social processes involving people, language and religion. As Schwandt (2000, p.197) states:

> We do not construct our interpretations in isolation, but against a backdrop of shared understandings, practices, language, and so forth.

We believed from the outset that our research participants, while all Indigenous, would have many differing understandings and experiences, as well as 'shared' meanings through common culture. We have therefore taken the approach that the patterns that emerge from shared meanings can be used to build trusted technologies – in this case archival systems and services for the Victorian Indigenous community. To this end, we aimed through qualitative research to discover the meanings which were shared by participants, as well as those that were not (consensus and dissonance).

User Needs Analysis

The team labelled the first stage of the project the 'user needs analysis' phase, since the term encapsulates the purpose: to understand the needs of Indigenous people in relation to preservation of their oral memory. User needs analysis is a form of grounded theory, involving the observation of the subjects of study at close quarters, and collection of data in everyday contexts. Some strengths of grounded theory are that it articulates: logical, predetermined steps for handling data collection and analysis; a means of correcting errors and omissions and of refining analytic ideas as the researcher progresses; and tools for studying social processes in natural settings (Charmaz, 2001).

By employing user needs analysis, eventually a shortlist of intensive needs was identified:

> Intensive [community] needs assessment takes an identified need and fully explores how important and broad that need is, where it came from, and what caused it (Stoecker, 2005, p.99).

In practice, interviewers began by speaking with individuals who have a good general knowledge of the broad topic of transmission of Indigenous knowledge and the significance of cultural memory, and by reading widely. A broad-ranging conversation (over a couple of hours) was guided to some degree by some key questions, but the aim of this exploratory stage was to canvas as many relevant issues as possible. The discussed themes required further research on the part of the interviewer (as they did, e.g., in relation to verifying what are current PROV protocols), and some acted as guides only (e.g., the concept of 'oral memory' was very hard to pin down in the early discussions).

The nominated issues were consolidated and re-arranged into a sequential interview schedule of semi-structured questions and statements, with an internal logic, which were then piloted further. The pilot interviews (three in number) helped to refine the clarity and flow of the questions. They were intelligible and conducive to all types of responses, including negative reactions, and extra on-the-spot observations which the researcher had not pre-empted. Even when the main interviews began, it was necessary to tweak a few fine details.

As the set of questions were settled on, the aim was to explore openly and without preconception what were contemporary interests and concerns, and what were not. We sought common understandings of key concepts.

The Sample

The sample is a purposive (or purposeful) one, comprising 72 Indigenous participants – a large number for a qualitative study. As Patton (1990, p.169) observes, whilst quantitative enquiry typically depends on larger samples selected randomly, qualitative samples focus on small samples selected purposefully. He argues that:

> the logic and power of purposeful sampling lies in selecting information-rich cases for study in depth. Information-rich cases are those from which one can learn a great deal about issues of central importance to the study, thus the term purposeful sample.

As this quotation implies, purposive samples are also often premised on the concept of 'theoretical sampling', as discussed by Glaser and Strauss (1967). Theoretical sampling means selecting subjects who represent the important characteristics that researchers consider of interest to the study. With this approach there is no compunction to sample multiple cases which do not extend or modify emerging theory (Pidgeon & Henwood 1996). In this study, key characteristics to be represented and balanced were gender, age (with key representation of Elders), place of abode (ensuring sufficient representation of rural areas where there are strong Indigenous populations, as well as city-dwelling Aboriginals), and close association with traditional culture and less close association.

Participants were recruited through the networks of the team's Indigenous Research Officer. She arranged personal interviews in workplaces (21% of the interviews), homes (21% also), educational institutions (21%), Indigenous organizations (19%), colleges of Technical and Further Education (10%), and rural centres (8%), i.e., in places familiar to the interviewees. She also provided on-going support to participants, assisted in framing questions appropriately, accompanied non-Indigenous interviewers at interviews at all times, liaised with interviewees regarding the checking of their interview transcripts, helped with the analysis of the data to ensure appropriate interpretation, and kept interviewees up-to-date with the whole project.

The interviews were audio-taped, with the permission of the interviewees, and then transcribed by an experienced transcription typist. Although the analysis did not constitute 'grounded theory', it was influenced by the 'constructivist grounded theory' approach of Charmaz (2003) which "recognises that the viewer creates the data and ensuing analysis through interaction with the viewed" (p.273). The analysis was a continuous process with the initial categories, determined after the first few interviews, being continually reassessed and expanded as more data were collected.

The early transcripts were read, and re-read, with margin notes indicating the key themes as they emerged. The initial themes were recorded in separate Word files, with definitions of each theme, or topic, attached to the relevant file. As more data were collected, these files not only expanded in number but also sometimes expanded or changed in their definitions. Some files were merged, or removed when it became obvious that the data from them represented a very insignificant contribution. The quotations in this chapter derive from these files.

As the interviews progressed, it became clear that a number of Indigenous interviewees believed that they were imparting useful knowledge to the non-Indigenous researchers (as well as to their community). The interview process was very familiar to them already:

> Now we've got a voice to say we have a history, and our history is this. It shouldn't be all negative stuff, it's very positive stuff and it needs to be passed on to the younger generation, because they're the ones coming through. Whereas before it was left there, and the Elders passed on, and it wasn't really passed on to the wider community (Participant 7).

Indigenous groups are thoroughly-researched, and know a lot about themselves and their communities as a result – more in fact than many white communities. Because the value of history is known, this research itself is facilitated:

> We really know our history. We had to know our history because we are so researched, and people ask us all the time… One of the things that I do say to people especially with our mob, we might have all our families here, but each one of those families has different knowledge of our country. So it's like a jigsaw puzzle. Somebody will have one parcel of it and someone will have another, and they connect (Participant 8).

Indirectly our temperate approach was commended, as being akin to an Indigenous approach, as the opening quotation to this chapter indicates. Time needs to be spent to earn the considered respect of the interviewee:

> I guess if it was non-Indigenous persons who were trusted within the community, [they could] start to build a trust in the community, like going out and talking to people like you are. Maybe sitting down, have a coffee, just dropping in and getting to know the communities. That's how you get trust in our areas. You know, someone just coming up and saying, 'I'm going to fill out a form', that's too confronting. I know most people would like someone to sit down with them have a cuppa, get to know them. That's more of the way that they like it (Participant 1).

In this section we have outlined the research paradigm and methods and described how the techniques were received by the community under scrutiny. We do not assert that our approach was original or unique, but we believe it was effective.

Privileging the voice of the community, moderating the power of the researcher

As the research project progressed, a partnership between interviewer and interviewee developed. The mediation of the project by the Indigenous Research Officer was crucial. All participants want the project to succeed. The project team set up a website to inform of progress, and it e-mails a newsletter to any interested people, including participants.

Efforts to share the responsibility for the success of the project are paralleled by a belief that oral history allows participants to have some control over the creation of their own history:

> It is an opportunity to democratise the nature of history, not simply by interviewing, but by seeing that involvement [by the researcher] as a prelude to a method which allows people to formulate their own meanings of their past experiences in a structured manner... (Grele, 1985, p. viii).

Everybody has a story to tell, as one interviewee pointed out, and may be worth recording:

> I guess it is a matter of degree. Less significant figures might have part of the truth, but [with] more significant figures you generally take it that they have a bigger picture of the truth. I don't actually think that you question the validity of lesser storytellers (Participant 2).

Academic oral historians concur:

> The oral tradition offers extraordinary insights into the lives and struggles of ordinary people (Grele, 1985, p.1).

As Lynette Russell notes, there has been a revival of interest amongst non-Indigenous researchers in Indigenous storytelling in the past 15 years, the emergence of a greater respect for the value of oral memory:

> There has been a palpable change over time and there is now a perception that the external threats which resulted in such horrors as the stolen generations has diminished. Storytelling is perhaps enjoying a resurgence... (Russell, 2005, p.9).

One thoughtful interviewee articulated the same change in the area of art at some length, which is worth quoting:

> Stories, I think places, associations to places, connections to country, all of those sorts of stories are still alive today. And I work with lots of artists now who are now starting to interpret those stories in symbols and images from their own understanding. To go back ten or fifteen years ago, I'd have to say those stories were sadly being lost.
>
> There has been a revival. I think it's coming through the arts, both performing and visual. I think it's where aboriginal people's roots are connected to...
>
> Art is a very important component to the aboriginal community life. I think when you scratch the surface, when you're working in community, you'll see

> that there are lots of aboriginal people who paint or act for whatever reason. It's about identifying or trying to piece stories together for themselves. I think art is a fantastic tool to embark on that journey (Participant 9).

The interviews stimulated some participants in fresh ways. The interviewers received the impression that the participants found the experience worthwhile. Two interviewees commented:

> I didn't think about it at all until [this] research,... and 'Heavens, I'm going to have to think.' I'd forgotten how close to myself it is. It's amazing that your questions to me have made me think about things that I wouldn't think about normally, and it's been an interesting interview (Participant 11).

> Telling our stories is important. I think individual stories of not necessarily famous people can benefit so many people. So a lot of people don't know a lot of stuff. If somebody feels comfortable telling their story then there should be a method for them to do it (Participant 12).

Red agreed with the interviewer that the project is a way of doing this. An example of a situation where the interview made the interviewee think about issues afresh involved Participant 12, who had not contemplated how to keep her own story in the long term. In response to the question of how she would like her community story kept, she replied:

> Kept? Now that's a question isn't it? I hope I learn how to write things down and also I have respect for how we culturally, historically, told our stories. So that's a tough question. I'd like it to be more on the visual side like audio or a video. With a transcript of course, but that's secondary. More visual (Participant 12).

One interviewee had undertaken extensive interviewing herself, for another purpose, and pointed to the possibility of an element of shared catharsis as part of the interview process:

> When I was doing the interviewing[23], I explained to people that the public would have access to those things, and they were quite in agreement. There wasn't one person who said No ... They wanted to get that stuff off their chest and heal. Unburden themselves. They also said, 'No, it's for everybody' (Participant 13).

---

[23] As part of the *Bringing Them Home* project (Human Rights and Equal Opportunity Commission, 1997)

There is enjoyment to be experienced in hearing stories that do not 'belong' to an individual interviewee. Listening to others provides entertainment to the open-minded, as well as having serious purposes:

> In terms of interpreting stories that are not from my country, I can become an observer and a listener to learn what other stories are being told about other pieces of country. Even though it's not mine, it's nice to hear some of those other stories... But we all have the right to be in a position to be able to receive that information. But going back to country, then I believe it is my right if people ask me to interpret something, or tell a story or give some definition, to what this all means, then I believe it is my place to do that (Participant 9).

This confident interviewee was didactic in several places, and the interviewer felt that he was being instructed by implication in basic storytelling etiquette. The lessons to be taken from this interview were about the value of sharing, appreciating group identity, the absence of exclusive personal ownership, and unquestioning acceptance of the rights of the community. Justifiably, other interviewees were angry (not making any effort to be polite) about the poverty of some past relationships between researchers and interviewees in other contexts.

Research does not always engender happy connections. An interviewer is privileged, and can present too omnipotently. In general interviewers must never assume superior knowledge:

> And that's another thing too with being researched, especially in my family line. We found that having an anthropologist there verifies [that] what we're saying is true. And that's in a European court of law. Because our history is an oral history handed down, because I was quite shattered with our anthropologist coming back and saying, 'Look we can't connect your actual ancestor with ... We cannot find stuff, and that has to be written down.' I said to him, 'Look you've shattered me because all my life I have known this, and now you're saying there is no evidence to it' (Participant 8).

Too often in the past the researcher has not only provided negative feedback, but none at all. Indigenous interviewees have had enough:

> I'm of the belief that people have done things, and used it and abused it, and worked it to death over the times. They've used us as guinea pigs. A lot of people have done research and papers and things like that. Coming from a mission, I've been through it all. People have done papers and you never get feedback or access to it (Participant 14).

A further cause for continual annoyance is deliberate theft of Indigenous knowledge:

> People come to the Centre [of work], they'll pick your brains, go back and write a thesis, and get top marks. The person they got the knowledge from doesn't get acknowledged for it. That happens quite often. It's not only with information, it's with art. A lot of things in the community where people take advantage. It is still happening (Participant 15).

The paradox about storytelling (that a story needs documenting as a surrogate in order to survive) has been mentioned already in this chapter. On occasion researchers have to accept that some knowledge will never be shared with researchers because it is too precious:

> It's no use having a story, for me, and then keeping it to yourself. But then that is so sacred it is only said within and to certain people within the family confines. So if someone from the university was to ask me, I'd say 'no'. It is very, very selective who it be told to, because you want that treasured.
>
> If you're telling a story, it's giving your heart away a bit. You come from a private space that usually you don't tell people (Participant 13).

There is a range of additional reasons why some oral knowledge may never be disclosed even within a local community, and certainly not beyond it. Such restraint is a form of respect for individual sensitivity, and a researcher has no choice but to follow the community embargo:

> There will be stories that will be taken to the grave for a whole range of reasons. I think it goes back to the era that some of these people grew up in, and talking about some of the previous government policies, particularly for those older people who are in the latter part of their lives now, looking at some of the things that happened back then, won't disclose because of that (Participant 9).

When asked if it would be too traumatic, Participant 9 replied:

> It could be. It could be fear of bringing shame to their family or community for whatever reason it might be... There is that degree of cynicism, scepticism, uncertainty, lack of trust, all sorts of things, so that they would rather hold those stories and take them with them to the grave... We have to respect their wishes for whatever reason it might be... But that's just the way it is and you have to accept it.

The argument in this section is that oral history can act as a shared meeting-place, as a democratic and empowering commons for communal knowledge. The interview process spurred some community members into fresh memory terrain, and for others it was an opportunity to demonstrate their moral control over the interview interactions. Abuse of community stories and Indigenous evidence by other researchers in the past has given interviewing a bad name, and it has been used so much for manipulative hegemony that it has led some storytellers to determine never to share their private knowledge with anyone at all.

Effects of research on the Indigenous community and research community

Abuse of past storytelling apart, there are further important effects of this research on the researched communities to note. As Randy Stoecker points out, the business of choosing appropriate researchers is not always easy:

> Communities… trying to fill a particular research need not only have to develop their own understanding of what they need, but they also need to really hunt to find a researcher who can fill that need (Stoecker, 2005, p.42).

Good research interactions require wise choices on all sides.

There are five effects of the project to summarise. They are that the first phase:

1. inevitably revived past painful experiences;
2. led to a degree of empathetic pain on the part of the interviewers;
3. illustrated the researcher's moral responsibility to recommend redress for past wrongs;
4. reaffirmed storytelling (or transmission of oral memory) as essential historical evidence, alongside complementary records and artefacts, and the non-Indigenous historian's efforts to make sense of the past; and
5. helped to articulate a permanent role for Indigenous storytelling as central to the survival of community identity.

These effects are elaborated further. This project carries the burden of the horrors of Indigenous experience which are ever close to the surface. We could not side-step them, and they affected community reactions. Inevitably the interviewees were reminded about the painful past:

> [Indigenous history] is pretty painful I think across the board. In fact I tend not to listen. I don't read Indigenous books, anything about Indigenous stuff because I work in [an] environment [where I am constantly exposed to social upheaval] and I have a great understanding of what's happened to [Indigenous people]. Just to keep reading it or even seeing 'The Rabbit Proof Fence'[24] – it's too painful. I don't want to even know about it, face it again (Participant 16).

The same interviewee raised the issue of how old the emotional scars might be, before they can be exposed fully:

> That's an interesting question. I think until we age on another two hundred years, then it may be that that access [to stories] is very restricted because it is still very near. It's not historical enough to be just general information, not enough distance. That's just my opinion. But that would change in another hundred years or two. I don't know about fifty years even. I'd say a hundred at least (Participant 16).

Another interviewee had clearly not thought about control over access to personal stories before. When asked, she was alarmed about being under the spotlight:

> That's a bit frightening actually. That's a bit scary. What if somebody does read your records and writes a story on you, and elaborates as all writers do? Good God, what hope have you got? So it would be good to have some sort of control (Participant 17).

In spite of the intense sad feelings aroused, nevertheless there was no dearth of Indigenous volunteers for our interviews. It is as well to remember that our research approach has the ability to remind non-Indigenous people of painful vicarious involvement also. Such was the feeling of the historian Peter Read, who has worked with the stolen generations and their traumatic memories for 25 years. He has been preparing (by interview) a biographical account of one Indigenous family which spans four generations, and he laments:

> In [my] 25 years of listening to oral history, apart from stories I've heard at massacre sites, I've never heard anything so confronting (Read, 2002, pp.58-9).

The experience of our researchers were no exception.

---

[24] A recent Australian film.

Graeme Davison posits a constructive role for the historical researcher faced with traumatic scenarios such as the European invasion of Indigenous Australia. In his view it is necessary that critical history assesses the past as objectively as possible, and embraces the moral responsibility to pass judgement on its horrors. Furthermore, historical researchers should make recommendations that might go some way towards redressing observed wrongs (Davison, 1988, p.74). It is no accident that this project incorporates the aim of providing usable results for a range of stakeholders, including the community itself, funding agencies, developers of policy and other practitioners. As mentioned above, the final phase involves recommending a system that would enable Koories to provide contextual information alongside the official record. The project has begun to build trust and understanding between archival institutions and Indigenous communities. Modelling archival systems that support community-based archival services is another aim.

On an abstract level there is a coalescence around the narrative role of the Indigenous storyteller and that of the historian. To some degree this research project has helped to publicise the role of storytelling as a constructive means of cultural transmission. It is possible to observe a shared function for storytelling by Indigenous communities and the objectives of the post-modern historian in practice:

> One finds an assumption that the ... workings of [historical] discourse are determined by ... a universal drive to impose meaningful reality on meaningless 'reality', to narrativize the dissociated fragments of contingent identities (Teows, 2001, p.8920).

Such a link emerged at the end of the interview with Participant 18, who was reminded of his nagging longing to find out more about his own background. He speaks of cycles of an inner urge for greater self-awareness, of a need to make sense of his heritage, as an Indigenous storyteller and as a family historian at the same time. The interviewer finished the questions, and asked Participant 18 if he wanted to add anything. He did:

> It's interesting, considering I've travelled since I was young and have just started to settle down now, I'm starting to want to find out more about all that stuff, so it is probably beautiful timing for this. [There is a time in everyone's life] when they want to go searching. I think it comes round every couple of years, but it gets stronger. It's like a little cycle that you go through. The more you go through that cycle, the stronger it gets. I've wanted to find out before, but it hasn't been as strong as now. Specially seeing a lot of other people who have that information. I've got a ten-year-old daughter as well, and she is always keen to know a lot of stuff so it is important that I am able to let her know as well (Participant 18).

One interviewee expressed the perspicacious view that Indigenous people will never be able to escape their past entirely, that its influence is unavoidably integral to temporal experience. In this excerpt storytelling and Indigenous history are inseparable:

> It's still part of your history, but it's been decisions that people before you have made, or been involved in, and therefore you can keep it within that context rather than someone being immediately involved in it… [If there is hurt later on] I think that's part and parcel of being aboriginal. I think it's part of having a past and having ownership to that past … At least you can rationalise it with the fact that that's the way things were then. That's the way they described us then. That's part of our history. There would also be pleasure in knowing that your forefathers did this, or practised that, or had some impact in some way on something else (Participant 20).

Non-Indigenous researchers may be free to select elements of their own past more casually for study, but such luxury is not available to Indigenous interviewees, for better or worse. It is hoped that this project will help to alleviate the past-in-the-present burden, always implicit in the act of storytelling, and a permanent mark of Indigenous identity. It should be assisted by the plan which this project proposes, to help to collect oral memories in an accessible repository under Indigenous control.

Conclusion

As described in this chapter, the research dialogue has been a joint, reflexive, and worthwhile experience. The first phase of this co-operative project – where user needs analysis was undertaken – has shown that the Indigenous community anticipates that a wide range of means of accessing recorded knowledge would be helpful to it, varying from existing archival norms, to an individual family retaining control over access to its own history and stories. A form of Indigenous repository is clearly favoured over deeply-distrusted 'government' institutions. The Koorie Heritage Trust has already begun to assume this mantle. In the interviews, a strong desire was expressed to be able to add fresh versions of 'stories', to set the official record straight, to acknowledge the innate dynamism of stories, and to create additional layers to stories. Future sensitive control over the online record is a fundamental expectation, requiring full and ongoing consultation.

It is hardly surprising that this chapter finds that Indigenous storytellers regard themselves as expert transmitters of culture. In order to respect that belief and to empower communities, any future modes of recording must accommodate the sensitivities of the storytellers, provide an element of entertainment, and function alongside irreplaceable oral modes of transmission. In their wide-ranging analysis of colonialist portrayals of Indigenous peoples by Western archaeologists, Ian McNiven and Lynette Russell (2005, p.241) have written recently that a corner has been turned, that in future it is likely that most, if not all, archaeological research projects focused on Indigenous heritage will be partnership projects.

Discussion of the problem of whether contrasting Western and Indigenous epistemologies and ontologies can be rationalised, will no doubt continue for some time. But it can be assumed that future joint investigations of Indigenous culture will be

> partnerships [which are] neither appropriationist nor hegemonic but mindful of the [Indigenous] host and [non-Indigenous] guest relationship and respectful of Indigenous cultural sensitivities (p.259).

The use of grounded theory assisted the research team to ensure that the interests of the researched communities were considered in all aspects of the project. The researchers were privileged to have access to Indigenous thinking about the problems posed by this topic. The research activities stimulated Indigenous ideas which the researchers were pleased to explore together. A challenge for the next two phases of the project is to respond to the expressed needs in constructive, practical, and useful ways. Sue McKemmish reminds that the time is ripe:

> Indigenous inscribing practices and oral ways of recording and remembering must... be addressed... The necessity to be inclusive... is underlined by the recordkeeping and archiving aspects of the stolen generations, reconciliation, documenting native title, and the preservation and transmission of indigenous community memory (McKemmish et al, 2005, p.331).

Acknowledgement

Whilst this chapter is based on the thoughts and experiences of specific author-members of the research team, the research team as a whole has been extremely supportive with encouragement, advice and discussions. We therefore gratefully acknowledge the ARC Linkage Project, 'Trust and Technology: Building an archival system for Indigenous oral memory' (T&T) team. This team includes the Chief Investigators Professor Lynette Russell, Centre for Australian Indigenous Studies, Monash University, Professor Sue McKemmish, Faculty of Information Technology, Monash University, Professor Don Schauder (2003-6), Associate Professor Graeme Johanson (from 2005), and Dr Kirsty Williamson (2003-4), with Partner Investigator Justine Heazlewood, Director and Keeper, Public Record Office Victoria. The industry partners are Public Record Office Victoria, the Koorie Heritage Trust Inc., the Australian Society of Archivists Indigenous Issues Special Interest Group, and the Victorian Koorie Records Taskforce. Past and current members of the Research Team include: from the Public Record Office Victoria Andrew Waugh, Rachel U'Ren (also of Faculty of Information Technology), Emma

Toon, and Merryn Edwards; from the Faculty of Information Technology, Dr Stefanie Kethers, Fiona Ross, Carol Jackway, Jen Sullivan, and Sharon Huebner (also from Koorie Heritage Trust); from the Centre for Australian Indigenous Studies Diane Singh, and the Australian Postgraduate Award (Industry) PhD researcher is Shannon Faulkhead. We would like to also thank our Advisory Committee.

Finally we acknowledge and thank the participants who agreed to be interviewed as part of the project, who shared their views and experiences with us.

References

Australian Broadcasting Corporation (2006). Dust Echoes; ancient stories, new voices. Retrieved 5 June from: www.abc.net.au/message/dustechoes/

Berger, P.L. & Luckman, T. (1967). The social construction of reality: A treatise in the sociology of knowledge. New York: Anchor Press.

Booth, W.J. (2006). Communities of memory; on witness, identity and justice. Ithaca, Cornell University Press.

Bruner, J. (1986). Actual Minds, Possible Worlds. Cambridge, Massachusetts: Harvard University Press.

Charmaz, K. (2003). Grounded theory: Objectivist and constructivist methods. In N. K. Denzin & Y. S. Lincoln (Eds.), Strategies of qualitative inquiry (2nd ed., pp. 249-291). Thousand Oaks: CA: Sage.

Charmaz, K. (2001). Grounded theory: methodology and theory construction. In N. Smelser & P. Baltes (Eds.), International encyclopedia of the social and behavioural sciences (pp. 6396-6399). Oxford: Elsevier Science.

Davison, G. (1988). Use and abuse of Australian history. Australian historical studies, 23 (91), 55-76.

Giddens, A. (1984). The constitution of society: outline of the theory of structuration. Berkeley: University of California Press.

Giddens, A. (1976). New rules of sociological method: a positive critique of interpretative sociologies. Cambridge: Polity Press.

Glaser, B. G., & Strauss, A. S. (1967). The discovery of grounded theory. Chicago: Aldine.

Grele, R.J. (Ed.). (1985). Envelopes of sound: The art of oral history (2nd ed.). Chicago: Precedent.

Hammersley, M. (1995). The politics of social research. London: Sage.

Human Rights and Equal Opportunity Commission (1997). Bringing them home: Report of the National inquiry into the separation of Aboriginal and Torres Strait Islander children from their families. HREOC: Sydney.

Kelly, G. (1963). The psychology of personal constructs, 1 & 2. New York: Norton.

Kingsolver, B. (1998). The Poisonwood Bible. London: Faber and Faber.

Lincoln, Y. S., & Guba, E. G. (1985). Naturalistic inquiry. Newbury, CA: Sage.

Madjar, I. & Walton, J. A. (2001). What is problematic about evidence? In J. M. Morse, J. M. Swanson & A. J. Kuzel (Eds.), The nature of qualitative evidence (pp.28-45). Thousand Oaks: California: Sage Publications.

McKemmish, S., Piggott, M., Reed, B., & Upward, F. (Eds.) (2005). Archives: Recordkeeping in society. Wagga Wagga, N.S.W.: Centre for Information Studies, Charles Sturt University.

McNiven, I.J. & Russell, L. (2005). Appropriated pasts: Indigenous Peoples and the Colonial Culture of Archaeology. Latham: AltaMira.

Ong, W.J. (1991). Orality and literacy: The technologizing of the word. London: Routledge.

Patton, M. Q. (1990). Qualitative evaluation and research methods (2nd ed.). Newbury Park: CA: Sage.

Pidgeon, N. & Henwood, K. (1996). Grounded theory: practical implementation. In J. T. Richardson (Ed.), Handbook of qualitative research methods for psychology and the social sciences (pp. 86-101). Leicester, England: British Psychological Society.

Read, P. (2002). Clio or Janus? Historians and the Stolen Generations. In K. Darien-Smith, (Ed.), Challenging histories: Reflections on Australian history. Special Issue of Australian Historical Studies, 118, 54-60.

Russell, L. (2005). Indigenous records and archives: Mutual obligations and building trust. Made Kept and Used: Celebrating 30 Years of the Australian Society of Archivists Seminar, held at the National Museum of Australia, Canberra, 5 April 2005.

Russell, L. (2004). Indigenous knowledge and archives: Accessing hidden history and understandings. Paper for the State Library of New South Wales and Jumbunna Indigenous House of Learning UTS, Libraries and Indigenous Knowledge Colloquium, Sydney, December 2004.

Saule, S. (2002). Ethnography. In K. Williamson, Research methods for students and professionals: Information management and systems (2nd ed., pp. 177-193). Wagga Wagga, NSW: Centre for Information Studies, Charles Sturt University.

Schwandt T. (2000). Three epistemological stances for qualitative inquiry: Interpretivism, hermeneutics, and constructionism. In N. K. Denzin & Y. S. Lincoln, (Eds.), Handbook of qualitative research (pp. 189-213). Thousand Oaks: CA: Sage.

Stillman, L. (2006). Understandings of technology in community-based organisations: A structurational analysis. PhD thesis in progress, Ch. 6.

Stillman, L. (2004). Community informatics. In Wikipedia. Retrieved 5 June 2006 from: en.wikipedia.org/wiki/Community_informatics

Stoecker, R. (2005). Research methods for community change: A project-based approach. Thousand Oaks: Sage Publications.

Sutton, R. I. (1997). The virtues of closet qualitative research. Organization Science, 8 (1), 97-106.

Teows, J.E. (2001). Linguistic turn and discourse analysis in history. In International Encyclopedia of the Social and Behavioural Sciences, 8916-8922.

Williamson, K. with Burstein, F. & McKemmish, S. (2002). The two major traditions of research. In K. Williamson, Research methods for students and professionals: Information management and systems (2nd ed., pp. 26-47). Wagga Wagga, NSW: Centre for Information Studies, Charles Sturt University.

Williamson, K. (1995). Maintenance of personal identity and local culture: The role of the telephone. In D.J. Wedemyer, (Ed.), Proceedings of the Pacific Telecommunications Council Seventeenth Annual Conference, 1995, Honolulu, Hawaii, pp 607-611.

Williamson, K. (2002a). Research methods for students and professionals: Information management and systems (2nd ed.). Wagga Wagga, NSW: Centre for Information Studies, Charles Sturt University.

Williamson, K. (2002b). Research techniques: Questionnaires and interviews. In K. Williamson, Research methods for students and professionals: Information management and systems (2nd ed., pp. 235-249). Wagga Wagga, NSW: Centre for Information Studies, Charles Sturt University.

Graeme Johanson, Kirsty Williamson and Don Schauder

Soalapule – The sharing of power: Reflections on community initiated research

Alison Greenaway, Jennifer Margaret and Robyn Allpress

> In October 2006 the Otara Network Action Committee (ONAC) initiated a research project to reflect on and document 'How ONAC works'. The project initiated on the basis of the 'Otara principles' was designed to ensure the first beneficiaries of the project would be people from Otara; that the project was owned by ONAC; that it would create opportunities for growth and development of people in Otara, a suburb of Manakau City, Aotearoa/New Zealand; and that people in ONAC would be empowered through the process of the research. An external researcher was invited to be a part of the team leading this project. What transpired was a fascinating multi layered reflection process that gives insight not only into community networking but also the way people build knowledge together.

This chapter tells the story of a community initiated research project in Otara, Manukau City, Aotearoa/New Zealand. The story is told part way through the research, by the three co-researchers[25] leading the research. We present our reflections through the first person plural personal pronoun (we), breaking out of this collective voice through use of quotes of individual researchers. This enables us to speak collectively and as individuals. Quotes from individual researchers also reveal the positionality of each researcher involved in the project, particularly our shifting insider/outsider positions (Denzin & Lincoln, 1994). We have also woven in voices of participants (and a non participant) of the research. The act of seeking out participants views about the research aided our reflection on the process, and provides examples of our methods of reflective research (Wadsworth, 1998; Ledwith, 2001). Our aim is for you, the reader to get a good sense of not only what we've been doing but some of the ways we've thought about and cared for the research process. We begin by introducing Otara, the reasons for the research and a bit about who we are. We then focus on the research steps taken and some of the ethical concerns we've explored. Underpinning this story and our research practice is a wariness of extractive research (Chambers, 1983); this informs our attempts to foster reciprocity through research (Spoonley 2003).

---

[25] Informed by methods of co-inquiry and action research (see Bray, 2000 and Reason & Bradbury 2001)

Otara, ONAC and the research sub group

Otara is located in Manukau City, New Zealand's most ethnically diverse and fastest growing city. Otara exemplifies the city's demographic trends – 42% of the population is below 20 years with high populations of Māori (20%) and Pacific peoples (63%) compared with the rest of the country[26].

Otara has a vibrant community that struggles with low incomes[27] and inadequate investment in the area (see Rankine, 2005). People are supported by a long history of community building practices, strong community identities and pride. External perceptions of Otara are mainly derived from the mainstream media in which it is most commonly portrayed as an impoverished and often violent place. However perceptions of Otara are shifting as more stories are told of a community with a positive vision, actively engaged in initiatives to create and maintain it as a safe and great place to live.

Otara has strong community networks. Monthly meetings of the Otara Network provide a forum for information sharing for community members and organisations, local government and social service agencies. The meetings are overseen by the Otara Network Action Committee (ONAC) which has been in existence since 2000.

ONAC formed out of a strong desire from people active in Otara for self determination and control of resources and projects. These aspirations were generated from experiences of external organisations and agencies holding on to power by using resources and operating in ways that did not acknowledge or respect people's wishes, e.g. poor or no consultation, projects and research that were of little or no benefit to people living and working in Otara. Residents and people working in community organisations in Otara wanted to change this dynamic; to work with Council and government agencies as equal partners.

ONAC is made up of representatives of community groups and agencies plus individual residents who attend the Otara Network. These people all hold a vision of how they would like Otara to be and are passionate about working for the best interests of the Otara community. Anyone can be a member of ONAC and the meetings are open. Membership changes constantly though there is a core group of thirteen people. Because of its open and flexible membership, sub-groups are formed to work on specific projects and issues such as economic development, community information technology and youth issues. The sub-groups work with the external agencies and organizations to progress action and report back regularly to ONAC.

---

[26] National figures are Māori 14.7% and Pacific peoples 6.5%. Figures for Pākehā (NZ European) are Otara 21%, national 80.1%. 2001 Census, Statistics New Zealand.

[27] The median personal income for people in Otara is below that of Manukau City and New Zealand (source StatisticsNZ)

- There are three key dimensions to ONAC's work:
- overseeing community projects and initiatives;
- community action; and strategic planning.

ONAC has developed the Otara Principles (included at the end of this chapter), which outline the values that are important to the community. The Principles are provided to external organisations as a basis for relationship building and are constantly referred to by ONAC internally. It is because of the strength of the Otara Network and ONAC that projects funded from a range of sources have come to Otara in recent years (Key informant, 2006).

Reasons for the research

After six years in existence ONAC had created a considerable body of community development knowledge and practice. There was a desire from within the group to record ONAC's story to date as a resource for the group and for other communities both within Aotearoa and overseas. It was thought that the process of telling ONAC stories would help to build a strong awareness amongst members of the history of ONAC, plus it would help to share what people have learnt with other communities looking to address issues in a similar way[28]. But who could do this research? The people most likely to were bound up in the work and too close to the action. It needed to be someone with the research skills who could look at things with a clear fresh eye and most importantly work well with the Otara people. The person to do this work required a style of working and values that fitted with the 'Otara Principles'.

Three members of ONAC, Robyn, Jennifer and Nita, were looking for ways to appropriately meet this desire. Robyn is a Community Advisor working for local government, Manukau City Council, in the Otara community. She has a coordination role in supporting ONAC and the action and projects that are undertaken by the group. Jennifer has a community liaison position at Manukau Institute of Technology, a tertiary education institute located in Otara. She began this role in 2000 and has been a member of ONAC since it was established. Nita works as the Injury Prevention Coordinator for Otara Health Inc., a primary health organisation, and has lived in Otara all her life. She joined ONAC in 2002 as part of the Otara Digital Opportunities Project.

In September 2005 Jennifer talked about ONAC with Alison, a researcher with Manaaki Whenua Landcare Research's Collaborative Learning Group. Alison has a long standing

---

[28] Our thinking was informed by our understanding of community story telling (see Ledwith, 2001) and process evaluation (see Lewin, 1952).

interest in community development and social change and she thought there was potential to do some research relating to community networks and sustainability.

> I discovered they had an interest in documenting and sharing with others how they operate as a committee that coordinates action initiatives for a community network. I was told of the achievements of this group and their recognition that they had learnt some important things about working as a group and facilitating a network of people attempting to improve their community. At the time I was looking for an opportunity to use some government funded research time (FRST: Building Capacity for Sustainable Development) to undertake an empirical study of community networks and capacity building for sustainable development. It seemed a good fit (Alison).

After the initial conversation, Jennifer talked to Robyn and Nita about this possibility and introduced them to Alison at the National Local Government Community Development Conference in September 2005.

Research relationships

Robyn, Nita and Jennifer formed the ONAC sub-group for the research. They took on a role as go-betweens in establishing and holding the relationship between ONAC and the external researcher. The purpose of this group was to work alongside Alison in shaping and undertaking the research process. The first step in this was having the research process mandated by ONAC. Because of their familiarity with ONAC's way of working the members of the sub-group knew the way in which the mandate for the research should be given.

In November 2005 Alison attended her first Otara Network meeting to get a feel for the community, its interests and issues.

> I sat in the back row for the two hours and said nothing apart from adding my voice to the common 'Amen'. Over tea I said a few hellos and was aware that subconsciously I was adjusting my posture and tone of voice in an attempt not to look like a 'Naive Journalist' or 'Wellington Bureaucrat' (perhaps the only two characters likely to get a colder reception than an 'Ivory Tower Academic'?) (Alison).

The idea for the research was also discussed with key ONAC leaders in November 2005 at an ONAC meeting without Alison.

> Within Otara there is a great deal of fear and suspicion of research because of previous negative experiences which have included lots of 'bad press' and processes which haven't honoured what has been shared by the community (people taking but not feeding back). We knew therefore that this could mean some resistance to the idea of researching ONAC and particularly to Alison coming in as an outside researcher (Robyn).

The research and Alison's role needed to be presented, discussed and accepted at an ONAC meeting. A key factor in it being accepted was that a number of the core members of ONAC who are trusted by the group were suggesting and supporting this process. When Alison was introduced to ONAC at their monthly meeting there were no major issues raised about the research at this meeting because Jennifer, Nita and Robyn had already held discussions with many ONAC members so they had an understanding of what was happening.

Jennifer discussed how she knew Alison and how the research idea had come about. Nita and Robyn both talked about the discussions of the sub group and made clear the idea for the research was driven by ONAC members, rather than Alison, and the sub-group would be guiding process. It was made clear the research would be beneficial to the group.

People asked how Alison was funded, and what her employers and funders would want the research to be used for. Other questions were 'Who would access the information given and the results published? What professional supervision did Alison receive and what structures did she have in place for dealing with ethical issues and considerations of the power dynamics in research?' Ownership of the research was discussed as well as ideas for how to manage the process of the research. People expressed wariness of being researched and frustrations with how researchers had operated in the past. The sub-group responded to these questions. Alison didn't get to talk at all through this discussion and the mandate for the research was given.

> I recognized how important it was for these questions to be openly addressed, the discussion helped me realise how aware people were of the possible detrimental implications of research. Whilst I had come prepared to face these challenges it was great to have the support of the others stepping in to deflect them (Alison).

It was important that the research questions and the process (what we are doing and why) were simple and that all the sub group members could explain it. This was both about ensuring participants could understand what it was about and reflecting the community ownership of the process.

> It was important for the sub group to reiterate why the research was happening and what it was about each time we talked about it with the community (Jennifer).

Undertaking the research

Once the mandate had been given we began working together as co-researchers. Jennifer, Nita and Robyn would set the agenda for the sub group meetings, which at the start, were held in the Tui Room in Otara (ONAC's usual meeting room). Alison filled the role of suggesting research tasks and methods. For example, it was Alison who suggested we do workshops followed by interviews and feed the analysis back to people through a concluding workshop (informed by ONAC's ways of working plus methods of co-inquiry, action and qualitative research, see Spoonley 2003; Smith 1999, Olsen & Shope 1991; Bishop, 1996).

The research design emerged out of our initial conversations identifying each other's needs and expectations. We realised the overarching research question was 'How does ONAC work?' It was the processes people wanted to focus on rather than documenting what ONAC does. We also came to realise that we were not at this stage asking the more evaluative question 'does ONAC work?' We were proceeding on the basis that ONAC does things that the people in ONAC think are worthwhile. This was a good starting point for building a common understanding amongst ONAC members of how those things had come about. We recognised that building a common story of ONAC's processes of operating and relating would be a useful first step for any future evaluative inquiry into the impacts of what ONAC does (see Greenaway and Witten, 2006 for discussion on the role of evaluative research for community projects).

A Challenge

In the second subgroup meeting in November, an ONAC member, who had not been at the ONAC meeting where Alison was first introduced, joined the group. He directed a strong challenge to Alison. The challenge was about Alison as an outsider coming in to research an already over researched community. He questioned what Alison and her organisation wanted out of the research.

> He seemed certain that Alison had predetermined the outcome for the research which was to fulfil her organisation's aims and intentions and not the community's. Alison had been clear about why she was involved and I felt that his testing of her was unsupportive and disruptive to the process that the sub-group had established and ONAC had mandated (Jennifer).

The other sub group members reacted strongly to this challenge, as they were ready to get underway with the research and felt that this person was obstructing progress. They also felt the community had moved on from these attitudes. This was a new type of research being done in Otara. ONAC had asked for it and was completely involved in determining the way the research would happen and the ownership of the material. At this meeting the challenger decided to leave it to the 'petticoat mafia' to get on with the research and that he would be involved in the research as a participant but not as a member of the sub group.

In subsequent ONAC meetings new comers would ask Alison 'what are we going to get out of this research'. Jennifer, Nita and Robyn would respond, asserting it was an important opportunity to reflect on their work. Alison supported this by stating what she could offer was to help create space for reflection and document what came out of this reflection. Story-telling and oral history are embedded in the practices of ONAC so there was already strong appreciation of this way of working.

The principles behind this research

There are underlying principles to the way ONAC works, which are documented as the Otara Principles. These formed the basis for the way we worked on the research together. In particular it is important that people in Otara are the first beneficiaries of the research. Otara provides the base, the motivation, and the commitment to its projects, therefore the people of Otara should benefit first and foremost from the outcomes. We are all very cognizant of the power that research can have representing people's experiences. So it was important for us that the control of the project sat strongly with members of ONAC and that the ownership of the research was clearly defined from the outset.

We were also aware of the opportunities for growth and development that could arise through the research. The primary motivation for this research is the empowerment of ONAC by creating space for critical reflection, learning and skill sharing about the processes ONAC has developed for working together.

> It was important to do this research to better ourselves and our community, and to be seen as an example for other groups and communities to follow. ONAC is an important voice who will speak for the community. We need to know whether it is working and whether our goals are being achieved. ONAC members are leaders and we are accountable to the community (Tai; participant).

Another key consideration in designing the research process was how it would impact on the group. We were particularly aware of how we needed to be able to allow tensions, conflict and painful history to be acknowledged in a safe way. Awareness of this influenced how we structured the workshops and the language we used for questions. It was also important to ensure participants felt control over what is shared publicly.

Flexibility on the part of both ONAC and Alison's employers to negotiate deadlines and outputs has been important. Linked to this is the appreciation that this research needs to be productive in a number of ways. We realised we need to show people in Otara, Manaaki Whenua Landcare Research and FRST the benefits of the research immediately through the workshops and the research process, through the final reporting process and eventually through a published paper.

The process of legitimising the research and maintaining integrity of the co-research relationship has meant that we have all taken care with how we present the research to various audiences. This has been complicated by the fact that Alison is also undertaking PhD research at the University of Auckland. When discussing the research with work or University colleagues, Alison makes a point of emphasising the shared ownership and co-research relationship.

What we did

Our research is designed to enable people to tell stories about ONAC and reflect on the processes and relationships that are important to ONAC. This meant we wanted to use a mixture of techniques to enable people to talk in a group as well as individually. The research design included three workshops, some document analysis and open ended interviews. A prime consideration in this design was to use activities that ONAC people are familiar with, that draw on ONAC's way of working together, and that would not take too much time to organise or participate in.

We started with two workshops. The first was designed so people would tell their own stories of how they got involved with ONAC. It focused mainly on engagement with ONAC – what motivated and enabled people to get involved and then what kept them involved. At this workshop we put a large timeline up on the wall of the Tui Room so that people could write on it when they got involved and the various projects they have been involved with. This timeline has been left on the wall of the room and over the months people have slowly added to it.

> The first workshop jostled our memories of what ONAC had accomplished. By listening to everyone talking, we remembered what had been achieved and how we had been involved. We discussed how we grew from each project. It was very positive and we need to do this more often (Debbie; participant).

The second workshop focused more on the collective stories of ONAC, looking at the roles, relationships and rules that have developed to form distinctive ONAC ways of working together.

> The process has been slow and the two workshops have been held a number of months apart. The timeframe has stretched out further than originally planned (we have already extended past our initial deadline of 6 months) but I don't think this is a problem, more of a luxury. It is giving us time to think about the results of the workshops as we go. We're in no hurry. Already some of the material has been used in a presentation to a Regional Networking Forum in Auckland. There is also interest in the results of the research from other organisations such as Manukau City Council and the Community Sector Taskforce (Robyn).

The research is currently at the phase between the second and third workshops. Alison has undertaken eight semi-structured interviews with a range of people with different connections to ONAC. She interviewed people who have been involved in ONAC quite intensively but are not currently involved, people who support ONAC but are not directly involved and then people who have had difficult relationships with ONAC in the past.

It has been valuable to hear from those outside of ONAC who represent a variety of perspectives on ONAC. Alison as the external researcher has conducted one to one interviews. This provided a less threatening opportunity for people to reflect on ONAC than if ONAC members had done the interviewing themselves.

As stated above there are very strong principles shaping the ethical stance we have taken for this research. We ensured the research design meets not only the University of Auckland's ethics committee requirements but also the requirements of ONAC's principled way of working. In doing, so we have questioned notions of maintaining confidentiality in research. The co-research relationship has meant members of ONAC (Robyn and Jennifer) have access to the interview transcripts and notes.

> This is unusual as a process because Robyn and Jennifer are 'players' rather than impartial observers, and I have to note that clear definition of roles is one of the issues around ONAC's operation. However, I am willing to roll along for the wider aspiration of better functioning (Anonymous).

Some of the interviewees had difficulties with the co-research approach to gathering and analysing the data and queried the legitimacy of the research.

> I would like to participate however on some reflection this is not appropriate seeing this research is not confidential and could in fact affect

the validity of the findings as people not just me may have to 'temper' a response to some of the questions hence honest feedback may not be forthcoming (Anonymous).

Our response was the research gains legitimacy by having both internal and external researchers developing themes and analysis from the interview data. We have weighed off giving interviewees a chance to express their opinions to a 'neutral' listener against ownership of the representation and analysis process.

Deciding who to involve in the research

We had lengthy discussions about who to involve at different stages of the research process. ONAC is an open group but we decided that for the first two workshops it was important that it was just those who had been involved for a long time who participated. This allowed for more depth in the discussions as people were working from a shared history. There was some questioning of this by ONAC members who weren't invited to participate in these stages. They accepted the rationale when learning that the third workshop will be open to everyone so that all members will have an opportunity to participate in the process. Communication about the process and progress of the research in ONAC meetings has been important to ensure everyone knows what was going on.

The value of the external researcher

The two workshops were designed by the subgroup and Alison. The group has looked to Alison to provide guidance and facilitation. She recorded (on a digital recorder) the discussions with permission of the participants and then wrote up the discussions. The style Alison used in leading the workshops has been very low key and allowed plenty of time for discussion and participation. While there was structure to the workshops there has been plenty of time and opportunity for everyone to contribute and enlarge on themes and talk about experiences. Alison was very empathetic to the community and open to its way of working. While having an unobtrusive style, she has known when to step in and provide guidance or move things along.

> We accepted Alison because she came in with a different approach. She's come in with us, explained why she's there. She doesn't push her way in (Yvonne; participant).

> Alison doesn't talk in 'research speak', keeps things simple and makes use of a framework that allows full participation. It's all about the group and they have been having fun (Robyn).

> For us (the sub-group) the opportunity to have an external researcher work with us is great. It has ensured we give time to talking about our processes, so the research didn't keep dropping to the end of the to-do list. Alison has brought research skills. She has distance from the group and a fresh perspective which has been valuable to our reflective process. Having her facilitate the workshops meant we could fully participate, which was important to us. Also, Alison's skills and experience in community development has meant she has contributed to our reflections and group process beyond the scope of the research (Jennifer).

The value of the research

Our meetings as co-researchers have been a place of learning, analysis, reflection and have contributed to building all of our skills. In terms of the research itself, stepping back from the day to day running of ONAC and reflecting on the group has been really valuable. We can see a number of benefits from the research to date, for example the group building and strengthening.

> The research has generated enthusiasm for and commitment to ONAC. It has been celebratory whilst also addressing some of the hard issues we have not been able to clearly focus on in the past. The research has created a degree of honesty that has been healing. We have had a chance to talk about our differences and still stick with it (Jennifer and Robyn).

> ONAC has been going for seven years and is the steering wheel of everything that happens in Otara. It's good to stop and look back, see if we've made changes and where those changes have been (Yvonne; participant).

Working as co-researchers

Nita had a change of employment and in her new role could not continue to be involved in the research sub-group. The three remaining co-researchers for this project are all Pākehā[29] women in full time employment. We have regularly reflected on our positions with this research and why it is that we are the ones making it happen. Some common skills and perspectives we share are linked to our being Pākehā women who acknowledge our colonial heritage. We also share an approach to our work that actively seeks to recognise and reconstruct the power relations that shape our work and lives. In addition, we are practiced at operating reflexively and value reflective practice. We have found this project

---

[29] Colonial descendants.

both refreshing and fun and are interested by the multiple layers of reflection with which we have been engaged.

Next steps in the project

We have just completed the interviews. We will undertake some initial analysis together as co-researchers and then develop the analysis further with the participants of the third workshop. We are still developing ideas of what the 'final report' might look like. Our aim is to produce a report that can be used for a number of purposes and for different audiences. We want an active useful resource that can be used for giving presentations, background papers etc. A range of media will be used so the resource might include photos, slices of interviews, music, artwork as well as written documents. The report will only represent the ONAC story to date so it needs to be stored in a way so other chapters can be added – e.g. a record of the projects so far, community issues and actions, copies of submissions, histories of people and community groups involved in ONAC.

As well as creating this resource there is a need to think about ways to integrate research into ONAC practice and to take action on the ideas that have come out of the process e.g. ONAC's approach to external relationships, and considerations for interaction within the group. This might take the form of discussions about some of these areas within the third workshop as well as establishing a regular (bi-annual or annual) reflection process for ONAC.

The process has already produced useful discussion for the group and some valuable insights into ONAC's approach and position. It has also led to the creation of resources and opportunities to share the learning, a key one being a presentation Nita and Jennifer (supported by other ONAC members) made to representatives of eighty community organisations at an Auckland City Strengthening Networks Forum in July 2006. We presented at the 2007 National Local Government Community Development Conference and are looking for other opportunities to share ONAC's story. We look forward to learning more through the second half of the research and aim for this also to be a constructive way of enhancing the relationships and processes by which ONAC works.

Closing thoughts

We are just over half way through our community based research process, thus we close this chapter with some final reflections as opposed to a conclusion. Our research process is a work in progress based on knowledge and experience drawn from many fields. We have focused on the attention we are paying to building research relationships of reciprocity based on ONAC principles. We have been able to create a space for fun and critical reflection on ONAC. This chapter outlined how we have incorporated integrity, clear principles from which to work, flexibility, creative insight and appropriate ways of meeting people's needs. In writing this chapter we created another space for reflecting on the research. We feel very privileged to have the time and space to do these many layers of reflection. This privilege (which is also an expectation from members of ONAC) is partially due to our common identity of professionally employed educated women. We continue to actively examine the limits to which this shared identity enables or inhibits learning across cultures.

The strength of our process is also in the levels of co-learning we are engaged with. We are the first to admit that we, the three women involved in the sub-group leading this research, are the ones who are currently benefiting most directly from the research process. However, what we have found is the learning process extends beyond the research project into ONAC and other community and research projects we are concurrently involved with. Thus we are achieving far more than documenting and sharing stories about how ONAC has worked in the past. As we learn together and share this with our networks we are gaining insights that shape how we act in community today as a community of practice (Wenger, 1998).

> What do I think of the research on ONAC and why it is important? It's necessary for the sole purpose of self review, evaluation, assessment and yes gratification. Only those who participate in ONAC will understand whether what they have been part of is working. To reflect is to look at your own performance and those who sit next to you. It gives you knowledge that what you and others have contributed to has helped, or not. It also gives direction to ONAC. We can get caught up in the needs of others who come to see us and seek support rather than focussing on the true needs of our community. We are change agents but we mustn't think that we can do it on our own. We always need guidance and this comes from each other. The research is necessary to ensure that we are thinking generally the same, that we want the same outcomes and that we can contribute to achieving the outcomes. The goal is for ONAC to support the process of change for the community of Otara.
>
> Does Otara want us to do that? We haven't asked them the question, and we more than likely won't because in the end we (this is me) do it for ourselves because we want the best for our community that we live in (Nita; participant).

References

Bishop, R. (1996). Whakawhanaungatanga: Collaborative Research Stories. Palmerston North: Dunmore Press.
Bray, J., Lee, J., Smith, L. & Yorks, L. (2000). Collaborative inquiry in practice: action, research and making meaning. Thousand Oaks: Sage Publications.

Chambers, R. (1983). Rural Development: Putting the Last First. London: Longman

Chile, L.M. (2006). The historical context of community development in Aotearoa. Community Development Journal 41, 407-425

Denzin, N.K. & Lincoln, Y. (Eds.). (1994). The Handbook of Qualitative Research. Thousand Oaks: Sage Publications.

Greenaway, A. and Witten, K. (2006). Meta-analysing community action projects in Aotearoa/New Zealand, Community Development Journal 41, 143-159

Kondrat, M. E. (1999). Who is the "Self" in Self-Aware: Professional Self-Awareness from a Critical Theory Perspective, Social Service Review 3(4), 451–77.

Ledwith, M. (2001). Community work as critical pedagogy: re-envisioning Freire and Gramsci. Community Development Journal 36 (3), 171-182.

Lewin, K. (1952). Field theory in social science: selected theoretical papers, edited by Dorwin Cartwright. London: Tavistock

Olson, K. & L. Shopes (1991) Crossing boundaries, building bridges: Doing oral history among working class women and men in S. Gluck and D. Patai (eds.) Women's Words: The Feminist Practice of Oral History. New York: Routledge.

Rankine, J. (2005). Housing and health in Auckland: a summary of selected research. Auckland Regional Public Health Service and Auckland District Health Board.

Reason, P. & Bradbury, H. (2001). Handbook of action research. London: Sage Publications.

Smith, L. (1999). Decolonizing Methodologies: Research and Indigenous Peoples. New York: Zed Books.

Spoonley, P. (2003). The challenge of cross cultural research. in C. Davidson and M. Tolich (eds.) Social Science Research in New Zealand: Many Paths to Understanding. Auckland: Pearson.

Wadsworth, Y. (1998) What is Participatory Action Research? Action Research International, Paper 2. Retrieved 1 July 2007 from www.scu.edu.au/schools/gcm/ar/ari/p-ywadsworth98.html.

Wenger, E. (1998) Communities of Practice, Cambridge: Cambridge University Press

Appendix

OTARA COMMUNITY PRINCIPLES

These principles were developed and adopted by the Otara Network Action Committee in May 2003. They were reviewed and updated in April 2007. The Principles are the important aspects and values that we wish to uphold. All principles are inter-dependent, that is, any single principle will not contradict another.

1. **Te Tiriti O Waitangi**

   The Otara community recognises the indigenous rights of mana/tangata whenua. Te Tiriti o Waitangi is our founding document and can be implemented in a number of ways. Community processes and projects will provide opportunities to implement the Tiriti in practical ways, and governance and management bodies will identify these opportunities on a project-by-project basis. This principle also recognises mana whenua/tangata whenua as having a special status that is in balance with the needs of multiculturalism and diversity.

2. **First beneficiaries**

   As Otara community provides the base, the motivation and the commitment to its projects, the people of Otara should benefit first and foremost from the outcomes.

3. **Leadership and working style**

   The Otara community values its distinct ways of leading and working together. It recognises that every member of the collective has a contribution to make towards decisions, and should be given the opportunity to contribute. All spokespeople and leaders will aim to represent that which is for the 'good' of the entire community.

   The Otara community has a mature style of teamwork where members of the collective will at different times play roles of leaders, workers, entertainers, elders, planners, strategists, etc. It places importance on consensus decision-making processes. This is called 'soalaupule' which literally means the sharing of power.

4. **Looking after the collective**

   Projects provide opportunities for community growth and development. However, the successes are dependent on the commitment of those involved. Participating groups will be accountable to each other as the successes of its projects are dependent on the support and full participation of *all* groups. In turn, projects will support those who participate fully to achieve their goals.

5. **Empowerment**

   The reason for involvement in projects is the empowerment of the Otara community. This includes acknowledging and respecting the existing strengths of individuals and the community as a whole. It involves enabling people to enhance their existing skills and fulfil their goals.

6. **Ownership**

   Otara takes responsibility for the issues it faces as a community. The community holds the knowledge and skills to provide appropriate solutions to these issues. The community works with external organisations who can support them in addressing these issues by contributing time, resources and information.

   The Otara community has existing structures and decision-making processes that are supported and strengthened through collaboration, recognition and acknowledgement.

7. **Relationships**

   Healthy working relationships between organisations, agencies and people are essential to achieving good outcomes for the community. This applies to relationships at all levels both within the community and externally.

   We recognise that strong relationships take time to build and maintain and require trust and understanding. We value relationships which are based on respect and integrity. An important component of relationships is an understanding of power between those involved. The community seeks to engage with other groups who acknowledge and value these Principles as the basis for working together.

8. **Accountability**

   We commit to meeting our accountabilities we expect that external groups will do likewise and that in circumstances where difficulties arise, good faith will prevail. We will accept advice and support from external groups and offer the same to them for the collective outcomes we all require. We encourage good and timely communication so that all parties are able to support each other towards meeting their accountabilities.

9. **Sustainability**

   Sustainability means exploring ways working towards a better life for current and future generations without compromising others (including the environment). Sustainability is about maintaining commitment to a long term vision through thinking about long term impacts, learning from the past and trying new ways of doing things. The Otara community understands the interconnectedness between issues and values a holistic approach to addressing issues. Sustainability is also about preparing present generations to take up their rightful place as future leaders of our families, local community and Aotearoa/New Zealand.

10. The Commons (The koha[30] principle)

The Commons is where we place resources that are created for the common benefit of Otara people and other communities. These resources may include the things and ideas that are developed as part of our projects. They may be offered to similar communities who are looking for ideas they can benefit from. In turn, other groups have created resources that Otara can use and even modify to suit its projects. Knowledge and resources held in the Commons can be protected by ensuring copyrights and intellectual property are explicitly stated.

---

[30] Koha = gift.

Methodology and process

17 ways that 'community talk' misguides research

Bernard Guerin and Pauline Guerin

> In this chapter, we discuss how community research is influenced by the ways we talk and think about communities and how they function. Based on our research and experiences with indigenous, ethnic and refugee communities in New Zealand and Australia, we explore two main groups of issues that we see as problematic in our understanding of communities. Within those, we identify 17 ways that our 'community talk' can misguide research. These broadly divide into two main issues. The first main issue is that how we talk about communities usually does not reflect the reality of people's lives in communities. The second issue is that the community talk can be strategic to access resources or to support an agenda. We conclude that researchers need to be aware of these influences when conducting research and that participatory and long-term research approaches are necessary to our understanding of social issues, particularly for indigenous, ethnic and refugee communities.

Governments, researchers, non-government organisations (NGOs) and others have been working hard to link with the communities that make up societies. These 'communities', however, are often those that are recognizable or obvious. For example, a common response to any problem with different communities such as Māori, Pacific Island, refugee, or migrant, is to send Government representatives around the country to conduct community meetings or to get in touch with the local community leaders. This is considered to constitute 'community involvement', 'community consultation' or 'community participation', and what is reported often forms key ingredients for Government social policy.

Similarly, there is a growing movement for researchers to involve communities in research collaboration rather than doing research 'on them' or 'through them'. There are definite advantages to this, although a few problems with such approaches are also now becoming clear (Cahill & Hart, 2006; Cartwright & Allotey, 2006; Merzel & D'Affitti, 2003; Quaghebeur, Masschelein & Nguyen, 2004; Seifer & Sisco, 2006; Uzochukwu, Akpala & Onwujekwe, 2004; Williamson & DeSouza, 2007). While some of these problems with community-based research have arisen from rushed attempts at collaboration, or from using the collaboration for other ends, part of the problem, we argue in this chapter, can arise from how communities are talked about (i.e., our 'discourses' surrounding communities) rather than anything to do with the communities themselves or resource or logistical problems.

While part of understanding communities comes from working with or alongside people in the community, involving the material processes of community decisions, resources, and relationship building, another important part comes from understanding the talk or discourses around and within communities. There are many subtleties to this 'community talk', and we will go through a number of these with examples from community research.

We loosely divide the subtleties of 'community talk' into 17 ways[31]. Broadly, there are two main issues in how 'community talk' can influence our research and understanding of communities:

- Talking about communities in certain ways can lead us to imagine communities and the people who form certain communities in a non-realistic way that then can misguide community research.
- Talking about communities can be strategically used to give certain impressions—by the community, government, researchers, or others—and this can interfere with and influence research and practice.

We will now explore 17 ways that talking about communities can be problematic, grouped into these two main categories. These are not all the ways that talking about communities can be problematic, nor do all these problems happen all the time. This discussion provides a basis for being more critical and reflective of our conversations about communities and how this can influence our research.

Communities are not what they are talked about

When we talk about 'communities', we are already talking in an abstract way or making generalised statements about communities that are not necessarily connected to the realities of lives in communities. There are numerous ways that 'communities' are talked about that are shorthand or abstracted from the real workings of communities (Della-Piana & Anderson, 1995; Green, Cohen & Pooley, 2006). For example, in saying "The community is unhappy with the government's approach" we are already abstracting from the people making up the community. These discourses are sometimes used to make things simple, but they also can misrepresent and misguide our research. If you go to work with a 'community' and expect a certain pattern which is not really there, many things can go wrong—and they often do.

First, there are some common ways we talk about communities, particularly indigenous, ethnic or refugee communities, that are good for talking but bad for reality. For example,

---

[31] We have used the structure of '17 ways' to organise this chapter in keeping with the structure that we have used in other publications (Guerin, 2001). While other structures could have been used to organise this chapter, the main ideas are the same.

people sometimes talk about a 'traditional' community although this does not mean old or old-fashioned, as is sometimes implied by such talk—'traditional' community organization is happening now all over the world, in both urban centres and rural areas. 'Traditional' communities were/are also not all rosy, but are often talked about as a sort of utopian group of people with mystical and idyllic practices. Conversely, 'modern', urban communities are not all bad either although they are sometimes portrayed that way in comparison to these pristine 'traditional' communities. It is also not the case that people in 'traditional' communities all like one another and get on perfectly—there are conflicts. Similarly, strangers in big cities are not all rude to each other and ignore each other—there are many contexts in which urban strangers act with respect and are caring towards each other. Interestingly, we also sometimes talk about 'traditional' research, which usually refers to scientific-influenced or positivistic approaches, which are also abstract and diverse but are construed as something uniform and homogenous and as the 'superior' method that we must all rally against. Ironically, the two uses of 'traditional' have nothing in common, except, perhaps, their over-simplification as discourses.

Second, migrant and refugee communities are often talked about as cohesive and tight communities, based on 'traditional' practices and social organization. However, outside of this talk, many, if not most, of the people who arrive as migrants or refugees have been part of communities that have changed or been disrupted before or after they arrived and we must not assume that people form part of intact or cohesive communities. Refugee communities, in particular, have often been disrupted for many years, there has been conflict and separation of the members during the conflict, they have lived in refugee camps where communities get dispersed, and there can be leaders or elders who have died, gone missing or have relocated elsewhere in the world. Among many indigenous communities, globalisation and various colonisation efforts have disrupted community and family relationships and practices. We will see later that it is sometimes in the interest of the community to portray themselves as cohesive, but the reality is that many of the community parameters have been changed or disrupted and anyone expecting to work with a cohesive community may miss important things going on.

Third, Jeffers, Hoggett and Harrison (1996) point out that 'community' often gets mixed with 'race' and 'ethnicity'. That is, people casually refer to a community when they are referring to a race or an ethnicity and, in that way, treat the community as cohesive and non-disrupted when in fact it may not be. That is, a 'community' is not always racially or ethnically determined, nor do all ethnic or racial groups form 'communities'. Communities may involve people of different 'races' and ethnicities in some capacity or another, such as urban, geographic communities. Referring to 'the Sudanese community' or 'the African community' misses this point. Similarly, what are called 'traditional' or kin-based communities are not all based on ethnicity, race or indigeneity. There are many examples, such as the Exclusive Brethren (a fundamentalist Christian group that resides in western societies but stays aloof), of tight, kin-based communities not based on any of these verbal category markers.

Fourth, referring to kin-based communities in terms of being 'traditional', 'ethnic' or 'indigenous' also leaves out that many are now mixed in with non-kin-based western communities. Most people are, and have been, exposed to very different concepts of what a community is and how to manage them, and over time communities will become (or already have been) changed or disrupted by this interaction with western communities. For example, Becker (1998) showed how two religious communities successfully adapted to a changing racial mix in the congregation, and how black-Americans were incorporated into formerly all-white congregations.

Fifth, almost all communities we know of and have worked with have families or individuals who lie outside of the 'community' by choice and are therefore not included when a 'community' is represented to researchers, government agencies or others. Some families or individuals prefer not to associate with an ethnic or racial community, some move away from the community for special schooling or other conditions, while some remove themselves because of conflict. None of these tend to get included in collaborations or research with the 'community' of interest. In fact, these families or individuals can then 'fall between the cracks' in that they are not included in social structures and access to resources for 'their community' and can also be excluded from mainstream resources because it is assumed that they are being looked after by 'their community.' In terms of research, inclusion or exclusion of such individuals and families presents challenges, both to the research process, and also to interpretation of results.

Sixth, Shelly (1996) pointed out in his study of people in a 'Vietnamese community' in Milwaukee that ethnic identity by itself was insufficient to sustain a 'community'. For example, 'New Zealanders' or 'Australians' might travel to another part of the world, perhaps Africa, and meet up with other Australians and New Zealanders, but this national identity is insufficient to sustain a community. National identity might help for support in the short-term but if there is little in common other than national identity, then a 'community' formation would not likely be sustained. Our verbal framing of ethnic, refugee and indigenous communities leads us to forget this point and implicitly assumes that because they are 'all the same ethnicity' that 'they' will succeed together.

Seventh, methods of community consultation vary widely: some communities work through councils, some work through meetings, others work through elders and yet others work through word of mouth. This means that Western methods of consultation—working through an executive meeting or a council—will not necessarily capture 'the community' depending on their background. For example, we found that research with a Somali community, with both, an executive and community structure as well as a group of elders, was most successful when done through word of mouth. We found that things were passed through the community quickly in this way and that is where people heard about things, not at a meeting. For example, when doing interviews with women on the topic of female circumcision, after the first few interviews, the main interviewer was phoned by many women asking to be included in the project, simply through word of mouth. The whole idea of the Somali community having a big meeting of everyone together, even if it was separate for males and females, was not one that we found worked, although the community did have meetings on occasion. We also found that not everyone agreed on research ideas and approaches and that it was important that individuals could still agree or not agree to participate in research. This was not a decision that a community council, or even a group of elders, could make and we needed, as researchers, to remember this point.

Eighth, our use of words to categorize communities, especially in terms of ethnicity, race or indigeneity, can lead people to assume that the researcher or whoever is working with that community needs to be someone from that 'community' and that they would be (automatically) better than someone not from that 'community'. For example, we have seen people assume that research with a Somali community would be best done by a Somali researcher. There are arguments against this assumption (Guerin, 2005, p.33) and evidence that in many contexts it is false (Andrade & Burnstein, 1973; Cuco & Pierce, 1977, p.51; Gatmon et al., 2001; Helms & Carter, 1991; Kim, 1990; Moon et al., 2000; Tom & Cronan, 1998). For example, just because someone is indigenous does not mean that they would prefer to have an interviewer who is indigenous or that they would somehow respond better with an indigenous interviewer. Nor can we assume that a non-ethnic or indigenous researcher will be preferable in certain cases. Whether such a matching works or not is contextual and cannot be assumed from the category words we use about the people involved. We need to find out what works best and not assume because of our 'community talk' that the same label is always better.

Finally, for this section, is our ninth point. There is some evidence from McComas (2003; also Carr & Halvorsen, 2001) and from our experience that people do not always take community meetings seriously but research and 'community consultations' held, for whatever reasons, via 'community meetings' can assume that results from these meetings are authoritative. McComas (2003) found that few people attended community meetings and when they interviewed people from the meetings they found a large number were sceptical of what was 'decided'. They found the people believed, perhaps correctly, that what came out of the meeting would not be taken seriously by those who are consulting and it would be thrown away and not used in the long run. People may well get up and say their piece in front of the meeting but doing so does not suggest that they believe it would actually help change anyone's view. While many communities do attend and utilize meetings, we must be careful of assuming that a verbal statement such as, 'there was a community meeting in which the community attended and discussed and voted the issues', reflects the reality of what actually happens.

'Community' is a strategy not a given

The second broad issue for this chapter is that there is evidence showing that the whole concept of, and way of talking about, 'community' is not just a given that applies to a group of people but that this concept can be used strategically for certain ends, be they good or bad. This means that talking about 'communities' can be even more in doubt than just natural misrepresentation from category mistakes and over-simplification.

Our tenth point, then, is that 'myths' about communities can be created. For example, migrating or refugee communities can have community myths, such as, that 'they will all return to their homeland one day', that 'they are a tight community', or that 'they are working together in unison' (Black, 2002). When talking with community leaders (a term discussed below), we might hear such stories about a community. Such myths can function to engender solidarity amongst members, to consolidate a certain strategy or course of action for the community, or to persuade government and other officials. For example, community leaders who present a story about how closely the community works together and how well they support each other is more likely to be successful at acquiring resources for 'the community' than is a community that is seen as having much internal conflict. These 'stories' are not necessarily malicious or seeking to do harm, but are part of the normal stories we use to facilitate life (Guerin, 2004).

Eleventh, McDonald and Armstrong (2001) and others found that there is much romanticising of community social support. In a similar way to our earlier point about 'traditional' or 'kin-based' communities not always getting on well together, also misguided is the idea that such communities will inevitably and automatically pull together to provide support for one another. This 'community cohesiveness' can be used by communities to argue for resources going to the community as a whole rather than to individuals. But it can also be used as a strategy by governments or funding bodies to forgo providing social and material support for these 'cohesive communities' since 'they prefer to look after each other'. We have heard service providers remark that 'these people have their own community, they can look after them better than we can', little realising that there was no strong community and the community social support was being romanticised for other reasons (some given below).

Our twelfth point is that using the 'community' category ignores the diversity of people contained. White (2002) points out that this can be especially so when referring to 'refugee communities'. Refugees come from all nations, all different types of conflict, some from natural disasters rather than human conflict, and to put people into a community category as refugees is strategic rather than a given natural category. There is also the question of when does someone stop being a refugee? At what point does a category no longer apply, and, as there is no correct answer, this again suggests that it is not a natural category and can be used in various ways. To refer to 'refugee communities' can be very misleading if one is not careful. What are the researchers or funders assuming when they consider a project relating to a 'refugee community'?

Thirteenth, Tuffin and Danks (1999) point out that referring to communities can strategically be a problem because one ends up talking about dual communities and thereby excluding one of the communities either with good or bad intent. For example, if one talks about the 'Somali community' then one also ends up constantly talking about the 'non-

Somali community', or worse, the 'New Zealand community' even though most Somali refugees in New Zealand are also New Zealanders with New Zealand passports. So the talk of a 'Somali community', strategically for good or bad, can exclude them from the other category of 'person residing in New Zealand' because two communities necessarily get invented in the discourse. For example, if we talk about things we find out about the 'Somali community', these things can imply that the 'not-Somali community' is *not* that or *is* that, which are not necessarily true. More specifically, if we learn that unemployed Somali have multiple family commitments that negatively impacts on their ability to find and maintain employment, this does not mean that non-Somali who are unemployed do not have those same family commitments (Guerin, Guerin, Diiriye & Abdi, 2005).

Fourteenth, Kelly (2003) provides some useful data from a Bosnian refugee 'community' that communities can be constructed in order to gain benefits even when there is no informal community in existence otherwise. In this case, the government had policies that funnelled benefits to communities rather than individuals, therefore leading the people in a 'community' to create a community image or to make themselves look inappropriately coherent. Similarly, community members in a Mexican community participation program were guided almost wholly by the resources they could gain locally rather than for the value of the program (Zakus, 1998). So the existence of policies with financial or other help available can create the communities in the first place, even if the people themselves in the families are not in contact normally and there is no informal support for interactions apart from the benefits they might gain. This is also known from colonization that government policies for 'communities' can lead to the construction of a community to match the policy (Guerin, 2004). On the other hand, that strategy of colonists providing support only to individuals has also led to the destruction of communities, which is equally problematic. Again, we need to find out which is best rather than be led by 'community talk'.

Fifteenth, we have seen a variation of the previous point in our community practice in the creation of unitary 'community committees' that do not have any real authority to represent the families and people (also see Kalka, 1991). In order to gain resources, communities that might not otherwise have a coherent committee or executive are forced to create one (McEwan, 2003). Problems then occur because these committees do not have a mandate and do not represent all the people gathered in that 'community', but those people do not have an option to work as individuals because of other points we have made above. Furthermore, in many cases, executive functions can become based along family or kin lines and be biased in these ways.

Sixteenth, similar points arise when investigating 'community development' or 'community care' programs (Hudson, 2004; Potter & Collie, 1989; Tuffin & Danks, 1999). These terms often are used to refer to coherent communities with identified leaders, all working together for a traditional or modern common good to facilitate the development or care of the community. These programs often, however, turn out to have many social and political underpinnings that were really facilitating the development (e.g., Page, 2003). This is not bad or wrong in itself, but it does mean that people involved can be misled by the rhetoric of 'community development' and 'community care'. It also means that attempts to transfer successful community development programs will not work because the real factors underpinning the cooperation and development—the hidden social and political underpinnings—are not going to transfer. What is verbally presented as the story of a community development project and its success is not telling us what was really making the project work (Page, 2003).

Finally, the concept of 'community leaders' or 'representatives' can also be used strategically (Jewkes & Murcott, 1998; Potter & Halliday, 1990; Potter & Reicher, 1987). Researchers may prefer to work with 'community leaders' making it sound like there is a singular person who can represent the community when in fact that person may not be a leader of the whole community and there may well be dissention within that community. Using the term 'community leader' gives one the verbal impression that one has consulted or that one has represented the larger community when that may not be the case. As pointed out earlier, researchers may look for community leaders to work with since that is simpler to do and it fits the western bureaucratic model easier. Potter and Halliday (1990) found that the media in particular utilized 'community leaders' to give particular slants on news, even when the label was unwarranted.

Conclusions

The conclusion from this chapter, in broad terms, is that there is a fundamental mismatch between how most people, and especially government and academics, talk about 'communities' and how 'communities' actually function, work and live (the same is true for talk about 'society', Bowers & Iwi, 1993). Our main point for this chapter is that this is especially so for refugee, ethnic, indigenous and migrant communities, although it can apply to many other named communities in our society, such as rural 'communities', a school 'community', or a community based around a profession such as the 'nursing community'.

'Communities' are neither static nor are they unitary. There are groups within communities, and individuals within these. Communities change and bureaucracies need to become more flexible to treat the exceptions and the variations. For example, our research in New Zealand with Somali reflected the issues and concerns that were relevant at that time. Since then, political chaos and violence has, yet again, plagued Somalia and this will likely have impacts for many Somali, all around the world. The settlement of Somali in New Zealand, now for over a decade, has implications for every aspect of Somali life such as identity, language, education, employment, youth, elderly, and research issues. When talked about, however, such diversity can be lost as well as the history and make-up of the 'community'. This is where, we believe, most of the problems with community-based research and interventions arise, that were alluded to at the start of this chapter. We are not arguing to stop such approaches, but to become less enamoured of the discourses surrounding communities and spend more time and resources instead on documenting the details and the contexts of communities, and people who comprise them, as they exist, *in the moment* (Guerin & Guerin, 2007). In the short term, casually and glibly using the term 'community' might make things easier to talk about, but in the long-term such attempts come unstuck and the hard work still needs to be done.

Acknowledgement

This chapter was supported by funding from the New Zealand Foundation for Research, Science and Technology (UOWX0203, *Strangers in Town: Enhancing Family and Community in a More Diverse New Zealand Society*), a Divisional Grant from the Division of Education, Arts and Social Sciences at the University of South Australia, and a research contract to the CRC: Desert Knowledge Core Project 4 *Sustainable Desert Settlements*.

References

Andrade, S. J., & Burnstein, A. G. (1973). Social congruence and empathy in paraprofessional and professional mental health workers. Community Mental Health Journal, 9, 388-397.

Becker, P.E. (1998). Making inclusive communities: Congregations and the 'problem' of race. Social Problems, 45, 451-472.

Black, R. (2002). Conceptions of 'home' and the political geography of refugee repatriation: Between assumption and contested reality in Bosnia-Herzegovina. Applied Geography, 22, 123-138.

Bowers, J., & Iwi, K. (1993). The discursive construction of society. Discourse & Society, 4, 357-393.

Cahill, C. & Hart, R. A. (Eds.). (2006). Pushing the Boundaries: Critical International Perspectives on Child and Youth Participation [Special Issue]. Children, Youth and Environments, 16(2).

Carr, D., & Halvorsen, K. (2001). An evaluation of three democratic, community-based approaches to citizen participation: Surveys, conversations with community groups, and community dinners. Society and Natural Resources, 14, 107-126.

Cartwright, E. & Allotey, P.(Eds.). (2006). Women's Health: New Frontiers in Advocacy & Social Justice Research, Haworth Press. Simultaneously published as a special issue of the journal Women & Health, 43(4).

Cowlishaw, G. (1999). Black modernity and bureaucratic culture. Australian Aboriginal Studies, 2, 15-24.

Cuca, R., & Pierce, C. S. (1977). Experiments in family planning: Lessons from the developing world. London: Johns Hopkins University Press.

Della-Piana, C. K., & Anderson, J. A. (1995). Performing community: Community service as cultural conversation. Communication Studies, 46, 187-200.

Gatmon, D., Jackson, D., Koshkarian, L., Martos-Perry, N., Molina, A., Patel, N., & Rodolfa, E. (2001). Exploring ethnic, gender, and sexual orientation variables in supervision: Do they really matter? Journal of Multicultural Counseling and Development, 29, 102-113.

Goodkind, J. R., & Foster-Fishman, P.G. (2002). Integrating diversity and fostering interdependence: Ecological lessons learned about refugee participation in multiethnic communities. Journal of Community Psychology, 30, 389-409.

Green, A., Cohen, L., & Pooley, J. A. (2006). In search of community in Western Australia: A qualitative study of adults' conceptualizations of their communities. The Australian Community Psychologist, 18, 58-70.

Guerin, B. (2001). Individuals as social relationships: 18 ways that acting alone can be thought of as social behavior. Review of General Psychology, 5, 406-428.

Guerin, B. (2004). Handbook for analyzing the social strategies of everyday life. Reno, Nevada: Context Press.

Guerin, B. (2005). Handbook of interventions for changing people and communities. Reno, Nevada: Context Press.

Guerin, B., & Guerin, P. (2007). Lessons learned from participatory discrimination research: Long-term observations and local interventions. The Australian Community Psychologist, 19, 137-149.

Guerin, P., & Guerin, B. (2007). Research with refugee communities: Going around in circles with methodology. The Australian Community Psychologist, 19, 150-162.

Guerin, P.B., Guerin, B., Diiriye, R. O., & Abdi, A. (2005). What skills do Somali refugees bring with them? New Zealand Journal of Employment Relations, 30, 37-49.

Helms, J. E., & Carter, R. T. (1991). Relationship of White and Black racial identity attitudes and demographics similarity to counselor preferences. Journal of Counseling Psychology, 38, 446-457.

Hudson, K. (2004). Behind the rhetoric of community development: How is it perceived and practices? Australian Journal of Social Issues, 39, 249-265.

Jeffers, S., Hoggett, P., & Harrison, L. (1996). Race, ethnicity and community in three localities. New Community, 22, 111-126.

Jewkes, R., & Murcott, A. (1998). Community representatives: Representing the 'community'? Social Science & Medicine, 46, 843-858.

Kalka, I. (1991). The politics of the 'community' among Gujarati Hindus in London. New Community, 17, 377-385.

Kelly, L. (2003). Bosnian refugees in Britain: Questioning community. Sociology, 37, 35-47.

Kim, C. S. (1990). The role of the non-western anthropologist reconsidered: Illusion versus reality. Current Anthropology, 31, 196-201.

MacQueen, K. M., McLellan, E., Metzger, D. S., Kegeles, S., Strauss, R. P., Scotti, R., Blancahrd, L., & Trotter, R. T. (2001). What is a community? An evidence-based definition for participatory public health. American Journal of Public Health, 91, 1929-1938.

McComas, K. A. (2003). Trivial pursuits: Participant views of public meetings. Journal of Public Relations Research, 15, 91-115.

McDonald, K. B., & Armstrong, E. M. (2001). De-romanticizing Black intergenerational support: The questionable expectations of welfare reform. Journal of Marriage and Family, 63, 213-223.

McEwan, C. (2003). 'Bringing government to the people': Women, local governance and community participation in South Africa. Geoforum, 34, 469-481.

Merzel, C., & D'Affitti, J. (2003). Reconsidering community-based health promotion: Promise, performance, and potential. Public Health Matters, 93, 557-574.

Moon, L. T., Wagner, W. G., & Kazelskis, R. (2000). Counseling sexually abused girls: The impact of sex of counselor. Child Abuse & Neglect, 24, 753-765.

Page, B. (2003). Communities as the agents of commodification: The Kumbo Water Authority in Northwest Cameroon. Geoforum, 34, 469-481.

Potter, J., & Collie, F. (1989). 'Community care' as persuasive rhetoric: A study of discourse. Disability, Handicap and Society, 4, 57-64.

Potter, J., & Halliday, Q. (1990). Community leaders: A device for warranting versions of crowd events. Journal of Pragmatics, 14, 905-921.

Potter, J., & Reicher, S. (1987). Discourses of community and conflict: The organization of social categories in accounts of a 'riot'. British Journal of Social Psychology, 26, 25-40.

Quaghebeur, K., Masschelein, J., & Nguyen, H. H. (2004). Paradox of participation: Giving or taking part? Journal of Community & Applied Social Psychology, 14, 154-165.

Seifer, S. D., & Sisco, S. (Eds.). (2006). Mining the Challenges of CBPR for Improvements in Urban Health [Special Issue]. Journal of Urban Health, 83(6).

Shelley, N. M. (2001). Building community from "scratch": Forces at work among urban Vietnamese refugees in Milwaukee. Sociological Inquiry, 71, 473-492.

Tom, T. L., & Cronan, T. A. (1998). The effects of ethnic similarity on tutor-tutee interactions. Journal of Community Psychology, 26, 119-129.

Tuffin, K., & Danks, J. (1999). Community care and mental disorder: An analysis of discursive resources. British Journal of Social Psychology, 38, 289-302.

Uzochukwu, B. S. C., Akpala, C. O., & Onwujekwe, O. E. (2004). How do health workers and community members perceive and practice community participation in the Bamako Initiative programme in Nigeria? A case study of Oji River local government area. Social Science & Medicine, 59, 157-162.

White, A. (2002). Organic functionalism, 'community' and place: Refugee studies and the geographical constitution of refugee identities. Geoforum, 33, 73-83.

Williamson, A. & DeSouza, R. (Eds). (2007). Researching with communities. London: Muddy Creek Press.

Zakus, J. D. L. (1998). Resource dependency and community participation in primary health care. Social Science & Medicine, 46, 475-494.

Direct qualitative analysis of data from digital audio sources

Andy Williamson and Ruth DeSouza

> New technologies offer increasing potential for supporting qualitative researchers in their work. Combining high quality digital audio recording with computer-based textual analysis software presents researchers with the opportunity to work directly from audio. The author's present an example of coding directly from audio and explore the advantages of such a process, such as preserving the richness of the conversation and its value for analyzing large focus groups where English is not the first language for the majority of participants. Coding directly from audio also offers potential time saving, narrowing the delay between conducting focus groups and interviews and being able to analyze rich data, an important consideration in commercial or participatory research, where feedback loops need to be shortened.

Technology, we are told, is becoming ubiquitous. It encroaches into many aspects of our daily lives. Increasingly it seems we are being called on to learn a new way of doing what we did before. For a disadvantaged community, this was by way of a government funded initiative to introduce computer literacy and access to community groups. In this chapter, we present a brief exemplar of how we, as a technology research team, harnessed improvements in digital and computer based audio technology to help evaluate how that community was coming to terms with information and communication technologies (ICT). We note the limitations of this chapter in that it is brief and therefore unable to articulate all of the issues and learnings in detail. Also, the project was a commercial evaluation project with a limited timeframe, meaning that the processes used and lessons learned are not necessarily directly transferable to purely academic research or to larger scale projects.

There is an emerging awareness of the efficacy and usefulness of digital tools in qualitative research. Brown (2002) charts the rise of digital technology and suggests some impacts and strategies for researchers who wish to utilize it to enhance their practice. Productivity of the research team is also a motivation for the transition to digital audio, removing the time, cost and re-working by the researcher of traditional transcription methods (Mitchell, Peterson, & Kaya, 2004). Masten and Plowman (2003) go further, suggesting that digital tools offer the potential for re-conceptualizing the way that qualitative data is analyzed. They also note that much literature alluding to the use of digital technology is simply advocating the replacement of traditional research methods and practices with digital ones, rather than incorporating new possibilities offered by new technologies or extending the current repertoire. Such digital methods offer benefits to qualitative researchers in terms of privileging the voice of research participants by retaining a direct link between original voice and the analysis (Crichton & Childs, 2005).

A new range of textual analysis products computerize (rather than simplify or automate) the qualitative researcher's toolkit. There are three functions that are available which include direct transcription, voice recognition and text management. Examples of qualitative analysis software include QSR's NVivo (www.qsr.com.au), Atlas-TI (www.atlasti.com) or Qualrus (www.qualrus.com) and others (see the CAQDAS website at caqdas.soc.surrey.ac.uk). Software such as Transana (www.transana.org) and Express Scribe (www.nch.com.au) facilitate the direct transcription of audio. Dragon Naturally Speaking (www.scansoft.com/naturallyspeaking) allows voice to be directly converted to text; however it is limited to the voice in which a particular computer is trained and useless for group interactions. This means that transcription still takes time and the richness of the original recording is lost in the conversion to text. Transcribing large focus-groups with a number of competing speakers, strong accents and significant background noise inevitably results in a loss of richness.

This chapter describes a qualitative research project that accepted Masten and Plowman's (2003) challenge to be innovative in research design. In this research project textual coding took place directly from digital audio files, rather than transcribing these prior to coding. The chapter provides a brief overview of the project, the methods employed in data collection and data analysis, including an explanation of the processes used that made coding directly from audio a viable option. It will then go on to discuss issues of quality and rigor and identify lessons learned such that these might assist other researchers considering employing a similar process.

Background

The authors were asked to carry out a review of a recently established community informatics project. This project was government funded and designed to provide ICT, training and support to a number of community groups in a socio-economically disadvantaged community. The evaluation project was made up of two parts; first, a review of the project management and project processes (which is not discussed here) and, second, to discover what the project meant to the participants themselves. It is this second part of the project that forms the background to this chapter.

Successful community informatics projects are embedded within communities and support the aspirations of the community that they serve (Day, 2003). This project was seen as achieving two aims by introducing ICT skills into a community. The first resulting in an immediate increase in motivation for and access to technology as a tool amongst the direct participants. Second, to assist in building the long term ICT skills capacity in the wider community, thereby increasing economic development. Obtaining feedback directly from the participants was useful both locally to know that the project was succeeding and nationally in terms of future policy development and funding.

The brief for the research team, therefore, was to understand what the project meant to the participants from their own point of view. The research team spent a number of months visiting the community, attending workshops and hui (a Māori term for a community meeting) and over this period of time provided information to the community on what the evaluation was about and what their role was (and was not). This occurred in parallel to the first part of the research project and the participants were provided with draft copies of this material as soon as it became available.

Potential participants in our research were identified as anyone involved in any of the 22 community groups who were participating in the project. Representatives of funding and management bodies were excluded from the second phase of the research.

The Focus Group

Because the ICT project had not advanced as quickly as was hoped by the sponsors, the research team decided that a single focus group would be sufficient. This was followed up by informal and semi-formal interviews with a number of the participants.

The focus group itself consisted of approximately 25 participants and was run as a hui or community meeting (which was the standard practice for the community). The session lasted for two and half hours and a number of participants came and went as the session progressed. Two members of the research team attended, one was allocated the role of facilitator and the other was responsible for note taking and recording the session but also co-facilitated at times due to specialist knowledge of the project and because they had built rapport with the community prior to the study formally commencing. The hui took place in a moderately sized meeting room, with participants around the outside (the room was just about at full capacity).

A structure for the semi-structured focus group was developed by the researchers who facilitated the group and by a third member of the team. The majority of participants spoke English as an additional language. The process ensured that at the beginning of the focus group interview the purpose of the research was reiterated and the option of not taking part was restated. It was made clear that participants could stop the interview and the recording at any time. Participants were supplied with an Information Sheet that explained the nature and purpose of the research and with a Consent Form.

Data Collection

Data was collected in written form (as observations and notes) and the focus group was digitally recorded using professional digital audio recording equipment with two high-quality microphones. The decision to use this equipment was taken because of concerns held by the researchers relating to the size of the group, the fact that many of the participants were not native English speakers and the nature of the environment in which the focus group was held (as it turned out, it rained torrentially onto the tin roof during parts of the focus group). Whilst CD-writing equipment was used in this example, we have subsequently repeated this process using digital audio recorders and software to segment the recorded audio – they key factor to be aware of is the quality and reliability of the microphones and recording equipment.

Processing the Audio

Because this was a commercial evaluation project grounded in a vulnerable community, innovative and expedient methods were required for the recording and analysis of the focus group process. A rapid turnaround of material was required so that ownership of the research process and the intellectual capital that informed the process was validated and remained with the participants. Digital recording and coding directly were thought to facilitate that aim and reverting to traditional transcriptions practices could occur if this new method failed.

The design of the process called for the digital recording to be segmented into easily accessible tracks (fortunately this was automated by the equipment used). The reasoning behind this was that any part of the focus group could be reached quickly through hyperlinks without having to search or skip through large portions of audio. Upon completion of the focus group, the CDs were 'finalized' to prevent over-recording. At this point there existed 150 minutes of audio data and the CDs were now in a standard format that could be played on any household CD player (itself useful for reflection and group analysis).

The next stage was to migrate these files into a more user-friendly computer-based format. MP3 was chosen as being flexible, reasonably sized and of sufficient quality for the nature of the project. Specialist software was used to convert the CD audio to 150 individual MP3 files and these were stored in a secure folder on the lead researcher's computer (the research team was obviously cognizant of confidentiality and ethical issues and wanted to ensure that there was no likelihood of unwanted access to these files). A document was created which was designed to contain hyperlinks to the source audio files, so that when it was edited in Microsoft Word, the user could simply click on a link to go straight to the sound file. This file also contained space for notation and comments. This process acted not only to rigorously review and assess the data but also as a first-pass analysis of the themes that might emerge from the focus group. Once completed, the file was converted to a Rich Text File (RTF), to be imported into NVivo, and to an HTML file so that it could be viewed through a web browser.

In parallel with this process, the researcher's notes were typed and distributed to the participants for their information and feedback. These notes also formed one of the input documents to the analysis process.

Data Analysis

The researchers' epistemological position was interpretative and participatory. A qualitative approach was used because the project was not intended to produce quantifiable statistics on how the ICT is (or could be) used. Rather it was an attempt to identify qualitative factors that identify real and perceived social benefits. The research was grounded in the concepts of action research because:

> [it] is the application of fact-finding to practical problem-solving in a social situation with a view to improving the quality of action within it, involving the collaboration and cooperation of researchers, practitioners and laymen (Burns, 1997, p.346).

It is important for the qualitative researcher to immerse themselves in their data (Tolich & Davidson, 1999). This was no different for the research team using audio than it would be for a textual transcript. Indeed, the key value of the audio data was felt to be the depth of the research experience that was captured and, therefore, able to be articulated (this includes tone, non-syntactical gestures and participant interactions). The single-minute tracks made this particularly simple because it was extremely easy to repeat a segment or skip back and forward. It was also easy for the researchers to quickly recall different parts of the focus group interview to compare and contrast comments that were made, which Belisle (1998) suggests is a key benefit of digital audio.

During the analysis, drop markers (think of these as digital post-it notes) were generated. These contained not only key textual references and summaries of the focus group but also emerging themes and keywords and were constructed iteratively as segments were repeatedly analyzed. This demonstrates the benefits of immediate recall; not only does the audio recreate the focus group for the researcher, there is no delay in the research process whilst waiting for transcripts to be prepared, edited and corrected. Qualitative researchers recognize that good data is perishable, as Strauss and Corbin (1990) observed, data analysis and collection are symbiotic processes.

The RTF file was now ready to be imported into NVivo along with the notes from the focus group. This document contained an outline of the focus group and the researcher's thoughts, linking directly to the source audio. Unfortunately, NVivo's ability to process audio files (and any other externally linked file, for that matter) proved significantly poorer than we were led to believe. Whilst this is entirely possible, NVivo chose to ignore our existing hyperlinks that converted intact to the RTF. NVivo provides a proprietary feature called 'data bites'. These are in effect simple hyperlinks to external documents but they had to be re-created. This process was made more frustrating by the primitive design of NVivo's interface, which required us to re-navigate the folder structure each time a data bite was added. It must be said that this proved a serious flaw in the viability of NVivo for this purpose, it seemed to us that the feature was poorly thought through and even more poorly implemented. Eventually, although some data bites were set up, it was decided to be expedient and use the HTML file to navigate sound files whilst generating code from the documents imported into NVivo.

At this point, textual links and links to audio data were 'free-coded' in NVivo, so that the emergent themes could be identified. This process was blind reviewed by a second member of the project team to ensure consistency and check for bias in the original coding. Once a broad group of free-codes had been created, the research team analyzed these to determine relationships and hierarchies, eventually determining five key themes.

Epistemology

It is important in a community-based project that the researchers are both participants in the process and observers within the study. The researchers saw their role in this project as 'paddling a waka' (a traditional Māori canoe) alongside the participants, acknowledging our own role as guests but also developing relationships with the participants. This approach is consistent with that recommended by Guba and Lincoln (1989, p.11), who promote that "participants [are] accorded the privilege of sharing their constructions and working toward a common, consensual, more fully informed and sophisticated, joint construction, [where] they [are] accorded a full measure of conceptual parity."

Knowledge acquired from qualitative research methods seeks to understand the participant's view. It can, therefore, provide a suitable framework for identifying issues that are of concern. By using such a qualitative research method, the participants would be able to maintain control over meanings and the naming of their own realities in relation to their experience of the project. Researchers have an overt and political commitment to the participants in their research and a commitment to ensuring that the research process is non-hierarchical, reciprocal, negotiated, emancipatory and subjective (Mirza, 1998).

Whilst we consider the end result to be substantially the same as for traditional research practices (coding from a transcript), and indeed would have had no issue with using traditional transcription, we did feel the need to privilege the lifeworld of our research participants. It was for this reason that we wished to work with the original audio as it allowed us to capture subtle intonations and culturally specific use of language that could have been missed or even lost in a transcription. Theories that have arisen from a particular perspective are not necessarily inclusive of voices from the margins, where culture or ethnicity are defining dimensions of the experience of being in the world (Allen, 1999). Our standpoint aligned with Allen, noting that cultures are discursive objects and it is important that as researchers we do not support systems of injustice by "unintentionally reproducing ideological discourses under assumptions of descriptive neutrality" (Allen, 1999, p.232).

It is important to analyze not just the content of the knowledge that is produced through research, but also the process in which research is conceived, produced and justified as knowledge. This is because research is "an active process, engaged in by embodied subjects, with emotions and theoretical and political commitments" (Gill, 1998, p.24), that have an impact on the process. The narratives used by participants reflect both their social location and the cultural resources that they have access to, and will also have an impact on the process (Jackson, 1998). As researchers, the choice of methodology and the research design are influenced by our own identities and "we inevitably bring our biographies and our subjectivities to every stage of the research process, and this influences the questions we ask and in the ways in which we try and find answers" (Cameron, Frazer, Harvey, Rampton, & Richardson, 1992, p.5). Researchers also have a pivotal role in shaping the research encounter through the theoretical, ontological, personal and cultural frameworks that they hold (Luttrell, 2000). The question is how can they faithfully represent the voices of the researched in a way that is both rigorous and valid?

Research needs to faithfully represent the community being studied as well as be rigorous and valid, so that it can attract the attention of those who are able to do something about the concerns raised. Qualitative research by its very nature always carries the possibilities of alternative explanations and a measure of uncertainty. Research is more complex when participants are drawn from diverse groups and it was important for the researchers to be aware of the need to produce clear, refined analyses which were not seen as being assessed from ethnocentric frameworks.

Ensuring Rigor

Lincoln and Guba (1985) recommend the use of four criteria to ensure rigor in qualitative research projects, namely: Credibility, transferability, auditability and confirmability. To ensure credibility, member checking with research participants occurred and feedback from participants as to the reliability of the study was obtained during the research process. Lincoln and Guba also recommend prolonged involvement with participants, in order to ensure that researchers have learned about the culture they are studying, and peer debriefing. This took the form of team members attending regular hui and spending time being immersed in the community and the project. Re-enforcing this building of participant relationships, the project team also used independent supervisors, experienced in the research method used. Given the leading-edge nature of the project being researched, transferability was difficult to ascertain, however, this was achieved to some degree through the experience of some participants and the expertise of the research team. Finally, auditability and confirmability ensure that the research findings match the data. This was achieved by having another researcher review the research notes and audio files, the codes and the decision trails so that the process of the research could be clearly followed.

Lessons Learned and Conclusions

The project has demonstrated that there is significant potential for the use of direct analysis from digital audio and that such a process offers significant advantages where richness and timeliness are important. We consider that the key lessons learned from this process were:

- Audio preserves the richness;
- Immediacy of access was of critical importance in the analysis phase;
- The ability to carry out iterative passes of audio segments and add comments and notations as they emerged was vital;
- Text and sound can be accessed by multiple researchers but security (and anonymity) can be protected;
- Computer based audio files, linked to textual analysis provides a strong audit trail;
- Test that the software does what you want (and expect) it to do. If doing something new and innovative, the risk is greater, so ensure that you have a contingency; and
- Using a commercial-quality recorder and high-quality microphones meant that we captured the detail and didn't lose our focus group to thunderous rain. In terms of audio equipment, you really do get what you pay for.

The direct use of the audio files during the analysis and coding process allowed for the full richness of the focus group to emerge. Audio was not transcribed verbatim, rather it was annotated and the raw audio used directly for analysis. Summaries were then posted or e-mailed to participants and participants were given the opportunity to make changes as required.

The research team's reflection on this experience is that the emergence of new, high-quality digital audio and computer-based qualitative research tools enabled the voices of the research participants to be captured and privileged in the emergent themes of the project. The participants in the process have indicated to us that the information we have captured and the themes we have described have accurately reflected their views. Furthermore, the ICT skills available to the research team meant that the use of emerging digital technologies was able to close the gap between focus group and data analysis, ensuring that the experience remained fresh in the minds of the research team.

Acknowledgement

This chapter emerged from research undertaken in a community setting in Aotearoa New Zealand. Whilst the chapter is about process rather than the research or the community, the authors acknowledge the members of that community, their mana and their role in this process. The knowledge gained from this project belongs to that community and our role was simply to assist them in forming and articulating it.

References

Allen, D. G. (1999). Knowledge, politics, culture and gender: a discourse perspective. Canadian Journal of Nursing Research, 30(4), 227-234.

Belisle, P.(1998, December). Digital recording of qualitative interviews. Quirks Marketing Research Review.

Brown, D. (2002). Going Digital and Staying Qualitative: Some Alternative Strategies for Digitizing the Qualitative Research Process. Forum Qualitative Sozialforschung, 3(2), Retrieved 5 Jun 2005 from www.qualitative-research.net/fqs-texte/2002-2002/2002-2002brown-e.htm.

Burns, R. B. (1997). Introduction to research methods (3rd ed.). Melbourne, VIC: Addison Wesley Longman Australia.

Cameron, D., Frazer, E., Harvey, P., Rampton, M. B. H., & Richardson, K. (1992). Introduction. In T. Crowley, T.J. Taylor & M. Williamsburg (Eds.), Researching language; Issues of power and method (pp.1-29). London: Routledge.

Crichton, S., & Childs, E. (2005). Clipping and coding audio files: A research method to enable participant voice. International Journal of Qualitative Methods, 4(3), Retrieved 5 Jun 2005 from www.ualberta.ca/~iiqm/backissues/2004_2003/html/crichton.htm.

Day, P.(2003). Community (information and communication) technology: Policy, partnership and practice. In S. Marshall, W. Taylor & Y. Xinghuo (Eds.), Using Community Informatics to Transform Regions. Melbourne, VIC: Idea Group.

Gill, R. (1998). Dialogues and differences: Writing, reflexivity and the crisis of representation. In K. Henwood, C. Griffin & A. Phoenix (Eds.), Standpoints and differences: Essays in the practice of feminist psychology (pp.18-45). Sage: London.

Guba, E. G., & Lincoln, Y. S. (1989). Fourth generation evaluation. California: Sage Publications.

Jackson, S. (1998). Telling stories: Memory, narrative and experience in feminist research and theory. In K. Henwood, C. Griffin & A. Phoenix (Eds.), Standpoints and differences: Essays in the practice of feminist psychology (pp.45-65). Sage: London.

Lincoln, Y. S., & Guba, E. (1985). Naturalistic inquiry. Beverley Hills: Sage.

Luttrell, W. (2000). "Good enough": Methods for ethnographic research. Harvard Educational Review, 70(4), 499-523.

Masten, D., & Plowman, T. (2003). Digital ethnography: The next wave in understanding the consumer experience. Design Management Journal, 14(2), 75-81.

Mirza, M. (1998). 'Same voices, same lives?': Revisiting black feminist standpoint epistemology. In P.Connolly & B. Troyna (Eds.), Researching racism in education; politics, theory, practice (pp.55-67). Buckingham: Open university press.

Mitchell, S. G., Peterson, J. A., & Kaya, S. (2004). Making the switch to digital audio. International Journal of Qualitative Methods, 3(4), Retrieved 8 Jun 2005 from www.ualberta.ca/~iiqm/backissues/2003_2004/html/mitchell.html.

Strauss, A., & Corbin, J. (1990). Basics of qualitative research, grounded theory procedures and techniques. California: Sage.

Tolich, M., & Davidson, C. (1999). Starting fieldwork: An introduction to qualitative research in New Zealand. Auckland, NZ: OUP.

Researching inequalities: Lessons from an ethnographic study

Ghazala Mir

> Studies exploring health inequalities have often demonstrated the inappropriateness of service provision in relation to the needs of disadvantaged communities. However, the research methods used to explore these issues have been subject to less scrutiny. This chapter considers whether research methods used for a study of long-term illness in a Pakistani community in the UK were appropriate and sensitive to the needs and priorities of Pakistani people. Findings in relation to fieldwork revealed the value of ethnographic methodology in providing context to data from semi-structured interviews. However, attitudes towards research within the Pakistani community, which formed part of this context, indicated that many Pakistani respondents felt disengaged from and cynical about the research process. They also felt vulnerable to exploitation and to abuse of trust from researchers and other professionals. These findings have implications for the methodological approaches adopted during research and their acceptability to research subjects in marginalised communities. Research methods and designs that engage individuals and offer reciprocity through practical outcomes that meet their needs are suggested as more appropriate than traditional qualitative methods.

This chapter aims to critically evaluate methods used in an ethnographic study of long-term illness within a Pakistani community in the UK and to draw from these more general lessons about research in socially excluded groups. The study adopted a complex range of data sources to explore whether and to what extent religious identity influenced the processes of communication and decision-making about long-term illness management. This research question was prompted by the high level of certain long-term conditions within this social group (Department of Health/HM Treasury, 2002; Acheson, 1998), evidence that communication is a particular issue in relation to access to services and management of self-care (Mir & Tovey, 2001) and the primacy of religious identity within the Pakistani community (Modood et al., 1997).

The following sections describe fieldwork for the study and draw on findings about these to highlight the strengths and weaknesses of the methodology adopted. These are considered in the context of attitudes to research within the Pakistani community concerned. Possible responses to these weaknesses are considered along with the more general implications for how studies are designed and conducted within this and other marginalised groups.

Ethnographic methodology

Qualitative methodology is particularly valuable when an area is under-researched, complex relationships are involved, and when the life experience of participants is central to the development of knowledge (Ryan et al 2001). Ethnographic approaches provide detailed accounts of the concrete experience of life within a particular culture in order to discover and understand the beliefs and social rules that are used as resources within it. Ethnographic fieldwork combines observation, informal 'interviews' and in-depth case studies as a powerful means of investigating complex questions relating to experiences, relationships and social processes (Hammersley &Atkinson, 1995).

Importantly, this methodology recognises the social context of an individual's life and the fact that people are 'patients' for very little of their illness experience. The perceptions of significant others and the personal and social circumstances within which individuals live are recognised as crucial to understanding communication patterns and decision-making processes (Charmaz & Olsen, 1997; Donovan &Blake, 1992) and necessary to developing effective care interventions (Rybarczyk et al., 1999). Triangulation – comparing and combining data from different sources about the same issue – supports researchers to reveal and examine assumptions made by individual research participants or by researchers themselves. This helps to develop a more sophisticated understanding of people's behaviour and beliefs than would otherwise be possible (Hammersley, 1992).

The inclusion of diverse data sources during fieldwork for this study (see Table 1), helped build a detailed picture of the context in which long-term illness was managed and the influence of religious identity within this, whilst taking account of other influences such as gender, age and social class. The suitability of specific aspects of this methodology is explored in the sections below, taking account of the data generated, respondents' attitudes towards the methods used and ethical considerations highlighted during fieldwork.

Table 1: Types of data source

Source of data	Details
Interviews and contacts with adults recently diagnosed with chronic illness	1-3 semi-structured interviews with 31 respondents and informal contacts over 12-16 months
Interviews with carers/family members	11 semi-structured interviews
Professional interviews and 'shadowing'[32] of appropriate professionals in both practice	10 semi-structured interviews (GPs, interpreters, community health visitors; diabetes, cardiology, oncology and mental health consultants; specialist

---

[32] 'Shadowing' involved spending time with health professionals in their workplace in order to observe and discuss the detailed processes and practices involved in their day-to-day activities.

and community settings	nurses; dieticians; podiatrist) and 12 observations of healthcare settings(diabetes clinic, cardiac rehabilitation clinic, community health clinics
Interviews with key informants	13 semi-structured interviews
Community-based ethnographic work	Fieldwork over 27 months
Messages from local, national and international email groups set up for and by Muslims	11 groups with varying levels of mail followed over the fieldwork period
Local information and policy relating to health facilities, ethnicity or the Pakistani community	Documents collected over the period of the study and attendance at related local events.

Semi-structured interviews

Semi-structured interviews were carried out with 30 Pakistani people, living in the Harehills area of Leeds, who had been diagnosed with a long-term illness in the last year. Twenty-two of these individuals were interviewed a second time six months later and 20 a third time, a year to 16 months after their original interview. The three interviews helped build a very detailed picture of respondents along with an understanding of their most important concerns and values. This approach also enabled tailoring of questions to individual respondents based on previous interviews. All Pakistani people with long-term illness lived within a two-mile radius of Harehills, which constituted the fieldwork area. Interviews were conducted by two Pakistani researchers in English, Urdu, Punjabi and Mirpuri (a dialect spoken by many respondents originating from the Kashmir province of Pakistan).

Important issues relating to the makeup of the Pakistani community were discovered through recruitment of individuals to this part of the study. Fieldwork demonstrated that the term 'Pakistani' is misleading in relation to community membership. A number of people who considered themselves to be part of the local Pakistani Muslim community in fact originated from India and East Africa. Whilst retaining strong and separate ethnic identities, these individuals nevertheless used and contributed to the same social networks as the majority Pakistani population because of their religious identity, which differentiated them from the majority Indian and African populations in the fieldwork area. This confirmed and provided further evidence of the primacy of religious over ethnic identity for Pakistani Muslims (see Modood, 1997). A decision was consequently made to include in the sample respondents who identified with and formed part of the social networks within the Pakistani community, even though they were born in India, East Africa or the UK. Their inclusion reflected the geographical and historical diversity that a single Pakistani community may contain.

Semi-structured interviews allowed in-depth discussion of issues such as responses to diagnosis and the meaning of illness, sources of information, communication patterns in family, social and clinical settings, management of illness in daily life and the influence of significant others on communication and decision-making. Interview accounts were compared with fieldwork observations relating to the same themes, providing a means of triangulation. Informal contact and fieldwork observations did not require respondents to dedicate time or effort to the research process and there was no evidence that they were perceived as intrusive. However, as a method, semi-structured interviews raised practical and ethical issues that are considered in detail below.

The need for participatory techniques

Semi-structured interviews generated a good deal of valuable data from most respondents. However, interviewees who had little experience of research could be bemused or perplexed by the process and, despite researchers' best efforts, some participants did not engage in an in-depth discussion. This was particularly noticeable with respondents who had little formal education. Open-ended questions could generate very little response in these cases and it was clear that respondents were neither engaged by the process nor stimulated to share their feelings or experiences.

Examples of the difficulties faced in relation to semi-structured interviews with some Pakistani patients are given below:

- NS and QL seemed amused and gave joke answers to questions about feelings or family dynamics.
- NC felt that talking at length was not appropriate unless he had something definite to say: 'There's no point just saying something for the sake of it'
- In response to specific questions IN and NJ, two elderly people with long-term illness, sometimes began to talk about other issues related to their health or about a certain word in the question but in an unrelated way.

These difficulties indicated that some respondents did not wish to answer direct questions about their feelings or family relationships or felt they had little to contribute to the research. In some cases responses indicated resistance to the process in which participants were being asked to engage. The third example above suggests some people found it difficult to focus on the question being asked, perhaps because of age or illness. In each example, what appears clear is that for a variety of reasons these dynamics prevented interviews from being 'conversations with a purpose' (Burgess 1988) since individuals were not always involved in a conversation and interviews became more a question and answer session. In this situation, individuals appeared to be subjected to research rather than enabled to participate in it.

As a way of addressing these problems different ways of eliciting the views of research participants were explored and a more sophisticated approach to data generation adopted.

Johnson and Webster (2000) recommend participatory research techniques as a way of involving people from socially excluded, particularly non-literate, groups in a process of which they may have little experience. This approach uses visual stimuli and practical activities to generate data about views and experiences, empowering participants to share their knowledge in a way that traditional research methods do not always achieve. Participatory methods support respondents to take control of their interactions with researchers.

The use of concrete keywords, taken from previous interviews with this respondent group, was an important means of achieving this kind of participation. Three participatory techniques were used in the third interviews:

- A set of cards developed from analysis of previous interviews, which identified problems people could face when trying to manage their health. Pictures as well as Urdu and English keywords were used on these cards. This allowed involvement of individuals who did not speak or read either language as well as those who were literate in one or both languages. Respondents were asked to identify cards which showed problems they faced and then to place them in priority order.

- A second set of cards in similar format was used to ask patients about influences on decision-making. Keywords were again developed from the variety of influences mentioned in the full sample of previous interviews. Respondents were asked to identify the most important influence on their decision-making and place this in a central position. They then placed other cards near or distant to this central card, depending on the level of influence they felt each person or thing had (see Figure 1).

A map of the fieldwork area used to find out how much people knew about health facilities and community organisations in the area and their views about the quality of services offered. The map was also used to find out about other places in the community that were important to health or social activity and the extent to which individuals mixed with people from other ethnic and religious groups. Places already mentioned in previous interviews, and the respondent's own home, were pre-identified on a personalised map as a starting point for discussion.

Figure 1: Participatory techniques - "Influences on decision-making"

These activities were piloted in two User Advisory Groups established for the study and were well-received. During fieldwork, most respondents who were reticent in semi-structured interviews gradually became familiar with the activities and took control of the process. For example, NL and TBl began to tell the researcher where to put the card after originally feeling the researcher should 'put them wherever you like'.

The words on the cards acted as prompts but the method allowed a greater number of prompts than would be possible in a semi-structured interview. In addition the priority attached to each card was made explicit through the process of accepting or rejecting cards and placing them in a particular order. In contrast, data from previous interviews had reflected needs and problems but often not the order of priority in which they were held by patients. The cards also placed more pressure on individuals to be specific about difficulties they faced. For example, TBl moved from stating a number of times that 'Nothing is difficult' to expressing in detail how he felt financial worries contributed to his illness by taking away his 'peace of mind' and ability to work less hours. He explained that these worries often occupied his thoughts but were a subject about which he spoke to no-one and this 'thinking' was also, he felt, a cause of illness. Comments in relation to a particular card could also help make explicit what respondents saw as the underlying reason for an identified problem:

> NL	Every thing is difficult for me.
> Q	Which is difficult from these [cards]? ...
> NL	Walking and talking both have become difficult for me.
> Q	How? Is it because of the language?
> NL	No I am old. I am seventy years old. I have breathing problems. The other thing is I am on medication. Doctor gives me the medicine but it doesn't have any effect.
> Q	Right, so is 'treatment' a problem then?
> NL	Treatment means, when somebody doesn't understand your illness then medicine doesn't do any good... The difficulty is in talking, difficulty is in time ... Doctor prescribes the wrong medicine

Q	Is that your family doctor or the doctor in the hospital as well?
NL	All of them... They all just pass their time. They don't give you the medicine.

(NL – male with coronary heart disease and diabetes)

The extract above is taken from an interview with a respondent who was at times difficult to follow. The use of cards in this interview enabled researchers to identify mobility, speech and treatment as three priority areas of difficulty in relation to this respondent's condition. The additional comments provide insight into the respondent's feelings that these were problems partly because of his age but also because the doctors who treated him did not give sufficient time or attention to understanding his condition and therefore could not treat him appropriately. These ideas were supported by evidence elsewhere in this and other interviews with the respondent.

This approach to communicating with respondents was therefore of value in drawing out the views of individuals who generally did not communicate their thoughts and feelings in response to a straightforward question. It was not entirely effective in all cases, however. A small number of respondents who did not speak in any depth during semi-structured interviews were also not stimulated to talk at any length through participatory methods. The use of maps of the area, whilst providing a visual focus for discussion, could also be difficult for people who could not read or people with visual difficulties.

Interviewees were asked to evaluate these methods after the interview. Some respondents preferred straightforward questions and answers rather than the participatory approach, which they felt demanded more concentration and where the answers had to be more specific:

> I did find it harder, I am not sure how I should have answered you ....I have to read myself and then concentrate. I have to think a lot *(HX - female with diabetes)*.

However, others preferred the participatory techniques which they said they did not find difficult. Overall, better quality data was generated through this approach. In addition to encouraging greater participation from individual respondents, these activities enabled data to be gathered that could be compared across the group of people with long-term illness. This made it possible to construct a hierarchy of problems and influences on self-care management for this respondent group as a whole. The map exercise gave an overview of the most important community sites for social and health activities and the level of knowledge about community-based organisations within the respondent group. Furthermore, the process of selecting cards inevitably prompted individuals to talk about their reasons for choosing a particular card and revealed in more subtle detail the reasons why some problems or influences might be more significant than others.

Power relationships

A number of Pakistani respondents expressed feelings of vulnerability and lack of control in their relationships with health and social care professionals. Those with limited English felt vulnerable to having their trust abused by professionals, who might use information against them, or being held responsible for things in which they had unwittingly become involved. Unequal power relationships between Pakistani respondents and health practitioners emerged as an important theme during analysis for the study, affecting those who spoke English fluently as well as others.

Fieldwork revealed that similar dynamics existed in respondents' relationships with researchers. For example, AB initially refused to take part in the research because she had heard locally about a bilingual professional working with Social Services to take the children of Pakistani parents into care. NI expressed similar fears about unexpected consequences after he gave consent to interview his GP. He asked, half-jokingly, "They won't come to take me away in handcuffs will they?"

Greater trust in the aims of the research was apparent in cases where respondents already had knowledge of the researcher through previous community links or where support was provided with health-related issues. Involvement of Pakistani people from the fieldwork area on the Advisory Group and Users Advisory Groups for the project was also helpful in achieving transparency about the research activity and outcomes. Two Users Advisory Groups (male and female, following the gendered nature of groups in Pakistani communities) were also vital to validation of research tools and of findings.

A community-based conference at the end of the project was of further help in terms of increasing the credibility of, and trust in, the researchers. The event was organised so that Pakistani respondents were supported to express their views about service provision directly to healthcare professionals. Feedback from Pakistani participants revealed that this approach was considered very useful and a rare chance to have a voice in discussions about service development.

Triangulation

Triangulation was built into the research design both through the use of diverse data sources and through accounts from different people involved in managing a single individual's condition. In addition to fieldwork in family and community settings, a cross section of primary and secondary care health professionals from various health services related to long-term illness were included in the study (see Table 1).

People with long-term illness were asked to identify a carer and health professional who was most involved in supporting them to gain information and make decisions about their health. Eleven carers were interviewed and ten people with long-term illness gave consent for researchers to interview a professional who had influenced their health behaviour and decisions.

Semi-structured interviews, observations and shadowing activities gave valuable insights into the perspectives of professionals, not just in relation to the healthcare of Pakistani people with long-term illness as a whole but also into their relationships with individuals. Along with 'patient' and carer interviews, this data enabled triangulation of different perspectives on long-term illness management during analysis. However, the balance between different perspectives gained from such diverse data sources as Muslim e-lists and media representations of Muslims raised further issues about how to manage these different perspectives during analysis.

Managing 'regimes of truth'

A particular issue relating to triangulation during analysis for this study was the balance to be achieved between religious and secular perspectives in the data. Exploring the views of Muslims within a secular sociological framework results in a conception of Islam as a social construction and of Muslim understandings of truth and knowledge as functional in nature (Asad, 1993). The absence of Islamic interpretations from a sociological framework has the potential to allow interpretations of religious acts and beliefs by researchers that conflict with the way they are presented in Islamic scriptures and understood by Muslims. An acceptance of destiny can consequently be equated with fatalism and the specific roles for men and women in Muslim societies be construed as necessarily oppressive of women (Mir & Tovey, 2003; Said, 1995).

Diverse interpretations of the behaviour of Muslims was of particular relevance to local, national and international events involving Muslims over the three year period in which the research was conducted. Disturbances involving Pakistani youth in Harehills (the fieldwork area) and the terrorist attack in New York in 2001 had a particular impact on the Pakistani community in the fieldwork area. The significance of these events and the way in which they were interpreted was discussed within community settings, through e-lists organised by Muslim groups and, of course, in the media. Data from elists and community settings often provided alternative perspectives to those in the mainstream media and highlighted the dominance of a secular framework in the UK within which the beliefs and actions of Muslims were interpreted.

The generally negative representation of Muslims presented in the media was often seen as an indication, by respondents in the fieldwork area as well as by e-list participants, of the social position Pakistani people, and Muslims generally, held in the UK. This aspect of fieldwork contributed significantly to findings about adverse influences on the psychosocial capital of Pakistani people (Marmot, 2004) and the relevance of this to health inequalities within this community. Stereotypes about Islam and Muslim women were reflected in clinical settings, highlighting healthcare as one arena of many in which the beliefs of Pakistani respondents were undermined on a daily basis.

This context raised questions about how, at the stage of analysis, the interplay between differing 'regimes of truth' (Hammersley & Atkinson, 1995) should be explored and how to balance differing views about what is true and false. An ethnographic approach went some way towards enabling different constructions of knowledge to co-exist – for example, Islamic and sociological or positive and negative interpretations of the behaviour of Pakistani community members. It allowed the adoption of a framework which attempted to understand Pakistani Muslims on their own terms, emphasising their 'subjective meanings' as social agents (Hammersley & Atkinson, 1995).

The approach adopted allowed exploration of the validity of these different views in the context of the empirical data, irrespective of their origin and irrespective of how dominant or marginalized a particular view may be in UK society as a whole. Both frameworks were thus treated as possible ways of knowing the world that may struggle for wider acceptance and resist each other in the process. This approach helped avoid analysis that naturalised and reproduced the inferior position given to Islamic interpretations and the unequal social relations that disadvantage Pakistani communities in the UK (Said, 1995; see also Donnelly, 2002). Managing the tension between different perspectives helped increase the credibility of findings at the same time as interpretations that built on the common ground between them were formulated.

Ethical concerns

A further issue raised by the frequent contact with Pakistani respondents in the 'patient' sample highlighted ethical concerns about the benefit of the research to these participants. The author's previous experience of research within this community (Mir et al., 2001; Mir &Tovey, 2003) had revealed a high level of cynicism about benefits to the Pakistani community from research carried out within it and this view was evident from some respondents in this study:

> So, what's going to happen when you've finished the research – is it going to end up as a big report on a shelf somewhere? *(RS – male with diabetes)*

Whilst highlighting the needs of minority ethnic communities, research recommendations over the past two decades have sometimes resulted in few and piecemeal outcomes within mainstream service provision in the UK (Mir et al., 2001). It is, perhaps, not surprising therefore that some respondents took part mainly out of politeness and a wish to support the researchers rather than because they expected any benefits from the study itself. Low expectations of research outcomes were a particular problem for this study, which aimed to interview people with long-term illness on three separate occasions and thus drew heavily on their time and resources.

To address the problem, researchers offered to help individuals with health-related issues with which they might need support over the period of the study. This offer was taken up by a number of respondents and the resulting activity contributed to ethnographic data collection. Support activity highlighted a range of issues that people felt were relevant to their health, such as helping to pursue a claim for central heating, referring a complaint to the Community Health Council[33], providing transport and interpreting for people at the diabetes clinic and finding a support group for someone with coronary heart disease.

This activity also revealed that some respondents needed help with longstanding problems in which a number of other professionals had already been involved without success. The perseverance and time needed to help solve these problems was considerable and the lack of skilled support available to Pakistani people in the fieldwork area became apparent. If researchers were not prepared to do anything about these issues, their reasons for asking about problems was called into question:

Q	Do you want to ask any thing uncle? [34]
NE[35]	No we don't want to ask anything.
NE's wife	No we don't want to ask anything.
NE	We don't have any other demand. Our demand is to get us a house. If you could do that then thanks to you. If you can't do that then coming repeatedly is useless. Otherwise it is waste of time for you and us. The questions are fine but the illnesses don't go away with answering these questions.

Similar concerns about the benefits of research were apparent in many of the thirteen community organisations which were also included as data sources. Involvement in community groups was undertaken during fieldwork to gain an understanding of how community networks operated in relation to health. In addition information and literature was gathered to gain an overview of how Pakistani community networks fit into the wider network of community activity.

Community groups were selected as a focus for fieldwork activity because of a link to health or else to faith. Researchers gathered data through volunteering, attendance at regular meetings or one-off events and informal contact with group members or facilitators. Involvement through volunteering was validated as a mutually beneficial means of gathering data a number of times during the fieldwork period. One group organiser contrasted this method with her experience of other research projects, which had expected her to organise women to be interviewed, on top of everything else for which she

---

[33] An independent body within the NHS, established to represent the interests of health service users in localities across the UK.

[34] This extract is translated from Punjabi: the term 'uncle' is used to show respect for an elderly person.

[35] NE - male with asthma and coronary heart disease.

was responsible, without offering any extra resources. Not only did volunteering build in an element of reciprocity to the research design, it also enabled collection of valuable data, through the role of participant observer, about group dynamics and about interactions between Pakistani individuals and community-based services. Much information about the quality and type of service people with long-term illness were receiving from overstretched community-based organisations was gathered in this way.

Discussion

My aim in this chapter was to highlight practical and ethical problems in the use of research methods commonly used for qualitative studies in Pakistani communities. The research methodology adopted for this study was complex and presented numerous opportunities for reflexivity and for drawing lessons about the appropriateness of the approach. In some respects findings can be seen to support those of previous studies about research in socially excluded communities. However, in other areas the findings present fresh insights into the dynamics of researcher-respondent relationships.

This chapter began by outlining the value of ethnographic methodology in providing context to the experiences of Pakistani respondents. Evidence from fieldwork confirmed that lack of support to address unmet needs, unequal power relationships and low social status form part of this context for many people in Pakistani communities. The evidence presented here demonstrates that research methods are capable of reinforcing this context and that researchers will need to specifically address these issues both in the design and implementation of fieldwork and during the process of analysis and dissemination. As with research in other disadvantaged groups, care is needed to ensure that Pakistani respondents are not perceived simply as the objects of study, that they can contribute effectively and that they are empowered by research projects (Hill, 2004).

The potential for exploitation has been highlighted by writers and activists in the fields of feminism and disability studies and greater accountability demanded to avoid studies that primarily serve the interests of researchers themselves (Hill, 2004; Barnes, 1996). In studies of ethnicity and health inequalities there has been less consideration of these issues, though research on minority ethnic women has sometimes drawn on feminist research perspectives concerning power relationships (Mulder et al., 2000; Egharevba., 2001). Whereas standards of professionalism and problems with communication have been highlighted in relation to health and social care practitioners by numerous studies on ethnicity and health, particularly in relation to respondents who do not speak English well and who do not understand professional systems (see Mir &Tovey, 2003), findings presented here suggest that these issues are no less important in relationships between researchers and respondents in minority ethnic communities.

Perhaps the principal finding of the research relating to methodology, and one in which the significance of researcher-respondent relationships is evident, is the need to take account of the priorities of people from Pakistani communities at all stages of the research process. As Mulder et al. (2000) note in their research with Bolivian women, constant checks are needed to ensure that the desire to obtain specific data does not take precedence over the interests of research participants and damage the ability to work fairly or collaboratively with the community being studied. Evidence presented here demonstrates that respondents may agree to take part in studies for a variety of reasons, including politeness or a wish to support researchers. They may also give consent to researchers even though they are fearful of unintended consequences or feel vulnerable and powerless. Without a negotiation of the diverse interests and agendas of participants, and support to become engaged, the response of some respondents may be tacit resistance to the process. Furthermore, unless researchers respond to the critiques of research and concerns of respondents from socially excluded groups, they become guilty of mirroring and perpetuating the social disadvantage that members of this group already experience (Mulder et al., 2000).

Ryan et al. (2001) establish acceptability of the research to respondents as a criterion for evaluation of qualitative research on health. Innovative methods of engaging and empowering people at all levels of a research project, such as the participatory techniques used in this study and the User Advisory Groups, go some way to addressing these challenges and identifying the priorities of people from such communities. However, adapting existing techniques is not the same as fundamentally changing the relationship between researchers and respondents. Evidence from Pakistani respondents suggests that the absence of reciprocity in their relationships with researchers diminished the acceptability and thus credibility of both research and researchers. As Egharevba (2001) points out, shared ethnicity does not automatically bestow credibility or trust in researchers, whereas willingness to engage with the needs of respondents may help prevent exploitation in these relationships and raise the standing of research within this social group.

If acceptability to respondents is a standard for the quality of a methodology, evidence from this study suggests that approaches in which reciprocity has not been considered can be deemed methodologically weak in relation to the Pakistani community. Studies that take up the time and energy of people from this community, whilst offering no tangible benefit to them, risk reinforcing the existing perception that research is carried out primarily for the benefit of researchers.

The nature of what can appropriately be offered to respondents when considering reciprocal arrangements can not be assumed. Whereas Hill (2004) found that emotional support and willingness to engage in 'mutual disclosure' was important to women prisoners, evidence from this study suggests that support to meet immediate and practical needs was the priority of many Pakistani respondents. Egharevbar's (2001) study of South Asian female students indicates that this priority is not necessarily restricted to those with limited English and may be a reflection of limited social capital and capacity to meet practical needs within South Asian communities.

Findings indicate that helping to meet the needs of Pakistani respondents impacts positively on their relationships with researchers and increases acceptability of the research. This dynamic highlights an important issue in researcher-respondent relationships that was mirrored in relationships between Pakistani people and healthcare professionals - the process of identifying need was often not considered a worthwhile activity unless linked to outcomes that improved people's lives. The means by which such outcomes may be achieved during the research process needs further exploration. Both Hill (2004) and Egharevbar (2001) made use of their own skills to provide benefits to respondents but how far this contributed to their data for analysis is unclear.

Attempts to incorporate the priorities and concerns of Pakistani people into the research process for this study affected methodology in a number of ways. The tools used to engage with Pakistani respondents developed from traditional semi-structured interviews to more participatory techniques, which were combined with practical support for health-related needs. All these became methods for collecting data which shaped not only how data was generated but also the kind of data gathered.

The practical support was not only of direct benefit to research participants but also highlighted the way they conceptualised their health needs and the process, if any, through which particular needs could be met. In a social group that consistently experiences unmet need, findings that indicate how needs can be met more effectively are perhaps more relevant than a more sophisticated understanding of what those needs are. This approach may be understood as translating 'practice into research' and findings suggest that this may be more appropriate within Pakistani communities than methodologies which result in research recommendations that struggle to find their way into practice.

Conclusion

Lessons highlighted for research in marginalized communities through this study converge on the quality of the relationship between researchers and respondents and the impact of this relationship on research design. The evidence suggests that culturally competent researchers should identify the priorities and concerns of people from marginalized communities and ensure that they respond to these. The use of participatory methods can empower individuals, who may feel unwilling or unable to respond to abstract questions, to engage in the research process. An opportunity to influence this process can also be offered through User Advisory Groups. These can help to increase transparency and address the lack of trust in research that may exist within some communities.

The importance of reciprocity in culturally competent research has also been demonstrated by findings from this study. Evidence suggests that building this into research design can enhance the quality of data gathered and go some way to establishing more equal power relationships between researchers and respondents. This shift in power needs to be carried through to analysis and writing up of research and can involve managing the tension between different knowledge frameworks.

Interpretations that have been formulated in collaboration with all stakeholders will not only be more valid but are likely also to increase the credibility of research itself amongst those taking part. Such credibility is particularly important for researchers working with communities that feel they have benefited relatively little from past studies. Establishing the value of research within these communities will involve ensuring that they are empowered through the research process and that dissemination strategies promote their voice in ways that influence policy and practice.

References

Acheson, Sir Donald (Chair). (1998). Independent Inquiry into Inequalities in Health The Stationery Office, London. www.archive.official-documents.co.uk/document/doh/ih/part2h.htm (Accessed June 2006)

Asad, T. 1993, Genealogies of religion: discipline and reasons of power in Christianity and Islam Johns Hopkins University Press, Baltimore.

Barnes C. (1996). Disability and the myth of the independent researcher, Disability and Society, vol. 11 (1), pp.107-110.

Bryman, A. & Burgess, R. (1994). Analysing Qualitative Data, Routledge, London.

Burgess, R. (1988). Conversations with a purpose: the ethnographic interview in educational research, Studies in Qualitative Methodology, 1, pp.137-155.

Denzin, N. K. & Lincoln, Y. S. (eds). (1994). Handbook of qualitative research Sage, Thousand Oaks, California; London.

Department of Health/HM Treasury. (2002). Tackling Health Inequalities: Cross Cutting Review, Department of Health/HM Treasury.

Donnelly, T. (2002). Representing 'Others': avoiding the reproduction of unequal social relations in research [Post-Colonial Research], Nurse Researcher, vol. 9, no. 3, pp.57-67.

Donovan, J.L. & Blake, D.R. (1992).Patient Noncompliance - Deviance or Reasoned Decision-Making, Social Science and Medicine, vol. 34, no. 5, pp.507-513.

Hammersley, M. (1992), What's Wrong with Ethnography Routledge, London.

Hammersley, M. & Atkinson, P.(1995). Ethnography Routledge, London.

INVOLVE. (2004). Brief Summary and Checklist for Researchers, Research Commissioners and Research Groups for Involving Vulnerable and Marginalised People. www.invo.org.uk/pdfs/Brief Summary and Checklist for Researchersver2.pdf . (Accessed June 2005)

Johnson, V. & Webster, J. (2000), Reaching the Parts ... Community Mapping, Working Together to Tackle Social Exclusion and Food Poverty Sustain; Oxfam, London.

Marmot, M.G. (2004). Status Syndrome - How Our Position on the Social Gradient Affects Longevity and Health Bloomsbury.

Mir, G., Nocon, A., & Ahmad, W. (2001). Learning Difficulties and Ethnicity, Department of Health, London.

Mir, G. & Tovey, P.(2003), Asian Carers' Experience of Medical and Social Care: The Case of Cerebral Palsy, British Journal of Social Work, 33(465), p.479.

Modood, T., Berthoud, R., Lakey, J., Nazroo, J., Smith, P., Virdee, S., & Beishon, S. (1997). Ethnic Minorities in Britain: Diversity and Disadvantage Policy Studies Institute, London.

Nazroo, J. (1997). The Health of Britain's Ethnic Minorities Policy Studies Institute, London

Ryan, M., Scott, D.A., Reeves, C., Bate, A., van Teijlingen, E.R., Russell, E.M., Napper, M., & Robb, C.M. (2001). Eliciting public preferences for healthcare: a systematic review of techniques. Health Technology Assessment 5(5), 17-24.

Rybarczyk, B., DeMarco, G., DeLaCruz, M., and Lapidos, S. (1999). Comparing mind-body wellness interventions for older adults with long-term illness: Classroom versus home instruction, Behavioral Medicine, 24(4), 181-190.

Said, E. (1995). Orientalism. London: Penguin Books.

Lessons in research collaboration: Strengths Model research in New Zealand

Monika Divis

> Affinity Services (a community mental health organisation) entered into a joint collaborative research project with The University of Auckland's School of Population Health to investigate how the Western based Strengths Model could be applied as a recovery intervention for New Zealand Chinese people experiencing mental illness. The collaboration process was a valuable learning experience for Affinity Services. It revealed areas worthy of consideration for future research collaborations between Affinity Services as a community organisation and academia. Through the collaborative process, we found that, it was imperative to develop common understandings about the feasibility, objectives and anticipated benefits of the research. It was also vital to establish clear communication pathways and a clear outline of the timeline, process and responsibilities of all stakeholders involved in the project. Due to unanticipated events during the course of the project, it was necessary to alter the research design and timeframe in order to complete the project. At the conclusion of the project, we found it valuable to receive feedback about the outcomes of the research from the researchers and discuss the implications of the findings for our practice.

Affinity Services (formerly, Baptist Action Te Korowai Aroha) is a community based non-governmental organisation dedicated to working towards recovery outcomes alongside people affected by mental illness. Affinity Services Ltd provides services under the framework and principles of Charles Rapp's Strengths Model (Rapp & Gosha, 2006) & Mary Ellen Copeland's 'Wellness Recovery Action Planning' (WRAP) (Copeland, 1997).

In early 2004, Affinity Services was approached by The University of Auckland's School of Population Health requesting its participation in a joint collaborative research project. The proposed project was to investigate how the Strengths Model could be utilised as a recovery intervention for New Zealand Chinese people experiencing mental illness. The Strengths Model is a Western model of intervention (Rapp & Goscha, 2006; Rapp & Chamberlain, 1985; Rapp & Wintersteen, 1989). It is designed to assist the mental health practitioner and service user to identify the service user's individual and environmental strengths, their future goals and aspirations and to secure the resources needed to achieve those goals (Rapp & Goscha, 2006). The Strengths Model has been found to facilitate integration into the community, reduce psychiatric hospitalisation, significantly improve overall physical and mental wellbeing, social functioning and improve quality of life (Barry, Zeber, Blow & Valenstein, 2003; Bjorkman, Hansson & Sandlund, 2002; Stanard, 1999).

The collaborative research project between Affinity Services and The University of Auckland aimed to test the hypothesis that Chinese mental health service users receiving the Western Strengths Model intervention would have clinically significant and sustained improvement in their psychosocial wellbeing and daily functioning. The process of establishing and working collaboratively with researchers from an academic institutional setting on this research project was a valuable learning experience for Affinity Services. This chapter outlines the learning experiences of this process from a community mental health organisations perspective,

Recognise Differences in Values and Practice

The process of the collaborative research made apparent the differences between the values and practices of the academic research approach and those governing our community organisation. One of the more apparent differences was that the researchers with their academic affiliation must adhere to rigorous guidelines and structures in order to secure funding and ethical approval and meet employment obligations. For community organisations, any project undertaken beyond the core contractual obligations must be relevant to the organisations vision and useful to the organisation's stakeholders (Henderson, Dougal, & Henderson, 2006). The research findings and the process must be applicable to the community organisations practice, especially if the organisation is constrained by limited funds or funding criteria that does not allow for research activities (Tennant, Sanders, O'Brien, & Castle, 2006). These differences are not necessarily in opposition; our organisation viewed the project as an opportunity to further enhance our practice and valued the researcher's contributions particularly in establishing independent and rigorous evidence of our practice which also served to validate our work.

Researchers entering into partnership with community organisations need also be mindful of specific cultural practices related to ethnicity. Chinese mental health practitioners involved in the research considered it pertinent that participants of the research receive a token as a show of appreciation for the value of their contribution to the research project. They felt that it would be inappropriate for a researcher to enter the participant's environment, take information from them and leave them with nothing in return. Giving the participant a token acknowledgement would demonstrate both respect for the person and their traditional cultural practice.

Establishing and Managing Communication

We (the community mental health organisation) were approached by the researcher (from The University of Auckland) with a pre-established set of objectives and an outline of a possible research design. The researcher presented the concept of the proposed project at an initial meeting which included a cross-section of staff from our organisation (i.e., senior management, strengths model practitioners, research coordinator, and service user representation). At this meeting we discussed the general structure of our service and the feasibility of the proposed project. Both parties agreed that the proposed project was worthwhile and highly feasible. Thus, began our collaborative project. Subsequent meetings held over the next 18 months included all relevant stakeholders depending on the agenda at hand. More often than not the researchers came to our premises and would organise catering for these meetings. This kind gesture was much appreciated by staff involved with the project.

As the project unfolded we encountered only a handful of challenges and these were resolved promptly as they arose. We found that it was important to effectively manage communication between the two parties. For a period of approximately six months at the outset of the project a number of staff from our organisation liaised independently with the researcher and research assistant. This resulted in communications not being relayed to all relevant people and in some instances being misunderstood, which delayed required actions (for example, recruitment and data collection). We found that the project progressed more effortlessly (to timeline and with less communication confusions) when one person from each party took on an overall coordination and liaison role with individual communications with others as required.

The research process was challenging for some practitioners, due, in part, to an initial lack of understanding about the purpose of the research and their role in the research process. This confusion translated into an increase in perceived pressure and workload for these practitioners and affected both new and existing employees. A few practitioners, new to the organisation felt overwhelmed contending with all that was involved in orienting themselves to their new role with Affinity Services (for example, learning the process requirements of the job role, establishing relationships with service users and other staff) as well as learning the research process and dealing with the researcher as yet another stakeholder.

More experienced employees involved with the research project were also affected by uncertainty about their role in the research process and lack of understanding about the purpose of the research. Furthermore, some perceived these role and purpose misinterpretations as contrary to their values in their work with service users which in turn led to a lack of enthusiasm on their part for the project. For example, the practitioner's role in the project was to inform service users on their caseload about the research project, to give the service user the participant information sheet and to inform the service user that a researcher would contact them in the next few days to discuss the project with them in more detail. Some practitioners misunderstood that their role was to recruit service users as participants of the project and because of their desire not to jeopardise the process of establishing a constructive and therapeutic relationship with the service user; were reluctant to promote the research to service users. In addition, they felt that the perceived pressure to promote the research took the focus away from their core work with the service user, which in turn, undermined their integrity in their work with the service user.

Written information about the project had been received by our organisation from the researcher, in the form of the submitted Ethics Committee proposal. This format contributed to the lack of clarity about the practitioners' roles and the process, as it required practitioners taking time to examine and decipher the information pertaining to them. In response to the perceived lack of clarity about the process and roles, this document was used to develop a flow chart outlining the process and roles and responsibilities of both the researchers and the practitioners. In retrospect, developing common understandings and anticipating roles and expectations of all stakeholders (both as individuals and as parties) at the outset and presenting this information in a simple format would have eliminated many of these misinterpretations.

Expect the Unexpected

We strived to work within a limited timeframe for data collection and found that the number of participants recruited in this timeframe was not sufficient to draw sound statistical conclusions of changes in psychosocial functioning. During this period, there was a low rate of response by existing service users and a low rate of new service users entering the service. Furthermore, for those recruited later in the project the timeframe available for the research was not adequate for six-month follow up data collection. As a result, the researchers revised the research design to include more qualitative methods and obtained ethical approval for the changes.

Present Research Findings for Feedback

At the completion of the project, the researchers presented initial research findings to the mental health practitioners involved with the project. These findings included interpretations of data from focus groups that some practitioners had participated in. The presentation of these findings gave the practitioners an opportunity to reflect and feedback how accurately their contributions and experiences were represented and interpreted. It also provided practitioners an opportunity to discuss ways in which the findings could enhance their work practice.

Influence of Approach and Research Design

After completion of this project, we (the community organisation) decided to continue working collaboratively with the researcher. We initiated and collaborated in the formation of the research project including framing the research questions and objectives. On reflection, this lead to a more worthwhile research from our perspective, in that, the objectives related directly to the needs of our organisation.

Again in reflection, we found that the design of a research project can shape the nature of the relationship between the researcher and the community organisation. Compared to the first project; (which utilised service user self-rated, practitioner-rated and researcher-rated questionnaires and individual and focus group interviews with service users, practitioners and significant others (family members)), the second proposed project was a participatory action research design. This design allows an opportunity for all levels of the organisation (service users, practitioners, management and significant others) to be involved in a decision making and problem solving capacity within the research process. This process positions all involved as 'experts' with researchers playing the roles of facilitator of the process and evaluator of the process and outcomes (DePoy & Gitlin, 2005).

Key Learning Experiences and Recommendations

Overall, we found working collaboratively with researchers affiliated with an academic institution a worthwhile experience. The resulting findings validated the work of practitioners' involved and further enhanced implementation of the Strengths Model as a recovery intervention for Chinese people experiencing mental illness. Our key learning's from the process of collaboration and recommendations for future research projects are:

Both community organisations and academia should be aware, sensitive and respectful of any differences in their respective values and practices. This also extends to cultural differences for ethnic groups which may be involved in the project. It is important to establish common understandings between parties at the outset of a research project. This can include articulating the anticipated benefits and limitations for all parties, and outlining anticipated roles and expectations of all stakeholders (individuals and parties). The common understandings can be reviewed as necessary throughout the course of the research project.

Managing communication effectively ensures that the project progresses more smoothly. This can be enhanced by ensuring that all key stakeholders attend initial meetings and that subsequent meetings include all relevant stakeholders (depending on the agenda at hand). Communication can also be managed more effectively when one or two people coordinate the project and are the point of contact for each party.

Practitioners from our organisation involved with the project benefited from having clear, easy to follow information about the research. Uncertainty about the process and responsibilities can be alleviated by presenting information (including individuals responsibilities and a clear statement of the objectives and benefits of the project) using a flow chart format.

Establishing and distributing a proposed timeline of the project to all involved, sets clear guidelines for progress, however, unanticipated events (such as slow recruitment) may require modifications to the implementation of the research, thus, both parties need to maintain some degree of flexibility to ensure that the project remains feasible.

Partnerships between community organisations and academia can be influenced by the way the researcher approaches the community group and the research design used to collect data. Researchers intending to establish partnerships with community organisations can encourage a more mutually beneficial partnership for the community organisation by enquiring about what is of interest or relevance to them as a community organisation.

Finally, it is very important that the researchers present findings of the research to the community organisation and participate in a discussion forum about the potential application and implications of the outcomes of the research for practice.

In essence, from a community mental health organisations perspective, it is important for both researchers and community organisations to consider differences in values and practices, establish relevant research objectives and research design and develop and maintain clear communications, in order to ensure a mutually beneficial and feasible research partnership.

Acknowledgement

I would like to acknowledge Barbara Anderson (CEO, Affinity Services) for her incredible passion for and promotion of appropriate support for the wellbeing of people living with mental illness. Her courage and determination in her belief that people with mental illness can recover, reclaim and transform their lives is inspirational and has lead to many innovative services and positive outcomes. I am extremely grateful for the encouragement and confidence you offer me. I am also grateful for the opportunity to work collaboratively with Dr Samson Tse, I have learned much from our work together and greatly admire your purposeful, flexible and sensitive approach.

References

Barry, K. L., Zeber, J. E., Blow, F. C., & Valenstein, M. (2003). Effect of Strengths Model Versus Assertive Community Treatment Model on Participant Outcomes and Utilization: Two-Year Follow-Up. Psychiatric Rehabilitation Journal, 26(3), 268-277.
Bjorkman, T., Hansson, L., & Sandlund, M. (2002). Outcome of Case Management Based on the Strengths Model Compared to Standard Care. A Randomised Controlled Trial. Social Psychiatry and Psychiatric Epidemiology, 37, 147-152.
Copeland, M. E. (1997). Wellness Recovery Action Plan. Brattleboro, VT: Peach Press.
DePoy, E., &. Gitlin, L. N. (1998). Introduction to Research: Multiple Strategies for Health and Human Services. St Louis: Mosby-Year Book.
Henderson, M., Dougal, T., & Henderson, S. (2006). Leading Through Values: Linking Company Culture to Business Strategy. Auckland: HarperCollins Publishers New Zealand.

Rapp, C. A., & Chamberlain, R. (1985). Case Management Services to the Chronically Mentally Ill. Social Work, 30, 417-422.

Rapp, C. A., & Gosha, R. J. (2006). The Strengths Model: Case Management with People with Psychiatric Disabilities (2nd Ed.). New York: Oxford University Press.

Rapp, C. A., & Wintersteen, R. (1989). The Strengths Model of Case Management. Psychosocial Rehabilitation Journal, 13, 23-32.

Stanard, R. P. (1999). The Effect of Training in a Strengths Model of Case Management on Service User Outcomes in a Community Mental Health Centre. Community Mental Health Journal, 35(2), 169-179.

Tennant, M., Sanders, J,. O'Brien, M., & Castle, C. (2006). Defining the Nonprofit Sector: New Zealand. Working Papers of the John Hopkins Comparative Nonprofit Sector Project No. 45, Baltimore: The Johns Hopkins Centre for Civil Society Studies.

Researching communities with community participation in a metropolitan municipality in South Africa

Udo Richard Averweg

> In terms of the initiatives of South Africa's State President's ICT program, the development of an e-Government strategy for local government will ensure greater efficiencies and working smarter to ensure that a municipality is in touch with its citizens. There is considerable interest in the use of Internet technologies to support citizens' needs. The networking capability offered by the Internet and related technologies have the potential to transform structures and operation of government and local government organisations.
>
> eThekwini Municipality, the most populous metropolitan municipality in South Africa, sees the national e-Government strategy and its website as important management tools and for improved citizen service delivery and communications in the various communities in its geographical area. In order to research to research eThekwini Municipality citizens ICT needs and capabilities for implementing an e-Governance strategy, a survey instrument was developed. The survey instrument was administered by eThekwini Municipality community members to 465 citizens in eThekwini Municipality Area (EMA). The author reports on citizen information needs for communities in the EMA. From these results the author suggests some management implications for consideration when implementing an e-Governance strategy in the EMA to cater for supporting these communities' needs.

Information and communication technologies (ICT) are playing an increasingly important role in the daily lives of citizens, revolutionising work and leisure and changing the rules of doing business. ICTs encompass all technologies that facilitate the processing and transfer of information and communication services (United Nations, 2002). In the realm of government, ICT applications are promising to enhance the delivery of public goods and services to citizens not only by improving the process and management of government but also by redefining the traditional concepts of citizenship and democracy (Pascual, 2003). The spread of ICT brings hope that governments can transform (Pacific Council on International Policy, 2002).

Electronic service delivery (ESD) is a method of delivering services and conducting business with customers, suppliers and stakeholders to achieve local government developmental goals of improved customer service and business efficiency. The eThekwini Municipality sees the e-Government strategy (Ethekwini Municipality Integrated Development Plan 2003-2007, 2003) and its website[36] as important management tools for improved citizen service delivery and communications.

Research Background

An editorial in the *South African Business Day* on 26 August 2003 reports that the City of Durban on the east coast of South Africa in the eThekwini Municipality Area (EMA), is quietly installing one of the largest networks in the country to link up scores of municipal centres all over greater Durban. The more technologically savvy can already access a wealth of city information via the Internet, by browsing the website either from home personal computers (PCs) or an increasing number of web-linked computers at municipal libraries. The editorial states that Durban 'is also pumping tens of millions of rands into promoting the local technology sector'. It is against this background that research was conducted to glean a clearer understanding of the implication of ICT for e-Government adoption in the EMA.

eThekwini Municipality Area (EMA) of South Africa

eThekwini Municipality's population is 3,09 million citizens (Statistics South Africa, 2001). The population is an amalgamation of racial and cultural diversity. The Black African community comprises 68,3%, Coloured citizens 2,8%, Asian citizens 19,9% and White citizens 9,0% (Statistics South Africa, 2001). Thirty-eight percent of the population is under 19 years of age (Ethekwini Municipality Integrated Development Plan 2003-2007, 2003). Ethekwini Municipality has a capital budget of ZAR1,95 billion (approximately U$0,28 billion) and an operating budget of ZAR7,80 billion (approximately U$1,11 billion) for the 2003/4 financial year (eThekwini Municipality Integrated Development Plan 2003-2007, 2003). Durban is South Africa's major port and the second largest industrial hub after Johannesburg. The EMA's gross geographic product income is ZAR25,529 (approximately U$3,647) per person per annum which is higher than the South African average of ZAR17,756 (approximately U$2,537) per person per annum.

Erwin and Averweg (2003) report that there is a need for organisations to adapt to constantly changing business conditions. The Ethekwini Municipality: Quality of Life Household Survey 2002/2003 (2003) reveals the needs and problems impacting the quality of life of EMA citizens. Some issues raised include new housing requirements,

---

[36] See www.durban.gov.za

water and sanitation supply and lack of recreation facilities (Ethekwini Municipal Area Development Profile, 2002). This survey reveals that there is also a growing need for information in the EMA. Among the solutions to fulfil this need, ICT is seen as an effective mechanism to access municipal information and development information in general. As reflected in section 7 of this paper, most EMA citizens receive municipal information via a municipal magazine (*MetroBeat* publication is published monthly by Communications Department, eThekwini Municipality) delivered to their post box. However, EMA citizens indicated that they would like to receive information via the electronic information exchange mechanism in the form of the Internet.

There is a growing number of EMA citizens accessing the eThekwini Municipality website through other initiatives, eg Carnegie e-Community project, aims to improve the quality of life of municipal citizens and access to information by placing computers in municipal libraries. South African websites which seek a local and global reach have to cater for the digital divide which exists between the technological 'haves' and 'have nots' (Averweg *et al.*, 2003). The mere existence of gaps in levels of ICT practices between rich and poor across and within countries is not an automatic reason to argue that ICT should be placed near the top of the development agenda (Manyanga, 2002). In looking at the difference in access between developed and developing countries, Gumucio-Dagron (2003) notes that the "divide has never been only a 'digital' or technological divide. It is a social, economic and political fracture". The authors suggest that a comparable situation exists (in microcosm form) in the EMA. Bridging the digital divide in the EMA is not the end. It is not even the beginning of the end. The authors suggest that perhaps it is the end of the beginning to bring positive changes in the development of a municipal information society.

e-Government and e-Governance

e-Government is about transformation that helps citizens and businesses find new opportunities in the world's knowledge economy (Pacific Council on International Policy, 2002). Governments have not been immune to the impact ICT have in our society (Rivera-Sanchez & Sriramesh, 2003). Governments that define e-Government as simply moving services online 'miss larger opportunities which will determine competitive advantage in the long run' (Caldow, 2002). Definitions of e-Government range from 'the use of information technology (IT) to free movement of information to overcome the physical bounds of traditional paper and physical based systems' to 'the use of technology to enhance the access to and delivery of government services to benefit citizens, business partners and employees (Deloitte and Touche, 2003). Ultimately, e-Government aims to enhance access to and delivery of government services to benefit citizens (Pascual, 2003). e-Government needs to find a positive developmental role. Without this, e-Government runs the risk of being a 21st century 'rusting tractor', cast aside as it fails to fulfil its promise (Heeks, 2003). e-Government services focus on four main customers: citizens, the business community, government employees and government agencies. The focus of this paper is on (local government) citizens in the EMA.

e-Governance refers to a local government's inventiveness to electronically govern areas under its jurisdiction (Manyanga, 2002). This effectively means the public sector's use of innovative ICT (*eg.* Internet) to deliver to all citizens improved services, reliable information and greater knowledge in order to facilitate access to the governing process and encourage deeper citizen participation.

Research Goals

ICT can be defined as electronic means of capturing, processing, storing and communicating information (Heeks, 1999). e-Readiness can be defined in terms of availability of ICT infrastructure, the accessibility of ICT to the general citizen population and the effect of the legal and regulatory framework on ICT use (Manyanga, 2002). In building a model of ICT, two separate elements exist: the technology itself and the information on which it operates. Heeks (1999) suggests that in order to make this model useful, two further processes should be added: processes of purposeful activity and the people to undertake those processes. Together these constitute an 'information system', such as a support system that helps citizens interact with their local municipality.

The eThekwini Municipality embarked on an initiative to understand the needs of its users and non-users in utilising ICT as a tool to improve service delivery and establishing effective communication between itself and its constituencies. Prospective techniques help practitioners work on an e-Government project that is still at the planning stage (Heeks, 2003). This paper reports on this initiative, findings from a survey conducted and suggested management recommendations that relate to the adoption of an e-Government strategy in the EMA. With the high failure rate of e-Government projects, Heeks (2003) notes that it carries direct and indirect financial costs, it damages morale, credibility and trust, preventing the benefits of e-Government from being delivered.

The focus of this study is on citizen's capabilities to use ICT to acquire or share information with the municipality and general community development in the EMA. The primary goals of this research are to gauge (1) e-Readiness of the citizens to use ICT as a communication medium; (2) the technological capabilities of ICT users and non-users; and (3) obstacles and barriers which may impact e-Government implementation (social, cultural, *etc*).

Research Method and Data Gathering

A survey instrument was developed to gauge EMA citizen's ICT needs and capabilities. This survey tool represents an attempt to obtain a snapshot of the current ICT status of EMA citizens. The authors' rationale is that social, cultural and other contextual factors are often ignored in the development of ICT strategies. In order to overcome this shortcoming, it was considered important to bring these factors 'on board' for planning the eThekwini Municipality's e-Government strategy. The survey instrument comprises two sections:

>**Section 1: General Information**: Section 1 contains three subsections: (1) citizen personal information; (2) experience in using a computer and access to the Internet; and (3) focus on the eThekwini Municipality website.

>**Section 2: Citizen's Information Needs**: Section 2 contains three subsections: (1) how citizens currently receive and will like to receive information about the eThekwini Municipality; (2) how citizens currently interact and will like to interact with the eThekwini Municipality; and (3) identifying where citizens will prefer the eThekwini Municipality to provide access to PCs.

During May 2003, the questionnaire was administered face-to-face to 465 EMA citizens by the second author and seven temporary staff members. The duration of each interview was approximately ten minutes. The selected sample was on a random basis to gather quantitative data to develop qualitative information. Interviews were conducted at EMA customer service offices and municipal libraries. The requirement for effective e-Governance requires a good understanding of the cultural or social background of its end-users (citizens in its communities). The citizen survey thus focused on the e-Readiness of EMA citizens to 'tap' into the new methods of communication for e-Governance.

Results and Discussion

ICT survey results are the reflection of e-Readiness of EMA's citizens to use ICT as a communication medium with the eThekwini Municipality and among themselves. Table 1 reflects the race grouping where EMA respondents reported surveyed having a household PC.

Table 1: Race Grouping of EMA respondents surveyed having a household PC

(Source: Ethekwini Municipality: Quality of Life Household Survey 2002/2003, 2003)

Race Grouping	Percentage (%) of respondents who have a household PC
Black	10,5%
Asian	39,5%
Coloured	28,6%
White	76,7%
Average	**21,7%**

From Table 1, White citizens surveyed reported the highest percentage (76,7%) of PCs in their household. A significant percentage (89,5%) of Black citizens surveyed do not have a PC in their household (eThekwini Municipality: Quality of Life Household Survey 2002/2003, 2003). The average percentage of respondents surveyed that have PCs in their household is 21,7%.

Table 2: Race grouping and gender of respondents surveyed

Race Grouping	Percentage (%) of male respondents	Percentage (%) of female respondents
Black	49,0%	51,0%
Asian	52,9%	47,1%
Coloured	42,9%	57,1%
White	36,8%	63,2%
Average	**48,2%**	**51,8%**

Table 2 reflects the demographics (race grouping and gender) of the respondents (EMA citizens) who participated in the authors' ICT survey. Using SPSS software, the race groupings were weighted to actual population composition of the EMA. The gender composition of the sample surveyed was 48,2% males and 51,8% females.

The computer experience of respondents surveyed by race grouping is reflected in Table 3. Some 58,7% of respondents surveyed reported that they have some computer experience. Computer experience by White citizens is relatively high (85,7%) followed by Asian citizens (77,5%). Black citizens reported the least (46,8%) computer experience.

Table 3: Computer experience of respondents surveyed by race grouping

Race Grouping	Percentage (%) of respondents who have some computer experience
Black	46,8%
Asian	77,5%
Coloured	64,3%
White	85,7%
Average	**58,7%**

Table 4 reflects respondents surveyed who are employed have the highest percentage (49,6%) of computer experience. This is followed by citizens who are studying (21,4%).

Table 4: Computer experience of respondents surveyed by occupation status

Occupation status	Percentage (%) of respondents who have some computer experience
At school	4,1%
Studying	21,4%
Employed	49,6%
Self-employed	11,2%
Not working	12,3%
Pensioner	1,4%
Total	100,0%

Table 5 reflects respondents surveyed who indicated they have completed matriculation have the highest percentage (51,3%) of computer experience. It is interesting to note that those respondents surveyed who have no education, do have some computer experience (1,1%). Inadequate computer literacy and the lack of access to ICT are widely recognised as an increasingly daunting obstacle to the economic, civic and political development of Africa (Badshah &Thumler, 2003).

Table 5: Computer experience of respondents surveyed by highest level of education

Level of Education	Percentage (%) of respondents who have some computer experience
No education	1,1%
Primary	0,4%
Secondary	10,5%
Completed matriculation	51,3%
Not working	10,9%
Diploma/Degree	25,8%
Total	100,0%

The concept of e-Government involves using ICT (*eg.* Internet) to deliver public services (Rivera-Sanchez & Sriramesh, 2003). Table 6 reflects the age grouping of respondents surveyed that have Internet access. Respondents with the highest percentage (43,2%) are those in the '21 - 30' age grouping. The second highest age grouping is '31 - 40' which reflects that 21,0% of respondents surveyed have Internet access. This tends to suggest that EMA citizens surveyed receive Internet exposure during their post-matriculation studies and in their employment environments.

Table 6: Age grouping of respondents surveyed with Internet access

Age grouping	Percentage (%) of respondents with Internet access
Under 21	16,7%
21 - 30	43,2%
31 - 40	21,0%
41 - 50	11,1%
51 - 60	6,2%
61 - 65	1,2%
Above 65	0,6%
Total	100,0%

From Table 6, of the respondents surveyed with Internet access, 16,7% reported that they had visited eThekwini Municipality's. Table 7 reflects current delivery mechanisms that EMA citizens receive information about eThekwini Municipality. A significant number (69,6%) of respondents surveyed receive municipal information (*MetroBeat* publication) delivered to their post boxes.

Table 7: Current delivery mechanisms for receiving information about eThekwini Municipality

Delivery mechanism	Percentage (%) of respondents
Telephone	4,3%
Post Office	69,6%
Municipal customer service office	7,6%
Municipal publication	13,3%
Community meeting	4,4%
Internet	0,1%
School/Tertiary	0,7%
Total	100,0%

From Table 8, 47,9% of respondents surveyed reported that they are satisfied with the current manner in which they receive information from eThekwini Municipality about eThekwini Municipality. Heeks (1999) cautions that as an aid to entrepreneurs in the developing world 'poor entrepreneurs need more than money, skills and infrastructure in order to make use of the data delivered by ICT". E-Government must be about meeting the needs of citizens and quality of life (Pacific Council on International Policy, 2002).

Table 8: Citizen's satisfaction level with the current manner of receiving information about eThekwini Municipality

Satisfaction Level	Percentage (%) of respondents
Not Satisfied	9,2%
Average Satisfaction	37,1%
Satisfied	47,9%
Don't know	5,8%
Total	100,0%

Table 9 reflects respondent's preferred information delivery mechanisms for receiving information about eThekwini Municipality. Some 63,0% of respondents surveyed reported that they would like to continue receiving information via the South African Post Office. It is interesting to note that only 5,0% of respondents surveyed reported that they would like to receive information via the Internet. On the contrary, when respondents surveyed were asked whether in future they would like to interact with eThekwini Municipality specifically via the Internet, 64,3% of these respondents reported positively.

Table 9: Preferred delivery mechanisms for receiving information about eThekwini Municipality and associated percentage

Delivery mechanism	Percentage (%) of respondents
Telephone	9,0%
Post Office	63,0%
Municipal customer service office	3,0%
Municipal publication	11,0%
Community meeting	5,0%
Internet	5,0%
e-Mail/SMS	4,0%
Total	100,0%

The aim is not simply to deliver services electronically in the EMA but to encourage its citizens to start learning about the Internet via its website and thereafter make use of the Internet for other services. The success of the Internet should be measured in terms of accessibility and contribution to social progress, rather than in terms of numbers of connected individuals (Kamel &Hussein, 2000). Evidence suggests that countries that have experienced the most rapid diffusion of ICT have also experienced the most rapid rates of employment and output growth (Baily &Lawrence, 2001). The eThekwini Municipality Integrated Development Plan 2003-2007 (2003) states that its strategic commitment is to develop a smart city as part of the process of economic development and 'a shift to service and knowledge-based activities'.

In response to the question regarding the preferred location where respondents surveyed will like to have PCs installed, 51,0% of respondents surveyed reported in municipal libraries, 20,0% in schools and 13,0% in shopping centres/malls (see Table 10). Some respondents stated 'the idea of computers in libraries and shopping centres is good, they take their time to resolve queries', 'timing bad sometimes' and there is rather a need to 'upgrade township services'. Experience shows that to implement public access centres extensively, is a big challenge (Fernández-Maldonaldo, 2003).

Table 10. Preferred locations for PC installation and associated percentage

Preferred location for PC installation	Percentage (%) of respondents
Municipal library	51,0%
School	20,0%
Municipal customer service office	8,0%
Clinic	8,0%
Shopping Centre/Mall	13,0%
Total	100,0%

The authors' survey focused on establishing a better understanding of how ICT can contribute to eThekwini Municipality's citizen service delivery and development communication. The main objective was to establish how EMA citizens perceive new technology and their willingness to 'try out' ICT as a new form of communication (e-Readiness). Readiness for e-Government is not only a governmental issue (Pacific Council on International Policy, 2002). This survey also analysed the social factors that are related to the eThekwini Municipality's progressiveness with e-Government and some future challenges for governance using ICT within EMA. Some suggested management implications are now discussed.

Management Implications

From this study and in implementing an e-Government strategy in the EMA, the authors suggest the following serves as important considerations:

- **Physical access.** Access to communications and the Internet is a cornerstone of a municipal information society. Digital inclusion cannot be achieved without providing all EMA citizens access with affordable ICT appliances to the information highway. The findings of the authors' research shows that respondents surveyed prefer to have access to PCs installed in municipal libraries;

- **Appropriate technology.** Establishing the appropriate method of interaction must be identified to ensure that the technology reaches all EMA citizens. The challenge is to chart an appropriate course which does not perpetuate Gumucio-Dagron's 'new apartheid' syndrome (Gumucio-Dagron, 2003);
- **Affordability.** The communication mechanism, whether in regional centres or via PCs, should be affordable to EMA citizens (end-users);
- **Human Capital.** Training and re-skilling will be necessary. As many EMA citizens lack ICT skills and/or do not have access to PCs, demonstrations on how to effectively utilise ICT technology (*eg.* e-Mail/SMS) must be provided. Furthermore attention must be afforded to the training of teachers to adapt to the new learning environment. ICT demands that citizens are perpetually in a learning environment;
- **Relevant Content.** The content developed must be locally relevant to its constituency, especially in terms of language. Averweg *et al.* (2003) suggest that a website must facilitate access by end-users not familiar with Internet norms and whose home language is not English. To bridge the digital divide through e-Government, e-Government must be relevant to citizens. The latter's motivation for using ICT should stem from citizens having their needs addressed (Pascual, 2003). For these citizens' needs, the authors suggest community-focused applications, content management and knowledge sharing;
- **Integration.** ICT must not act as a further burden to EMA citizen's lives. ICT should be integrated into priority sectors of the EMA economy and into citizen's daily lives. This should be coupled with efforts to de-mystify and de-demonise ICT for people to accept it as an everyday tool and not an end to itself (OleKambainei and Sintim-Misa, 2003). It is suggested by the authors that the challenge here will be to balance the demands of a few very literate and demanding citizens with a majority who may probably never move to the electronic world. One suggestion is to focus on ICT-based trade as a precursor to fully-fledged e-Commerce. Kamel and Hussein (2000) report that with continuous developments in ICT, there are 'remarkable contributions to the growing global environment with implications on individual and societal aspects of life';
- **Socio-economic factors.** The South African government has a responsibility for the well-being of its employees that cannot be ignored as new technology is introduced. The socio-economic status of EMA citizens (end-users) should be considered. By evaluating their e-Readiness, this will determine the usability of e-Government tools. Innovations in ICT have had remarkable effects on socio-economic development (Kamel and Hussein, 2000). The socio-economic status of website users determines their requirements (Averweg *et al.*, 2003);
- **Political will.** Nothing is more critical to the success of e-Government that political will (Pacific Council on International Policy, 2002). The political will of EMA citizens, eThekwini Municipal Councillors, eThekwini Municipal officials, social groups and the business community will need to be secured to facilitate a successful e-Government implementation project; and

- **Legal and regulatory framework**. Government regulations affecting technology use and changes that need to be made to create an environment that fosters ICT usage must be considered. The effect of legal and regulatory framework on ICT use should be geared to facilitate the growth of the digital age.

Against this backdrop, the authors suggest four contextual factors that are primary to the acceptance of e-Governance in the EMA:

- **Usefulness**. EMA citizens must be convinced of the relevant advantage of using ICT. Embracing ICT should be perceived as easier, faster and less expensive than current processes. ICT needs to be understood and considered to be useful by EMA citizens;
- **Ease of use**. EMA citizens must be comfortable with the use of ICT. If the appropriate skills and understanding of ICT are in place, then the use of ICT will be easier thereby making its acceptance in the EMA more likely;
- **Intention**. EMA citizens must intend embracing ICT and have a positive attitude towards it. Citizens who view ICT which has no potential in what they are doing are unlikely to accept the potential of ICT; and
- **External variables**. These are factors affecting EMA citizen's acceptance of ICT, which are beyond the individual's control.

It is important that innovative ICT be adopted by EMA to deliver to all its citizens improved services, reliable information and greater knowledge in order to facilitate the e-Governance process by encouraging citizen participation.

Some Concluding Remarks

Public participation is an important element in the stages of the e-Government process, from defining a society's vision and priorities for e-Government to determining e-Readiness and managing e-Government projects (Pacific Council on International Policy, 2002). e-Government is not just about municipal websites, e-Mail and SMS. It is not about service delivery using ICT via the Internet. It is not about digital access to eThekwini Municipality information. It is about how EMA citizens change in relating to their eThekwini Municipality and the degree to which e-Governance changes citizens relating to each other in a municipal information society.

This research indicates that South African local governments need to assess their respective e-Readiness to adopt e-Government strategies or implementation plans. Research needs to be conducted by South African municipalities regarding issues that may impact their e-Government development strategies. This will facilitate an appropriate ICT infrastructure being made available. To seek building an ICT capacity without a solid foundation of research and development is nothing but building a skyscraper in quicksand

(Okpaku, 2003). It will also identify skills gaps required to use ICT effectively and some social, cultural barriers for an effective e-Government strategy within each South African municipality. Should the appropriate research be undertaken, South African municipalities will be able to ensure they adopt an appropriate ICT infrastructure for their citizens thereby improving ESD and narrowing the digital divide.

References

Averweg, U. R., Barraclough C. A. and Spencer, A. F. O., 2003. Towards creating a Municiapl Information Society: The Development of 'eThekwini Online' in South Africa. Proceedings of the World Forum on Information Society (WFIS), Geneva, Switzerland, 8-10 December.

Badshah, A. and Thumler, J., 2003. Digital Bridge to Africa – The Digital Diaspora Network for Africa (DDN-A). In Joseph O. Okpaku (ed) Information and Communication Technologies for African Development, Chapter 12, ICT Task Force Series 2, United Nations ICT Task Force.

Baily, M. N. and Lawrence, R. Z., 2001. Do we have a new e-conomy? NBER Working Paper No. 8243, National Bureau for Economic Research, Cambridge, Massachusetts, USA.

Caldow, J., 2002. Seven e-government milestones. In Eileen M. Miller (ed) Delivering the Vision: Public Services for the Information Society and the Knowledge Economy.

Deloitte and Touche, 2003. At the Dawn of e-Government: The Citizen as Customer. Available from the World Wide Web at www.publicnet.co.uk/publicnet/fe000620.htm

Erwin, G. and Averweg, U., 2003. E-Commerce and Executive Information Systems: A Managerial Perspective. In Sam Lubbe (ed) The Economic and Social Impacts of E-Commerce, Chapter VII, 103-120, Idea Group Publishing, Hershey, USA.

Ethekwini Municipal Area Development Profile, 2002. Changing Durban for Good. Urban Strategy Department, eThekwini Municipality, Durban, South Africa, February.

Ethekwini Municipality Integrated Development Plan 2003-2007, 2003. Available from the World Wide Web at http://www.durban.gov.za/council/transformation/download.htm

Ethekwini Municipality: Quality of Life Household Survey 2002/2003, 2003. Unpublished report by URBAN-ECON, Development Economists, Durban, South Africa.

Fernández-Maldonado, A. M., 2003. Satisfying the Demand for ICT Connectivity of Low-Income Groups. In Akhtar Badshah, Sarbuland Khan and Mario Garrido (eds) Connected for Development, Information Kiosks and Sustainability, ICT Task Force Series 4, United Nations ICT Task Force.

Gumucio-Dagron, A., 2003. Take Five: A handful of essentials for ICTs in Development. Available from World Wide Web at www.geocities.com/agumucio/ArtTakeFive.html

Heeks, R., 1999. Information and Communication Technologies, Poverty and Development. Available from the World Wide Web at idpm.man.ac.uk/publications/wp/di/di_wp05.shtml

Heeks, R., 2003. Learning From Our Mistakes. E-Government Bulletin, Issue 135, ISSN 1476-6310, 17 April. Available from World Wide Web at www.headstar.com/egb

Kamel, S. and Hussein, M., 2000. The Impact of Information & Communication Technology on a Developing Economy. BITWorld 2000 Conference Proceedings, Universidad Iberoamericana Sante Fe, Mexico City, Mexico, 1-3 June.

Manyanga, S., 2002. Understanding The Implications of Information and Communication Technology (ICT) For Local Governance: The Example of eThekwini Municipality, Durban. Master of Science dissertation in Urban and Regional Planning (Development Planning),

Department of Town and Regional Planning, University of Natal, Durban, South Africa.

Okpaku, J. O., 2003. Information and Communications Technologies as Tools for African Self-Development. ICT Task Force Series 2, United Nations ICT Task Force.

OleKambainei, E. and Sintim-Misa, M. A., 2003. Info-communication for Development in Africa. In Joseph O. Okpaku (ed) Information and Communication Technologies for African Development, Chapter 9, ICT Task Force Series 2, United Nations ICT Task Force.

Pacific Council on International Policy, 2002. Roadmap for E-Government in the Developing World, The Working Group on E-Government in the Developing World, The Western Partner of the Council on Foreign Relations, Los Angeles, USA, April.

Pascual, P. J., 2003. e-governance. UNDP – Asia-Pacific Development Information Programme. World Summit on the Information Society, Geneva 2003 – Tunis 2005, Kuala Lumpur, Malaysia.

Rivera-Sanchez, M. and Sriramesh, K., 2003. Information Society and E-Governance: The Case Study of a Knowledge-Based Economy – Singapore. Proceedings of the World Forum on Information Society (WFIS), Geneva, Switzerland, 8-10 December.

Statistics South Africa, 2001. Census 2001 Digital Census Atlas. Available from World Wide Web at gis-data.durban.gov.za/census/index.html

United Nations, 2002. Towards a Knowledge-based Economy. Regional Assessment Report. ISBN 92-1-116823-6, United Nations Publication.

Blending commitment, passion and structure: Engaging cultural linguistic communities in collaborative research

Joanna Ochocka and Rich Janzen

This chapter provides an overview of a five-year research study in progress called *Taking Culture Seriously in Community Mental Health,* is a collaboration between community and academia conducted in two sites in Ontario, Canada. Canada is one of the world's leading immigrant and refugee receiving societies and Ontario the leading destination of most newcomers. The resulting cultural diversity presents challenges and opportunities for the mental health care system and for cultural linguistic communities in Canada. This presented research initiative brings together leading academics, clinical and community practitioners and cultural-linguistic communities to explore, develop, pilot and evaluate mental health services and supports that are culturally effective for the multicultural Canada.

The purpose of this chapter is to use this research imitative as a case study to demonstrate the theoretical and practical considerations of cultural linguistic community engagement in collaborative research. First we present four interrelated components of this research initiative embedded in Participatory Action Research (PAR) approach: research, training, knowledge mobilization and evaluation. Next we illustrate seven concrete mechanisms of community engagement as a means of implementing the Participatory Action Research approach. We assert that the commitment to a value-driven approach to research, together with a mutually agreed upon structure to implement the mechanisms of engagement, form a comprehensive framework that respects cultural linguistic communities in collaborative research. We find that community engagement is not simply an effort at the start. It is an ongoing process that is constantly evaluated by communities. The chapter ends with critical reflections on community engagement.

Involving diverse cultural linguistic communities in community-based research is becoming increasingly common in multicultural societies (Trimble & Fisher, 2006). Ideally, community-based research strives to engage cultural linguistic community members in such a way that traditional research power differentials between professional and non-professional researchers are minimized, and that the control and benefits of the research agenda are equitably shared (Ochocka, Janzen & Nelson, 2002). Even within academia there is a budding discussion of the need to balance research's academic excellence with its practical relevance to community members (Social Sciences and Humanities Research Council of Canada, 2003).

The challenge, however, lies in putting these ideals into practice. How can researchers ensure that the voice and choice of community members (including cultural linguistic minorities) are upheld and that research is conducted with respect and safety? What values and structures should be adopted to help ensure that community members stand to benefit from research as much as professional researchers ("You get a PhD and what do we get?")? Examples are clearly needed to demonstrate how research has come to be relevant for cultural linguistic community members—seeing relevance as the gateway to community engagement.

The purpose of this chapter is to speak into this gap. The chapter features a Community University Research Alliance (CURA) in Canada, and outlines the theoretical and practical considerations of cultural linguistic community engagement in a mental health research project. The chapter begins with a brief overview of the research project in progress. Next we discuss the participatory action research approach used in this project, linking this theory to the project's four components of engagement. The seven concrete mechanisms used to facilitate community engagement are then reviewed, followed by a critical reflection on the successes and challenges of implementing these mechanisms to date.

Project Overview

Canada is one of the world's leading immigrant and refugee receiving societies, accepting roughly 225,000 immigrants each of the past five years. About 18% of Canada's residents are born outside of the country, with recent immigrants increasingly coming from non-traditional, non-Western European sources. Given these recent source countries, visible minorities are growing six times faster than the total Canadian population (Statistics Canada, 2003). The province of Ontario is the primary destination of most newcomers, receiving approximately half of Canada's immigrants.

The resulting cultural diversity presents challenges and opportunities for the mental health care system (Campinha-Bacote, 2002; Beiser, 2003) and for cultural linguistic communities in Canada (Weerasingthe, 2003). A five-year (2005-2009) research initiative called *Taking Culture Seriously in Community Mental Health* investigates these challenges and opportunities. The intersection of mental health and cultural diversity is explored through the active involvement of cultural linguistic communities, and by privileging their voice (see, Janzen, Ochocka & the *Taking Culture Seriously* Partners, 2007).

The overall purpose of the *Taking Culture Seriously* project is to explore, develop, pilot and evaluate how best to provide community-based mental health services and supports that will be effective for people from culturally diverse backgrounds. Five cultural linguistic communities are actively collaborating in this project: Sikh Punjabi, Mandarin, Somali, Polish and Latin American. They were chosen based on demographics across sites (both newer and established communities with sufficient numbers), geographic distribution of world region of origin, differences in migration experiences (immigrants versus refugees, voluntary versus forced migration), and visible minority status. In addition to these cultural linguistic communities, this project also brings together leading academics and practitioners located in the study's two sites (Toronto and Waterloo Region) in Ontario, Canada.

The project is funded for five years as a Community University Research Alliance (CURA) grant from the Social Sciences and Humanities Research Council (SSHRC), and by the Ontario Trillium Foundation. There are three phases planned: research, development of demonstration projects (that will seek to be funded outside of this CURA) and the evaluation of demonstration projects. The project is currently in the research phase.

Participatory Action Research as a Guiding Approach

From the inception, we wanted to have a successful process that engaged various stakeholders including cultural linguistic communities, that was appropriately sensitive to and respectful of cultural differences and issues, and that had a rigorous methodology producing credible recommendations for future actions. We have applied a participatory action research (PAR) approach, an approach that is value-driven and rooted in tradition of democratic pluralism, social change and empowerment (Ochocka et.al., 2002; Nelson, Ochocka, Janzen, , Trainor & Lauzon, 2004). We were committed to break down barriers between researchers and researched, to balance community relevance with academic excellence and to combine knowledge production with action for social change to improve health and human welfare (Ochocka, 2005).

Participatory Action Research (PAR) is one sub-division within a broader area of participatory approaches to research (Minkler & Wallerstein, 2003). It combines social investigation, education, and social change to define and address social problems. It is both a research ideology and a strategy for conducting research, emphasising a set of beliefs regarding the role of social research in addressing social injustice (Jason at al., 2006). PAR can be defined as a "research approach that involves active participation of stakeholders, those whose lives are affected by the issue being studies, in all phases of research for the purpose of producing useful results to make positive changes" (Nelson, Ochocka, Griffin & Lord, 1998, p.12). It also emphasises the attitudes of researchers, "which in turn determine how, by and for whom research is conducted" (Cornwall & Jewkes, 1995), and specific guidelines for planning and implementing research projects (Taylor & Botschner, 1998).

PAR provided this CURA a needed theoretical framework by which ethno-cultural communities could play an active role in conducting research, designing interventions/programs, and establishing power and control over their lives. Most individuals who are recent immigrants experience discrimination, isolation and loss of political and economic resources and power (Trimble & Fisher, 2006) therefore their engagement in researching and strategic planning for future interventions was critical. PAR is also an ideal approach to work collaboratively with other groups of stakeholders including mental health practitioners, cultural and community mental health service providers, and multidisciplinary academic researchers. It is ideal because it engages in mutual respect and mutual learning of all involved and defines research as an initiative that seek to involve communities and create better practice.

From our previous work, we recognized four values guiding PAR:

1. Empowerment;
2. supportive relationships;
3. action and social change; and
4. learning as an ongoing process (Nelson et al., 1998; Ochocka, et al., 2002).

Stating these values up front clarified the researchers' assumptions, and offered community partners concrete guidelines to foresee how the research would be conducted in the everyday activities of the project. The social action orientation of PAR helped to broaden and deepen the dialogue between researchers and communities about social issues beyond the project theme area. The focus on educational opportunities and practical implications from research, assisted communities in seeing reasons and benefits of contributing to this collaborative alliance.

Community engagement in this project has been facilitated through an intentional and ongoing emphasis on four inter-related components. These four components are standard for all CURA projects funded by the Social Sciences and Humanities Research Council: research, training, knowledge mobilization and evaluation. However in our research project, these components were applied to a sensitive research topic (mental health) and to a number of newcomer communities (a potentially marginalized group). Each of the four components is described below. The components can also be seen to shape the overall project structure outlined in figure 1.

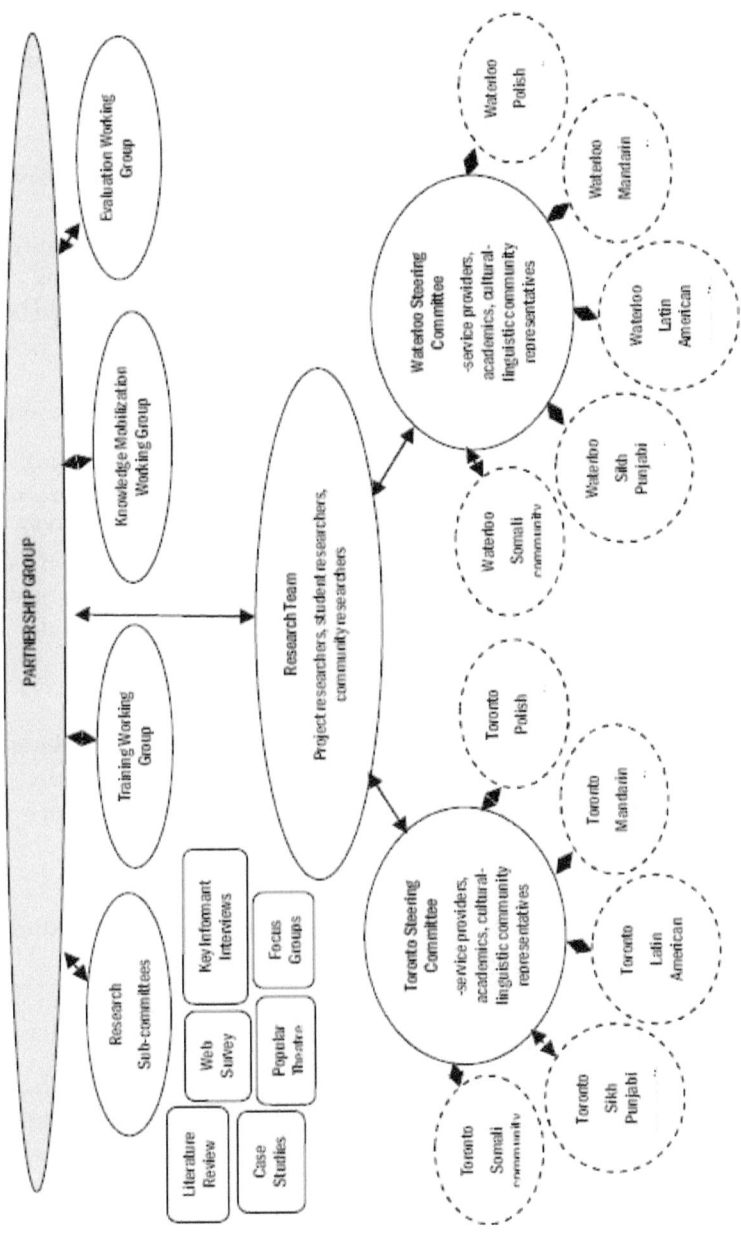

Figure 1: *Taking Culture Seriously* Project Structure

Research

The purpose of the research component is to build a framework for community mental health practice that can guide formal services and informal supports to be culturally empowering. The specific aims are:

1. to develop an understanding of culturally diverse conceptualizations of mental health;
2. to describe the level of awareness about and understanding of community mental health practices to meet the needs of people from various world regions;
3. to develop a framework and strategies for Canadian community mental health practice that are culturally empowering; and
4. to implement and evaluate innovative demonstration projects.

There are three phases of the CURA project. Phase I is exploratory research, using comparative needs assessment (Posavac & Carey, 2003) in order for communities to identify their needs and resources. It also uses critical ethnography (Tedlock, 2000) as a means to describe the lived experiences of research participants. Phases II focuses on creating innovative demonstration projects (based on the emerging framework) and writing funding proposals. Phase III will develop an evaluation framework and the innovative demonstration projects will be evaluate

Research methods in Phase I include a review of international literature, key informant interviews, a service provider survey, community focus groups, and individual case studies within each cultural linguistic community. Each method is led and implemented by a small sub-committee group.

Additional activities include theatre, community forums, conferences, and meetings with managers of mental health institutions and agencies.

Training

The overall purpose of education and training component is for all involved to share in learning and enhance their skills in community-base research. This project enriches research, teaching methods and curricula in universities and increases skills and capacities of non-researcher. Up to eight students at the master's and doctoral level a year are involved through hands-on research and related experience. In addition 10 community researchers are employed by the project to enhance immigrants' employability through training in research, knowledge dissemination and evaluation as well as to make the research culturally appropriate.

The partnership group has an ongoing learning component as a regular item at each partnership group meeting. There are regular bulletins linking to resources, conferences, and other events/initiatives related to mental health and cultural diversity. Community partners are engaged in collaborative conference presentations and writing activities. A small training-working group plans and manages all these internal education opportunities (formal and informal).

Knowledge Mobilization

The overall purpose for knowledge mobilization is to translate knowledge into active service within the community (SSHRC, 2003). In this project two knowledge mobilization-related objectives are implemented: 1) sharing knowledge, resources and expertise among universities, service organizations, and cultural-linguistic communities, and 2) promoting the use of this knowledge to improve both research and mental health services, and to reinforce community decision-making and problem-solving capacity. As such, knowledge mobilization stresses utilization and application.

Knowledge mobilization involves a combination of innovative strategies that speak to the unique cultures of academics, mental health practitioners, public policy makers, and mostly to citizens who belong to diverse ethno-cultural communities. These different expressions of dissemination are essential to ensure that these four main target audiences are informed and connected in an ongoing way. These dissemination strategies are prioritized and implemented by a knowledge mobilization working group.

Evaluation

There are two types of evaluations in this CURA project. One is an internal CURA evaluation. The purpose of this evaluation is to investigate the activities and outcomes of the CURA project and how the collaborative processes and efforts of the community and university have contributed to the project's achievements. The evaluation has started by collaboratively developing a program logic model (Rush & Ogborne, 1991) in which CURA partners link CURA activities with CURA objectives and finalize performance indicators. Methods for the evaluation component include a CURA activity tracking tool; an annual focus group of the partnership group, of research steering committees and of both community researchers and students, evaluation forms to be completed by participants at both CURA conferences; and a confidential mail-in survey sent annually to all CURA partners. In addition a limited access and anonymous feedback forum is included in the CURA website for ongoing reflection of the CURA process by community members. An evaluation working group is overseeing all CURA evaluation activities.

The second type of evaluation focuses on evaluating all new demonstration projects that will be created in Phase II. This evaluation will be implemented in Phase III of the projects (year 4 and 5) according to the evaluation framework developed by an evaluation subcommittee formed from CURA Partners. Evaluation framework will be designed to contribute to the common needs of the CURA project and to the specific needs of each demonstration projects.

Mechanisms of Engagement

Early in the conceptualization of the project, a number of concrete mechanisms of engagement were set in place as a means of implementing the principles of participatory action research. These structures sought to facilitate the active voice and choice of cultural linguistic community members in practical and respectful ways. When reading the description of these mechanisms below, notice that their implementation was not merely a mechanical process. Rather, these mechanisms represent an ongoing negotiation—all a part of dynamic relationship building that is expected to continue throughout the project. Note also that some mechanisms focus on engaging individual cultural linguistic communities while others on communities combined. This observation is reflective of the project's broader multicultural vision, while still working individually with the project's five selected communities.

Partnership Group

At the heart of the *Taking Culture Seriously* project is the partnership group. Formed by the project's lead organization, the Centre for Research and Education in Human Services (CREHS), the partnership group was built on a history of past collaboration. This group is comprised of representatives from all participating community and academic organizations and is ultimately responsible for the conceptualization and conduct of the project. Initially starting with 17 individuals, the partnership has now grown to include 43 individuals representing 38 distinct organizations, including academic/research centres (5), community mental health organizations (5), community and cultural linguistic organizations/groups (25), and provincial umbrella organizations (3) (see www.crehscura.com for complete list).

The partnership group meets four times each year, with partners also participating on subcommittees and working groups. Monthly partnership bulletins are circulated electronically, updating partners of all developments of the project and inviting the participation in newly developing areas. A private "members only" section of the project website was added to further facilitate partnership communication.

All original partners contributed to developing the grant proposal through a series of face-to-face meetings and teleconferences. Once funding was approved, an early task of the partnership group was to develop guiding principles of working together. Through the leadership of the knowledge mobilization working group, the partnership group also developed an authorship and dissemination policy, with an explicit emphasis on ensuring equity and fairness for students and community members, including grievance procedures (see Jacobson, et al., in press).

Cultural Linguistic Community Visits

In order to broaden the involvement of cultural linguistic communities within the project, a series of face-to-face meetings were held with community members from the five selected cultural linguistic communities. The meetings were facilitated by CREHS staff with occasional co-facilitation from other project partners. These community visits are seen to be part of an ongoing effort within the research project to deepen the engagement of community members.

The first wave of visits was held during the proposal development stage. A mixed-community meeting was organized with key leaders (suggested by each community) from the five selected cultural linguistic communities and in both study sites. About 10-15 community leaders attended each event and almost all of them stayed with the project as steering committee members or community researchers. Some participants had collaborated with proposal partners on past research and served as brokers of trust between researchers and their community. The objectives of these meetings was to present the research proposal ideas, to have community leaders subsequently shape the research agenda, and to discuss preliminary affirmation of community involvement in the proposed project. We also discussed in depth the benefits and shortcomings of each community's involvement in this project.

Once funding was approved, a second wave of visits immediately followed. A series of 10 meetings was organized, this time separately with each of the five cultural linguistic communities in both project sites. Meetings varied in terms of 1) location ('within' the community, e.g., ethno-specific organizations, temples or 'outside' e.g., the project partner's organizations), 2) length (1-5 hours), number of participants (4-15), 3) membership composition (formal leaders versus lay members), and 4) atmosphere (formal versus informal). In some communities follow-up meetings were organized to engage additional community members, resulting in a total of 17 meetings involving a total of over 200 people. Discussions during the meeting were generally lively, if not at times challenging, with community members often 'testing' project partners as to the benefit (and potential harm) of the research to their community. Project partners welcomed these challenges, inviting community members to help shape the research agenda through their involvement in the other pre-determined mechanisms outlined below.

Steering Committees

Within both the Toronto and Waterloo sites, a steering committee has been formed to provide guidance to all project activities within that site. Steering committees members included mixed stakeholders including representatives from each of the five cultural linguistic communities. Membership totalled 15 in Toronto, and 13 in Waterloo, with meetings held five times each year. In both communities an 'ex-officio' membership list was also created of local mental health service providers interested in being updated on the project's progress but not attending meetings.

The role of the steering committees is to give input into the formulation of research methods and tools, data collection and analysis, dissemination strategies, and the development and evaluation of demonstration project within their respective site. In community-based research projects these cross stakeholder steering committees can be seen as "mini-laboratories" of the broader community, where the challenges of innovative interventions can be played out and tested before implementation (Taylor & Botschner, 1998).

The cultural linguistic community representatives play a critical role in ensuring that all research activities remain relevant to their own community's interests. At each meeting representatives give project and non-project related updates about developments within their respective communities, thereby balancing the updates given by the research team. Representatives also provide critique of how research plans could best engage their community members in a safe and respectful manner. But their contribution goes beyond their participation in meetings. Representatives are also active 'behind the scenes', including: hiring community researchers/facilitators, promoting the project at community gatherings and events, recruiting research participants, advising and modelling how to navigate the micro-politics within their community, and some even co-facilitating focus groups within their community.

Community Researchers/Facilitators

Another mechanism of engagement was to hire, train and support cultural linguistic community members as community researchers/facilitators. CREHS regularly involves community members who are 'living the issue under study' as research team members (Reeve, et al., 2002). Their experiential knowledge can help to safeguard against insensitive research practice, can serve to challenge traditional power imbalances between researchers and community members, and can increase data quality (Ochocka, et al., 2002). For this project, a total of 10 people were hired, one from each of the five cultural linguistic communities in both study sites. The community researchers/facilitators met bi-monthly together with professional researchers for intense training, discussion and mutual support.

The dual researcher/facilitator title is reflective of their dual role. On the one hand, they are *researchers* involved in traditional research activities within their respective community settings (i.e., participant recruitment, facilitation of focus groups and individual interviews, data analysis, presentation of findings). But more than dispassionate technicians, they are also agents of change, *facilitating* a community response to the issue of mental health. In short, community researchers/facilitators are key actors of community engagement, serving as an important link between the research project and the participating community.

More than a strategy of community engagement, the hiring of community researchers/facilitators is a value-driven exercise. Their hire demonstrates a commitment to the value of community capacity- building, both in terms of leaving a legacy of community-based research skills within the community, as well as providing some (admittedly relatively modest) financial gain. Given the restrictions of the project's academic funder, the original research grant proposal budgeted little for these staff positions. However, additional funding was secured from another source to hire the 10 community researchers/facilitators on a part-time basis over a three-year period.

Community Forums

Upon completion of data gathering and analysis, the *Taking Culture Seriously* project is planning to organize a series of forums with cultural linguistic community members. The purpose of these forums is to share and verify research findings, and to generate discussion and commitment to linking these findings into action. One forum is to be held for each of the five cultural linguistic communities in both project sites (for a total of 10 forums). These culture-specific forums allows each community to first safely discuss their community's response to mental health issues without fear of public stigmatization. Community researchers/facilitators and steering committee representatives will play a key role in planning and facilitating these events. Two additional public forums will be held in each study site to facilitate cross-cultural discussions and to build linkages and partnerships between local mental health organizations and cultural linguistic communities.

Community forums are a potentially powerful community engagement strategy (Lukas & Hoskins, 2003). Their power lies in creating space for community members to hear each other's opinions, to develop strategies for change and to offer community members hope for future action, leadership and commitment to implement concrete strategies. As in past CREHS community forums (e.g., Janzen & Ochocka, 2003; Janzen, Hogarth & Hatzipantelis, 2005), the forums in this project will be organized as a part of longer-term engagement strategy, in this case through demonstration projects.

Demonstration Projects

Another important mechanism of community engagement built into this research study design is to develop, implement and evaluate innovative demonstration projects. Building on the results of the community forums, these demonstration projects will seek to model mental health practice that is culturally empowering. It is expected that a number of demonstration projects will be developed, involving a variety of partnerships among cultural linguistic communities and mental health practitioners. Prospective government and non-governmental funders have already expressed interest in receiving these demonstration project proposals.

These demonstration projects are built into the core of the *Taking Culture Seriously* project, not as an addendum. The demonstration projects therefore represent the project's commitment to utilization and action. This message is critical for cultural linguistic community engagement. Not only could cultural linguistic communities contribute to what culturally effective practice *should* look like, they could also participate in actually *implementing* these ideas. Demonstration projects therefore will offer cultural linguistic community members the opportunity to be the beneficiaries of research, both in terms of gaining new resources (financial and expertise), as well as in maintaining control over the development of mental health inventions that made sense for their community.

Community-Based Coordination

The six mechanisms of engagement mentioned above reflect the progression of the research process starting from establishing the project (partnership group, community site visits) to development of data collection tools, collection of data, analysis and interpretation (steering committee, community researchers/facilitators), communication of findings (community forums) and acting on research (demonstration projects). A final mechanism is also important. It is also critical that the project is managed by a community-based organization. The Centre for Research and Education in Human Services (CREHS) is a leader in PAR in Canada and has a long history of working with communities on relevant policy research. CREHS has a provincial and national reputation of working collaboratively with stakeholders, including ethno-cultural groups, mental health consumer/survivors, cultural and mental health service providers and academics. Having a community based research centre to coordinate and link all partners creates a safe and trusted community place for the study and all its players.

A team of three researchers (CURA Director, one CURA co-investigator and CURA Coordinator) provide strong project coordination linking all committees and working groups together, and overseeing all project activities including engagement of cultural linguistic communities.

Reflections on Engagement

Taken together, the mechanisms described above have already begun to facilitate community engagement. For example, the site visits were crucial in terms of building understanding, trust and respect between project researchers and community members. Hiring community researchers and community participation on steering committees allow a process of shifting the project ownership from researchers to collective alliance. The ongoing communication, the focus on outcomes (developing demonstration projects) and the culture of ongoing learning culture were crucial in terms of building understanding, trust and respect between project researchers and cultural linguistic community members. At this moment of the project, the engagement seems to be successful; all 10 communities in both sites are actively participating in the project.

Much work has been invested to implement the mechanisms described above, beyond the effort of typical academic based research. And it is an ongoing work. There are many meetings and work between meetings; there are many extra efforts in making sure that everyone is updated, heard, involved and at the same time that the study is moving ahead according to it pre-determined timelines. There is flexibility as the steps of engagement are tailored to each of the five participating cultural linguistic communities.

What is more, we have found that community engagement is not simply an effort at the beginning of a research project. It is an ongoing process that is constantly evaluated by the communities involved. It requires a commitment to "walk the talk" in implementing values of PAR and in collective sharing of all the responsibilities and benefits of the research agenda. It requires being open to flexibility in the research design and methodology and to active listening and constant acting. It also requires good organization skills, task management and a commitment to the larger vision.

Beyond hard work, however, there seems to be another important ingredient to ensure success. Effective community engagement seems to be directly linked to deeper values and assumptions about research. Engagement is more likely if community members see that professional researchers view the research project as a strategic social movement—in our case a movement with political goals of facilitating socio-political awareness and systemic change by reducing stigma and discrimination. Having this intellectual and safe place where people can gather, learn from each other, and create social change has contributed to helping make the *Taking Culture Seriously* project appealing to cultural linguistic community members.

This extensive community engagement is not without dilemmas and challenges. For example, in our project to date there is little involvement of communities in partnership group. Also after engaging communities in the focus group discussions, there are raised expectations expressed. Community members would like to see more groups discussion to be facilitated with them and with others regarding mental health issues. It is good to have mechanisms of community forums and demonstration projects planned, but in some cases the pace of the project timetable is too slow to maintain the momentum and acting on needs expressed from community engagement. There seems to be urgency to develop other mechanisms beyond the project plans and also a danger of building hope and not delivering.

Conclusions

Collaborative research initiatives combining community and university partners are increasingly seen as a promising means of increasing the likelihood that research-based knowledge is mobilized into active service in the broader society. Community engagement is very important in making research relevant. PAR seems to be helpful approach that facilitates successful and respectful community engagement. Its emphasis on multiple perspectives, on collaborative process of constructing knowledge and a strong focus on social action, attracts communities to actively participate.

The mechanisms we described in this chapter helped to facilitate community engagement. They provide clear avenues for involvement, voice and control of cultural linguistic communities. However the secret lies not in their mechanical implementation. The mechanisms were embedded in a mutually agreed upon structure of collaboration, that ensured that all four project components remained inter-connected: research, training, knowledge mobilization and evaluation. What is more, the success of engagement hinged on the researchers' value commitment to power sharing and authentic relationship building. Both structures and values are needed for successful and respectful community engagement.

Initially and continuously cultural linguistic communities judge research projects on good organization, mutual values, shared vision and culturally appropriate processes of engagement. But ultimately the final actions and products, and their relevance for communities, provide the basis for judging community and university collaborations. We will need to be continually mindful of this as we progress on our *Taking Culture Seriously* research project. And through the experience, we look forward to sharpening our knowledge about community engagement in collaborative research.

Acknowledgement

The community engagement strategies described in this chapter emerged from a research project entitled 'Taking Culture Seriously in Community Mental Health' (www.crehscura.com). This Community University Research Alliance (CURA) is funded by the Social Sciences and Humanities Research Council of Canada and the Ontario Trillium Foundation. We would like to acknowledge the CURA partners for their part in shaping the ideas presented in this chapter (see www.crehscura.com for a complete list of partners). In particularly we would like to acknowledge Laura Simich, Centre for Addiction and Mental Health, who submitted the original chapter abstract. Direct request for further information about the study can be made to the authors (rich@crehs.on.ca or joanna@crehs.on.ca)

References

Beiser, M., (2003). Why Should Researchers Care About Culture? Canadian Journal of Psychiatry, 48, 154-160.

Campinha-Bacote, J. (2002). Cultural competence in psychiatric nursing: Have you "ASKED" the right questions? Journal of the American Psychiatric Nurses Association, 8, 183-187.

Cornwall, A. & Jawkes, R. (1995). What is participatory research? Social Science and Medicine, 41, 1667-1676.

Jacobson, N., Ochocka, J., Wise J., Janzen, R. & the Taking Culture Seriously Partners (in press). Inspiring knowledge mobilization through a communications policy: The case of a Community University Research Alliance. Progress in Community Health Partnerships: Research, Education and Action.

Janzen R. & Ochocka, J. (2003). Immigrant youth in Waterloo Region. In P.Anisef & K.M. Kilbride (Eds.), Managing two worlds: The experience and concerns of immigrant youth in Ontario. Toronto: Canadian Scholar's Press.

Janzen R., Ochocka, J. & the "Taking Culture Seriously" Partners (2007). The road toward cultural empowerment: An invitation to inclusion. In D. Zinga (Ed.) Navigating Multiculturalism

Negotiating Change. Cambridge Scholars Press.

Janzen, R., Hogarth, K. & Hatzipantelis, M. (2005). Needs Assessment as Community Mobilization: The Immigrant Skills Initiative of Waterloo Region. Presentation at Crossing Borders, Crossing Boundaries. Joint CES/AES Conference (Canadian Evaluation Society; American Evaluation Association), Toronto, Ontario.

Jason, L., Keys, Ch., Suarez-Baltcazar, Y., Taylor, R. & Davis, M. (2006). Participatory community research; Theories and methods in action. American Psychology Association, Washington, DC.

Lukas, C. & Hoskins, L. (2003). The wilder nonprofit field guide to conducting community forums: Engaging citizens, mobilizing communities. Minnesota: Wilder Publishing.

Minkler, M. & Wallerstein, N. (2003). Community-based participatory research for health. Jossey-Bass A Wiley Imprint, San Francisco, CA.

Nelson, G., Ochocka, J., Griffin, K. &Lord, J. (1998). Nothing about me without me: Participatory action research with self-help/mutual aid organizations for psychiatric consumer/survivors. American Community Psychology Journal, 26, 881-912.

Nelson, G., Ochocka, J., Janzen, R., Trainer, J. & Lauzon, S.(2004). Comprehensive evaluation framework for mental health consumer/survivor organizations: Values, conceptualisation, design, and action. Canadian Journal of Program Evaluation, 19(3), 29-53

Ochocka, J (2005). Keynote presentation. CURA Launch, Centre for Research and Education in Human Services, Kitchener, ON, March 9, 2005

Ochocka, J., Janzen, R. & Nelson, G. (2002). Sharing power and knowledge: Professional and mental health consumer/survivor researchers working together in a participatory action research project. Psychiatric Rehabilitation Journal. 25(4), 379-387

Posavac, E.J. & Carey, R.G. (2003). Program evaluation methods and case studies. Upper Saddle River, NJ: Prentice Hall.

Reeve, P.Cornell, S., D'Costa, B, Janzen, R. & Ochocka, J. (2002). From our perspective: Consumer researchers speak about their experience in a community mental health research project. Psychiatric Rehabilitation Journal, 25(4), 403-408.

Rush, B. & Ogborne, A. (1991). Program logic models: Expanding their role and structure for program planning and evaluation. Canadian Journal of Program Evaluation, 62(2), 93-105

Social Sciences and Humanities Research Council of Canada. From granting council to knowledge council. 2003. Ottawa, Ontario. Accessed March 2, 2006 at www.sshrc.ca/web/whatsnew/initiatives/transformation/consultation_framework_e.pdf

Statistics Canada. (January, 2003). Canada's ethnocultural portrait: The changing mosaic. Census analysis series.

Taylor, A. R. & Botschner, J.V. (1998). Ontario community support association: Evaluation handbook. Kitchener, ON: Centre for Research and Education in Human Services.

Tedlock, B. (2000). Ethnography and ethnographic representation. In Norman K. Denzin, and Yvonna S. Lincoln (eds.) Handbook of Qualitative Research. Thousand Oaks: Sage

Trimble, J.E. & Fisher, C.B. (2006). The handbook of ethical research with ethnocultural populations & communities. California: Sage Publications.

Weerasingthe, S., & Williams, L.S. (2003, April). Health and the intersection of diversity. A challenge paper on selected program policy, and research issues. Paper presented at the Intersections of Diversity Conference, Niagara Falls, Ontario.

Moving towards increased cultural competency in public health research

Lisa Gibbs, Elizabeth Waters, Andre Renzaho and Maree Kulkens

> There has been a renewed focus in recent decades on collaborative approaches in community-based public health research and interventions. This is an important grounding for addressing the needs of culturally and linguistically diverse (CALD) communities. But how well do we as researchers prepare for the complexities of working with CALD communities? And what sort of support do we need to meet the challenges of the task? Cultural competence refers to the extent to which researchers, practitioners and organisations have the necessary skills, knowledge, attitudes and policies to work effectively in cross-cultural situations. The shift towards cultural competence in public health is evidenced by the development of policies and guidelines by government bodies and leading research institutions in countries such as Canada, the United States, Australia and New Zealand. This chapter will draw on these guidelines, on models of cultural competency used in welfare and health service delivery, and on collaborative research approaches. A framework for moving towards cultural competence in public health research and health promotion interventions will be discussed, drawing case study examples from the co-authors' community-based experiences. This will highlight the complexities but also the importance of adopting culturally competent strategies in public health research and health promotion interventions. The need for supporting government and funding structures will also be proposed.

Migration patterns in recent decades have led to increased cultural diversity internationally with some countries moving towards a population without a majority cultural group (Daunt, 2003). This presents a challenge for public health researchers who aim to represent the population as a whole, to address health inequalities and to ensure that public health interventions are relevant and accessible to all population groups. Governments are recognising the need to establish guidelines for addressing the health needs of culturally and linguistically diverse communities. For example, in New Zealand the Health Research Council produced Guidelines on Pacific Health Research (Pacific Health Research Committee, 2004) after extensive consultation. It is presented as an evolving document to guide dialogue between the researchers and the people (populations) involved in the research. Within this document it explores ethical principles of culturally competent research, stating that "the overarching principle is that relationships are the foundation of all ethical conduct" (p.1). The United States Government released National Standards for Culturally and Linguistically Appropriate Services in Health Care in 2001

(Cross, Bazron, Dennis, & Isaacs, 1989). This involved a four year development process including extensive consultation with consumers, stakeholders and advisers. In Australia, the National Health and Medical Research Council (NHMRC) recently released Cultural Competence: A guide for policy, partnerships and participation (National Health and Medical Research Council, 2006). This guide was developed to "help policy makers and managers with culturally competent policy and planning at all levels of the health system" (p.3).There has also been a renewed focus in recent decades on collaborative approaches in community-based public health research (Baum, 1998; Israel, Schulz, Parker, & Becker, 1998). This is an important grounding for addressing the needs of culturally and linguistically diverse (CALD) communities. But how well do we as researchers prepare for the complexities of working with CALD communities? And what sort of support do we need to meet the challenges of the task?

This chapter will propose strategies for moving towards a culturally competent approach to community-based public health research. In particular, the involvement of CALD communities as active partners in all stages of the research process will be recommended. Proposed approaches will be informed by existing cultural competence literature in relation to health service delivery. The realities of research within CALD communities will be discussed via case studies of the authors' research experiences. In addition, the need for supporting infrastructure in terms of funding models will be discussed.

Culturally and linguistically diverse communities

As developed countries embrace cultural and linguistic diversity, the need for consideration of health inequalities and differing health needs increases. In New Zealand, almost 1 in 5 residents were born overseas (Statistics New Zealand, 2001). The main countries of overseas birthplace were England, Australia, Samoa, China and Scotland. The fastest growing communities were those from China, South Africa, India, Fiji and Korea. The languages most widely spoken after English were Maori, Samoan, French, Yue (Cantonese) and German (Statistics New Zealand, 2001). In Australia, almost a quarter (23%) of the Australian population were born overseas, 14% in countries where English is not the first language (Australian Bureau of Statistics, 2004). While there are large well-established CALD communities, such as those from Italy and Greece, the fastest growing CALD populations are those from Iraq, India and China (Australian Bureau of Statistics, 2004). The ever increasing migration from developing to developed countries has created a 'paradox of assimilation' (Fuentes-Afflick, Hessol, & Eperez-Stable, 1999; Peak & Weeks, 2002). New migrants from developing countries (except for refugees and humanitarian entrants) display better health outcomes than comparable native-born populations in the host (developed) country despite their low socio-economic status and poor health profile prior to migration. This phenomenon is known as the 'healthy immigrant effect' and is extensively described in Australia (Australian Bureau of Statistics, 1998; Australian Institute of Health and Welfare, 2000; Bennett, 1993; Taylor, Chey, Bauman, & Webster, 1999), the United States (Abraido-Lanza, Dohrenwend, Ng-Mak, & Turner, 1999; Fuentes-Afflick et al., 1999; Muening & Fahs, 2002; Singh & Siahpush, 2001) and Canada

(McDonald & Kennedy, 2004; Newbold & Danforth, 2003). It has been suggested that health screening and healthier behaviours prior to migration, and the tendency for the wealthiest and healthiest individuals in a given population group to migrate (McDonald & Kennedy, 2004), may account for the phenomenon. However, the significant health advantages enjoyed by new migrants to developed countries disappear with continued length of stay. Migrants' mortality and morbidity indicators become worse than that of the host population as the length of stay increases or the migrant population moves from first to second generation (Harris, 1999; Razum, Zeeb, & Rohrmann, 2000). This highlights the need for public health interventions before the acculturation effect takes place.

For those who have migrated as refugees or humanitarian entrants, health issues are likely to arise from the circumstances in their country of origin such as war, persecution, famine, trauma, and the subsequent stresses of resettlement.

Cultural competence models

In order to understand and address health disparities affecting CALD communities it is necessary to conduct targeted research with these communities. As a starting point, it is useful to consider existing definitions and models of cultural competence.

> Cultural and linguistic competence is a set of congruent behaviors, attitudes, and policies that come together in a system, agency, or among professionals that enables effective work in cross-cultural situations. 'Culture' refers to integrated patterns of human behavior that include the language, thoughts, communications, actions, customs, beliefs, values, and institutions of racial, ethnic, religious, or social groups. 'Competence' implies having the capacity to function effectively as an individual and an organization within the context of the cultural beliefs, behaviors, and needs presented by consumers and their communities (OPHS Office of Minority Health, 2001, based on Cross et al., 1989).

Over the last three decades there have been a number of cultural competence models proposed (Cross, Bazron, Dennis, & Isaacs, 1989; Klimidis et al., 1999; National Center for Cultural Competence, 2004; Porteous, 2004; Rees & Ruiz, 2003; Renzaho, 2001; US Department of Health and Human Services, 2001). However, the most comprehensive and most cited model in the literature is the 'cultural competence continuum' by Cross and colleagues (see Figure 1) (Cross et al., 1989). This model is symbolic of the different stages of cultural competence, each stage representing a higher level of achievement on the continuum. It does not provide guidance on how to achieve this progress but is an important reminder of the complexities involved in developing cultural competence and the level of proficiency to which we should aspire. Strategies for progressing through the stages are discussed later in this chapter.

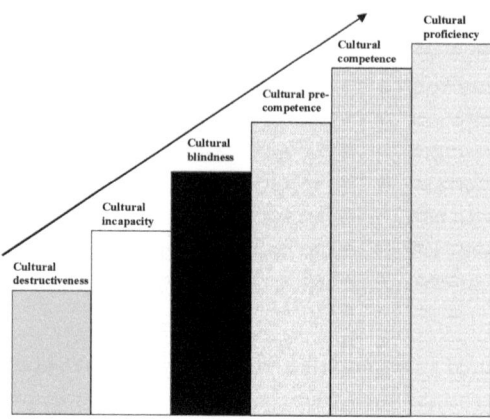

Figure 1 Cultural Competence Continuum (Adapted from Cross, et al., 1989)

Note:

- Cultural destructiveness is equivalent to forced assimilation whereby there is only one cultural trend that is acknowledged while purposefully outlawing any other cultural approaches.
- Cultural incapacity puts boundaries on cultural approaches in an equal manner, acknowledges their existence but without engaging them.
- Cultural blindness adopts the "one approach fits all" model whereby the assumption is that people are all alike and what works for one cultural group should also work for the other.
- Cultural pre-competence is a form of integration whereby learning about each other in terms of barriers and solutions is encouraged.
- Cultural competence is a form of incorporation, learning from the pre-competencies to develop policies and best practice.
- Cultural proficiency not only seeks to change policies and practices but also promote and seek to improve cultural relations and networks among diverse groups.

All these models are pitched within cross-cultural and welfare perspectives. They have been developed and used in the context of health service delivery to CALD communities. They cover the areas of mental health (Hays, 2001; Kinzie, Tran, Breckenridge, & Bloom, 1980; McKenzie et al., 1999; Patel et al., 2000), chronic disease (Bennett, 1993; Renzaho & Hawthorne, 1999; Rozman, 2001; Thow & Waters, 2005) and refugee and migrant health in general (Editorial, 1996; Porteous, 2004; Renzaho, 2002; Spruill & Davis, 2005). As discussed later in this chapter, key features of the models can also be applied to community-based public health research to support participative processes. They allow for the increased complexity of collaboration when the researchers and community groups have different cultural backgrounds.

> The member of the in-group looks in one single glance through the normal social situations occurring to him and... he catches immediately the ready-made recipe appropriate to its solution... For those who have grown up within the cultural pattern, not only the recipes and their efficiency but also the typical and anonymous attitudes required by them are an unquestioned 'matter of course' which gives them both security and assurance (Schutz, 1976).

The challenge for public health researchers is how to engage with particular CALD communities without creating ethnospecific models of engagement. From a policy perspective, these are more costly than cultural competence models. As Zola (1983) notes:

> ... everyone has a cultural heritage which is part and parcel of an individual's health practices. The practical answer is not to learn in detail the infinitive varieties of culture but to be aware of these varieties and how they might affect one's health practices. I am totally opposed to training anyone in the details of a particular ethnic group, for this will ultimately squeeze people into unreal categories, and typecast their culture just as we have rigidified diagnoses. What I favour is making practitioners sensitive to the patient's heritage, their own heritage and to what happens when different heritage come together (p.227).

An additional consideration is the fact that migration can occur due to war and persecution, family reasons or work reasons. Many new arrivals are dealing with issues arising from conflicts in countries-of-origin, the impact of trauma and the stresses of resettlement.

Moving towards culturally competent research

Building cultural competence into community-based public health research is a gradual process that takes time and experience (see Case Study 1).

> ### Case study 1: Gradual increase in cultural competence
>
> *Fun 'n healthy in Moreland!* is a cluster randomised controlled trial of a child health promotion and obesity prevention intervention. It involves 23 primary schools in an inner urban area of Melbourne, Australia. It is a culturally diverse community with a lower proportion of residents speaking English at home than in Victoria overall. 48% of participating children had one or more parents born overseas, the main countries being Lebanon, Italy, Turkey and China. This is a partnership project between Moreland Community Health Service and Deakin University. The first stage of the project was to collect a range of baseline data measuring the home and school physical activity and food environments, as well as child and parent knowledge, attitudes and behaviours in relation to eating and physical activity. Reference groups were established initially. Community Health Service staff contributed knowledge of the community's health needs. School principals provided information about families' communication strategies. However, no-one thought to mention during the planning period that the scheduled collection of baseline data coincided with Ramadan – a time of fasting followed by feasting for the Muslim community! Clearly this would have distorted the measures of healthy eating. Fortunately, the principal of the Islamic school pointed out the clash 2 weeks before the measures were taken so it was possible to delay data collection until the end of Ramadan. It was then possible to appoint staff from the same religious community onto the project team. This has been hugely beneficial in ensuring the project is consistent with local religious practices. For example, the *fun 'n healthy in Moreland!* team now provide practical Ramadan guidelines to schools and families. The guidelines cover:
>
> - nutritional information to parents about breakfast foods that are likely to provide sustained energy during the day to fasting children
> - reduced physical activity demands at school for fasting children
> - a separate space for fasting children to engage in quiet reading or sedentary activities while other children are eating their snacks and lunch.

In the initial phases, research teams may benefit from working in partnership with a research team or agency which has had more experience with this approach. However, it is encouraging to note that the key principles of cultural competence are consistent with those of participative research processes commonly employed in public health research. To demonstrate consistency between the two approaches, key features of the NHMRC Guide to Cultural Competence in Health (National Health and Medical Research Council, 2006) are presented in Table 1 alongside corresponding principles of participative research, as described in Israel and colleagues' review of community-based research (Israel et al., 1998):

...a fundamental characteristic of community-based research as defined here is the emphasis on the participation and influence of non-academic researchers in the process of creating knowledge (p177).

Table 1: Aligning the principles and key features of participative research with those of cultural competence

Participative research (Israel et al., 1998)	Cultural competence in health (National Health and Medical Research Council, 2006)
Recognises community as a unit of identity	Engages consumers and communities
Builds on strengths and resources within the community	Builds on strengths – know the community, know what works
Facilitates collaborative partnerships in all phases of the research	Develop reciprocal relationships
Integrates knowledge and action for mutual benefit of all partners	Knowledge transfer occurs as part of a reciprocal relationship that values different contributions.
Promotes a co-learning and empowering process that attends to social inequalities	Involves peer education, community development and capacity building. Acknowledges rights of all consumers to access health services and health information.
Involves a cyclical and iterative process	Establish long-term relationships that support systematic identification and response to issues rather than ad hoc approaches
Addresses health from both positive and ecological perspectives	Flexible approach, develop understanding of cultural differences in different contexts.
Disseminates findings and knowledge gained to all partners	Shared learning. Uses leadership and accountability for sustained change – including government mandates, organisational and professional accountability and infrastructure, and individual practice.

Table 1 shows consistencies between key aspects of participative research and cultural competence. The central themes of collaborative processes and mutual knowledge transfer are clear in both approaches. Despite the parallels, additional complexities are involved in developing participative processes cross-culturally. For example, identification and consultation with the appropriate community representatives and research participants (Lipson & Meleis, 1999) (see Case Study 2), recognising different cultural understandings of health and illness and working styles, and accounting for potentially interacting influences of gender and culture.

> **Case study 2: Consultation with community leaders**
>
> Engaging CALD communities in all aspects of research planning, implementation and evaluation is critical. As a starting point, identifying and engaging with key community leaders, both informal and formal, not only assists in ensuring the project is relevant within the cultural context, but will also provide guidance on specific health behaviours, practices and beliefs which may not be reflected within the literature. This approach has been particularly beneficial in informing Teeth Tales: a community-based health promotion study, aimed at improving the oral health of preschool aged children and their families. This study was focussed on examining the barriers to improved oral health for CALD communities and people from lower socio-economic backgrounds. Nearly one third of Moreland's population were born in a non-English speaking country. Evidence indicates that children enter their school years with untreated tooth decay (approximately 80% by the age of 4 years old) (Harris, Nicoll, Adair, & Pine, 2004) and the prevalence is higher among CALD communities and those from lower socio-economic communities (Armfield, Roberts-Thomson, & Spencer, 2003).
>
> In the early stages of this study a number of consultations took place with community groups to gain a clearer understanding of the factors and barriers that contribute to both positive and negative oral health practices. Key religious and community leaders were engaged to further understand cultural behaviours and practices relating to oral health. Through these consultations we were made aware of a particular cultural practice called *miswak*, which had not previously been evident through the literature.
>
> The *miswak* chewing stick has been used since ancient times and has a very strong traditional and religious background. The *miswak* is chewed on one end until it becomes frayed into a brush-like form, which is then used to clean the teeth in a similar manner to a toothbrush. It is believed to have a range of health benefits and is commonly used multiple times during the day coinciding with prayer time. Consultations with the Muslim leaders identified a strong level of *miswak* use across the Muslim community (World Health Organisation, 2000). Limited research is available about the *miswak*, both within Australia and internationally. These initial consultations have led to the development of a research study into the oral health practices of CALD communities, focussing on families with young children.

Strategies for shifting from a generic research approach, referred to as cultural blindness, to approaches which achieve increasing levels of cultural competence are outlined in Table 2. While there are likely to be different ways of moving towards cultural competence, Table 2 provides direction to researchers committed to conducting research which successfully engages with CALD communities. The strategies draw upon existing models of cultural competence, in particular Cross et al. (1989), NHMRC (National Health and Medical Research Council, 2006) and the Health Research Council of New Zealand (Pacific Health Research Committee, 2004). The strategies described at each level build upon and enhance the previous level and thereby reflect a gradual progression towards cultural proficiency.

Table 2: Progressing from generic through to culturally proficient public health research (Modified from Cross et al (1989), NHMRC (2006), Pacific Health Research Committee (2004))

Conceptual framework	Stages of Research	Cultural blindness	Cultural pre-competence	Cultural competence	Cultural proficiency
Defining the health problem	Forming partnerships	Involve other researchers, lead agencies, community organisations	Liaise with representatives of cultural organisations and/or community leaders of relevant cultural groups (ideally before a specific study has been identified or initiated)	Work through gatekeepers to establish peer educators matched to the culture, language, gender, age and life stage of the research participants	Cultural competence strategies embedded within organisational policies, infrastructure and accountabilities, and within individual work practices.
	Defining the research question	Evidence-based priority health issue	Refined in consultation with representatives of cultural group	Identified and initiated by cultural group. Explore their understandings of health and illness, perception of the problems and possible strategies.	
Identifying predisposing and protective factors	Identifying data sources and target populations	Identify potential sources and ways of collecting data in order to address the research question.	Build a profile of the target community in terms of linguistic, religious, cultural and migration issues, and test or qualify its validity with the community. Develop an understanding of the cultural values and meaning given to research issues.	Recognise the influence of the researchers' own cultural framework. Recognise diversity within cultural groups. Allow for effects of acculturation over time and changed context. Clarify values re levels of access to information based on culture, gender, age or life stage.	
	Appointing staff	Appoint competent staff to various roles within research team	Wherever possible include members of the target community as staff at all levels in the research team. Recruit through ethnic media, word of mouth through community groups and networks. Consideration needs to be given to confidentiality issues particularly within small communities	Be respectful of the role of community leaders, negotiate access to research participants and potential peer leaders. Recognise potential power imbalances. Account for complexities of culture and gender – eg women's voice restricted in interactions with men. Recognise cultural differences in working styles and consultation expectations. Reimburse community consultants and peer educators for expertise, time, travel and resources.	
	Recruitment of sample	Mailout, advertisements, telephone calls, flyers.	Personal contact, oral communication, ethnic media, multilingual staff, interpreters, peer educators, clear support from community leaders. Recruitment in community settings. Translated materials accompanied by	Recognise differences in defining language and cultural identity – may change following marriage. Different understandings of research may need to be addressed to ensure informed consent. Fear of authority may affect willingness to sign consent form – may need to record verbal consent.	

Developing, implementing and evaluating culturally appropriate responsive interventions	Data collection	Methodology determined by data requirements, comparative data, resource and time constraints	English versions. Observe etiquette of place and community. Methodology responsive to linguistic and socioeconomic considerations, eg. Use interpreters and translated materials to address language differences. Provide child care and transport to enable participation	Methodology responsive to cultural and migration considerations. For example, some cultures may prefer to be consulted as a family group rather than as individuals. May not be appropriate to use professional interpreters in small communities where privacy and confidentiality cannot be guaranteed
	Development of intervention (where approp)	Informed by the evidence and the baseline data	Feedback from community representatives about the design and implementation of the intervention	Involvement of peer educators in the development of the intervention. Implementation of the intervention by community organisations and providers.
	Analysis/Evaluation	Guided by standards of research rigour and researcher understanding	Feedback from community representatives about initial findings and analysis	Involvement of peer educators in the analysis and interpretation of the data. Feedback from research participants to establish the confirmability of the results.
Scaling up culturally appropriate and effective programs	Reporting/disseminating findings	Report summary of findings to participants & all stakeholders. Inform policy direction.	Mutual knowledge transfer process with cultural community. Dissemination of findings in a manner agreed with cultural representatives. Inform policy direction.	Reciprocity of information providing opportunities for the communities of interest to discuss findings and generate solutions. Policy development arising from findings. Establishment of sustainable programs.

Essentially, the goal of cultural competence as reflected in Table 1 is to involve all levels of the community within all stages of the research, i.e. as 'inside' researchers. Ideally, in these circumstances the community will drive the research agenda. This affords significant advantages to the research study. It provides ready access to community understandings and priorities that can be used to direct the research processes, findings and applications. Realistically, not all communities or members of communities wish to take an active role in research but their level of participation ideally should be an informed decision made by them rather than the researcher. The opportunity to make an informed decision and to contribute in a meaningful way requires that researchers are reflective about culture. This does not just refer to the complex interacting cultural influences on the community involved. Critically, the researcher needs to be reflective about cultural influences on their own working styles, values and assumptions. In doing so it becomes possible to consider a more adaptive approach. For example, in the Teeth Tales project (see Case Study 2), community leaders and community members have been actively involved in developing the research question, study design and methodology. They were consulted through informal discussions over the phone or in their home or community setting with the project worker. However, they are not willing to commit to "sitting around a table" in structured meetings with other advisors. This involvement has evolved through gradually developed relationships. In some cases contact was made with the community via approaches to religious and community leaders. In other cases, by involvement in community settings such as kindergartens and playgroups. It is also anticipated that some community members who are recruited as research participants will also be invited to actively contribute to research decision-making. It should be noted that the research study is being conducted in partnership between a University and a Community Health Service. This partnership with a community organisation provides entry to community settings and clear opportunities for applications of research findings to community services. These are important considerations in the engagement of communities.

Infrastructure

Additional time, strategies and resources need to be allocated for culturally competent research. Initially, this will enable identification and recruitment of appropriate cultural advisers and research participants (see Case Study 3). Adequate recruitment rates of cultural groups are unlikely to be achieved using standard recruitment practices. The recruitment aspect of the study needs to be specifically designed in consultation with the community representatives to address the cultural values, linguistic needs and practical constraints of the target population.

In general, comprehensive, overlapping strategies are required (Keyzer et al., 2005) and should include personal contact (Brown, Long, Gould, Weitz, & Milliken, 2000; Daunt, 2003; Lipson & Meleis, 1999; Marshall & While, 1994) and oral communication (National Health and Medical Research Council, 2006) wherever possible. If staff do not speak the language of the target group they should be accompanied by an interpreter (National Health and Medical Research Council, 2006), with clear support from community contacts. Ideally, a peer educator matched to the religion, culture, gender, age and life stage of the research participant should be involved in information sessions and recruitment. It is also helpful to obtain permission from community leaders to approach potential research participants in the community settings where members of the community congregate such as playgroups, churches and schools (B. Brown et al., 2000; Daunt, 2003; Green et al., 2003; Lindenberg, Solorzano, Vilaro, & Westbrook, 2001).

Case study 3: Recruitment

In a series of studies of parental uptake of child unintentional poisoning strategies, parents were recruited informally at maternal and child health centres and community playgroups, sometimes in the base of high-rise public housing (Gibbs et al., 2005). Community representatives, peer educators and kindergarten staff were involved in planning and conducting the recruitment. Talking to parents about their strategies for protecting their child from unintentional poisoning was potentially sensitive given the participants' vulnerable circumstances and fear of authority in some cases. However, a series of factors made the focus group discussions and interviews comfortable and informative:

- the security of a familiar environment, such as the home or kindergarten setting
- the support of the community representatives
- the morning tea provided by the researcher
- and the willingness of the researcher to chat while the children played alongside.

The inevitable background noise in this setting did present challenges for transcribing the tapes afterwards but this was overcome by clearly repeating what people said, which also proved to be a useful active listening strategy.

Additional time, strategies and resources will be required to enable the development of trust in the research and the researcher (Lipson & Meleis, 1999), understanding of different belief systems, values (A. Renzaho, 2004), lifestyles and work practices (Daunt, 2003; Eide & Allen, 2005; Keyzer et al., 2005; Marshall & While, 1994; National Health and Medical Research Council, 2006), cultural meanings given to symptoms and diseases (Kleinman, 1988; MacLachlan, 1997), culturally appropriate instruments and tools (Lipson & Meleis, 1999), and different approaches to cultural consultations in community-based research (Israel et al., 1998; Kirmayer, Groleau, Guzder, Blake, & Jarvis, 2003). For example, the different cultural meanings given to obesity are reasonably well documented, particularly in relation to some cultural backgrounds. African Americans associate *plumpness* and *bigness* with health, prosperity and a great achievement (Styles, 1980). They see overweight as acceptable and culturally desirable (McGee & Hale, 1980; Robbins, Vaccarino, Zhang, & Kasl, 2000) or a defence strategy against young "toughs" for women living in low-income housing (J. Brown, 1993). Therefore, while the obesity epidemic has continued to shape health policies in developed countries, obesity is not always seen as a disease or a negative state (Renzaho, 2004). As Brown (1993) puts it:

> Fatness is symbolically linked to psychological dimensions such as self-worth and sexuality in many societies of the world, but the nature of that symbolic association is not constant. In pre-industrial societies, thinness is stigmatised as a symptom of starvation or as a sign of AIDS in contemporary central Africa. Among middle and upper class women in the United States [as in all developed countries], thinness represents the moral success of self-control over one's body (p.186).

From a cultural competence perspective, public health researchers are confronted with the question of how to mediate the inherent tension between some cultural values and health risks. For example, raising awareness of obesity potentially conflicts with preservation of cultural values related to the body image and size, and gender related social contexts.

Culturally competent public health research is unlikely to be achievable without a supportive government and funding infrastructure. It also requires commitment from the wider academic infrastructure such as those who publish research findings. Funding allocations need to reflect the increased time and resources required to undertake culturally competent research (National Health and Medical Research Council, 2006). Research being conducted through academic institutions may benefit from the added support of student placements and higher degree students (Brown et al., 2000).

Furthermore, government and funding bodies are in a position to generate a shift towards cultural competence in public health research by working collaboratively with CALD communities in the development of research priorities. Establishing supportive policies and setting requirements for evidence of cultural competence in research funding models and tender documents will further support the process (Israel et al., 1998).

Conclusion

Increased global migration necessitates a shift from public health research embedded in the majority population to research which is culturally competent. This requires considerable expertise and impacts upon the entire research process. Existing models of cultural competence in health service delivery, in conjunction with models of participative/collaborative research, provide a useful guide to culturally competent strategies. Research teams new to this area would benefit from forming an alliance with researchers experienced in working cross-culturally, to guide the transition to cultural competence. The subsequent richness of the data, the depth of the findings, and the wider applications of the research will enhance the research experience and the relevance of the work being conducted. It will contribute to the impact and sustainability of subsequent interventions and policy changes. Shifts to cultural competence in government and in research funding bodies would support this necessary shift in focus.

References

Abraido-Lanza, A., Dohrenwend, B., Ng-Mak, D., & Turner, J. (1999). The Latino mortality paradox: a test of the 'salmon-bias' and healthy migrant hypotheses'. American Journal of Public Health, 89, 1543-1548.

Armfield, J. M., Roberts-Thomson, K. F., & Spencer, A. J. (2003). The Child Dental Health Survey, Australia 1999: Trends across the 1990's. AIHW Cat. No. DEN 95. Adelaide: The University of Adelaide (AIHW Dental Statistics and Research Series No. 27).

Australian Bureau of Statistics. (1998). Deaths. Canberra: ABS.

Australian Bureau of Statistics. (2004). Migration, Australia 2003-2003. Canberra: Commonwealth of Australia.

Australian Institute of Health and Welfare. (2000). Australia's health 2000: biennial health report of the Australian Institute of Health and Welfare. Canberra: AIHW.

Baum, F. (1998). The New Public Health: An Australian Perspective (1 ed.). Melbourne: Oxford University Press.

Bennett, S. (1993). Inequalities in risk factors and cardiovascular mortality among Australia's immigrants. Australian Journal of Public Health, 17, 251-261.

Brown, B., Long, H., Gould, H., Weitz, T., & Milliken, N. (2000). A Conceptual Model for the Recruitment of Diverse Women into Research Studies. Journal of Women's Health and Gender-Based Medicine, 9, 625-632.

Brown, J. (1993). Cultural perspectives on the etiology and treatment of obesity. In A. J. Stunkard & T. A. Wadden (Eds.), Obesity: Theory and therapy (Second ed., pp. 179-193). New York: Raven Press, Ltd.

Cross, T., Bazron, B., Dennis, K., & Isaacs, M. (1989). Towards a Culturally Competent System of Care, Volume 1. Washington, DC: CASSP Technical Assistance Center. Center for Child Health and Mental Health Policy, Georgetown University Child Development Center.

Cross, T., Bazron, B., Dennis, K., & Isaacs, M. (1989). Towards a Culturally Competent System of Care: Vol I. Washington, DC: National Technical Assistance Centre for Children's Mental Health, Georgetown University Child Development Centre.

Daunt, D. (2003). Ethnicity and Recruitment Rates in Clinical Research Studies. Applied Nursing Research, 16, 189-195.

Editorial. (1996). Asylum Seekers: General Health Status and Problems with Access to Health. Med J Aust., 165, 634-637.

Eide, P., & Allen, C. (2005). Recruiting Transcultural Qualitative Research Participants: A Conceptual Model. International Journal of Qalitative Methods, 4, 1-10.

Fuentes-Afflick, E., Hessol, N. A., & Eperez-Stable, E. (1999). Testing the epidemiologic paradox of low birth weight in Latinos. Arch Pediatr Adolesc Med, 153, 147-153.

Gibbs, L., Waters, E., Sherrard, J., Ozanne-Smith, J., Robinson, J., Young, S., et al. (2005). Understanding parental motivators and barriers to uptake of child poison safety strategies: a qualitative study. Injury Prevention, 11, 373 - 377.

Green, J., Waters, E., Haikerwal, A., O'Neill, C., Raman, S., Booth, M., et al. (2003). Social, cultural and environmental influences on child activity and eating in Australian migrant communities. Child: Care, Health and Development, 29, 441-448.

Harris, K. M. (1999). The health status and risk behaviors of adolescents in immigrant families. In D. J. Hernandez (Ed.), Children of immigrants. (pp. 286-315.). Washington, D.C.: National Academies Press.

Harris, R., Nicoll, A. D., Adair, P. M., & Pine, C. M. (2004). Risk factors for dental caries in young children: a systematic review of the literature. Community dental health., 21, 71-85.

Hays, P. A. (2001). Addressing cultural complexities in practice: a framework for clinicians and counsellors. Washington D.C.: American Psychology Association.

Israel, B., Schulz, A., Parker, E., & Becker, A. (1998). Review of Community-Based Research: Assessing Partnership Approaches to Improve Public Health. Annual Review of Public Health, 19, 173-202.

Keyzer, J., Melnikow, J., Kupperman, M., Birch, S., Kuenneth, C., Nuovo, J., et al. (2005). Recruitment Strategies for Minority Participation: Challenges and Cost Lessons from the Power Interview. Ethnicity and Disease, 15, 395-406.

Kinzie, J. D., Tran, A. K., Breckenridge, A., & Bloom, J. D. (1980). An Indochinese refugee psychiatric clinic: culturally accepted treatment approaches. Am J Psychiatry, 137, 1429-1432.

Kirmayer, L., Groleau, D., Guzder, J., Blake, C., & Jarvis, E. (2003). Cultural consultation: a model of mental health service for multicultural societies. Can J Psychiatry, 48, 145-153.

Kleinman, A. (1988). Rethinking psychiatry. New York: Free Press.

Klimidis, S., Lewis, J., Miletic, T., McKenzie, S., Stolk, Y., & Minas, I. H. (1999). Mental health service use by ethnic communities in Victoria. Part 1. Melbourne: The Victorian Transcultural Psychiatry Unit & Centre for Cultural Studies in Health, The University of Melbourne.

Lindenberg, C., Solorzano, R., Vilaro, F., & Westbrook, L. (2001). Challenges and Strategies for Conducting Intervention Research with Culturally Diverse Populations. Journal of Transcultural Nursing, 12, 132-139.

Lipson, J. G., & Meleis, A. I. (1999). Research with immigrants and refugees. In A. S. Hinshaw, S. L. Feetham & J. L. F. Shaver (Eds.), Handbook of Clinical Nursing (pp. 87-106). London: Sage Publications.

MacLachlan, M. (1997). Culture and health. Chichester: John Wiley & Sons Ltd.

Marshall, S., & While, A. (1994). Interviewing respondents who have English as a second language: challenges encountered and suggestions for other researchers. Journal of Advanced Nursing, 19, 566-571.

McDonald, J. T., & Kennedy, S. (2004). 'Insights into the healthy immigrant effect: health status and health service use of immigrants to Canada'. Social Science and Medicine, 59, 1613-1627.

McGee, D., & Hale, H. (1980). Social factors and obesity among black women. Free Inquiry, 8, 83-87.

McKenzie, D., Klimidis, S., Lewis, J., Minas, H., Stuart, G., & Renzaho, A. (1999). The continuity of mental health care in immigrant and Australian born patients in Victoria. Paper presented at the First National Conference of the Australian Transcultural Mental Health Network, Melbourne, October 1999.

Muening, P., & Fahs, M. (2002). Health status and hospital utilization among immigrants to New York City. Prev Med, 35, 225-232.

National Center for Cultural Competence. (2004). Health Bridging the Cultural Divide in Health Care Settings: The Essential Role of Cultural Broker Programs: Georgetown University Center for Child and Human Development, Georgetown University Medical Center.

National Health and Medical Research Council. (2006). Cultural Competence in Health: A guide for policy, partnerships and participation: Commonwealth of Australia.

Newbold, K. B., & Danforth, J. (2003). Health status and Canada's immigrant population. Social

Science and Medicine, 57, 1981-1995.

OPHS Office of Minority Health. (2001). National Standards for Culturally and Linguistically Appropriate Services in Health Care. Washington D.C.: U.S. Department of Health and Human Services.

Pacific Health Research Committee. (2004). Guidelines on Pacific Health Research. Auckland: Health Research Council.

Patel, N., Bennet, E., Dennis, M., Dosanjh, N., Mahtani, A., Miller, A., et al. (2000). Clinical psychology, race and culture: a training manual. Leicester: British Psychology Society.

Peak, C., & Weeks, J. (2002). Does community context influence reproductive outcomes of Mexican origin women in San Diego, California? J Immigr Health., 4(3), 125-136.

Porteous, S. (2004). Access to mainstream services by culturally and linguistically diverse communities in Manningham, Whitehorse and Knox. Migration Information Centre.

Razum, O., Zeeb, H., & Rohrmann, S. (2000). The 'healthy migrant effect'-not merely a fallacy of inaccurate denominator figures. Int J Epidemiol., 29, 191-192.

Rees, C., & Ruiz, S. (2003). Compendium of Cultural Competence Initiatives in Health Care. Menlo Park, CA: The Henry J. Kaiser Family Foundation.

Renzaho, A. (2004). Fat, rich and beautiful: changing socio-cultural paradigms associated with obesity risk, nutritional status and refugee children from sub-Saharan Africa. Health & Place, 10, 105-113.

Renzaho, A. M. N. (2001). The Western Region Health Centre's Refugee Health Service Model: A report and evaluation documenting the service. Melbourne: Centre for Culture, Ethnicty and Health.

Renzaho, A. M. N. (2002). Addressing the needs of refugees and humanitarian entrants in Victoria: An evaluation of health and community services. Melbourne: Centre for Culture, Ethnicity and Health.

Renzaho, A. M. N. (2004). Fat, rich and beautiful: changing socio-cultural paradigms associated with obesity risk, nutritional status and refugee children from sub-Saharan Africa. Health and Place, 10, 115-113.

Renzaho, A. M. N., & Hawthorne, G. (1999). Does non-English Speaking background make a difference to patient outcome in ischaemic heart disease? , The University of Melbourne, Melbourne.

Robbins, J. M., Vaccarino, V., Zhang, H., & Kasl, S. V. (2000). Excess type 2 diabetes in African American women and men aged 40-74 and socioeconomic status: evidence from Third National Health and Nutrition Examination Survey. J Epidemiol Community Health, 54, 839-845.

Rozman, M. (2001). Ethiopian Community Diabetes Project. Melbourne: Western Region Community Health Centre.

Schutz, A. (1976). The Stranger. In G. Bowker & J. Carrier (Eds.), Race and Ethnic Relations. London: Hutchison.

Singh, G. K., & Siahpush, M. (2001). All-cause and cause-specific mortality of immigrants and native born in the United States. Am J Public Health, 91, 392-399.

Spruill, I., & Davis, B. L. (2005). Cultural Competence: Myth or Mandate. Online Journal of Health Ethics, 1(1).

Statistics New Zealand. (2001). 2001 Census Snapshot 1: Cultural Diversity. Retrieved 09 August, 2007

Styles, M. H. (1980). Soul, black women and food. In A. S. Kaplan (Ed.), A women's conflict: the special relationship between women and food (pp. 161-176). Englewood Cliffs, NJ: Prentice

Hall.

Taylor, R., Chey, T., Bauman, A., & Webster, I. (1999). Socio-economic, migrant and geographic differentials in coronary heart disease occurence in New South Wales. Aust N Z Public health, 23, 20-26.

Thow, A., & Waters, A. (2005). Diabetes in culturally and linguistically diverse Australians: Identification of communities at high risk (cat. no. CVD 30). In. Canberra: Australian Institute of Health and Welfare.

U.S. Department of Health and Human Services. (2001). National Standards for Culturally and Linguistically Appropriate Services in Health Care. Washington, D.C.: Office of Minority Health.

World Health Organisation. (2000). Consensus Statement on Oral Hygiene. International Dental Journal, 50, 139.

Zola, I. (1983). Oh where, oh where has ethnicity gone? In I. Zola (Ed.), Sociomedical inquiries. Philadelphia: Temple University Press.

Lisa Gibbs, Elizabeth Waters, Andre Renzaho and Maree Kulkens

Innovative assessment of human development: The case of Bougainville

Jim Chalmers, Udoy Sankar Saikia and Gouranga Dasvarma

> This chapter reflects on the process of the forthcoming UNDP Bougainville Human Development Report, which provides a baseline study of population groups who have recently emerged from a decade-long civil war. The human development view is that education and health are economically important; but more than this, they are an investment in human capability – not just "human capital" that can bring productivity gains. Accordingly, the research process was designed to enhance choices and capabilities of the communities. The starting point was that Bougainvilleans' life skills enabled them to survive when cut off from the world in terms of health, educational and technological support during their long struggle for autonomy in 1988-1999. We wanted to foreground these "literacies" by investigating them alongside the text-based skills that declined when schools became a casualty of war. Methodologically too, the intent was to put emphasis on human lives as assets, not on insufficiencies. The project consults broadly with communities; and key empirical and historical modes of investigation have been undertaken by local civil society actors, and local activists and thinkers. With a conviction that national ownership is contingent on the quality of engagement as well as on quantity, data collection teams were engaged, not only in data collection but also in research design. They are also thoroughly involved in the analysis. In addition to analysing primary data collected as above, selected authors were asked to write papers covering the various themes of the report. The contributing authors were briefed with the intent to draw insights from their local experiences and struggles. In sum, the chapter elaborates how the tradition of Human Development Reports is a factor of uncompromised universal values in combination with processes of localization that open spaces for cultural groupings to fill in the broad categories, and in ways that shape their particular drives for recognition.

Central to any description of Bougainville is an understanding of its recent history of civil conflict referred to as "The Crisis" (PNG HSSP, 2005). This was caused by dissatisfaction among local community over their share in profits gained from the operation of a huge copper mine, and by the environmental damage it caused. This discontent was coupled with ethnic tensions between Bougainvilleans who identify closely with the people in the Solomon Islands and people from other provinces of Papua New Guinea (PNG) (PNG HSSP, 2005). The civil conflict continued until 1998 when a negotiated settlement was agreed between all parties except one group known as Mekamui Defense Force. The nine-year long conflict involved nearly everyone, physically destroying one of the country's most developed provinces, and devastating the socio-economic, political and governance structures. Autonomous elections in June 2005 have resulted in substantial improvements in the political environment- an action which will give them a semi-independent status from Papua New Guinea. The elected autonomous government has a strong mandate; and political leaders are actively engaged in priority setting and managing divisions. These transformations mark a current need to move forward with activities that support the capacity to deliver long-term public and private services. One set of activities involves the Human Development Report (HDR) for the Autonomous Region of Bougainville (ARB), which, significantly, was requested by the Autonomous Government.

Although a national level Human Development Report was produced by the United Nations Development Programme (UNDP) for Papua New Guinea in 1998, Bougainville was not included due to the Crisis. The present Report consulted widely, undertaking to support the priorities of the ARB Action Plan. In selecting *the role of communities in education* as its theme, the Report undertook to identify and recommend the most relevant forms of education, an approach that relies on understanding the linkages between learning/education and *kastom* (custom). A key formation of *kastom* in Bougainville is belonging; and, in turn, the chief determinant of belonging is shared emotional experience. The implications and applications of this set of principles is even more marked in places with a recent history of diaspora, such as Bougainville. Such experience escalates people's impressions of a "common enemy" who ostensibly broke up and scattered their lives. The civil war and the peace process in Bougainville can be expected to continue to play a key role in social self-identity, not simply because of the damage caused by war, but also because the development of shared emotional experience goes back to colonial times.

Historical discontinuities, such as colonial experiences and the war and peace experiences are of particular importance to the process of Bougainvillean identity. Bougainville has endured occupation by many foreign forces- Germany, Britain, Australia and Japan. Another very significant discontinuity concerns changes to the matrilineal social system, mostly brought about by the increasing dominance of the cash economy. The fact that men have been given more opportunities to prosper from the formal economy means that women's customary power is at risk. When cash earnings become the predominant form of power in social contexts where land has been the basis of customary authority and power, the relative value of land and its customary custodians (who are the women in Bougainville) diminishes.

Customary land is not divisible and so has no actual cash value. The implication is that women have lost their customary power with the advent of a business society and the wage economy, in the particular context of the huge Panguna copper mine. But discontinuities don't run in a straight line: during the crisis Bougainville women renewed their customary authority and their power. This is because when the blockade was imposed it brought about ever greater prevalence of barter and other non-cash exchange mechanisms, and, predictably, individuals reverted to producing more of what they consume.

While there is good evidence that wellbeing suffered in terms of physical ill health, there is also anecdotal proof that wellbeing gained in terms of belonging, dignity, etc. Women played a key role in this process of cultural renewal; thus a further implication for the Report and its methodology, was the need to reflect very carefully on the significance of the shift in moral authority and leadership when the matrilineal system loses its economic power, and how educational curricula need to address this change in women's status in speaking to the blend of *kastom* and modernity.

How the Report's theme was identified

While the BHDR is an independent report, the process and outcomes of the Bougainville Human Development Report (BHDR) were participatory and fully-inclusive. For purposes of comparison across regions and countries, HDRs follow an established structure and set of indices; however, the reports are very flexible and tailored to local contexts, especially through the selection of the theme.

It is useful to emphasise an earlier point that the theme of "basic skills and life skills" was decided on during a process of close consultations with Government partners, civil society, and development agencies, and that the key reference point in decision-making was the Medium Term Development Strategy 2005-2010 (MTDS) of the National Government, together with the Strategic Action Plan 2006-2010 of the Autonomous Bougainville Government (ABG).

In harmony with the National Government's Poverty Reduction Strategy, the MTDS is focused on rural development, poverty reduction and empowerment through human resource development. The MTDS priorities blend income earning opportunities with basic education and informal adult education.

In keeping with a sequenced road map for autonomy, the ABG Action Plan puts the spotlight on villagers improving their own wellbeing. Support for this is identified in terms of government priorities of inclusiveness, participation, self-reliance, and mutuality. Goal 3 of the Action Plan sets out the primary means for achieving this, by building "A peaceful, law abiding, inclusive society of clever, well-educated and healthy people" (ABG, 2005:19). To help make this possible, the Action Plan allocates cost estimates for Education of 23.24% of the Total Cost Estimates for 2006. By 2010, education will comprise 33.4% of the total cost estimates for planned actions. Clearly, over the coming five years, education will remain a key priority for the ABG. Its mandate to implement this expectation is set out by the 1995 Organic Law on Provincial and Local Level Government, which devolves responsibility for many elements of service delivery, including in education. The broad target groups for picking up responsibility are communities themselves. More specifically, the intent is to encourage and support the inclusion of customary experts in the formal education system. The purpose of this is to build demand for formal education through narrowing the gap between formal and informal learning. Customary experts refer to canoe-builders, drum-makers, agronomists, story-tellers, and so on.

Before elaborating on the focus of the consultative process on education and learning, it is useful to say characterise the more general process of consulting with communities. The intent or end goal of covering the widest possible range of stakeholders invariably boils down to ensuring that the voice of the community predominates. In this case it was achieved first by carefully searching and selecting Bougainvilleans as the subject of consultations rather than 'Bougainville experts' in PNG and NZ or Australia. Cutting across the solidarity aspect of this aim was the tension expressed by Bougainvilleans who experienced the 10 year war first-hand against those whose families had left for other parts of PNG or elsewhere. The consultation strategy was to select regardless of this specific experience and support reconciliation by staging consultations in alternative venues in the Autonomous Region and the mainland of PNG. Second, the goal was to select 'unofficial' as well as 'official' voices, with the intent of uncovering versions of social history that expressed the widest possible range of experiences of the conflict and post-conflict aspirations – regional, factional, empowered, disempowered, women, men, youth, elders, and so on. Civil society organisations (CSOs) are particularly well-developed in the Autonomous Region and so the consultation process was able to draw extensively on active participants in the political life of Bougainville. The CSOs are also especially well-organised, which made it possible for the consultation process to integrate with existing complementarities. Thus, the selection of CSOs was organic in the sense that the three organisations, although discrete and independent of each other, had frequently collaborated in previous projects.

The nature of the research that the Bougainvillean collaborators undertook was designed to enhance choices and capabilities. In particular, this refers to the population who missed out on formal education when schools were closed by the war. Conventional or universal literacy measurements would fail to capture their life skills because they test enrolment and completion rates. And since many Bougainvilleans had not completed formal schooling, conventional literacy tests would not measure what they could in fact read. The project assumed that Bougainvilleans had reading and writing and numeracy capabilities, but they would not be uncovered unless specific tests were used to probe these skills. In sum, the research component of the report was designed to show the baseline of human resources in the Region. And the purpose was to emphasise the importance of social inclusion of a vulnerable population (the under-formally-educated).

The consultative process that confirmed education as the Report's priority went further again. It also undertook to consult widely in order to learn *which aspects* of education are most appropriate for Bougainville. The President and senior ministers in the ABG insisted that they were not interested in replicating the formal education systems of industrialized states. They want learning programmes that combine elements of proven value in indigenous knowledge systems (*kastom*) together with the most relevant of progressive modalities used in international spheres of education. A similar concern was raised by the community, as Ahai reports, that culture and tradition emerge as very important in the vision of a new Bougainville:

> Cultural reclamation – to reclaim that which has been lost through paternalistic attitudes of missionaries and the euro centric social and economic systems. Programs of cultural reclamation and development focused on educating children and youth about their cultural foundations (stories about land ownership, customary marriage practices, clan and inter clan genealogies, traditional medicine, myths, legends and creation stories, hunting and fishing practices, custom songs, chants and dances, different types of custom festivities, counting systems, custom arts and craft, annual cycle of plants and animals- traditional calendar, traditional peace making processes, traditional knowledge and the environment, language etc) (Ahai, 1999, pp.124-125).

Consequently, discussions were held with lead international agencies in education – in particular the United Nations Educational, Scientific and Cultural Organisation (UNESCO) and the International Literacy Institute (ILI).[37] The views of these agencies were found to be highly relevant. They view literacy as 'a gateway' that makes it possible for individuals to learn skills wherever they may be, in school, or in a place of work. These kinds of 'literacies' enable individuals to assume their rights and responsibilities in their community (UNESCO, 2004).

The academic literature was also trawled for new approaches to literacies.[38] The key finding, which is also reflected in UNESCO's approach, is that literacies are no longer being seen as a rigid set of instructions; the view now is that literacies are a set of skills that reflects and is shaped by community life and values. Literacies are being recognized as skills and learning strategies that link up with particular situations – sites where they were learned, and where the skills had particular end purposes[39].

These preparatory consultations enabled the Report to be well-focused on the appropriate nature of education for Bougainville. And this focus was further tightened by the decision to identify the target group as those youths who missed out on schooling during the decade long civil war.

---

[37] The ILI was established in 1994 by UNESCO and the University of Pennsylvania/Graduate School of Education

[38] Exponents of new literacy studies include Brian Street, Harvey Graff, and James Gee.

[39] Luke and Freebody (2000) define literacy as: The flexible and sustainable mastery of a repertoire of practices with texts of traditional and new communications technologies via spoken language, print and multimedia. www.education.tas.gov.au/english/liteng.htm [Date accessed 20th September 2006]

The Report's target group is currently aged between 15 and 30 years old. They endured heavy exposure to the conflict, but they also played a key role in negotiating the successful peace plan[40]. It is interesting to reflect on the skills they brought to that process; because it is "the effective uses of language" that new literacy studies highlight above all else[41]. And since oral traditions play a strong role in Bougainville literacies, this element features strongly in the Report's inquiries.

Policy-makers are increasingly demanding localized information – as near as possible to individual level. Only then can they identify gaps and inequities. The Report helps make this possible. Through surveying the most vulnerable groups – those who couldn't go to school because of the war – it will help planners to build policies for inclusion. And through providing a complementary survey on communities' access to services and on the scope of everyday activities, the Report will help planners to glimpse the different priorities of people in different communities.

Further, by investigating the likelihood that people can read an election pamphlet, the Report will help make better governance, especially in terms of how it feels to be governed. Societies are fragile things. Governance depends on consensus but also on meaningful participation. Similarly, a strong economy needs skilled human resources. By surveying numeracies, the Report will help planners strategise for improved income generation, particularly in the informal sector. And, if mining is to once more underpin economic growth, as most of the stakeholders predict, this aim will be improved by the baseline survey of human resources that the Report provides.

In the final instance, the Report captures synergies across the key areas of human development priorities; and this is expected to help planners to investigate, integrate, and further develop more targeted approaches to programming in capacity development, poverty reduction, conflict prevention, civil society, gender equity, empowerment and governance. Contributing to the production of disaggregated data will help confirm the importance of doing diagnosis at local levels, and in turn, it will help satisfy the growing demand by national level analytical and diagnostic tools for locally relevant data. Last but importantly, the Report brings about an opportunity to localize the Millennium Development Goals through making available better profiling of skills[42].

---

[40] An enhanced ability to resolve conflict has been recognized by a delegation to the ARB from Nagaland, India in March 2006; Naga peoples have long been seeking a successful outcome to their autonomy struggle.

[41] For instance in the Queensland state school system, see Luke and Freebody (2000)

[42] Typically HDRs are users rather than producers of primary data but surveys are being undertaken in this case due to lack of information, Fieldwork, being conducted by local NGOs, will commence in May 2006; the Report publication date is December 2006.

The BHDR process

This section explicates the tactics designed to support local preparation of the Report, or, to use development language, the ways that communities were supported to take ownership of the Report's preparation. The explicit principles of the HDR process are national ownership, participatory and inclusive participation, independence of analysis, quality of analysis, flexibility and creativity in presentation, and sustained follow-up. These principles were followed in the preparation of the Bougainville Report as follows:

National ownership

The key instrumentalities were broad consultations, production of primary data from two surveys, and production of background / working papers.

- **Consultations** – Formal and informal consultations aimed at consensus on the theme and the methodology were held on a continuous basis with senior political leaders in the ABG, with Bougainville Peace and Restoration Office (BPRO), with Local Level Government (LLG) and the Council of Elders (COE) in the ARB, with civil society leaders in the ARB, with radio and newspaper media in the ARB, with donors as end users, and with UN international resources including HDR offices in Sri Lanka and New York, UNDP country offices world-wide, UNICEF in PNG, and UNESCO in New York and Montreal.
- **Production of primary data** – In the absence of disaggregated lower level data sets, the BHDR recruited and trained local organizations in Bougainville to produce information that national and ARB planners' need. An instrument (Social and Economic Conditions Survey) produced by National Statistical Office (NSO) of Papua New Guinea was also used to collect data on the access of Census Units to public services; and Council of Elders (COEs) were briefed into this objective as the principal providers of information about access of Census Units.
- **Production of background/working papers** – With the aim of capturing existing knowledge and producing new knowledge by Bougainvilleans on the subject of the BHDR theme of education / basic skills, the BHDR identified and briefed 17 contributing writers most of whom were local.

Inclusive participation

As noted, the BHDR has had a clear mandate to support a new Government in Autonomous Bougainville with a strong and broad mandate to govern, and to this end the BHDR has worked to provide localized data sets on human development. These are expected to further enhance the ability of the ABG to be inclusive in ways that consolidate the peace process while building autonomy. Further, the theme of the BHDR (skills for sustainable development) has been chosen in consultation with political and planning leaders on grounds that ensure inclusiveness and pluralism.

Capacity-building is the key instrument being used to assure active engagement by a fully inclusive representative group. This includes training/capacity-building workshops held in Buka for data collection agencies, and other workshops (in Buka and in Port Moresby) for contributing writers.

Independence of analysis

The chief mechanisms of independence of analysis include:

- Recruitment of international consultants with expertise in population studies and development studies,
- Recruitment of Bougainvillean and PNG contributing writers, from academia, education, and civil society, who collectively bring broad and relevant expertise in both formal and informal education subjects.
- Clear editorial policy of independence was imparted to contributing writers and to data collection agencies. This was reinforced through workshop agenda items focused on HDR traditions of excellence, and on academic methodologies and ethics that underlie independence of analysis.

Quality of analysis

Quality of analysis was assured by the selection process of contributing writers which was concentrated on identifying researchers and education professionals who demonstrate lively and sustained historical interest and concern, as well as their ability to put forward pragmatic solutions concerning the well being of Bougainvilleans and their elected Government.

Quality of analysis was further assured by the participation of Peer reviewers, as follows:

Peer review process

The peer review is a demand-driven exercise that is able to greatly improve the content of HDRs using thematic and/or regional expertise, who provide crucial external support comments on the contents of the HDR. The key moment in the HDR process where the peer review took place is following the last Report draft. There are several other pieces of information that were provided to reviewers including Working Papers for the BHDR process, which contain information on the context of preparation (capacity at the national level, involvement of the UNDP office, availability of statistics, involvement of the government, etc) and the intended audience. The basis of the reviews is six principles that address overall quality of the analysis contained in the reports, whether it is based on objective research, the relevance of that analysis to the country and region, and the effectiveness of the BHDR as an advocacy document. The aim of the peer review exercise is to generate valuable outputs that include:

- Obtaining credibility and legitimation from experts and potential target audiences
- Provide an opportunity for Country Offices and HDR teams to engage in valuable discussions that can translate into higher levels of national ownership
- Generating valuable conceptual and technical exchanges
- Opening spaces for advocacy in favor of strategic issues, such as social inclusion, political participation, poverty reduction and human security.

Special vulnerabilities related to the Crisis

As noted, during briefings for the Report, the political and civic leaders have emphasized the fact that "relevancy" in education and learning encompasses the renewal of strong relationships between youths and their families and communities. In other words, the leadership has no desire to inherit the industrial society malady of alienated individualism. We have seen that the war did fragment family relationships. It caused physical separation and sometimes ideological splits. Criticizing the individual oriented western social and economic system for undermining the traditional values of Bougainvillean society, Ahai writes:

> School systems cultured students to operate as individuals through such practices as punishments if students shared each others' work and through the practice of examination which rewards individual success rather than group achievements. The contradiction is that in later years when students join the labour force as workers, the system hires foreign consultants to teach Bougainvileans how to work as a team or in groups- teaching them the very traditional values of co-operation which education systematically decultured in the children (Ahai, 1999, p.120).

But there were elements of the shared emotional experiences that served to enhance social identity processes. This means that the priorities of education and learning for the target group are fundamentally about re-entry or socialization into the kind of society that Bougainville has become – not what it was. And the backdrop to this, for all of us, is that all regions of the world have been brought into the proximity of a global society where knowledge-based technologies are the norm. But this does not and should not invalidate the emphasis that leaders want on localized interpretation of a knowledge-based society. There has been a general agreement among the members of the civil society that education in Bougainville should be firmly grounded in community life with orientation towards practical, village based skills promoting self-reliance (Ahai, 1999).

When it comes to assessing the vulnerabilities of populations exposed to war, experts have identified ways that conflicts change youths' and children's senses of reality. They may experience developmental delays and have problems with reading, comprehension, and abstraction (Somasundaram and van de Put, 2005, p.66; WHO, 2005). Adolescence is a particularly vulnerable (transitional) period in people's lives. Concentration loss, hostility, and loss of memory are relatively common in this age group. In places where communities put special significance on education and learning, as they have historically done in Bougainville, the fall-out of war is that hopeful attitudes about the future frequently turn skeptical. Adolescents are particularly vulnerable to substance abuse and exploitation for religious, militant or political purposes (Somasundaram and van de Put, 2005).

The exposure that Bougainville children had to the brutality of war, and the discontinuities they experienced in family life, is a significant challenge when building relevant formal and informal learning programmes. But, education has a special role to play in this challenge. Emphasising the importance of inclusion of peace education programme for school going children in Bougainville, Ahai (1999, p.139) mentions that most of the current school age population will have mostly been born during the ten year old conflict and have distant memory of peaceful life. The international community has recognized the role of education in such societies, observing that those "countries considered 'at-risk' of not achieving the 'Education for All' (EFA) goal of universal primary completion by 2015 are either engulfed in conflict currently…or recovering from recent conflicts" (Sommers, 2002, p.4 cited in Dupuy, 2006, p.1). It is also recognized that of the 100 million children in the world who do not attend school, half are victims of war (UNESCO, 2004 cited in Dupuy, 2006, p.1). For these reasons, education has become the focus of strategies to prevent conflict and promote social reconciliation in the aftermath. One of the characteristics needed in post-war education systems is that they need to work hard to include population groups prevented from attending school by war. It is a basic right of those students, but inclusion in learning programmes also help to transform grievances. In addition, inclusion can build social capital – "which is vital to building stable and peaceful communities" – by renewing linkages through participation in school-related events and the socialization processes that schools precipitate. "Without social capital, crises-affected groups are unable to live together or cooperate to rebuild their lives, communities and nations" (Baxter and Triplehorn, 2004, p.51 cited in Dupuy, 2006, p.3). But the question of relevancy is again of paramount importance. If people perceive that formal education is being driven by external interventions, then it will be seen as irrelevant – and the social capital associated with participation in community schooling will not accumulate.

Women in Bougainville suffered extensively during the conflict. But at the same time as most of the women were left behind by their male counterparts who were busy fighting in the mountains, they learnt to adapt to a new way of living. The women discovered and learnt new ways of how to rely on natural resources (Havini, 2004, p.73). Moreover the elderly people who did not go to war utilized their opportunity to pass on their knowledge and skills to young women to survive by adopting a traditional way of life and this has created a new communal respect for traditional knowledge and skills added to the pride of the Bougainvillean (Havini, 2004, p.70). Through remarkable initiatives of ordinary citizens, including women, Bougainville has managed to survive and overcome many obstacles to reclaim the land for its indigenous people and rebuild its society into a modern construct of nationhood (Havini, 2004, p.75). The women in Bougainville who were formerly patronised or ignored by a colonial society, began to speak for themselves with a clear voice, reclaiming their traditional matrilineal roles (Havini, 2004, pp.xi-xiv). But the end of war does not automatically lead to the end of insecurity for populations affected by armed conflict and it appears that women in Bougainville are suffering the consequences of men's disillusionment with change (Tonissen, 2000). Unfortunately violence against women is on the rise and there are fears that high levels of violence may be a long term consequence of the nine-year conflict (Tonissen, 2000). It is therefore important that the post-conflict environment which has created a new social structure and ways of working in Bougainville makes adequate provisions for gender equity, especially through education strategies.

Social inclusion and capabilities

The Report for Bougainville is focused on the "youths" who missed out on much of their formal education because of the war. It is imperative to include them in plans for reconstruction despite any cost/benefit analysis that might say otherwise. There is evidence that policy can make a difference when it comes to social inclusion (CASE, 2002:1). A feature of social inclusion as a policy goal is that it involves several dimensions of deprivation and participation, including consumption, production, political activity and social engagement. The capabilities approach to human development spans all these levels. Beyond economic redistribution, we're starting to learn that exclusion is very much about feeling powerless to change situations. Perceptions of exclusion probably amount to more than what the metrics of material poverty show up. As a driver of social integration / fragmentation, feelings of injustice demand to be taken seriously, which the Report does.

The multi-dimensional quality of social exclusion is getting increasing attention from planners, but they mostly concentrate on consumption and production, which neglects how exclusion is experienced. The Report addresses this gap in analysis by targeting the "youths" who were made more vulnerable by missing out on schooling during the crisis. At the centre of the decision to target them is recognition that "feeling left out" amounts to more than what the metrics of material poverty show.

BHDR Methodology

The BHDR methodology encompasses three dimensions:

1. Human Development Indices built mainly from 2000 census tables (The household survey that National Statistical Office of PNG was intending to undertake in June 2006 is not expected to produce the data in time for primary use by BHDR);
2. differential diagnosis of skills at the level of individuals; this activity tailors the concept of poverty to Bougainville contexts, acknowledging that most people are

landholders, and recognizing that land fertility assures most families grow enough for their needs; and
3. surveying the social-economic conditions of community life in terms of access to essential public services. This aim is to directly support the Patrol initiative of the ABG, which plans to provide periodic visits by public servants to every village in Bougainville.

By localizing skill sets, BHDR has adopted locally appropriate measures / indicators of deprivation; an inquiry of individual capabilities and choices based on the quantification of self-reported assessments, supplemented by focus group inquiries that measure how individuals' map their capabilities. The approach is asset-based; the aim is to encourage householders to identify their functioning / capabilities; then by a process of deduction, analysts have generated the constraints or conditions.

In sum, the methodology requires two kinds of questionnaires: one to interview village heads or representative voices about what villagers do day-to-day; the other to qualitatively map individual capabilities and aspirations.

In a nutshell, the BHDR aims to provide differential diagnostics or baseline data that will help planners to understand the diversity of the human development challenges, which different villages face in distinct ways. Internationally, it is still a rare undertaking to diagnose diversity at such local depth; and BHDR represents a UNDP breakthrough initiative at sub-national level.

Conclusion

Producing a Human Development Report at a sub-national level is quite challenging and this challenge is greater if the province or the region is in the process of rebuilding after a long and devastating conflict. The entire process of BHDR has taken up this challenge by emphasising the role of communities, and individuals from those communities, in the report's preparation. The process has also tried to enhance the paper contributors' awareness of the human development principle, which considers not only the economic importance of education and health, but also their importance as investments in human capability - not just "human capital" that can bring productivity gains. In other words the intent was to put emphasis on human lives as assets and not on the insufficiencies of individuals. In sum, the research process was designed to enhance choices and capabilities through a participatory and fully-inclusive approach. By following such an approach, it is expected that BHDR will be successful in reflecting the communities' aspirations in the nation building process to the fullest extent.

References

Ahai, N.A. (1999). Grassroots Development Visions for a new Bougainville. In G. Harris et al. (Ed.), Building Peace in Bougainville (pp.113-138). The Centre for Peace Studies, University of New England, Australia and the National Research Institute, Papua New Guinea.

ABG. (2005). Strategic Action Plan 2006-2010. Autonomous Bougainville Government.

CASE. (2002). Understanding Social Exclusion, Centre for Analysis of Social Exclusion. Retrieved 18 March-2006 from CASEbrief. sticerd.lse.ac.uk/dps/case/cb/CASEbrief23.pdf.

Dupuy, K, (2006). Education, Peace, Conflict, and Children: Knowledge Base and Knowledge Gaps. Retrieved 18 March-2006 from kendup.googlepages.com/Reddbarnapaper.doc

Havini, M.T. (2004). Preface. In J.T. Sirivi and M.T. Havini (Ed), Mothers of the Land (pp.xi-xiv). Research School of Pacific and Asian Studies, The Australian National University: Pandanus Books.

Havini, M.T. (2004). Women in Community During the Blockade. In J.T. Sirivi and M.T. Havini (Ed), Mothers of the Land (pp.69-72). Research School of Pacific and Asian Studies, The Australian National University: Pandanus Books.

Luke, A, and P.Freebody. (2000). Literate Futures: the Queensland State Literacy Strategy. Queensland Education Department, Australia.

PNG HSSP.(2005). Bougainville Province Situational Analysis. PNG Health Service Support Program Pty Ltd.

Sirivi, J.T. (2004). Building a Jungle Society In J.T. Sirivi and M.T. Havini (Ed), Mothers of the Land (pp.73-76). Research School of Pacific and Asian Studies, The Australian National University: PANDANUS BOOKS.

Somasundaram, D. J. and W.A. van de Put. (2005). Management of trauma in special populations after a disaster, presented at the Symposium After the Tsunami, February, Bangkok. Retrieved 18 March-2006 from www.psychiatrist.copm/supplenet/v67s0210.pdf

Tonissen, M. (2000). The relationship between development and violence against women in post-conflict Bougainville. Development Bulletin, no.53, pp.26-28.

UNESCO (2004). Who are Excluded and Why? Retrieved 18 March-2006 from portal.unesco.org/educatino/en/ev.php-URL ID=28705&URL DO=DO TOPIC&URL SECTION=201 html

WHO, (2005). Conference on the Health Aspects of the Tsunami Disaster in Asia, Phuket, Thailand, 4- 6 May. Retrieved 18 March-2006 from www.who.int/hac/events/tsunamiconf/presentations/en/

Using interviews effectively in Community Informatics

Larry Stillman

> One of the most important techniques for finding out people's views and knowledge in a research project is though good interviewing. Even if you are caught up with the necessity of rushing to meet community or funding deadlines, you should put great effort into ensuring that your preparation for the interview, the actual interview, and the interview write-up are of a high quality. What you should aim for is an interview record that has integrity and cannot be challenged as erroneous or misleading. Information that is of low quality will always be problematic, whether you use it for community work or for high-level research purposes. High-quality interviews will be valuable for their immediate and future use.

This chapter reviews practical techniques concerning the preparation for and conduct of the interview, management of the electronic files, as well as the use of Grounded Theory for data management and analysis, linked to collaborative approaches to research with a community.

Why interview?

Community Informatics is a type of social practice that adapts Information and Communication Technologies to people's and community's needs (Stoecker & Stillman 2007) and as such, it uses many research techniques familiar from other forms of social research.

How to study a 'community' —primarily through the window of the knowledge held by its people and institutions—has long been a controversial and intractable issue in sociology, 'because there is no way to disentangle the research method from the investigator himself (sic)' (Vidich, Bensman et al., 1970, p.345). Thus, the difficulty of agreeing just what constitutes a community and how people interpret that community impacts upon any study of human action, including the study of the relationship between people and technology. Stoecker has observed that in Community Informatics, as with many other sorts of community work, 'community' is most often a community-of-interest of people with a problem to solve. And within such communities, we work with a huge variety of formal and informal community-based organisations that serve the interests of different communities (such as people with addiction problems, nursing mothers, a bowling club, or a community house) (Stoecker, 2005). Frequently too, we work with other stakeholders, such as funders and governments who have a direct interest in a Community Informatics project.

Peter Day and Doug Schuler, representing a mix of theory and practice from either side of the Atlantic, thus suggest that:

> Community and voluntary sector groups and organizations form the bedrock of community life through the planning, organization, provision, and support of community activities and services. Although usually under-resourced and over-stretched the community and voluntary sector play a significant role in building and sustaining community (Schuler & Day 2004, p.13).

Steps have been taken, again by Day and others such as Stoecker, with an explicit social justice[43] bent (Stoecker 2005), to develop participative, and overwhelmingly qualitative techniques for investigating and working with communities in a structured way, such as co-opting members of communities to help form research questions and manage research data (Stoecker &Stillman 2006).

In such forms of community-based research, the interview, alongside the focus group or workshop is one of the most important and efficient ways to gather detailed individual opinions from people who collectively, help constitute different communities, or who have relationships with different communities. The findings from interviews can also be used in many different ways, such as reporting to public meetings, in policy development and advocacy, or in the preparation of reports and scholarly materials such as journal articles.

Who should be interviewed?

Whether interviews are conducted by the researcher alone or in conjunction with members of the community and its stakeholders, there are some core considerations to be taken into account. One obvious question is: who to interview? At times, there is little choice because the researcher make be directed as part of a consultancy, to interview particular people. At other times, the skill of the researcher will be required to select—or at least locate and seek the cooperation of—some type of sample of organisations or people in

---

[43] What is social justice? 'From the perspective of working to remove disadvantage, it is social justice is what faces you in the morning. It is awakening in a house with adequate water supply, cooking facilities and sanitation. It is the ability to nourish your children and send them to school where their education not only equips them for employment but reinforces their knowledge and understanding of their cultural inheritance. It is the prospect of genuine employment and good health: a life of choices and opportunity, free from discrimination' (Dodson 1993).

a community to cover some criteria of representative ness (for example, large and small organisations, or men as distinct from women volunteers).

Additionally, the relationship of the interviewee to the community also needs to be considered. For example, when a sensitive issue is being researched, is it appropriate that community members close to the project in the research are also privy to personal interview data from those they know, even if personal attributions can be stripped from the interview transcript? How dispassionately can they, if they are responsible for the direction of a project, consider interview data about sensitive issues which directly affect them? Such issues need to be carefully considered in developing your research plan and negotiated with a community reference group.

There is also the danger of an interview being seen as means of exploiting community knowledge. Smith, a Māori researcher, argues that argues that on a practical level, even with the best of intentions, 'research within late-modern and late-colonial conditions continues relentlessly and brings with it a new wave of exploration, discovery, exploitation and appropriation. Researchers enter communities armed with goodwill in their front pockets and patents in their back pockets...no matter how appalling their behaviours, how insensitive and offensive their personal actions may be, their acts and intentions are always justified as being "for the good of mankind"' (Smith, 1999, p.24).

Community Informatics often works with disadvantaged communities, indigenous or otherwise, and we consequently need to guard against our own forms of colonisation. We need to be prepared to allow communities to develop research at their own pace and through their own processes of governance, in conjunction with outsiders so that far more equitable power relations are established. This includes the development of relationships of reciprocity and trust that allow for productive interviews. This means that in some circumstances, the notion of the 'individual' is subsumed to a collective viewpoint or expression, and that expectations about the utility of interviews will have to be somewhat modified in some circumstances (Stillman & Craig 2006).

Furthermore, ethical and practical issues must be considered for situations which require the interpretive skills of a third person to engage in a conversation with an interviewee, for example, through an interpreter. You should be prepared to spend some time investigating and preparing for ethical, cross-cultural issues that affect both you and the interviewee. Ethics Guides or Statements exist for many disciplines and many of us are additionally guided by our own university or institutional ethics requirements for informed consent and the safe storage of data which provide another barrier against the exploitation of research subjects.

Interview Preparation

In Community Informatics, the intention of research is find out information that will ultimately solve a community's information or technology issues. However, discussing social-technical issues is not easy, given how complex the issues can be, and how many people struggle with what they see as 'technical' terminology or concepts. Because of this, an interview should not be gone into 'cold', but rather, careful thought be given to how you will draw out the interviewee's insights and knowledge for the problems that you are investigating. There is no reason why your interaction with interviewees cannot be made as personalised, if professional, as possible, so that a mutually empathetic relationship is established. This can also lead to more fruitful long-term relationships in a community. It consequently makes sense to try to find out something about the person you are interviewing beforehand, particularly their exposure to different ICTs, before the interview and the organisation with which he or she is involved. There is no reason in fact, as part of your overall methods, that you should not meet that person at another event (such as a committee meeting), and introduce yourself. In any case, it is likely that if you are working with a university, you will be required to send interviewees Ethics Forms, and this can be another the opportunity to introduce yourself and 'break the ice'.

Questions used in a community-based research project can also be developed in consultation with a community reference group itself, and this can also has also help secure their active engagement with the project and co-ownership of the research process. In particular, as has already been suggested, care needs to be taken in developing interviews which discuss ICTs: not everyone has the same degree of knowledge of technical issues, and jargon should be avoided. For example, in negotiating a series of small evaluations of ICT community needs of small organisations, I have suggested to management that I interview each staff member, board member, and a number of service network stakeholders, in order to get a rounded picture of the community organisations' needs and ICT culture. Additionally, it may be that there is an annual report of other information available, and this can be matched to some of the questions you wish to ask.

Furthermore, in posing interview questions, the interviewer needs to develop manageable questions which can be answered by an interviewee. Given the nature of human conversation, they need to be short, clear and simple, and devoid of jargon. Developing such questions takes care, and your questions tested before going into the field (Minichiello, 1995). In fact, it is likely that you can only discuss about 10 topics or questions at the most in a semi-structured interview, particularly if you are exploring issues on which depth opinions or attitudes as sought. Furthermore, as data accumulates and you find very similar answers to questions as you conduct interviews, questions can be dropped and modified, as new questions arise from the substance of the interview data. Since you are not conducting rigorous quantitative research, there is no reason to continue asking about questions or topics that are saturated with the same answer, unless you wish to quantify that answer (but remember that unless you have a scientific sample, your quantification is only provisional and indicative of a trend).

Interview Environment

Interviews, if possible, should be conducted in a quiet and private space known to the interviewee. In some situations this may be very difficult to achieve, for example, in open-plan offices, or where private space is at a premium. Whatever the circumstances, you should try to find somewhere where there is minimal interference from external noise or distractions (turn off mobile phones), and a café, attractive as it may be, is not a private place! Because so much of interviewing is also about being aware of non-verbal cues such as body gestures (also called the 'silent language' (Hall, 1959)), interviewing by phone, except for the most factual of information, can be problematic. Personal presence can also reduce any fears of being interviewed. It could well be that people's confidence and attention spans cannot survive a phone interview with a stranger. However, on occasion, I have conducted phone interviews with people whom I have met beforehand, including international interviews.

The Interview

What is an interview?

Interviews are not an ordinary way of talking with someone, though we seek to make the discussion as comfortable as possible. The interview is a special type of conservation (which may be structured or unstructured) to obtain freely-offered information (Minichiello, 1995). Because of this, and the fact that the interviewer and interviewee have only a short amount of time to establish rapport, it can be a challenge to interview a relative stranger. It can also be quite confronting for an interviewee if he or she is not used to such forms of conversation, or with whom there are substantial cultural (and linguistic) differences that can set up barriers and misunderstandings to any form of open conversation. You also need to consider the difference between a one-on-one interview (such as that between you, as the researcher, and the person being interviewed), or an interview with several people acting as 'questioners': how appropriate is it to set in place a three-way conversation, particularly when the dynamics of three people (who may be strangers to each other), can come into play? In community-based research, such as that which seeks to directly co-opt community members as research partners, how appropriate is it to pass on the responsibility of interviews to other members of the community? The circumstances may not always be appropriate, such as when more sensitive opinions are being sought. Such questions need to be carefully considered before you begin the interview.

How long should an interview be? If you wish to develop long-term project relationships, it is particularly important that you accommodate to interview's needs, and not the other way round. There is a real danger of letting an interview drag on when there is nothing more to be gained by it. 45 minutes is probably the limit for many people. I have been in interview situations where if I had been in charge, I would have terminated the interview quite early, when it became clear that there was nothing to be gained by further questions.

In other situations, when it is clear that the interviewee has changed his or her mind about being interviewed, the session should be politely finished. Some people are much more confident in explaining themselves and can be highly articulate, while others have great problems in explaining things. But as an interviewer, you must accept people as they are, and accept that some interviews will be much richer than others. Your expectations will not always be met. People's time is also valuable, and it is also important to keep their interest so that formulaic or non-committal responses are avoided. It is also is very important to be aware of any cues such as shuffling of feet or staring out the window to indicate that boredom or frustration are setting in.

Conducting and Recording an interview

Traditionally, interviewers have written down a verbatim account of what they have heard, either during or directly after the interview. However, it is obvious that the accuracy of the account that is put on paper depends on a high degree of skill by the interviewer to listen, talk, and write (much of Sigmund Freud's work, for example, was based on relatively few, but deeply explored and interpreted interviews). And of course, with all three processes going on, there is also a high degree of filtering and interpretation.

This is where newer technology can be of great assistance. Different types of tape recorder have been around since the 1930s, but it is only recently, with very small and portable digital recorders, that the recording technology has become relatively unobtrusive. I have also been involved in interviews where instead of a data recorder, a small video recorder has been used. This was held in the interviewer's hand or placed in a corner (on a shelf for example), but not refocused or otherwise controlled during the interview so as to have minimal interference on the conduct of the interview. The rationale for using the video was to capture non-verbal language and additionally, to video additional materials that were used in this project (drawings and so on), as well as capture the local environment. The use of video also requires a further ethical consideration: is the person going to be identified in any further use of the video, or is the video just for recording their views and environment? This has to be clarified with the interviewee. Other options are also becoming available. Social software such as Skype now gives the researcher the opportunity to conduct (and record) interviews at a distance through a computer, but all the provisos already discussed apply, and as well, if the connection is poor, or disconnection occurs, the flow of an interview will be affected. Whether or not you wish to use a video link is also dependent on bandwidth and whether or not this will be more of a hindrance than a help.

Whatever brand of digital recorder you purchase (and more and more mp3 players and mobile phones have this capacity), it should be one that can make high-quality recordings of at least an hour long and be downloaded to your computer. You should also practice with a colleague or friend, and know how to use the recorder without fumbling. And always have fresh batteries in the recorder before the interview starts, pencils and notebooks. Nothing interferes with an interview like fumbling to change batteries. And also make sure that the recorder has sufficient memory left (with forgotten interviews left on the recorder).

Simply placing a data recorder on a table and then commencing an interview does not engender a positive atmosphere. You should make clear before hand that you wish to use a recorder as a way of writing an accurate account of the interview through being able to transcribe it post-interview and get the interviewee's permission to record beforehand, for example, in a letter of introduction. In addition, you should offer to share the transcription or account of the interview when it is written up with the interviewee, with the offer to let them comment on it before it is otherwise used. It may also be the case that the interview will be only used in an anonymous fashion, but this depends on the kind of research you are doing and the ethics requirements you are working with. In fact, people tend to be more open if they know that their views are going to be used anonymously as part of an aggregate report.

In my experience, after a moment or two, most interviewees lose their hesitation about being recorded. Setting the recorder on a table unobtrusively as possible (for example, next to a bag), helps with this. Interviewers need to remember that the focus is upon the person being spoken with, not themselves, and commenting on what is being said, or talking over the person both interrupt the flow of that the person has to offer as well as interfering with the quality of recording. It is surprising how hard it is to learn to not talk over another person, and you may wish to consider the effect this has when several people are involved in an interview. It takes some effort to resist verbal comments, promptings, and other 'noise' such as murmurs of agreement.

However, despite the usefulness of the recording, there is nothing like *listening* very carefully to what is being said, and directly after the interview, writing up an account of what seemed important to you to clarify later on. Over-reliance on the recording technology, rather than careful listening may make for a deficient account. It is surprising how quickly details can be forgotten if they are not written down.

Managing Interview Data

Data Recorders

The use of data recorders in interviewing means that the interviewer may need to acquire new skills in data management. In the past, before recorders, the interviewer's notes were used to write an interview account with reconstructed quotations and commentary, and this would be managed with other interview data to help with the research question. In writing up, for example, 20 or 20 interviews, this was already a substantial task. Today, however, being able to have a reasonably accurate transcription of an interview means that the richer has a much larger and potentially richer amount of data to work with, but converting such a large amount of information from voice data to an electronic text file can be a very large and daunting task. Twenty interviews can result in over 100 pages of text. Of course, it is possible that recorded interviews can be sent out to a transcription service, but the accuracy of the transcription should be carefully checked, and as well, the text annotated in the way described below. If you choose to record with a video recorder, there are similar issues around conversion of the video interview into a usable computer format separate to the actual tape. It can be very consuming, requires the right sort of software and is tricky for a novice to do. It also requires a computer with the memory to work with video manipulation, including the capacity to burn DVDs.

It is also important to distinguish in any discussion of this stage between speech recognition software and transcription software. Speech recognition software, in certain circumstances, provides for a high degree of accuracy when the recording played at the same time as the software. This is particularly the case when the software has been 'trained' to record one person's voice with a particular vocabulary, for example, a doctor dictating a medical report in a predetermined format. However, such software is not appropriate for free-ranging conversations between two people, where there are two different voices, vocabularies, and speeds of talking involved.

Furthermore, because this type of interview is not involved in the analysis of the sounds or speech, manipulating the quality of the recording to enhance the accuracy of the transcription (to remove extraneous noise) is not a methodological problem. However, if recordings are also being made for historical or audio broadcast purposes, the researcher should consider preserving an original, authentic, unedited audio file with backups in case of damage or loss.

Transcription

It is useful to go over the details of the upload and transcription process in some detail, in order to show what skills are necessary. In this case, I discuss the use of Sony data recorder. Files were uploaded from my data recorder to a PC and I use the free program, Express Scribe (www.nch.com.au/scribe). While it is possible to use the proprietary software that comes with the Sony recorder (and other brands), my colleagues and I have found Express Scribe, which is widely used as a transcription software is law and medicine very easy to use particularly because its 'Global' keystrokes can be run 'under' a word processing package such as Microsoft Word. The software that comes with data recorders I have used does not have this useful feature. Global keys allow the interviewer or other staff to type and control the flow of the recording (play, start, stop, fast, slow, rewind and so on) without having to move out of the Word window. This is a great time saver. Express Scribe also allows for a certain degree of noise scrubbing in its options for play back settings for the tone frequency which enhanced the accuracy of where there is background interference such as air-conditioning. I have also found it easiest so listen to a recording through good speakers rather than headphones, though this may not be your preference.

Depending on the type of data recorder used, Express Scribe may or may not load files automatically, but different options can be set. If you are short of storage space, converting files into an Open Source format such as ogg vorbis (www.vorbis.com/) will save space in comparison to very large wav files. Audacity software makes it easy to covert mp3 or wav formats (audacity.sourceforge.net) into ogg vorbis as well as manipulate the reproduction quality if you need to. Another software to use is dbPowerAmp (www.dbpoweramp.com/) for conversion into smaller-sized files. Smaller files are also easier to email.

In transcription, it is important to try to be as efficient as possible, given the many hours that will be spent doing it. An average of 5-8 hours will probably be spent on transcription of an hour-long interview if a high degree of accuracy is required. However, may not be necessary to transcribe the interviewer's questions and in some circumstances, the interviewee's remarks can be turned into a précis with only very pertinent remarks being transcribed verbatim. You can choose a different font to distinguish between the interviewer and interviewee, and always distinguish the two with a new paragraph for clarity.

The informants' words and colloquialisms should be transcribed verbatim—to the best of your ability—including indications and hesitations. Occasionally, however, clearly stumbles, repetitions, or prompts can be deleted (indicated by an ellipsis ...), and where clearly irrelevant material is introduced this can be summarised or an ellipsis inserted. Identifiers such as personal names and place names can be replaced by an em dash (—) in the de-identified version of the transcript.

Adding commentary to a transcription

There are some very useful features in Microsoft Word (and similar features can be adapted in other word processing packages) that can be used to develop accurate citation of text and commentary on the interview. First is the continuous line count feature in Word. In Word, go to 'File>Page Setup>Layout>Line Numbers'. This is an invaluable tool when it comes to cross-referencing interview data. (The same feature can be made operational in Open Office Writer by going to Tools>Line Numbering). Second, the Comments field in Word can also be very useful to add in your insights and (a similar function for Notes can be used in Open Office Writer). Care should be taken, as with any editing, not to forward your Notes or Comments to your interviewee unless you intend this to be the case. These can be removed from the version you send out, our make an Adobe Acrobat 'pdf' file. Comments and Notes can also be turned on and off for printing when managing your data. You may also find it useful to put a double space or 1.5 spaces between each line so that it is easy to write in comments, underline and so on. Spacing also helps with the cutting up of pages (see below).

Making sense out of the interview data through Grounded Theory

Once the transcription has been performed, checked, and sent to the interviewee for comment, you need to be able to manage the many pages of interview data. How you proceed in managing and interpreting the data is dependent upon your research purpose and the time and personnel resources that are available: obviously, a high-level research project such as a PhD demands much more close attention to accuracy and detail than a small project (for example, in evaluating the outcomes of a local Community Informatics project) with a very limited time frame. Whatever the particular circumstances, some discipline is required in order to make structured and useful sense of what you have. I have found that the Grounded Theory approach is intuitive and logical for many people and in my own experience it has been easy to show people how to use it.

Grounded Theory aims to generate explanations and theories and—as the name suggests—from bottom-up and this is well described in the classic work by Glaser and Straus (1967) and further theoretical perspectives are discussed in such works as that by Lincoln and Guba (1985). Some theorists also argue that because of its bottom up approach, it is ideally suited to a social justice orientation (Charmaz, 2001) and it is well suited for group work techniques.

For anyone moving from the theoretical to the practical application of a qualitative research methodology, I would advise getting to know a methodology such as Grounded Theory—through the tried and true method of manual card sorting (see below)—before moving onto more complex software tools such as Nvivo (www.qsr.com.au). Nvivo is a software package which is used to identify patterns and themes in qualitative data, but of course, it does not replace human, interpretive thought, so important in qualitative work. Furthermore, its utility for group work in a community setting is obviously limited, since it takes a high degree of skill to use and not everyone may have this sort of computer skill and with a focus on a computer screen, group communication can be difficult. Additionally, Nvivo is not cheap software: at least $US200 for students, and $US500 for institutions. Unless the researcher has institutional affiliation, this is an investment of funds which could be used elsewhere.

How Grounded Theory Works: the Constant Comparative Method

The Constant Comparative method takes units or slices of data, and as the name suggests, sets in place a process of constant comparison and checking. The actual physical act of annotating interviews, developing cards, sorting piles, and seeing an outcome develop can be a rich, if exhausting kinaesthetic experience that can be quite satisfying when the results are seen. The following steps can be undertaken:

Two copies of each interview should be made before hand-annotation commences. Only print on one side of the page. One set of interviews (kept in an arch file) can be viewed as a reference copy of the original text (and annotations made as necessary), and the other set of copies are the ones used in the coding and sorting exercises.

Using the second set of interviews, transcriptions should be carefully re-read, and highlighting and underlining in red or other colours used to indicate particularly interesting passages (some form of coding that makes sense to you could also be implemented). It is also likely that upon reading many interviews certain overarching themes or issues will become apparent: it is worth writing up a memo about these with references to salient passages in the interviews.

When confident that all the interviews have been annotated or marked for significant passages, the time has come to actually begin to sort, categorise and code the data. The marked-up relevant units (or data slices), are cut out and pasted onto large index cards[44], together with additional handwritten annotations that come to mind. This is the sort of task that a collaborative group could do together, to cut down the time taken and to get familiar with issues.

The goal is to make each card only contain one general concept or piece of data, 'interpretable in the absence of any additional information, other than a broad understanding of the context in which the inquiry is carried out' (Lincoln and Guba, 1985, p.345). Each card should be numbered according to the interview (assuming that they have also been anonymised), but also given a general record number. For example, card no. 60 could contain text from interview 7, lines: 111-123[45]. Keywords, representing what appeared to be emergent categories, and some notes about properties, as well as theoretical hunches can also be written on the cards, yellow sticky notes, or on memo pads. It is likely that several hundred cards will be generated from, for example, 20 interviews. It does not matter at this stage if many answers or comments appear to be the same (or different)—the fact that there are so many or so few is indicative of some trend in the interviews that have been conducted.

Cards should be then re-read and sorted into what appeared to be emerging common categories on the basis of content and suggested key words. An overall 'label' card can be created, with some propositions or statement on it describing what has been found as characteristic of each emerging category of data. Units of data can be compared again, and if necessary moved to a different pile. Obvious duplicates can be removed, though their frequency should be noted as they indicate a particular trend. Constant comparison of data

---

[44] In the literature this process is nicknamed the 3" x 5" card shuffle, though in my case, it is the 127mm x 203mm (5" x 8"), the half-page length and width of an A4 page.

[45] Having a card with an exact reference will make it very easy, at a later stage, to copy and paste interview text or comments into another format (but the line numbering won't be copied over into the new text, so be sure that you have an accurate citation in your quotation).

creates a memory for the researcher or researchers (at least for the length of the coding session) of the many possibilities offered by the data, but at the same time, given the depth of information (number of cards), and the process of comparison (see below), the test of trustworthiness and validity—also called 'confirmability' by Lincoln and Guba—is solved. There is a strong, triangulated, documented audit trail consisting of the 'data slices' or 'units', memos, and other written annotations that can be used, if necessary, in a form of reverse engineering to demonstrate how conclusions are reached (Lincoln & Guba, 1985, p.301ff and Appendix A).

Practice makes perfect, and I have noticed that the process of categorisation and coding takes far less time than the first time I did it. It is likely that at first there will be many separate piles, but you should aim to be parsimonious, so that a smaller number of manageable themes and their concepts or theories are the final result. Piles of annotated cards, the essence of many hours of interviews and thinking about them, and their accompanying memos, are the stuff upon which to basis a research report whether it is a report for local consumption, or more complex academic research. A key principle is at work here—ideas emerge *from the data*, rather than being forced *into the data*. This principle, in fact, is something similar to what is aimed for Community Informatics: outcomes that are in accord with the community, rather than being pushed onto a community. In a group setting, collaborative techniques such as knowledge matrix, in which issues and ideas are pasted or written onto a large sheet of paper or board, with references to specific citations in the interviews, could be used to facilitate this flow of ideas (Stillman, 2005).

Conclusions

The conduct of research for Community Informatics, including the conduct of the interview, cannot be considered in isolation from well-established methodologies which can be fruitfully adopted from the social sciences. It is very important to take the issue of developing good interviewing methodologies seriously, rather than as an add-on to projects, particularly when personal data may be the most critical data that you are looking for. Technical aids, such as the use of data recorders and software are very useful and practical tools, but they cannot substitute for the hard work involved in mining your data through careful work. Furthermore close attention to the management of data will result in rich findings, and the use of Grounded Theory is suggested as a practical technique, particularly because it can be adapted for group work if the circumstances are appropriate.

References

Charmaz, K. (2001). Grounded Theory: methodology and theory construction. International Encyclopedia of the Social & Behavioral Sciences. N. J. Smelser and P.B. Baltes. Oxford, Elsevier Science Ltd: 6396-6399.

Dodson, M. (1993). Annual Report of the [Australian] Aboriginal and Torres Strait islander Social Justice Commissioner.

Glaser, B. G. and A. L. Strauss (1967). The discovery of Grounded Theory : strategies for qualitative research. New York, Aldine.

Hall, E. T. (1959). The silent language. New York, Doubleday.

Lincoln, Y. S. and E. G. Guba (1985). Naturalistic inquiry. Beverly Hills, Calif., Sage Publications.

Minichiello, V. (1995). In-depth interviewing: principles, techniques, analysis. Melbourne, Longman.

Schuler, D. and P. Day (2004). Community practice in the network society : local action/ global interaction. London ; New York, Routledge.

Smith, L. T. (1999). Decolonizing methodologies : research and indigenous peoples. London ; New York, Zed Books

Stillman, L. (2005). "Participatory Action Research for Electronic Community Networking Projects." Community Development: Journal of the Community Development Society 36(1): 77-92.

Stillman, L. and B. Craig (2006). Incorporating Indigenous World Views in Community Informatics. OTM Workshops 2006, LNCS 4277. Montpellier, France, Springer Berlin / Heidelberg: 237-246.

Stoecker, R. (2005). Research methods for community change : a project-based approach. Thousand Oaks, Sage Publications.

Stoecker, R. and L. Stillman (2006). Who Leads, Who Remembers, Who Speaks? Constructing and sharing memory: community informatics, identity and empowerment, Prato 2006 (to appear 2007). Prato, Italy, Centre for Community Networking Research.

Stoecker, R. and L. Stillman (2007). Who Leads, Who Remembers, Who Speaks? Constructing and Sharing Memory Community Informatics, Identity and Empowerment L. Stillman and G. Johanson. Newcastle, UK, Cambridge Scholars Publishing.

Vidich, A., J. Bensman and M. Stein (1970). Reflections on community studies. Modern sociology : introductory readings. P. Worsley. Harmondsworth, Penguin: 345-349.

Larry Stillman

Engaging Asian communities in Aotearoa New Zealand: An exploration of what works in community research

Terry McGrath, Andrew Butcher, Yvette Koo, John Pickering and Hilary Smith

> An investigation into engaging Asian communities in Aotearoa New Zealand was commissioned by the Asia New Zealand Foundation (Asia:NZ) and contracted to International Student Ministries New Zealand Inc (ISM NZ), a Christian-based network of staff and volunteers around the country. A complex project structure was developed to reflect a philosophy of community-based participatory research appropriate to an organisation focusing on social justice. This also allowed the meaningful input of all research participants along an 'insider/outsider' continuum, as well as being appropriate in a project focusing on positive examples of engagement within a theoretical framework of social cohesion. The Christian background of ISM NZ appeared to be a generally positive aspect for the Asian community informants in the research, and ultimately the project design allowed a special depth of understanding to the research findings. The most important lessons learned from this project were the importance of a methodology which reflects the philosophy of the researchers, the need for a clear project structure to allow for flexibility and diversity, and the importance of incremental findings as a contribution to research results.

The Engaging Asian Communities research project was conceived from analysis of feedback in the *Seriously Asia* consultation project (Foley and Butler, 2004), carried out by the then Asia 2000 Foundation, now Asia New Zealand Foundation (Asia:NZ). Through *Seriously Asia*, a need was identified to obtain information on how Asian communities engage in New Zealand, using two key questions:

- What contributes to successful engagement?
- What creates barriers or impediments to good engagement?

Two of the principal researchers had specifically considered the engagement of international students in the community in previous research (McGrath & Butcher,

2004). This led to an invitation to International Student Ministries New Zealand Inc (ISM NZ) to tender for the Engaging Asian Communities project. A research team was assembled through ISM NZ and other networks, and an overall project design mapped out. A tender was submitted and was ultimately successful. The project was completed and published by Asia:NZ (McGrath, Butcher, Pickering & Smith, 2005).

The initial project structure proved to be the basis of the strength of the project, and was also the source of several issues which we needed to address as the project developed. In this paper we will first explain the structure of the project, before turning to a description of the issues which arose and how we addressed them in the research. These issues included the Christian background of ISM and the research philosophy of community-based participation; the 'insider/outsider' relationships between researchers and respondents in the project; the study's orientation towards positive outcomes; and our choice of a theoretical framework of social cohesion. Finally, we present a summary of lessons learned.

Project structure

ISM NZ is a national non-governmental organisation specialising in work amongst international students and communities that support international student welfare. ISM NZ works with churches, other agencies and education providers to enhance international student sojourn in Aotearoa New Zealand[46]. A network of ISM NZ groups is based around tertiary education campuses throughout the country. Due to the high number of Asian students currently studying in Aotearoa New Zealand (Education New Zealand, 2005), many of the staff and volunteers involved with ISM NZ are of Asian origin, and a number of these are now permanent residents. These members were able to form the basis of the Engaging Asian Communities project structure from which a multi-layered arrangement of participant roles and relationships developed, as can be seen in Figure 1. This shows a series of participants expanding outwards from the project leadership, and linked by arrows to emphasise the two-way direction of flows of information. We now turn to a description of the roles of each of the project participants.

---

[46] More information about ISM NZ can be seen on www.ism.org.nz

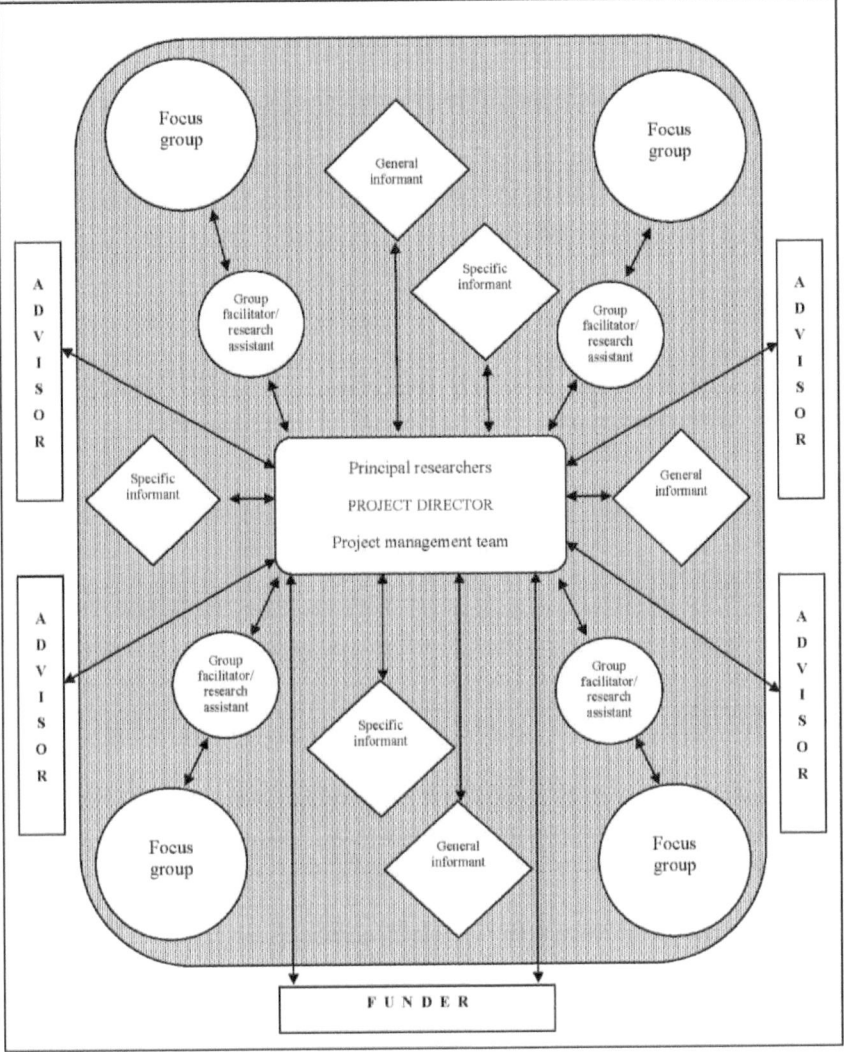

Figure 1

Leadership

The *project director* (Terry McGrath) kept an oversight of all of the different project management and research activities. He was also the director of ISM NZ, and was supported by the *project management team* who were staff at the ISM NZ office. Therefore, the team already had established working relationships and lines of communication, although a project of this complexity required high levels of input into the management of time and people.

Research team

The project director was also one of the four *principal researchers*, who carried out the major theoretical and analytical tasks of the project. The other principal researchers (Andrew Butcher, John Pickering and Hilary Smith) had a background in research on Asian migration and integration issues (see for example Butcher, Spoonley & Trlin, 2006; Pickering & Morgan, 2005; and Smith, 1996), and were brought into the project through personal and professional networks.

Informants

Three types of informant took part in the project, according to the type of information they could provide about engagement with Asian community groups in Aotearoa New Zealand. Interview schedules were developed for each of the three types:

- *Specific informants* (26 people) held a position (usually work-related) which gave them 'expert' knowledge about specific areas of engagement with Asian communities. Examples were people from city councils, city police departments, government ministries or departments, churches, charitable community trusts, etc. In some cases, the specific informants were also members of Asian communities themselves. They were contacted and interviewed by the principal researchers.

- *General informants* (10 people) were people from various Asian communities, who contributed their personal experience and opinions. In most cases, they had leadership roles within their communities but they were not asked to make their comments as representatives of these groups. General informants were also contacted and interviewed by the principal researchers.

- *Focus group participants* in a total of 17 groups were from a range of Asian community groups: Chinese (5 groups), Mixed (3 groups), Korean (1 group), Japanese (1 group), Filipino (1 group), Indian (1 group), Lao (1 group), Sri Lankan (1 group), Malaysian (1 group). There was also one group of 'Kiwi' non-Asian participants. The liaison between the focus group participants and the research team was carried out by *group facilitators*, who were usually also *research assistants*. These were mostly staff or volunteers in the national ISM NZ network.

Advisers

The research team was constantly seeking and receiving feedback through our interactions with research participants. In addition to this informal input, four outside sources of advice were part of the formal research design, these are discussed below.

Funding agency

The contract manager from Asia:NZ was involved in the design phase and provided suggestions for potential research participants. Both formal and informal meetings were held throughout the research process, which helped to ensure that the final product was in line with the expected project requirements.

Peer reviewers

Two senior academics working in related fields provided critique at the design phase and again at the draft report stage. Their comments and helpful insights, particularly at the draft report stage, assisted in maximising the clarity of the final report.

Quality assurance auditor

An accredited ISO 9000 auditor was contracted to carry out a quality assurance audit throughout the process. Four meetings were held with the project director and a formal report was completed at the end of the project. This was especially useful for the project management, as it ensured we kept to the project objectives and that there was integrity in our processes.

Advisory panel

In addition, specialist advice was also sought from a range of people from within the various Asian communities, drawn largely from the ISM network.

Although these advisory processes did not involve any major shifts in the course which the project was taking, they led to small changes and adjustments and enabled us to develop confidence in the overall direction of the research as it proceeded.

Issues raised in this research

A number of issues were raised as the project progressed, in most cases arising from the project structure outlined above. In this section, we describe these issues and how we addressed them in the research.

Organisational background

This project was carried out through a Christian organisation, a feature which was clear in the introduction to the research informants but was not highlighted in the research itself. The Christian background of the organisation appeared to elicit no reaction from the 'specific informants' in the research[47], and in fact as reported to several research facilitators it was a positive aspect for some Asian community informants. This may be because some respondents were closely linked to the ISM NZ network. It may also have reflected the Christian background of some Asian communities in Aotearoa New Zealand which have developed from families who chose to migrate to a 'Christian country', or others whose settlement was facilitated by church members in New Zealand, as has been the case for Korean families in Christchurch (Chang, Morris & Vokes, 2006, pp. 15-18).

A finding in this research was the strong importance of religious activity for all groups including non-Christian, and a recognition (which in some cases was expressed more strongly as an expectation) of religious activity as an expression of culture. In this context, the project respondents seemed to regard the idea of a Christian organisation carrying out the research in a positive light.

Philosophy of research

Since the project was carried out through an organisation which has a commitment to Christian social justice, it was important that this commitment be reflected in the philosophy of the research. We therefore took the approach of community-based participatory research, which Minkler and Wallerstein (2003, p.18) point out has developed from the Brazilian educator Freire's work in raising the 'critical consciousness' of marginalised people. Such an approach was particularly appropriate in a project researching Asian communities in Aotearoa New Zealand, which since the earliest days of settlement have been the target of discrimination through measures such the poll tax for nineteenth century Chinese gold miners; and more recently through media discussions of an 'Asian invasion' (Ip & Murphy, 2005). However, referring to 'Asian New Zealanders' as marginalised is also problematic:

- The term 'Asian' is itself a contested term (for a full discussion see Workshop Organising Team, 2005). For the project, we used the region as defined by Asia:NZ, which included South Asia, Southeast Asia, North Asia and East Asia.
- The term 'Asian migrants' includes communities as disparate as the descendants of the nineteenth century Chinese gold miners; late twentieth century refugees from Vietnam, Cambodia and Laos and their more recently arrived family members; current fee-paying students from the major source countries of China, South Korea, Japan, Thailand and Taiwan (Education New Zealand, 2007) who may be applying for permanent residence status; and recent skilled migrants from who largely come from China, India, the Philippines or South Korea (Department of Labour, 2005, p. 35)[48].

---

[47] Most of these 'specific informants' probably realised that the research contracting process would have provided assurances of ethically appropriate methods.

[48] These were the largest source countries from Asia, although the United Kingdom and South Africa were the largest source countries overall.

In spite of these issues, labelling Asian communities as 'marginalised' is supported by studies in Aotearoa New Zealand which have found that concerns for Asian communities in general include language difficulties, employment problems, disruption of family and social support networks, and acculturation attitudes; and for refugee communities there are additional problems caused by traumatic experiences prior to migration (Ho, Au, Bedford, & Cooper, 2003). In addition to the matters raised in the *Seriously Asia Report* which were the impetus of this project (Foley & Butler, 2004), such concerns for Asian communities would then reinforce our aim of carrying out a participatory style of research.

Researcher and respondent relationships

A specific area of sensitivity for the four principal researchers was that none of us is from an Asian background. We were aware that in the context of research with a cultural dimension, Māori researchers in Aotearoa New Zealand have called for 'de-colonising' research methodologies (Smith, 1999; Cram, 2001), and have particularly problematised the role of Pākehā researchers wishing to carry out research with Māori communities. Although we did not know of issues existing to the same extent for research with Asian communities, we acknowledged the fundamental 'outsider' status of the principal researchers. Consequently, our project team took on many aspects of the "insider/outsider team approach" as described by Clingerman (1999, p. 78), in which research team members are deliberately included for differences in "life experiences and interpretive perspectives".

A further important issue emerged. A considerable amount of migrant research has been carried out recently in Aotearoa New Zealand, especially in the Auckland area. We found that there was a well-worn track of looking for referrals for focus groups through government and local body agencies. Therefore, the participants likely to be identified through this route were suffering from 'focus group fatigue'. We decided to take a different route to ensure research participants were fresh and unaffected by previous research processes, and our procedure in getting research participants for focus groups depended heavily on our focus group facilitators. As 'insiders' themselves, they drew on their own community contacts.

The community-based participatory approach we took in the research also influenced the roles taken by the researchers in the project. Minkler and Wallerstein (2003, p. 4) point out that in contrast to 'outsider' research, in a community-based participatory research approach there is an effort to reduce the distinction between 'researcher' and 'researched', and participants have more involvement in all aspects of the research. In our project, people fulfilled different roles in the structure at different times. As noted above, the project director was also one of the principal researchers. One of the other principal researchers took on the role of group facilitator at the request of one of the community groups, and some project management staff were also involved as research assistants. In Auckland, an ISM NZ staff member took control of the running of the project.

An example of the usefulness of project members in multiple roles is provided by Yvette Koo, both a focus group facilitator and member of the project management team, who recalls:

> Interestingly, more than half of the people in my focus group found some solace and empathy as they shared with each other their difficult experiences as migrants here in New Zealand. These experiences mostly revolved around the area of discrimination, language, difficulty in adapting as well as the inability to find work according to qualifications.

Allowing a free reign for the stories to emerge is increasingly important in conducting research with migrants (see Connell & King, 1999, p. 19), and in many cases this is only possible by including an 'insider' on the research team. This reflects the specific advantages relating to language when 'insiders' are part of a research team. At the initial stages of the research it encourages issues around meaning to be clarified (Herod, 1999, pp. 318-320). In our project, some of the research assistants entered into discussion with the principal researchers about the terminology used in the interview schedules, in order to convey the terms most meaningfully to the Asian community respondents. As the research progresses there are other language benefits, for example, in line with Clingerman (2007, pp. 81-82), we found that the inclusion of 'insider' research assistants in our project allowed respondents to express themselves more comfortably (and went some way to compensate for what she describes as 'asymmetric language skills'), and also enabled clearer interpretation of the findings. In turn, the major conclusions of the project were translated into key languages as feedback to community participants.

The fluidity between roles as outlined above meant that the 'insider/outsider' dichotomy was not clearly defined in this project, but even the principal researchers were not always completely 'outsiders'. Their close involvement with Asian communities in religious activities (such as Christian congregations) or background experience (such as having lived in an Asian country and speaking some of the community language) reflected Herod's (1999, p. 326) view of "a continuum of 'outsiderness' along which researchers operate."

Orientation of the study

Our project aimed to identify examples of 'good' community engagement and although we also aimed to identify barriers to this, the focus was on what constitutes successful engagement. A list of principles for undertaking community development practice in Aotearoa New Zealand (Munford & Walsh-Tapiata 2006, pp. 428-429) includes "bringing about positive social change for all communities' and 'action and reflection'". They describe a structural analysis processes approach when working with marginalised community groups (p. 439):

> This includes taking groups through a process of locating themselves within the issue, naming clearly the issues to be addressed, identifying the vision for

change, analysing all the forces involved in the issues and working through and evaluating strategies for change. It concludes with reflection on the process and identifying how change can be sustained.

Our aim of identifying good examples of community engagement was an example of outcomes for sustainable change. Munford and Walsh-Tapiata (2006, p. 440) note that this approach helps determine the rights of both *tangata whenua* ('people of the land', or Māori) and *tauiwi* ('immigrants') to self-determination, as validated by the Treaty of Waitangi. This is particularly important for Asian community groups, given their historically disadvantaged status.

The importance of partnership and collaborative approaches in order to capture the complexities in community enquiry in such contexts is discussed by Matheson, Howden-Chapman & Dew, 2005, p. 10):

> The impact of historical events, power relationships and cultural mores defines people's situations, and people have an either implicit or explicit understanding of, or resignation to, their situation.

The historical 'model minority' attitude of some Asian community members (Wong, 2002; Ip & Pang, 2005) may have added a level of complication to such analyses, particularly for communities where there has been a nervousness in the well-established groups about the impacts of new migrants, for example in the long-established Chinese communities when faced with the 'Asian invasion' accusations of the 1990s (Wong, 2002). For some, this has now turned to the frustration expressed by Asian leader Mai Chen (Brown, 2003, p. 58):

> There's a whole generation of Asian New Zealanders who really strongly identify with their culture but who are New Zealanders ... And really, it's pretty tiring for them to constantly be told they can't make a full contribution. It's very uncomfortable and I don't think they're prepared to put up with it any more. Why should they?

Keeping the focus on positive examples of community engagement helped to avoid outcomes shaped by resignation or frustration, but rather directed to constructive and sustainable change.

Theoretical framework

The multi-disciplinary nature of the team ensured access to and the contribution of a wide range of literature in the research. Subsequently, the literature review became a useful by-product of the research, but the initial purpose of the review was to establish a theoretical and conceptual framework for the research. In the initial stages, the varied research backgrounds of the principal researchers provided a daunting range of options and directions for a study focusing on 'engagement'. Our decision was largely determined by the wide range of informants we wished to include in the project structure. We required a framework which would be comprehensive and flexible, to allow for the different types of knowledge and background our informants would bring to the project, yet would provide a meaningful direction for our questions and findings. We also needed it to allow a focus on the positive aspects of engagement, reflecting the study's orientation.

The framework we chose for the project came from work developed from Canadian social theorist Jane Jenson on social cohesion (Jensen, 1998). This work had recently been used in Aotearoa New Zealand and also had extensive international scholarship and public policy attention (see Spoonley et al., 2005; Peace et al., 2005). It was also aligned with indicators used in the Ministry of Social Development's annual *Social Report* (Ministry of Social Development, 2006). As one of the principal researchers had been involved in its development, we were particularly confident in our choice of this framework.

This framework provided us with useful indicators through which to help identify positive examples of Asian community engagement. We used the indicators in our explanations and discussions with the project informants, so the framework provided both clarity and rigour to the data collection process. In addition, one of the findings of this study was that there was no 'perfect' example of engagement with Asian communities in Aotearoa New Zealand. Therefore, a framework of indicators was valuable in identifying *degrees* of engagement for projects or programmes with Asian communities, and our study supported the development of the framework for future research in the area of social cohesion.

Conclusions

When the project had been completed, we were able to consider the degree to which it had been successful as an example of participatory community research. The feedback we received from participants and advisors (including funders) was that we had been successful, and our analysis of the process has led us to reflect on what we have learnt from the process.

Lessons learned

There were three main lessons which we learned in this project:

1   Methodology works well when it reflects the philosophy of the researchers

All aspects of this research methodology were developed out of the philosophical background of ISM NZ, the Christian-based organisation through which the project was carried out. The project structure utilised the wide-ranging networks of this grassroots organisation, and the way the structure was developed and managed followed a community-based participatory research approach in line with the organisational philosophy. This emphasised the importance of good relationships between all members in the structure.

2. *A clear project structure can allow for flexibility and diversity*

    This project had a complicated and flexible structure, although the roles and responsibilities for the members of each group were clearly defined. The flexibility of structure in the project combined with the diversity of participant and researcher backgrounds minimised the hierarchical distance among participants and allowed for an 'insider/outsider' continuum of perspectives. This enhanced analysis of the data brought a depth of understanding to the research findings.

3. *Incremental and informal findings may be as important as formal results*

    The process of this research project necessitated a high degree of interaction with Asian community members, and in some ways this tested our theories of 'engagement' as much as our formal data collection. Through the constant feedback from participants as the project developed, we learned a lot about positive engagement with Asian communities in Aotearoa New Zealand. Although they had not resulted in the stand-alone examples of positive community engagement that we had set out to find, we were nevertheless convinced of the usefulness of our findings.

Final thoughts

Social research of the type taken in this project allows near-strangers to ask the type of personal questions which would not be possible in other types of interactions. This can sometimes seem like meeting the researchers' interests while the other participants in the process remain the 'subjects'. Many of the informants and research assistants in this study took an active part in the process and outcomes of the project, thereby contributing towards the development of research skills among some members of Asian communities in Aotearoa New Zealand, and ensuring that the findings were meaningful to them as well as the funding agency who formally contracted the project.

Acknowledgements

We would like to thank the research participants who contributed their time and shared their experiences in this research process. We are also grateful for the support given by the project advisors Paul Spoonley, Noel Watts and Mario Garcia, and we appreciate the advice and input received from Rebecca Foley, formerly of Asia:NZ.

References

Butcher, A., Spoonley, P., & Trlin, A. (2006). Being accepted: The experience of social exclusion and discrimination by migrants and refugees in New Zealand. Occasional Publication No. 13, New

Settlers Programme, Massey University, Palmerston North.

Chang, S., Morris, C., & Vokes, R. (2006). Korean migrant families in Christchurch: Expectations and experiences. Families Commission Report No.11/06. Available www.nzfamilies.org.nz

Connell, J., & King, R. (1999). Island migration in a changing world. In R. King and J. Connell (Eds.), Small worlds, global lives: Islands and migration (pp.1-26). London: Cromwell Press.

Clingerman, E. (2007). An insider/outsider team approach in research with migrant farmworker women. Family Community Health, 30(Supplement 1):S75-S84.

Cram, F. (2001). Rangahau Māori: Tona tika, tona pono - The validity and integrity of Māori research. In M. Tolich (Ed.) Research ethics in Aotearoa New Zealand: Concepts, practice, critique (pp. 35-52). Auckland: Pearson Education New Zealand.

Department of Labour (Te Tari Mahi). (2005). Migration trends 2004/2005. Wellington: Author. Retrieved 9 September, 2007 from www.immigration.govt.nz

Education New Zealand. (2005). Student visa/permit approvals by month 1997- 16 September 2005. Retrieved 9 September, 2007, from www.educationnz.org.nz

Education New Zealand. (2007). Key indicators for Export Education Levy for full-year, 2003-2006. Retrieved 9 September, 2007 from www.educationnz.org.nz

Foley, R., & Butler, C. (Eds.). (2004) Seriously Asia (final report): Unleashing the energy of New Zealand's Asian links. Asia 2000 Foundation of New Zealand. Retrieved 9 September, 2007 from www.asianz.org.nz

Friere, P. (1970). Pedagogy of the oppressed. New York: Seabury Press.

Herod, A. (1999). Reflections on interviewing foreign elites: Praxis, positionality, validity, and the cult of the insider. Geoforum, 30: 313-327.

Ho, E., Au, S., Bedford, C., Cooper, J. (2003). Mental health issues for Asians in New Zealand: A literature review. Report prepared for the Mental Health Commission, Migration Research Group, University of Waikato. Retrieved 9 September, 2007 from www.mhc.govt.nz

Ip, M., & Murphy, N. (2005). Aliens at my table: Asians in the eyes of New Zealanders. Auckland: Penguin.

Ip, M., & Pang, D. (2005). New Zealand Chinese identity: Sojourners, model minority and multiple identities. In J. H. Liu, T, McCreanor, T.MacIntosh, & T. Teaiwa (Eds.), New Zealand identities: Departures and destinations (pp.174-190). Wellington: Victoria University Press.

Jensen, J. (1998). Mapping social cohesion: The state of Canadian research. CPRN StudyF03, Ottawa.

Larner, W., & Mayow, T. (2003). Strengthening communities through local partnerships: Building a collaborative research project. Social Policy Journal of New Zealand, 20: 119-133.

McGrath, T., Butcher A. (2004). Campus community linkages in Christchurch, Palmerston North and Wellington. Wellington: Education New Zealand.

McGrath, T., Butcher, A., Pickering, J., & Smith, H. (2005). Engaging Asian communities in New Zealand. Wellington: Asia New Zealand Foundation. Retrieved 9 September, 2007 from www.asianz.org.nz

Matheson, A., Howden-Chapman, P., & Dew, K. (2005). Engaging communities to reduce health inequalities: Why partnership? Social Policy Journal of New Zealand, 26: 1-16.

Minkler, M., & Wallerstein, N. (2003). Introduction to community based participatory research. In M. Minkler & N. Wallerstein (Eds.), Community based participatory research for health, (pp. 3-26). San Francisco: Jossey Bass.

Ministry of Social Development (Te Manatū Whakahiato Ora). (2006). The social report - Te Pūrongo oranga tangata, 2006: Indicators of social wellbeing in New Zealand. Retrieved 11 October, 2007 from www.socialreport.msd.govt.nz

Munford, R. & Walsh-Tapiata, W. (2006). Community development: Working in the bicultural context of Aotearoa New Zealand. Community Development Journal, 41(4): 426-442.

Pickering, J. W., Morgan, G. L. (2005). Practical solutions to barriers to effective pastoral care of Chinese students. Paper presented at the ISANA 16th Annual Conference: Internationalisation-Practical Solutions: A Trans Tasman workout, Christchurch, New Zealand.

Smith, H. A. (1996). English language acquisition in the Lao refugee community of Wellington: Recommendations for policy. New Zealand Social Policy Journal, 6: 200-215.

Smith, L. T. (1999). Decolonising methodologies: Research and indigenous peoples. Dunedin: Otago University Press.

Spoonley, P., Peace, R., Butcher, A., & O'Neill, D. (2005). Social Cohesion: A policy and indicator framework for assessing immigrant and host outcomes. Social Policy Journal of New Zealand, 24: 85-110.

Sullivan, M., Chao, S. S., Allen, C. A., Koné, A., Pierre-Louis, M., Krieger, J. (2003). Community-researcher partnerships: Perspectives from the field. In M. Minkler & N. Wallerstein (Eds.), Community based participatory research for health (pp. 113-130). San Francisco: Jossey Bass.

Wong, L. S. (2002). The moulding of the silent immigrants: New Zealand Born Chinese (NZBC). Paper presented at the Auckland University of Technology Chinese Centre, 15th May 2002. Retrieved October 11, 2007 from www.stevenyoung.co.nz

Workshop Organising Team. (2005). Issues and options paper: The use of the term 'Asian' in New Zealand and implications for research, policy development and community engagement. Auckland: University of Auckland.

Terry McGrath, Andrew Butcher, Yvette Koo, John Pickering and Hilary Smith

Contributors

Robyn Allpress

Robyn has worked in Otara, Manukau City, Aotearoa/New Zealand for 14 years, 7 of those as Community Advisor for Manukau City Council. This is a hands-on position, working alongside the community – developing projects, supporting networks, responding to community issues, initiating action and being the interface between the community and the Council. During the time of Robyn's involvement the Otara Community Network, which is overseen by the Otara Network Action Committee (ONAC), has grown to become the biggest community network in Manukau City.

Cheryl Anderson

Cheryl Anderson is Gudaga's full time project officer. She is an Indigenous woman who has spent most of her life living in Campbelltown, a satellite city on the southwest fringes of Sydney, Australia, where she is very active in the area's Indigenous community. She is the mother of four year old Catlyn.

Udo Richard Averweg

Udo Averweg is employed as an Information Technology (IT) Research Analyst at eThekwini Municipality, Durban, South Africa. He entered the IT industry during 1979 and holds a Masters Technology degree in Information Technology (cum laude), a second Masters degree in Science from the University of Natal and a third Masters degree in Commerce from the University of KwaZulu-Natal, South Africa. He is a professional member of the Computer Society of South Africa and has delivered IT research papers locally and internationally. During January 2000 Udo climbed to the summit of Africa's highest peak, Mount Kilimanjaro (5,895 metres), in Tanzania.

Alfred Joseph Banya

Dr Alfred Banya works in the Public Health Directorate of Lewisham Primary Care Trust in the UK. He is responsible for the development and expansion of community development for health activity across voluntary and statutory sector agencies. This includes developing and conducting training, and advising on best practice in community development. He was a lecturer in Medical Parasitology at Makerere University in Uganda prior to moving to the UK and working as a Senior Health Promotion Specialist in the 1990s. He is a member of the Royal Society of Medicine. His main interest is in identifying and utilising opportunities for partnership working between disadvantaged communities and professionals to improve health and reduce health inequalities. A focus of his PhD research was on the implications of UK government public health policy for partnerships between communities and health professionals. He has extensive experience in developing, managing and evaluating community-based health interventions.

Anthony Barnett

Anthony Barnett is Professor of Medicine and consultant physician/clinical director for Diabetes and Endocrinology at the University of Birmingham and The Heart of England NHS Foundation Trust. He heads one of the biggest diabetes units in the UK and has academic interests in genetics of diabetes, causes of diabetes vascular disease, new treatments for diabetes and its complications, and health service related research particularly regarding optimum provision of services for the South Asian community in the UK. He has published around 400 peer reviewed papers and has written many books and book chapters in his area of interest. He edits two educational journals aimed at the primary care multi-professional team and has also worked with the media.

Andrew Butcher

Andrew Butcher took up the role of Director, Research and Policy at the Asia New Zealand Foundation in December 2006. Prior to that he was a Senior Researcher in the New Zealand Inland Revenue Department. He has a doctorate in sociology and is the author and co-author of a number of internationally refereed articles and commissioned reports on the topic of international students and migrants.

Jim Chalmers

Dr Jim Chalmers has a research profile as a social constructionist through contributing to efforts to shed further light on how people make sense of their world, systems of representation (varieties of knowledge), and how such formations collide with power struggles in society, yet, present opportunities in related struggles for recognition and social inclusion. His work can be categorized as an ethical contextualist, inspired by how individuals experience culture, and by the efforts of scholars and practitioners to redraw boundaries occupied by the state, business, and civil society towards valorization of human development. His work is typically in the form of treatises written for international journals in the critical tradition, and includes a recent contribution for a collection of essays on modernism contributed by theorists who explore the fundamental tensions that defines this century between globalisation and experience. His field experience is predominantly in PNG, Sumatra, Borneo, India, Guatemala and Mexico with methodological interests in the achievement by communities of ever-increasing ownership over interventions.

Gary Collins

Dr Gary Collins is a Medical Statistician at the University of Oxford. His research interests cover translation, cultural adaptation, development and psychometric aspects of self-report health status measures. Recently, his research has focussed on examining the 'appropriateness', acceptability and cultural equivalence of health outcomes measures in languages spoken by Britain's minority ethnic groups, with special attention on those from the Indian subcontinent.

Elizabeth Comino

Elizabeth Comino, BVSc, MPH, PhD, is a senior research fellow at the University of New South Wales, Sydney. In 2002 she was awarded a Churchill Fellowship to study primary care research in the UK. She is an epidemiologist interested in access to and use of quality primary health care. She works with the Centres for Primary Health Care and Equity, UNSW and CHETRE, Liverpool Hospital. She leads a program of work at the Centres using population health data sets to provide information on use of primary health care. Dr Comino has extensive experience in the conduct of research in community, general practice and community health settings. She has used a range of study designs including intervention and descriptive study designs to improve access to and quality of health care for children and adults with a range of health care conditions including diabetes, asthma (children and adults), chronic obstructive pulmonary disease, anxiety and depression, and chronic pain. She has worked with the Aboriginal community in Macarthur since 2000 to support the establishment of the Aboriginal Home Visiting Team in the region and with Tharawal Aboriginal Corporation to support their activities. She is the lead investigator on the Gudaga Project. In developing and implementing this research she has worked closely with the Aboriginal Health Service, mainstream health services and the Tharawal Aboriginal Corporation.

Pippa Craig

Pippa Craig, BSc, DipNutrDiet, MHPEd, PhD, has worked on projects for improving services for and researching with the local Aboriginal community in South Western Sydney since 2000. She is a Chief Investigator on the Gudaga project. Dr Craig was involved in the establishment of the Aboriginal Home Visiting project which aims to address risk factors for conditions of high prevalence among urban Aboriginal children and to develop strategies to address these. She was also involved in another project that aimed to increase the use of primary health care services by the urban Aboriginal community in South Western Sydney. Outcomes were a package of Indigenous educational resources for local GPs, and a forum in which the local Aboriginal Controlled Health Service, local health services and GPs identified priority areas for future collaboration.

Gouranga Dasvarma

Dr Gouranga Dasvarma is a population and development specialist. He is a Senior Lecturer at Flinders University, Adelaide, Australia. He teaches demographic theories and methods, women's and children's health, human resource development, ageing, and population-development relations, and conducts research on population and development, fertility and family planning, mortality and population projections. He has supervised a large numbers of masters and `PhD theses. He has provided long and short term consultancies to various organisations including the United Nations Population Fund (UNFPA), Australian Agency for International Development (AusAID), the State Planning Department of South Australia, and to other international agencies such as the Ford Foundation and the Population Council. His current consultancy is with the United Nations Development Program (UNDP) in Papua New Guinea. He has worked in various countries including India, Indonesia, Cambodia and Papua New Guinea. He has published a large number journal papers, reports, and conference papers.

Peter Day

Peter is a senior lecturer at the University of Brighton and has a long history of academic and practical experience in the community technology movement. He is a founder member of the Community Informatics Research Network (CIRN) – an international network of researchers, practitioners and policy makers concerned with enabling communities through the use of Information and Communications Technologies (ICT). Peter is also a founder member of the Sussex Community Internet Project (SCIP) a community technology advocacy organisation and ICT service provider for the community and voluntary sector in Sussex, UK. He is the Principle Investigator and Project Manager of the Economic and Social Research Council (ESRC) funded Community Network Analysis project under the People at the Centre of Communication and IT research programme. He is also the Principle Investigator of a Brighton and Sussex Community Knowledge Exchange (BSCKE) funded Community Needs Analysis and ICT research project. Peter has undertaken commissioned research for the Community Development Foundation and IBM a jointly sponsored project, and for the Open Society Institute (Europe). He has published extensively in the field of community networking and community informatics.

Ruth DeSouza

Ruth DeSouza is a Senior Research Fellow coordinating both the Centre for Asian and Migrant Health Research and a Graduate Diploma in Addictions at AUT University in Auckland, New Zealand. A part-time PhD student, Ruth is a researcher and educator with experience drawn from a background in mental health nursing, teaching and counselling. She is actively involved in community activities and co-ordinates the Aotearoa Ethnic Network (AEN) and edits the AEN Journal. Ruth is a Councillor of the New Zealand Asian Studies Society, board member of the Asia New Zealand Foundation, member of the Waitakere City Council Mayoral Task Force on Family Violence, Deputy Chair of the West Auckland Living Skills Homes Trust Inc (WALSH Trust), Executive committee member of the Refugee Council of New Zealand and member of the International Marcé Society and the New Zealand coordinator for Postpartum Support International. Ruth has also recently been appointed to the Editorial Boards of the Journal of Diversity in Health and Social Care and Transcultural Nursing. Ruth is passionate about developing research processes that result in enhancing the well-being, capacity and capability of communities.

Monika Divis

Monika Divis was born and raised in Auckland, New Zealand. Her father migrated to New Zealand from the former Czechoslovakia and her mother is Fiji Indian. Monika gained a Bachelor of Arts and Bachelor of Science (conjoint) completing the requirements for majors in Psychology, Statistics, Pharmacology and Physiology from The University of Auckland. She then went on to complete a Master of Health Science (*hons*) specialising in mental health. Monika has worked in the community residential mental health care setting, and as a group facilitator and research coordinator. As a group facilitator, Monika was involved in development of an internationally recognised (TheMHS, 2005) innovative recovery program and facilitated Mary Ellen Copeland's W.R.A.P (Wellness Recovery Action Plan) groups. Monika has delivered trainings in areas including Charles Rapp's Strengths Model at introductory and advanced levels and group work practice. Monika views research as an avenue for continual learning and in her current role as research coordinator has conducted internal research projects and service evaluations using both qualitative and quantitative methods. Her research areas include implementation of the Strengths Model, evaluation of the use of Strengths Model from the service user perspective, evaluations of supported employment, residential mental health services, dual diagnosis and group work.

Jaya Earnest

Jaya is a science educator and sociologist and has more than twenty years experience working in universities and schools in India, Kenya, Uganda, Rwanda, East Timor and Australia as an educator, and researcher. Jaya was educated in India and England and in 2003 completed her PhD at Curtin University of Technology where she is a Senior Lecturer at the Centre for International Health. She is currently involved in research projects in India, Western Australia and East Timor.

Clair Farenden

Clair has a background in community development and participatory research. She has worked on various regeneration programmes to ensure local governments consult and work in partnership with communities, and has also been involved with voluntary and community sector projects that offer outreach and consultation programmes. Her experience covers many different geographical neighbourhoods and communities of interest on the south coast of England. She trained in Participatory Rural Appraisal in 2001 and has been working with and exploring these methods ever since as a way of including hard to reach people in research. She joined the CNA team at the University of Brighton in 2006 and has recently been involved in researching community networks and the use of communication technologies in a local geographical area.

Shannon Faulkhead

Shannon Faulkhead is a Koorie woman from Mildura, who is currently the postgraduate student attached to the Australian Research Council Linkage Project, 'Trust and Technology: Building an archival system for Indigenous oral memory' investigating Australian Indigenous oral testimonies and archives. Shannon's PhD research through Monash University is titled 'Narrative Creation and Koorie Victoria'. Prior to returning to study Shannon worked for nine years at the Koorie Heritage Trust Inc., an Aboriginal cultural centre in Victoria.

Robert Finger

Robert is a medical doctor and has been working for the Centre for International Health, Curtin University of Technology since August 2005, after completion of his medical degree in Germany and a Master of International Health at Curtin. He has been involved with research consultancies for UNAIDS/IOM in East Timor and UNICEF in Sri Lanka. Since having returned to Germany in mid 2006, he stays associated with the Centre as a research associate. His areas of interest are health in developing countries and healthcare delivery and utilization in settings with limited resources, with a focus on eye health.

Victoria Foster

Victoria Foster is lecturer in social policy at the University of Central Lancashire, UK. As well as having a particular interest in policy issues concerning children and the family, she is concerned with epistemology and with emancipatory approaches to knowledge production. Originally trained in Fine Art, her work explores the means by which the arts can be employed in sociological inquiry in order to further our understanding of the social world.

Lisa Gibbs

Dr Lisa Gibbs is interested in research which focuses on sociocultural differences and engagement of marginalised groups through health promoting community interventions. She is currently managing a range of child obesity prevention, child oral health, child injury prevention, and community health and wellbeing projects involving culturally diverse and low income communities, using mixed method evaluations. Her doctoral research explored men's experience of chronic illness and access to health services. These studies are all characterised by research partnerships with community organisations with a focus on developing cultural competence and community-based participatory approaches to research and interventions. She completed her B.Sc.(Hons) at University of Melbourne and her PhD at Deakin University.

Alison Greenaway

Alison is a Geographer, trained in political economy, with a long term interest in community development and collaborative research. Alison's work covers the fields of Urban Development and

Governing Climate Change. In her role with the Collaborative Learning Group at Manaaki Whenua Landcare Research she is working in a New Zealand Government Foundation for Research Science and Technology funded programme (Building Capacity for Sustainable Development) looking at community networking and how capacity is built for sustainable development.

Bernard Guerin

Bernard Guerin is currently Professor and Head of the School of Psychology at the University of South Australia, where he teaches community and social behaviour, language and discourse, and social science interventions. He trained at the Universities of Adelaide (Ph.D.) and Queensland (Postdoctoral), and then taught at James Cook University and the University of Waikato in New Zealand. He has published four books, the two most recent being *Handbook for Analyzing the Social Strategies of Everyday Life* (2004) and *Handbook of Interventions for Changing People and Communities* (2005). Most of his recent research has focused on communities, working with refugee (especially Somali), migrant, and indigenous Māori (especially Tūhoe) and indigenous Australian communities. He also has been working on a project with earth scientists on social aspects of household energy use. His goal has been to integrate social and community psychology with the other social sciences into an interdisciplinary framework that can be used for practical analysis and intervention.

Pauline Guerin

Pauline Guerin is currently Senior Lecturer in the School of Nursing & Midwifery at Flinders University in South Australia where she teaches developmental and health psychology and sociology. She has previously taught a wide variety of courses (such as psychology, communication, research methods, and planning and evaluation) to diverse student populations (including nursing, social work, psychology, occupational therapy, and health sciences). Pauline holds a Bachelor of Science in Psychology from DeSales University and a PhD in Psychology from Temple University, both in Pennsylvania in the USA. Pauline has held lecturing and research positions at the University of Waikato, the Waikato Institute of Technology and the University of South Australia. Pauline's research has included the use of physical activity in smoking cessation for New Zealand Māori women, Somali women's views on female circumcision, and a wide variety of projects on refugee resettlement. Pauline has published in the areas of reproductive health, mental health, refugee employment and community-based research approaches.

Elizabeth Harris

Elizabeth Harris originally trained as a social worker. She has worked in community based health services in urban, provincial and remote parts of Australia as well as in several Pacific Island countries. For the past eight years she has been the Director of CHETRE at University of New South Wales, Sydney, Australia. Her research interests are in developing and researching the effectiveness of interventions to reduce health inequality in policy and practice areas.

Maria Higgins

Maria Higgins is a Research Fellow at the Centre for Integrative Care, Glasgow Homoeopathic Hospital. Her clinical background is in nursing and academic background is in sociology/psychology focusing on health and medicine –a background which has facilitated an observation and interest in the frequent gap between clinical practice and research/academia. Subsequently she trained as a Dance Movement Therapist at the Laban Centre, London and became interested in how arts in health interventions could best be researched and 'measured' in an 'evidence – based' culture. Since then she has developed a particular interest in the application of innovative qualitative approaches to the research process at Glasgow University. She is currently working on a project using the Biographical Narrative Interpretive Method to evaluate services for people with Chronic Fatigue Syndrome and enable patients to express authentic stories and opinions within the research process.

Marion Horton

Marion Horton formed Marion Horton Associates and has worked since 1995 as an independent community development consultant, researcher and trainer. Marion specialises in a wide range of community development and adult education work, particularly rural and urban social exclusion, anti racist and citizenship initiatives both in the UK and internationally. She has worked with Gypsies and Travellers for the past five years. She is one of the founder partners of the Ad Ed Knowledge Company, a social enterprise for radical popular adult education and an associate of Access Matrix a leading research enterprise specialising in Black and Ethnic Minority research. She is an adviser to the Hungarian Association of Community Development and The Civil College in Hungary.

Lisa Jackson Pulver

Lisa Jackson Pulver, Grad Dip Applied Epidemiology, MPH, PhD, is a Koori woman whose people are from south western New South Wales. She is the Director of the Muru Marri Indigenous Health Unit within the School of Public Health and Community Medicine at UNSW. Professor Jackson Pulver is currently a team member of the ARC/NHMRC Research Network in Ageing Well; a Senior Research Fellow with the Australian Research Council's Ageing Research Centre; an Honorary Senior Research Fellow at the Prince of Wales Medical Research Institute; and a Visiting Fellow at the National Centre of Epidemiology and Population Health, ANU. Lisa is one of three Indigenous Advisors for the National Advisory Group on Aboriginal and Torres Strait Islander Statistics within the Australian Bureau of Statistics. Involvement in international committees and advisory groups includes membership on the International Organising Committee for the International Network of Indigenous Health, Knowledge and Development, a steering committee member for the International Indigenous Health Measurement and Data Group and a member of the Peoples Health Movement.

Gaby Jacobs

Gaby Jacobs PhD has a MA degree in social psychology and gender studies. She worked as a counselor at a women's health care center. In 2001 she finished her PhD on empowerment in feminist and humanist counseling. From 2001 until 2006 she has been a lecturer and researcher at the University for Humanistics in the Netherlands. Currently she is a lecturer in psychology at Keele University, UK. Her research topics include: community participation and empowerment in health promotion; 'normative' professional development and learning in health, social work, education and counseling.

Uzma Jamil

Uzma Jamil is an academic researcher with the Transcultural team of the Montreal Children's Hospital/McGill University Health Center. She is also a doctoral student in the sociology program at UQAM. Her current research focuses on South Asian Muslim immigrant communities in

Montreal and their construction of identity and belonging. Her previous research and publications focus on the interplay between human rights, religion and politics in Muslim societies.

Rich Janzen

Rich Janzen is Research Director at the Centre for Research and Education in Human Services in Waterloo, Ontario. He has been involved in over 50 applied research projects that used a participatory action research (PAR) approach. For Rich, research is a tool for social change – to find new ways of bringing people who are on the edge of society to live within community as full and equal members. Much of his research has focused on issues of immigrant settlement, access to professions and trades for immigrants, community mental health, and family support. Rich has an academic background in Community Psychology (MA).

Graeme Johanson

Associate Professor Graeme Johanson is Director of the Centre for Community Networking Research at Monash University, which hosts many projects which focus on the community-building capacities of information and communications technologies. His academic interests cover the definition of the nature of the cultural value chain in production of publications for Australia and the British Commonwealth, with regard to major economic, legal, political, institutional, management and literacy changes; up-to-date analysis of the relationships between expressions of research knowledge, their ideal forms of reproduction among scholarly communities of practice, and how best to manage them online; inexorable changes associated with information technologies in information management and librarianship; case studies in Australia of the effective use of information and communications technologies for community growth; collection of baseline data about levels of use of information and communication technologies by community-based organizations; modelling of frameworks for the recent emergence of international development informatics; and explication of the epistemology and ontology of the new discipline of community informatics, and its consequences for practice.

Mark Johnson

Mark R D Johnson is Professor of Diversity in Health & Social Care, and directs the Mary Seacole Research Centre, De Montfort University, Leicester. He works closely with practitioners, statutory Health and Local Authority bodies and community voluntary organisations to develop appropriate models of service delivery and professional training. He is working on collaborative research projects with community and academic agencies, and is co-Director of the Centre for Evidence in Ethnicity Health and Diversity. This Centre, run jointly with the University of Warwick, seeks to collate and validate both qualitative and quantitative research including material produced by community groups, for incorporation into professional evidence-based practice. It is working with the NHS to set up a Specialist Library for Ethnicity and Health in the National Library for Health, to make this widely available. His recent publications include reports on visual impairment, alcohol use among 'second generation' migrants, and health services for asylum seekers in the dispersal programme, as well as books, and reports for the Home Office and Department of Health on aspects of health inequality, 'race' and ethnicity.

Jennifer Knight

Jennifer Knight, BA (Hons), Dip Ed, MPH, PhD, is Gudaga's project manager. She is based at the Centre for Health Equity Training, Research and Evaluation (CHETRE) which is part of the

University of New South Wales' Centres for Primary Health Care and Equity. She has also held research positions at the University of Sydney and Macquarie University. Prior to entering the academic domain she worked in state politics for over ten years. Dr Knight was policy adviser to the New South Wales Minister for Health and Minister for Industrial Relations. She was also Director of the Legislative Council's Standing Committee on Social Issues, NSW Parliament where she headed inquiries into aboriginal representation in parliament, sexual violence, hepatitis C, adoption practices and rural suicide. Jennifer lives with her husband and young son, James and Elliott Smith, in Sydney, Australia.

Maree Kulkens

Ms Maree Kulkens is the manager of health promotion programs within a large inner urban community health service in Melbourne. She has extensive experience working with culturally and linguistically diverse communities and has developed a wide range of innovative health promotion programs and services in response to identified needs within these communities. In her work she is responsible for developing partnerships with a range of stakeholders including academic institutions, local and state government, health services and community groups to ensure a more coordinated and sustainable responses to community health. She completed her MPH with Deakin University and her final thesis paper titled: The benefits and challenges of participatory research to support health promotion planning within culturally and linguistically diverse communities; demonstrates her dedication to community based health promotion practices. She is actively involved in a number of community based public health research projects where participatory research methodologies have been incorporated to address key public health issues.

Yvette Koo

Yvette Koo is originally from Malaysia and is now permanently residing in New Zealand. She has a BA in Mass Communications from Australia and draws on her migrant experiences in regularly contributing to the work of International Student Ministries New Zealand Inc (ISM NZ). She is currently the Administrator for Malay Studies and assistant to the Chair of Malay Studies at Victoria University of Wellington.

Claudette Legault

Claudette Legault, MSW, RSW, Executive Director of the Metropolitan Immigrant Settlement Association (MISA), Halifax, Nova Scotia, Canada was one of the NGO representatives on the Atlantic Advisory Committee which oversaw the establishment of the Atlantic Metropolis Centre in January 2004 and continues to be active in the Centre. Ms. Legault has played a leadership role in regional and national immigration organizations including having served as President of the Atlantic Region Association of Immigrant Serving Agencies (ARAISA), Immigrant Serving Agencies of Metro (ISAM) and sits on the Board of the Canadian Immigrant Settlement Sector Alliance (CISSA), a national voice of the settlement sector representing 450 settlement and refugee agencies from across Canada. Ms Legault has a long history of working with community-based organizations and in 2005 was presented with the Nova Scotia Association of Social Workers Ron Stratford Award for "outstanding commitment to a holistic perspective emphasizing community-based social service." Ms. Legault is the community representative on Dalhousie University's School of Social Work Advisory Committee. Having worked extensively in Central America with refugees and displaced persons, Ms Legault was a founding member of the Central America Monitoring Group, a coalition of 16 organizations. The initiative received an international award for its advocacy and policy work having helped "establish what is today an accepted principle of sustainable human development –

that civil, political, social, economic and cultural rights are indivisible." Ms.Legault is co-author of an article (in press). *Where Does the Sun Set? Delivering Settlement Services using Technology.* Our Diverse Cities.

Cathy Lloyd

Cathy Lloyd is a Senior Lecturer at the Open University in the Faculty of Health and Social Care. Having chaired two of the nursing courses in the Faculty, she is currently leading the development of a new undergraduate level course entitled Promoting Public Health. She is the Principal Investigator on a project funded by Diabetes UK, which is developing alternative modes of data collection in South Asian people whose first language is not English, or where a written language may not exist, and where levels of literacy are an influential factor when self-report instruments are used. Her previous research studies include an RD Lawrence Fellowship (Diabetes UK) to investigate the role of stress in diabetes, an American Diabetes Association fellowship award to investigate the role of psychosocial factors in the development of diabetes complications, and several research studies in both the U.S. and the U.K. investigating the relationship between depression and diabetes. Her interest in South Asian people with diabetes stems from her experiences in measuring rates of depression in this community using self-completed questionnaires, and a study of non-attendance at diabetes clinics.

Jennifer Margaret

Jennifer has worked for the last 6 years in a community liaison role at Manukau Institute of Technology, New Zealand. Through this role she has been involved in community action and development within Otara and has been a member of the Otara Network Action Committee. Jennifer's background is in Adult and Community Education and social justice work, particularly in the area of supporting indigenous peoples' rights in Aotearoa New Zealand through working for change within the colonising culture.

Paula McGee

Paula McGee is Professor of Nursing at the University of Central England in the UK. Her clinical background is in acute medicine and the rehabilitation of stroke patients. She has two main research interests: advanced practice and cultural issues and has published a texts and article on both subjects. With regard to cultural issues, she has taught, researched and published on cultural issues in healthcare for over 20 years. In addition to her work in the University, she works with nurses to improve their practice and provides staff development on cultural issues in health and social care services both around the UK and in other countries. She is currently editor (with Professor Mark Johnson) of *Diversity in Health and Social Care*, an international peer review journal published by Radcliffe Press and associate editor of the Research Ethics Review.

Terry McGrath

Terry McGrath is currently National Coordinator of International Student Ministries Inc (ISM NZ) and International Student Chaplain at Massey University. He holds degrees in Science (Chemistry), History (Asian and Pacific) and Development Studies. His work has included consultancy, professional development, and the development of materials and programmes related to international student and migrant welfare, sojourn and cross cultural transitions. Terry is the recipient of a Massey Blue Award for services to international students.

Sue McKemmish

Professor Sue McKemmish, PhD, is Chair of Archival Systems, Monash University, and Director of the Monash University Centre for Organisational and Social Informatics. She is engaged in major research and standards initiatives relating to the use of metadata in records and archival systems (Clever Recordkeeping Metadata), information resource discovery (Breast Cancer Knowledge Online and Smart Information Portals), Indigenous archival services (Trust and Technology), and the nexus between memories communities, and technologies. She is particularly interested in working in collaborative teams to develop ICT solutions that genuinely meet the needs of individuals, organisations and society, and empower people in their working and personal lives. Sue McKemmish directs the postgraduate teaching programs in records and archives at Monash, has published extensively on recordkeeping in society, records continuum theory, recordkeeping metadata, and archival systems, and is a Laureate of the ASA.

Ghazala Mir

Ghazala Mir is a Senior Research Fellow at the Centre for Health and Social Care, University of Leeds, UK. Her main area of research is health inequalities affecting people from minority ethnic and religious communities and people with learning disabilities. She is particularly interested in research that explores the best way of meeting identified needs in practice. Ghazala is Director of the Ethnicity Training Network, which has been established to make good quality training on cultural competence easily available to practitioners. She currently sits on Advisory Boards for the UK Healthcare Commission, the Department of Health and the National Advisory Group on Learning Disabilities and Ethnicity.

Joanna Ochocka

Joanna Ochocka (Ph.D.) is Executive Director of the Centre for Research and Education in Human Services and Adjunct Faculty of Psychology at Wilfrid Laurier University in Waterloo, Ontario, Canada. Her primary areas of research include mental health, cultural diversity and community supports for marginalized populations. Joanna is one of the leaders in the country in the use of a participatory action research approach. She is co-author of the book: "Shifting the Paradigm in Community Mental Health". Currently she leads the Community University Research Alliance (CURA) on culture and mental health.

Catherine O'Donnell

Catherine O'Donnell is a Senior Lecturer in Primary Care R&D, General Practice & Primary Care, University of Glasgow. Her main research interests are in primary care structure, organisation and service delivery and the evaluation of primary care policy developments. Within these broad areas, she is interested in the changing skill-mix configurations required to delivery care in the 21st century; the boundaries between health care professionals; provision of unscheduled health care; and access to primary care, for deprived and socially excluded groups. Methodologically, she is interested in the use of mixed methods and in the integration of quantitative and qualitative methodologies (See www.gla.ac.uk/departments/generalpractice/odonnell.htm).

John Pickering

John Pickering has been involved in research, consultancy, chaplaincy, and professional development in the international education sector. He has worked as an international student advisor and helped to establish the New Zealand branch of a professional association for international education professionals, ISANA of which he is a life member. He has lived in Germany, Netherlands and Poland. He has a doctorate in physics and is currently employed as a Research Fellow and Manager in the Department of Medicine of the University of Otago.

Andre Renzaho

Dr Andre Renzaho is a senior research fellow at Deakin University. An experienced and active researcher covering a wide area of public health research, he has been sitting on a number of expert Panel committees and reference groups including the Nutrition in Culturally Diverse Communities by the Australian Department of Health and Ageing and Eat Well Victoria Partnership. Over the last six years Andre has convened, chaired or been involved in nine government sponsored steering committees covering the areas of Refugee Health Service Model, Language Services, Refugees and Humanitarian Entrants Research Strategy, Culturally Appropriate Aged Care, Healthy Eating Communication Strategy, Maternal and Child Health and Preschool Services Linkage, and the Somali Action Research. As the founder and director of the International Centre for Refugee Public Health and Nutrition, he has travelled extensively planning, implementing, documenting and evaluating public health and nutrition programs in more than 15 countries, focusing on cultural competence frameworks, knowledge, attitudes, practices and behaviours, public health outcomes, acculturation, nutritional status, socio-cultural influences, Complex Humanitarian Emergencies, and Human Rights-based approaches.

Lynette Russell

Professor Lynette Russell holds the Chair in Australian Indigenous Studies at Monash University and is Director of the Centre of Australian Indigenous Studies. She has published widely in the areas of Aboriginal History, archaeological-theory, post-colonialism and representations of race.

Udoy Sankar Saikia

Dr Udoy Sankar Saikia has specialised in population, gender and sustainable development. He is a lecturer at Flinders University, Adelaide, Australia. He has extensive work experience in population and development issues in tribal communities in Northeast India. His current research focuses on the demographic behaviour of new nations and indigenous communities. Initial findings from his research have shown that societies in new nations and in indigenous communities share a common sense of insecurity and a feared sense of identity loss, living as they do amid or in close proximity to much larger and dominant populations. This perceived sense of insecurity encourages members in these communities to adopt a defensive position vis-à-vis outside groups resulting in high fertility. Dr. Saikia worked as a fulltime consultant for Oxfam India (UK) and as a researcher at the grassroots level among tribal communities in Northeast India. He has experience of teaching in a wide range of topics such as primary health care in developing countries; gender, health and international development; population and environment, sustainable development; environment, economy and culture. He has supervised a number of PhD and postgraduate theses. He has been recently commissioned as an international consultant by the United Nations Development Program to compile the Human Development Report for Bougainville.

Don Schauder

Emeritus Professor Don Schauder, in the Faculty of Information Technology (FIT), Monash University, is past Associate Dean (Research) and a Fellow of the Library and Information Association of Australia. His research and teaching focus on the creation and use of knowledge by and for communities, whether local communities, communities of interest or communities of practice. Features of Don's career and the work of the research groups which he chairs include: Director of several libraries, the first being the South African Library for the Blind and the most recent RMIT University Library. He has a career-long concern with equity and access in the provision of information services; Frequently called upon to participate in governmental information policy processes (for example as a member of the Australian Government delegation to the UN World Summit on the Information Society, Tunis, 2005); Pioneer of electronic publishing and community networking (co-founder of INFORMIT Electronic Publishing, RMIT University and VICNET: Victoria's Network, State Library of Victoria). Current international projects include comparative study of libraries and museums as 'knowledge commons' resources in Australia and Singapore; information society policy in Vietnam; collaboration with the Development Informatics Laboratory of IITB (Indian Institute of Technology Bombay), Mumbai and with Monash South Africa on village-level community technology in India and Africa.

Diane Singh

Diane was born in the Murray River town of Echuca, Victoria, and is a member of the Yorta Yorta/Wemba Wemba communities from Victoria and New South Wales, but has lived in Melbourne since the late 1950s. After years of working in the health sector and return to study, she worked in the field of Indigenous Education and Employment with the then Department of Education, Employment, Training and Youth Affairs (DEETYA) in Melbourne and later as an Indigenous Education Officer with the University of Ballarat. Diane is currently working as the Community Liaison Officer at the Centre for Australian Indigenous Studies, (CAIS), Clayton, Victoria.

Hilary Smith

Hilary Smith is a language teacher and researcher, with a doctorate in linguistics. She has lived and worked in Tonga, Papua New Guinea, and the Lao PDR. Her areas of interest include Teaching English for Speakers of Other Languages (TESOL), language attitudes, language in education, language and settlement, and international development.

Larry Stillman

Larry Stillman has a background of community action and research in Australia. He has worked in non-profit organisations, as well as VICNET, the public internet service of the State Library of Victoria where he particularly focussed on multilingual and disability issues, including web accessibility. Since the mid-1990s he has played a leading role in community networking conferences and events in Australia, as well as building contacts with colleagues internationally, through the Community Informatics Research Network (CIRN). His PhD was a study of understandings of technology in Neighbourhood Houses, a type of community centre, as well as associated research in New Zealand. He has recently been funded to work on a major technology and social justice project with the Victorian Council of Social Service.

Randy Stoecker

Randy Stoecker is Associate Professor in the Department of Rural Sociology at the University of Wisconsin, with a joint appointment in the University of Wisconsin-Extension Center for Community and Economic Development. He has a Ph.D. in Sociology from the University of Minnesota, and a Masters of Science in Counselling from the University of Wisconsin-Whitewater. He moderates/edits COMM-ORG: The On-Line Conference on Community Organizing and

Development (comm-org.wisc.edu), and conducts trainings and speaks frequently on community organizing and development, participatory research/evaluation, and community information technology. He has led numerous participatory action research projects and empowerment evaluation processes with community development corporations, community organizing groups, community information technology programs, and other non-profits in North America and Australia. Randy has written extensively on community organizing and development and community-based research, including the books Defending Community (Temple University Press, 1994), Research Methods for Community Change (Sage Publications, 2005) and the co-authored book Community-Based Research in Higher Education (Jossey-Bass, 2003). You can find his complete vita at comm-org.wisc.edu/stoeckerfolio/stoeckvita.htm.

Jackie Sturt

Jackie Sturt trained as nurse in the early 1980s and spent 12 years working in the areas of diabetes, primary care and psychiatry. Her first degree, in Politics and sociology, was awarded by Oxford Brooks University in 1991. In 1997 she completed her PhD in primary care and health promotion. Jackie joined the Centre for Primary Health Care Studies and Warwick Diabetes Care in 2000. Research and teaching interests have focused on the development and evaluation of diabetes self-management interventions, the validation of diabetes management self-efficacy scales and user involvement in research. In 2004 she secured a 4yr Department of Health post-doctoral award to further her research programme in diabetes management self-efficacy. Jackie leads the Diabetes Manual cluster RCT, the SEGA complex intervention development study and the diabetes management self-efficacy instrument UK validation. She is a co-investigator on the Telecare RCT at Warwick and the ADCAD study to develop and evaluate alternative methods of data collection in minority ethnic populations, led by The Open University.

Madine VanderPlaat

Madine VanderPlaat, Associate Professor of Sociology and Women's and Gender Studies, Saint Mary's University, Halifax, Nova Scotia, Canada is one of the founding Directors of the Atlantic Metropolis Centre. Dr. VanderPlaat has worked extensively with the Public Health Agency of Canada developing the social justice dimensions of community based health promotion programs for women, children and families. She has been an academic advisor for a series of regional and national community-government Think Tanks on community capacity building, participation and governance. Her research and publication interests focus on immigrant families, citizen participation, social inclusion and civil society. Her recent research projects include an analysis of settlement patterns of sponsored parents/grandparents; an examination of integration outcomes for immigrant women in Canada; the development of a community of practice in ecosystem approaches to human health for coastal communities; an examination of the formal and informal community support services for abused and neglected older adults; and an exploration of parent-teen conflict in immigrant communities. Dr. VanderPlaat is a founding member of the Coastal Community Health Network (CCHN) with partnerships in Nova Scotia, Cuba, Chile and Brazil. She has also presented workshops and co-authored papers with faculty at the Human Rights and Health Research Unit at the National School for Public Health, Oswaldo Cruz Foundation in Rio de Janeiro, Brazil. She is a member of the Child and Youth Health Networks of Canada research team, and a Principal Investigator and Steering Committee member of the RURAL Centre.

Elizabeth Waters

Professor Elizabeth Waters is interested in public health research, practice and policy that aims to make a difference to health inequalities and health equity. She led the Australian NHMRC Working Group on the development of the 2005 NHMRC publication: Increasing cultural competence in health: a guide for policy, practice, and partnerships. She is actively involved in research partnerships with communities to develop programs and interventions where the process is culturally competence and the outcomes are multi-sectoral, and oriented towards addressing social determinants of health. She completed her MPH at Monash University and her DPhil at Oxford University. She is also the Coordinating Editor of the Cochrane Public Health Review Group which aims to summarise the evidence on upstream public health interventions with a focus on equity.

Andy Williamson

Andy is the Director of eDemocracy Programmes at the Hansard Society, the UK's leading independent, non-partisan political research and education charity. He has an extensive background in research and consultancy relating to information and communications technology (ICT), community informatics and social policy and was for ten years the Managing Director of New Zealand-based Wairua Consulting Limited. Andy has held numerous board positions, is an advisor to various governments and was co-founder of the Aotearoa Ethnic Network and AEN Journal. Andy's Doctoral research, undertaken at Monash University, Australia, developed a model for emergent citizen-focussed eDemocracy.

Kirsty Williamson

Dr Kirsty Williamson is the Director of the research group, Information and Telecommunications Needs Research (ITNR), a joint initiative of Monash and Charles Sturt Universities. Since the early 1990s, she has undertaken many research projects funded by a range of different organisations including the Australian Research Council (ARC), the Australian Commonwealth Department of Communications, Information Technology and the Arts (DCITA), Telstra, and various Australian library services including State Libraries and the Australian National Library. The ARC, through its Linkage Program, funded the Indigenous project about recording oral memory, together with the lead collaborating organisation, the Public Record Office of Victoria.

Don Wren

Don Wren is an eLearning Designer for SaskTel, Canada. His background is in Distance Education. He has worked at the University of Alaska and at the Saskatchewan Indian Federated College (now First Nations University of Canada) on a variety of Distance Education programs as technician, producer, and researcher. Don has a BA in History with minors in Anthropology and Canadian Studies and was one of the earliest graduates of the Canadian Studies program at the University of Alaska Anchorage. He was named the program's Honored Canadian Studies Student in 1995. His ethnohistorical research spans nearly 20 years. His primary area of interest is the "Influence of the Russian Orthodox Church on the Pribilof Islands." Don presented some of his findings at the Ioann Veniaminov (Saint Innocent) Bicentennial Symposium in the fall of 1997. Don earned a BA in Indian Studies from the Saskatchewan Indian Federated College (now First Nations University of Canada). He was awarded the President's Award for Indian Studies and received a Newberry Library Study Fellowship to participate in the D'Arcy McNickle Center for the Study of American Indian History seminar on "Tribal Communities and Spiritual Traditions". Don has posted some of his work on the web at: rocinak.sasktelwebsite.net.

www.ingramcontent.com/pod-product-compliance
Ingram Content Group UK Ltd.
Pitfield, Milton Keynes, MK11 3LW, UK
UKHW041258180426
11947UKWH00008B/558